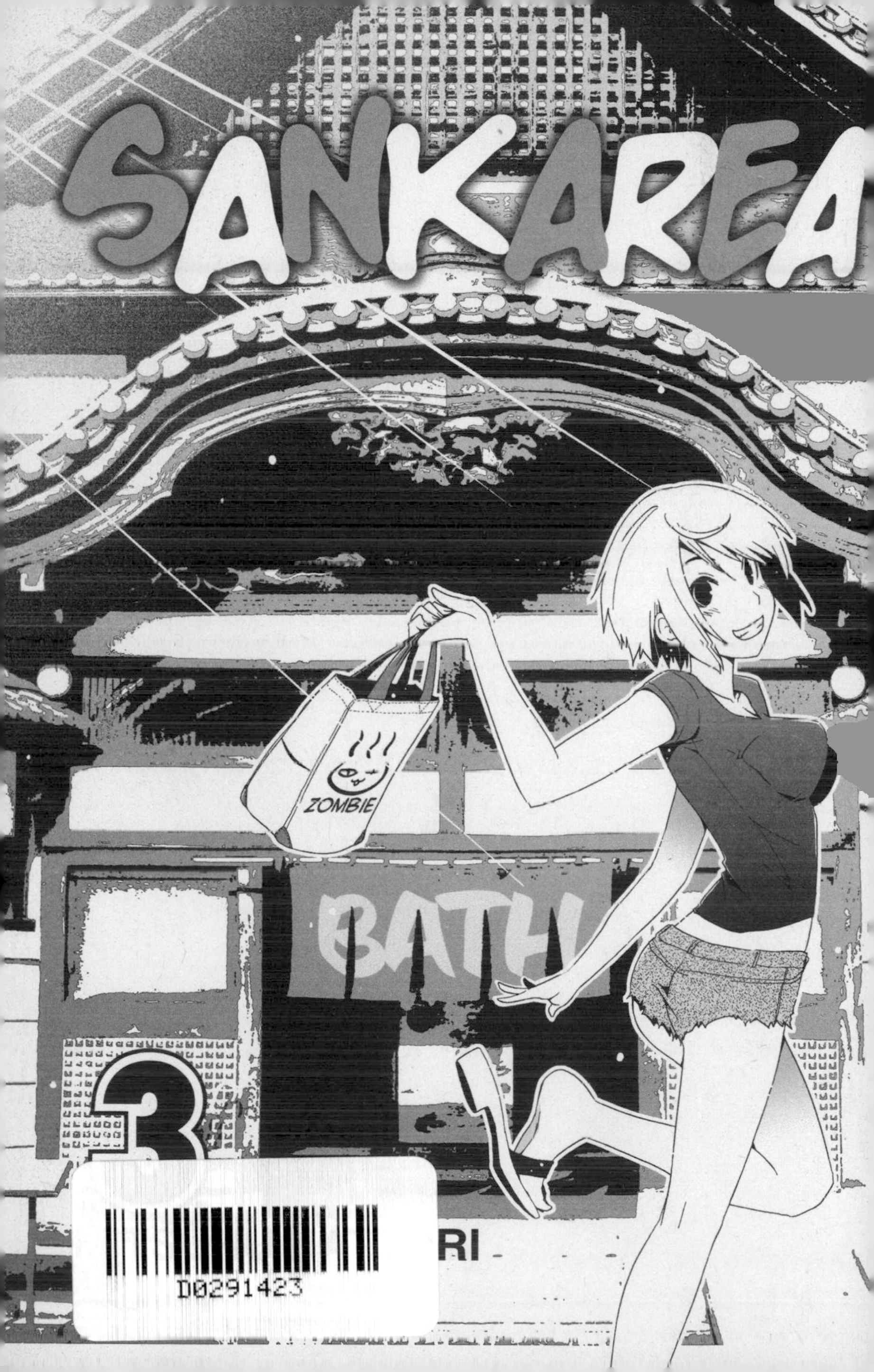
SANKAREA
3
ZOMBIE
BATH

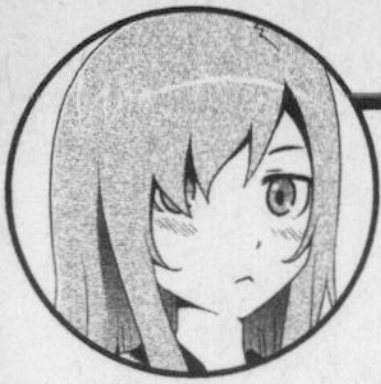

Furuya Mero

A reliable first-year middle school student, she manages all the housework for the Furuya family. She loves to read the Heart Sutra.

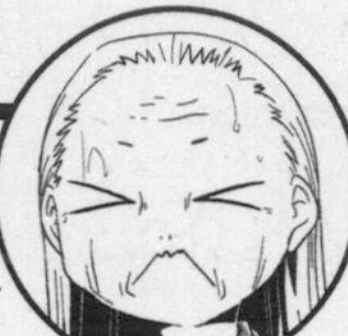

Grandpa

The most mysterious organism (?) of all in "Sankarea." He seems to be knowledgeable about zombies, though…

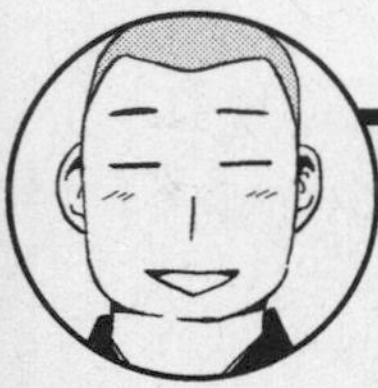

Dad

His real name is Furuya Dohn. He's the live-in head priest of Shiryohji Temple. He agreed to let Rea live with the family, saying, "Should be fine, right?"

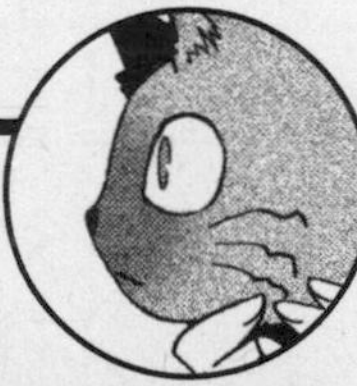

Bub

He died in an accident, but came back to life thanks to medicine made by Chihiro and Rea.

STORY

When she became a zombie, Rea had no place to go home to. Chihiro let her live with him at Shiryohji Temple, and they started a happy yet embarrassing life together. They couldn't discover how to stop her from decaying, but they did get to go out shopping together, and Rea enjoyed her freedom. Then, unable to let his daughter run away, Sanka Danichiroh laid a trap for them, goading Chihiro into a duel. Rea rushed to Chihiro's aid, and they managed to win. Rea is finally truly free.

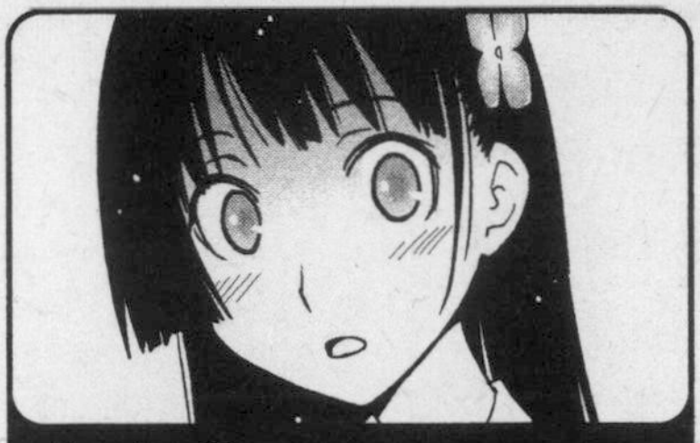

Sanka Rea

A first-year student at the private Sanka Girls' Academy. She's the daughter of a well-known family, but fell to her death trying to run from her father. Afterward, she returned to life as a zombie girl!

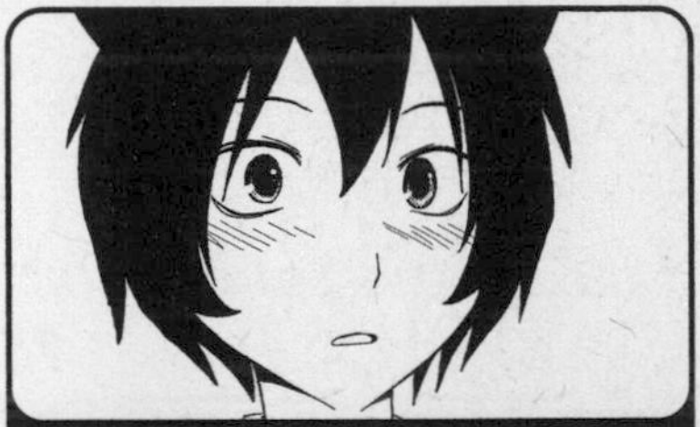

Furuya Chihiro

A first-year student at Shiyoh Public High School, he's an unusual boy who has loved zombies since he was little. He is currently trying all kinds of different things to protect Rea.

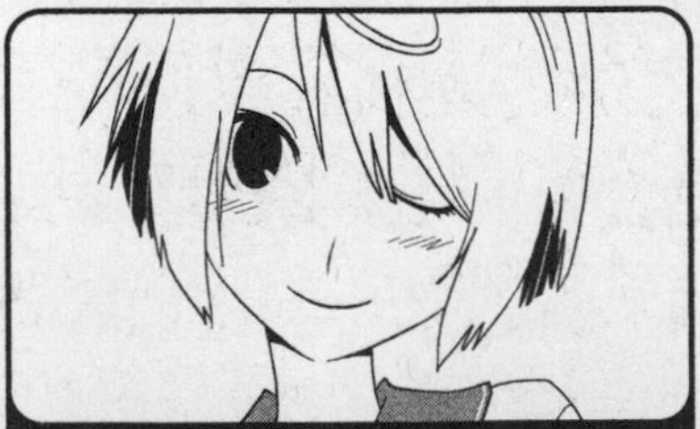

Saohji Ranko

Chihiro's cousin and childhood friend. She's a perky, energetic girl, and second-year student at Sanka Girls'. Her nickname is "Wanko."

MITSURU HATTORI presents

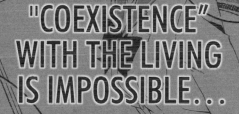

"COEXISTENCE" WITH THE LIVING IS IMPOSSIBLE...

CONTENTS

SERIALIZED IN BESSATSU
SHONEN MAGAZINE,
OCT. 2010 - FEB. 2011.

SANKAREA 3

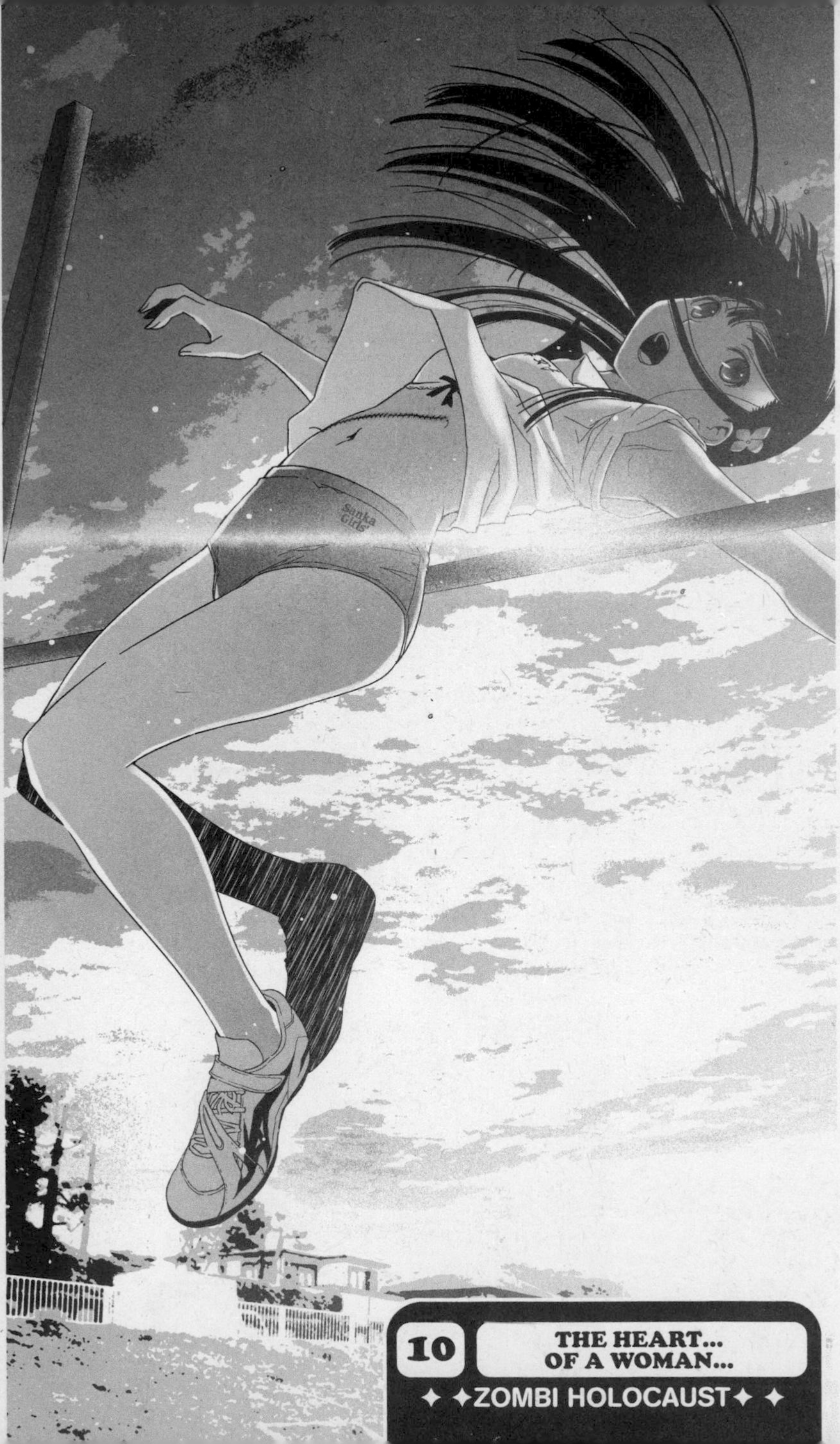
Sanka Girls
10
THE HEART... OF A WOMAN...
✦ ✦ZOMBI HOLOCAUST✦ ✦

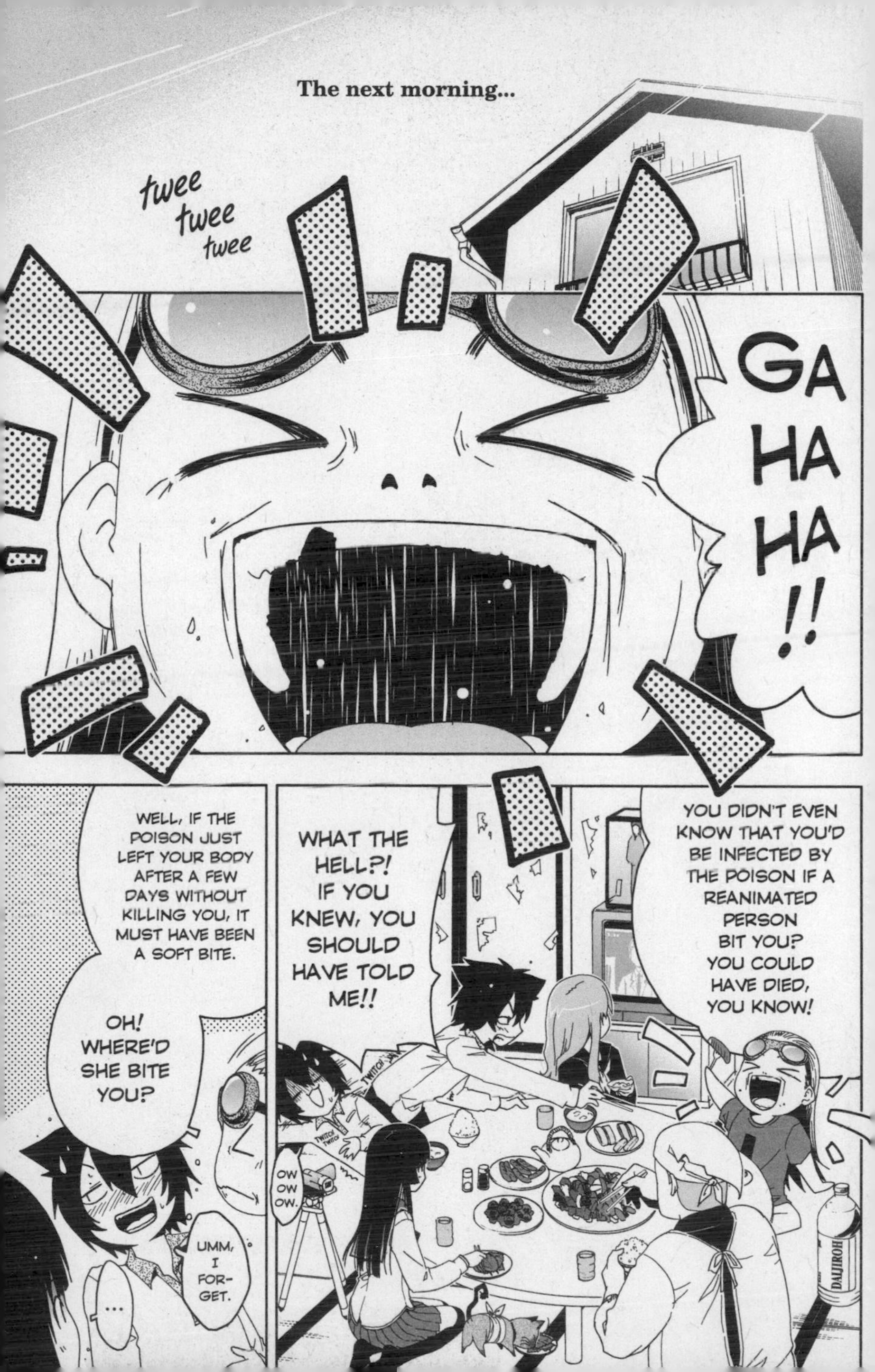
The next morning...
twee twee twee
GA HA HA HA!!
YOU DIDN'T EVEN KNOW THAT YOU'D BE INFECTED BY THE POISON IF A REANIMATED PERSON BIT YOU? YOU COULD HAVE DIED, YOU KNOW!
WHAT THE HELL?! IF YOU KNEW, YOU SHOULD HAVE TOLD ME!!
OW OW OW.
DAIJIROH
WELL, IF THE POISON JUST LEFT YOUR BODY AFTER A FEW DAYS WITHOUT KILLING YOU, IT MUST HAVE BEEN A SOFT BITE.
OH! WHERE'D SHE BITE YOU?
UMM, I FOR-GET.
...

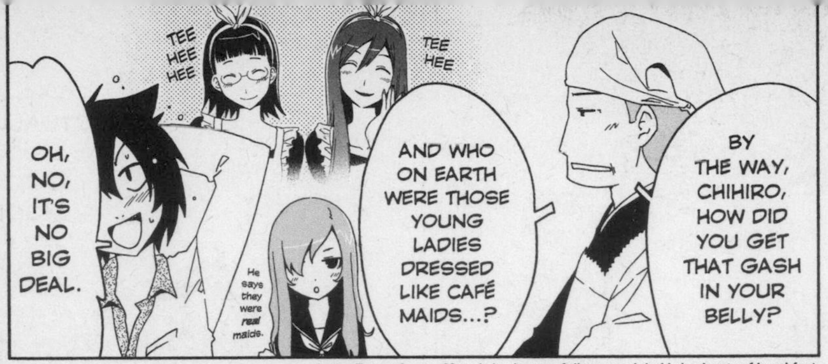
BY THE WAY, CHIHIRO, HOW DID YOU GET THAT GASH IN YOUR BELLY?
AND WHO ON EARTH WERE THOSE YOUNG LADIES DRESSED LIKE CAFÉ MAIDS...?
TEE HEE
TEE HEE HEE
He says they were *real* maids.
OH, NO, IT'S NO BIG DEAL.

In the Furuya home, Mero is in charge of dinner, and dad is in charge of breakfast.

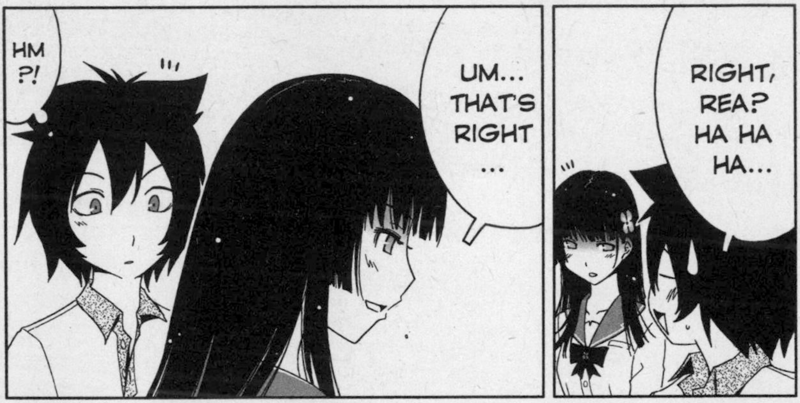
RIGHT, REA? HA HA HA...
UM... THAT'S RIGHT ...
HM ?!

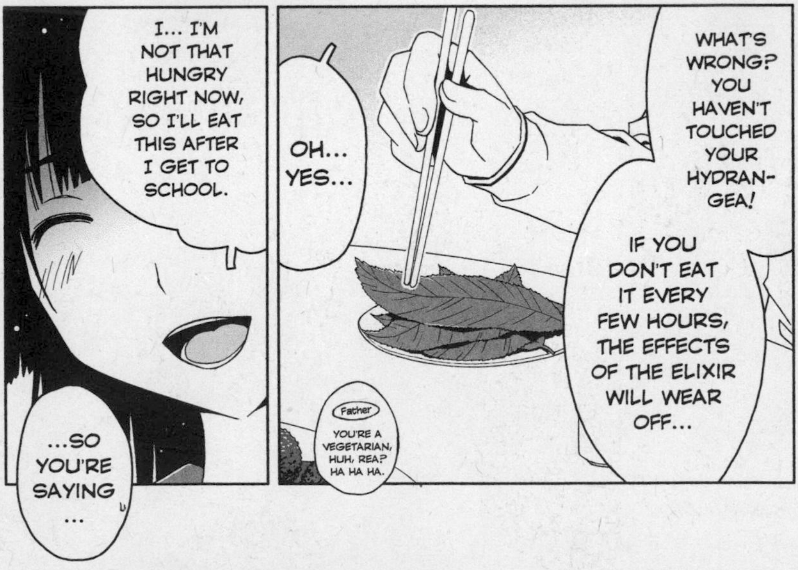
WHAT'S WRONG? YOU HAVEN'T TOUCHED YOUR HYDRAN-GEA!
IF YOU DON'T EAT IT EVERY FEW HOURS, THE EFFECTS OF THE ELIXIR WILL WEAR OFF...
OH... YES...
Father
YOU'RE A VEGETARIAN, HUH, REA? HA HA HA.
I... I'M NOT THAT HUNGRY RIGHT NOW, SO I'LL EAT THIS AFTER I GET TO SCHOOL.
...SO YOU'RE SAYING ...

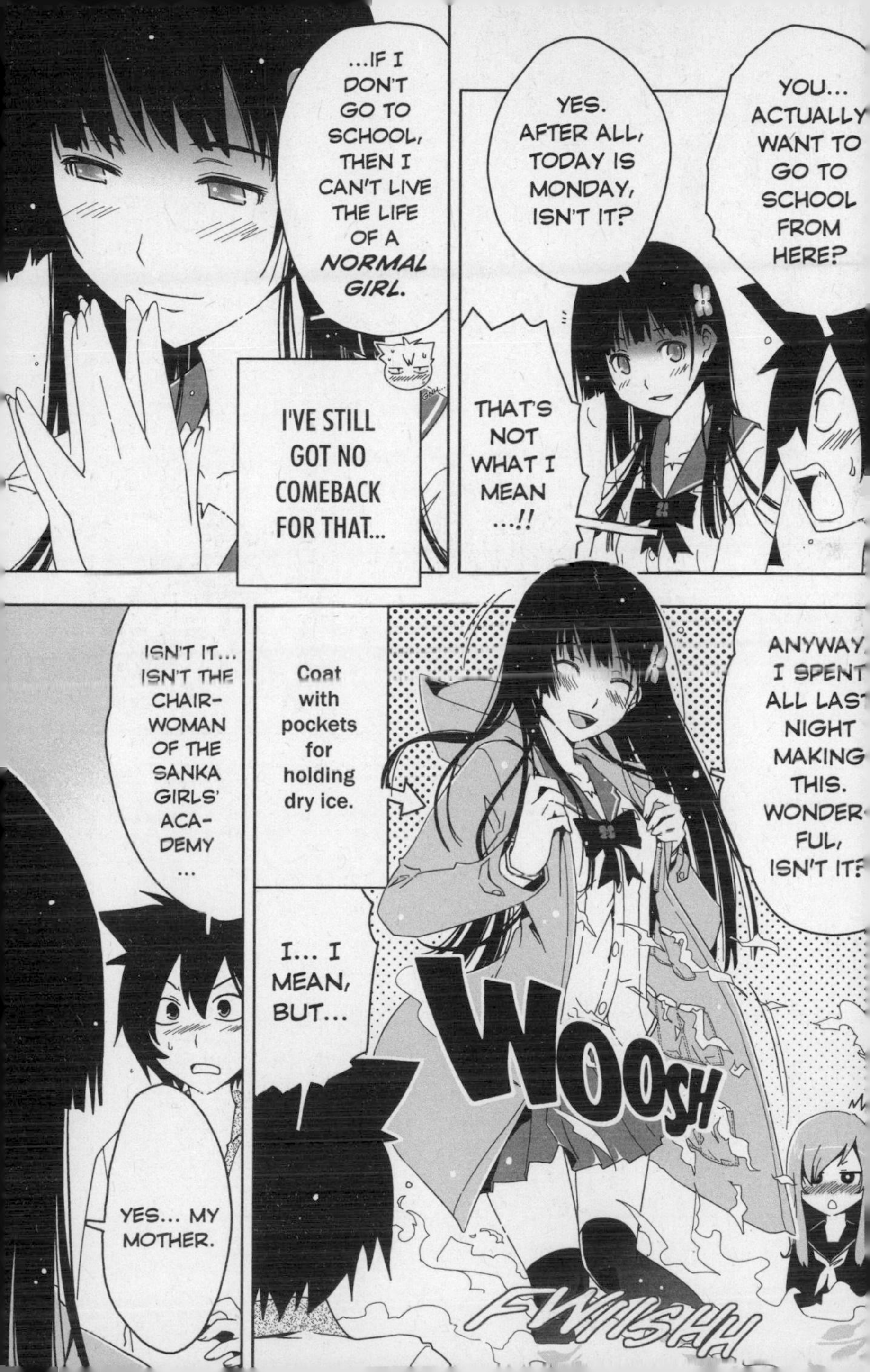
YOU... ACTUALLY WANT TO GO TO SCHOOL FROM HERE?
YES. AFTER ALL, TODAY IS MONDAY, ISN'T IT?
THAT'S NOT WHAT I MEAN ...!!
...IF I DON'T GO TO SCHOOL, THEN I CAN'T LIVE THE LIFE OF A NORMAL GIRL.
GNH...
I'VE STILL GOT NO COMEBACK FOR THAT...
ANYWAY, I SPENT ALL LAST NIGHT MAKING THIS. WONDERFUL, ISN'T IT?
Coat with pockets for holding dry ice.
WOOSH
FWISHH
I... I MEAN, BUT...
ISN'T IT... ISN'T THE CHAIRWOMAN OF THE SANKA GIRLS' ACADEMY ...
YES... MY MOTHER.

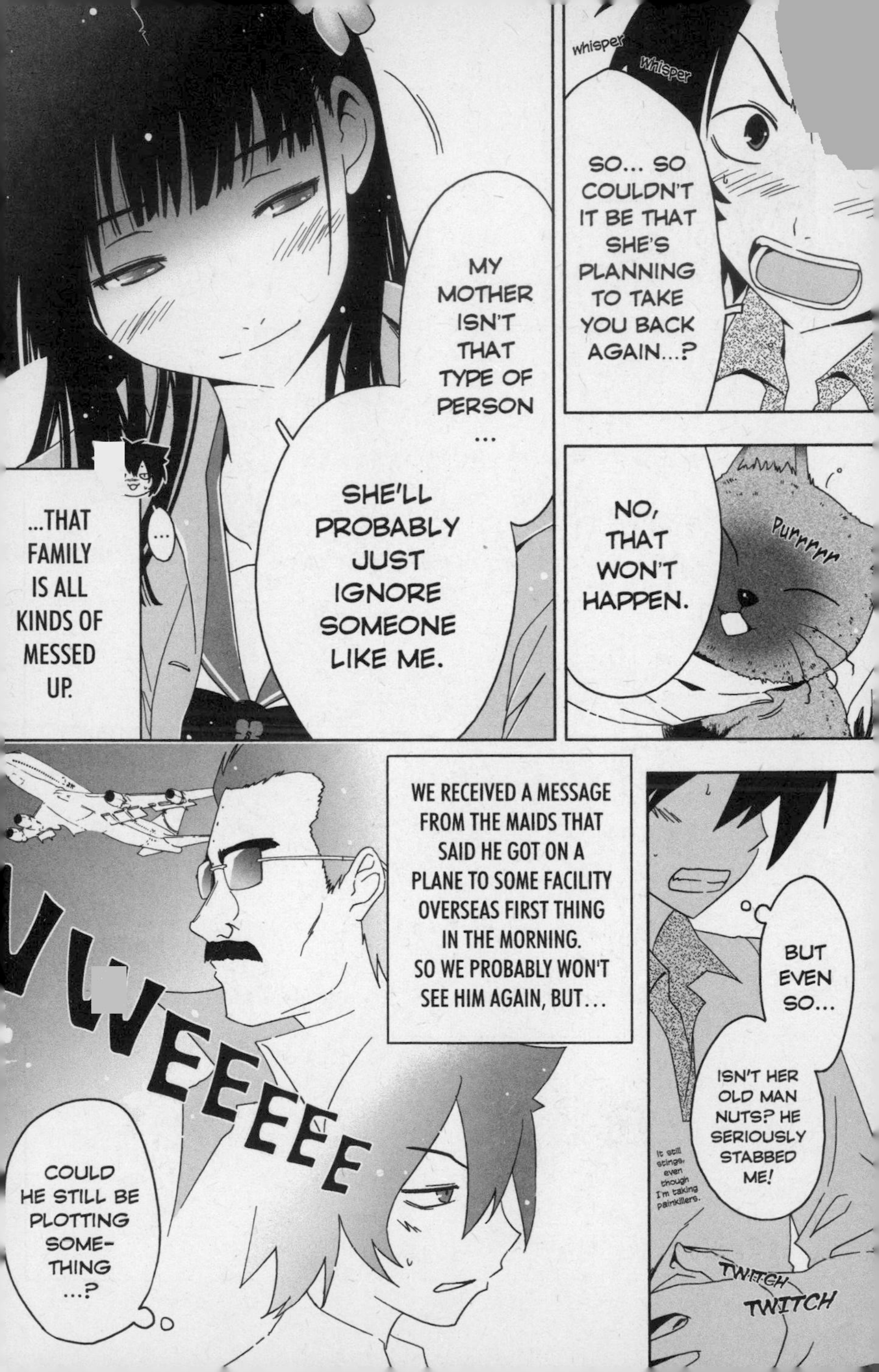
Whisper
Whisper
SO... SO COULDN'T IT BE THAT SHE'S PLANNING TO TAKE YOU BACK AGAIN...?
NO, THAT WON'T HAPPEN.
Purrrrrr
MY MOTHER ISN'T THAT TYPE OF PERSON...
SHE'LL PROBABLY JUST IGNORE SOMEONE LIKE ME.
...
...THAT FAMILY IS ALL KINDS OF MESSED UP.
BUT EVEN SO...
ISN'T HER OLD MAN NUTS? HE SERIOUSLY STABBED ME!
It still stings, even though I'm taking painkillers.
TWITCH
TWITCH
WE RECEIVED A MESSAGE FROM THE MAIDS THAT SAID HE GOT ON A PLANE TO SOME FACILITY OVERSEAS FIRST THING IN THE MORNING. SO WE PROBABLY WON'T SEE HIM AGAIN, BUT...
VWEEEEEE
COULD HE STILL BE PLOTTING SOMETHING...?

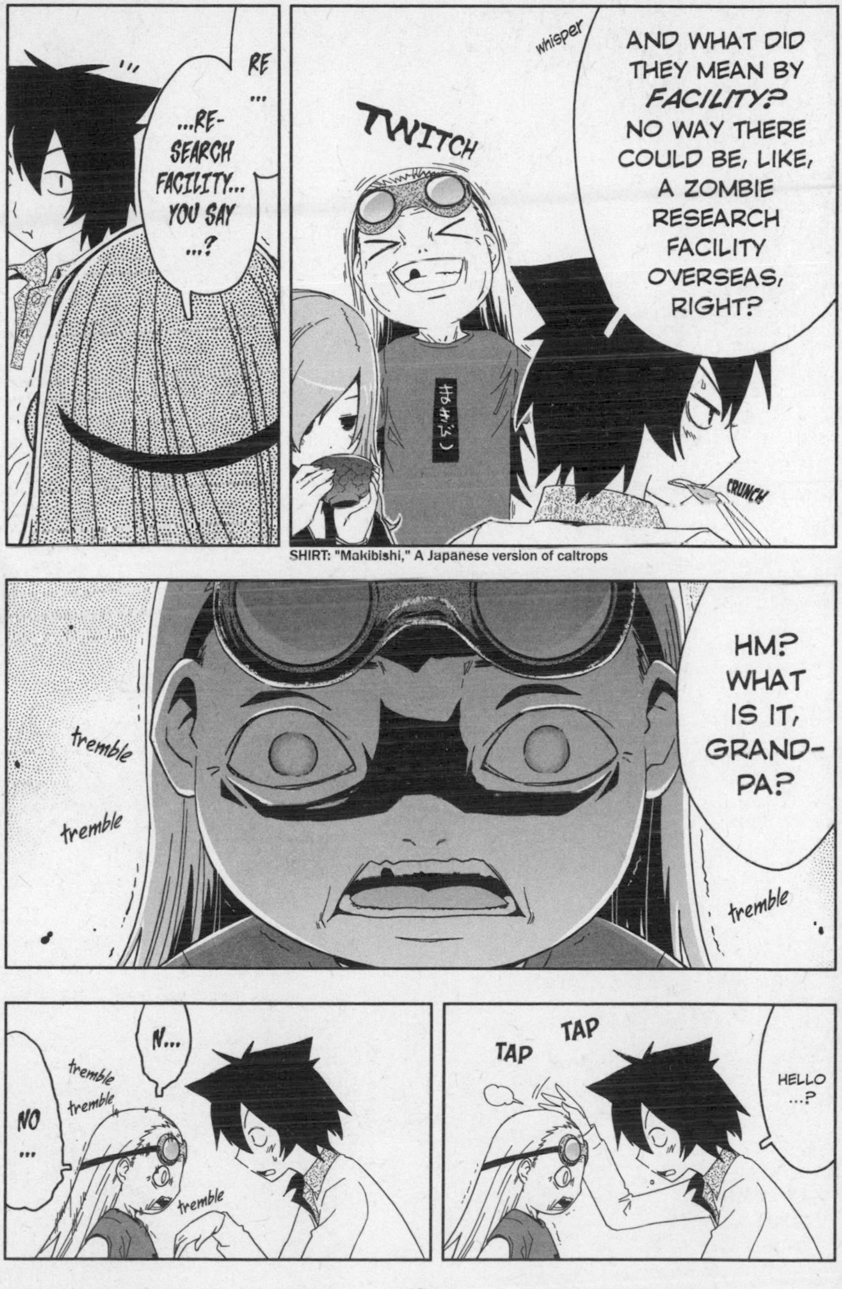
whisper
AND WHAT DID THEY MEAN BY FACILITY? NO WAY THERE COULD BE, LIKE, A ZOMBIE RESEARCH FACILITY OVERSEAS, RIGHT?
TWITCH
まきびし
CRUNCH
RE ...
...RE-SEARCH FACILITY... YOU SAY ...?
HM? WHAT IS IT, GRANDPA?
tremble
tremble
tremble
HELLO ...?
TAP
TAP
N...
tremble
tremble
NO ...
tremble

SHIRT: "Makibishi," A Japanese version of caltrops

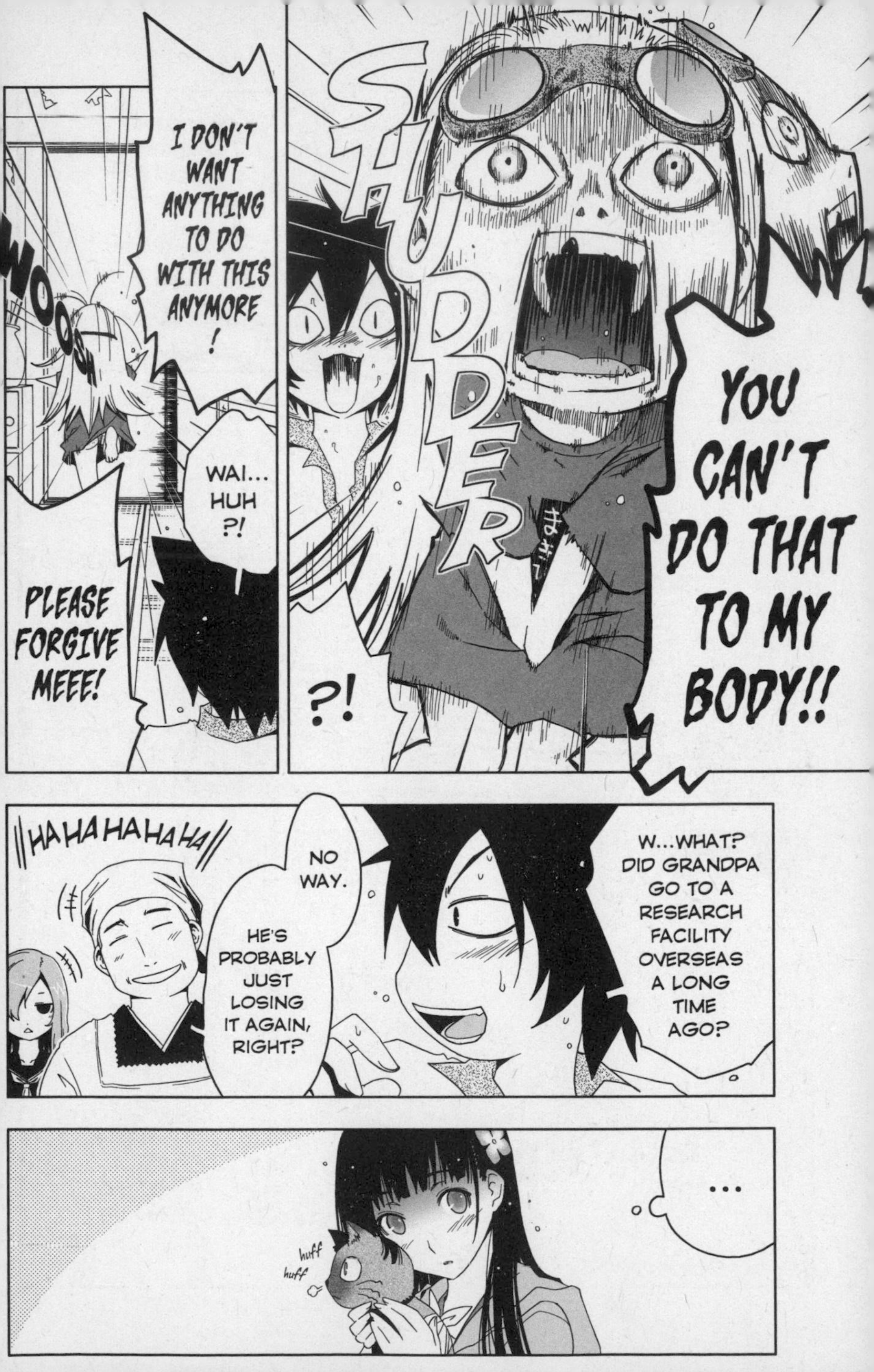
SHUDDER
YOU CAN'T DO THAT TO MY BODY!!
?!
I DON'T WANT ANYTHING TO DO WITH THIS ANYMORE!
WOOSH
WAI... HUH ?!
PLEASE FORGIVE MEEE!
W...WHAT? DID GRANDPA GO TO A RESEARCH FACILITY OVERSEAS A LONG TIME AGO?
NO WAY.
HE'S PROBABLY JUST LOSING IT AGAIN, RIGHT?
HAHAHAHAHAHA
...
huff huff

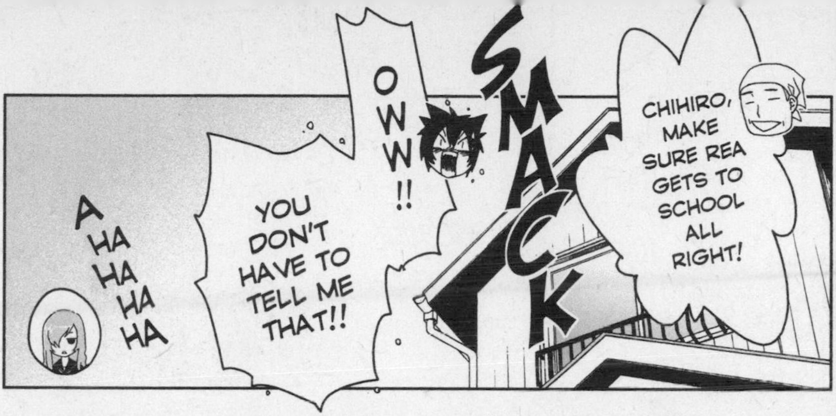
CHIHIRO, MAKE SURE REA GETS TO SCHOOL ALL RIGHT!
SMACK
OWW!!
YOU DON'T HAVE TO TELL ME THAT!!
A HA HA HA HA

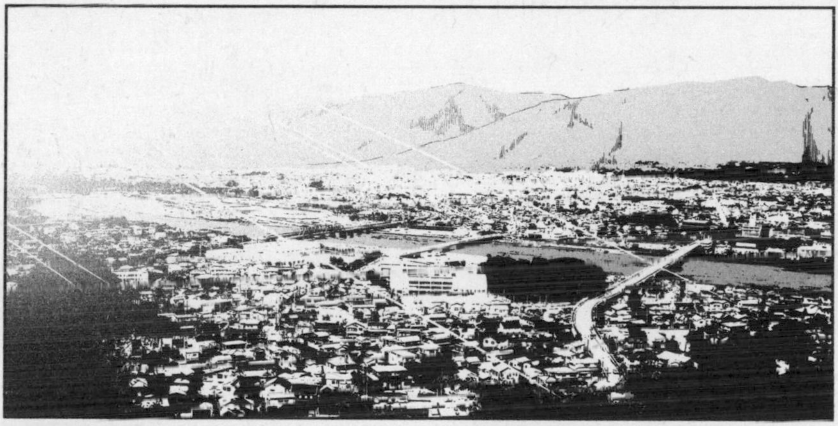

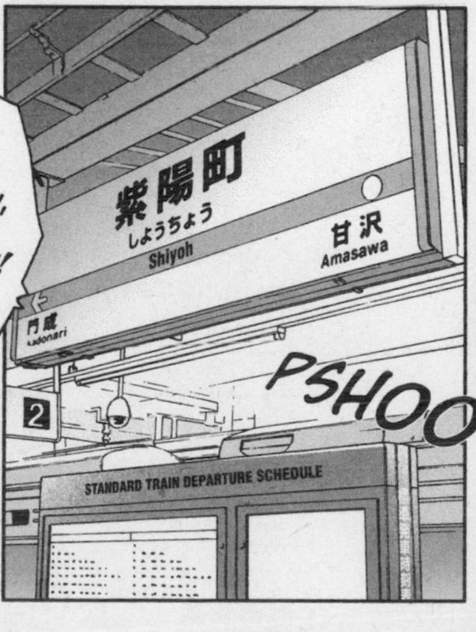
SHIYOH STATION, SHIYOH STATION!
紫陽町
しょうちょう
Shiyoh
甘沢
Amasawa
門成
2
PSHOO
STANDARD TRAIN DEPARTURE SCHEDULE

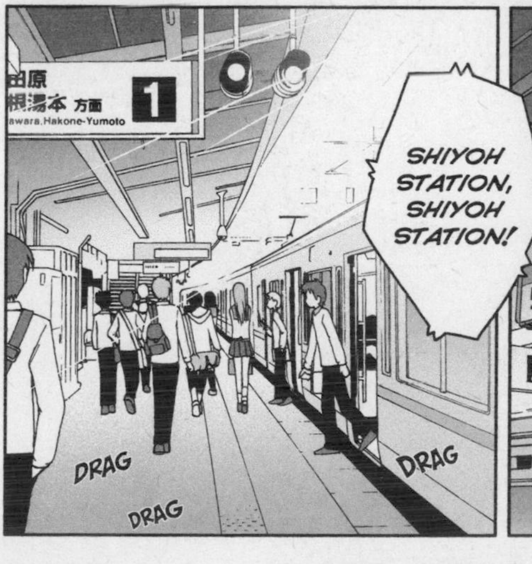
1
方面
Hakone-Yumoto
DRAG
DRAG
DRAG

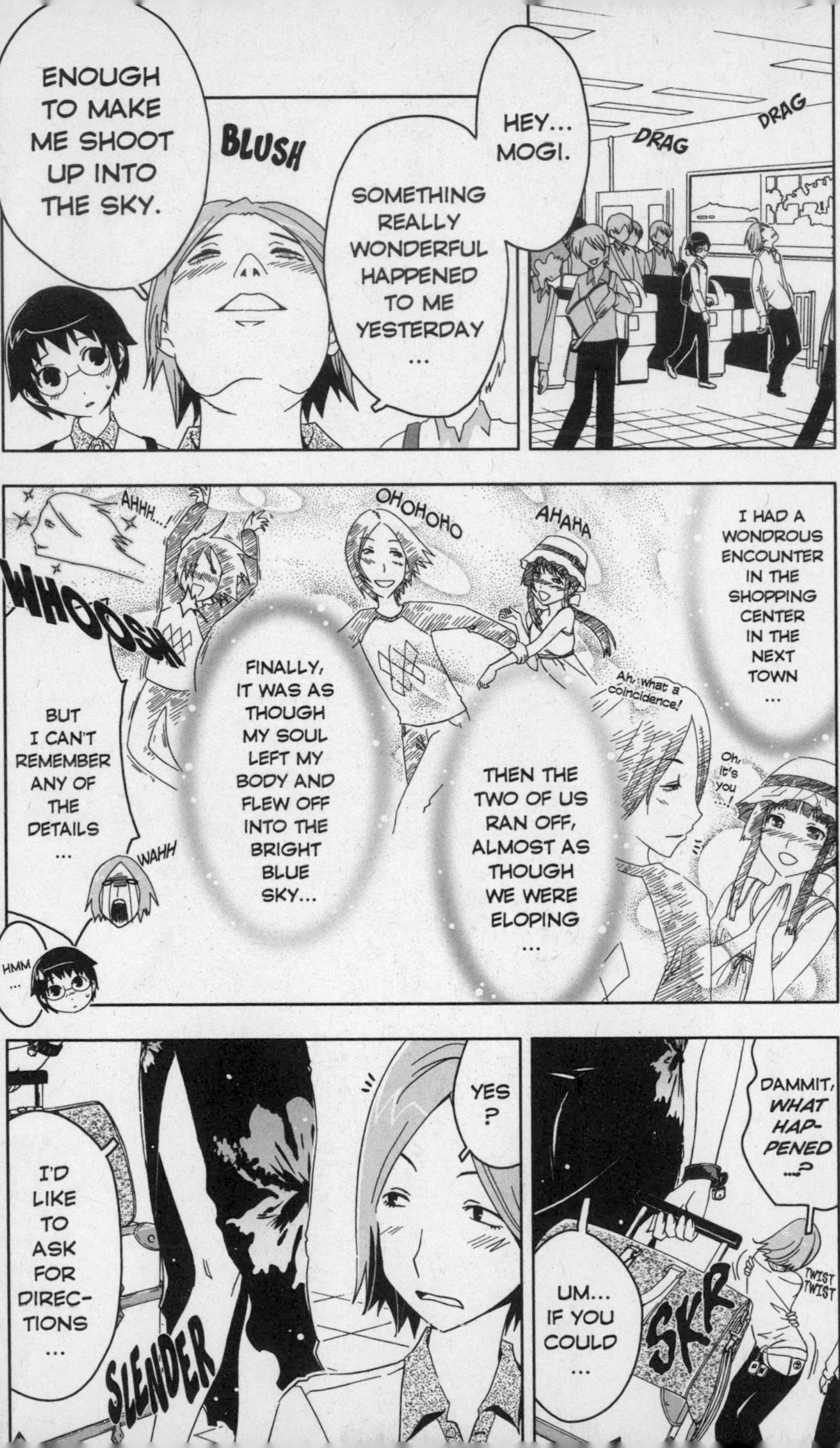
DRAG
DRAG
HEY... MOGI.
SOMETHING REALLY WONDERFUL HAPPENED TO ME YESTERDAY...
BLUSH
ENOUGH TO MAKE ME SHOOT UP INTO THE SKY.
I HAD A WONDROUS ENCOUNTER IN THE SHOPPING CENTER IN THE NEXT TOWN...
AHAHA
OHOHOHO
Ah, what a coincidence!
Oh, it's you...!
THEN THE TWO OF US RAN OFF, ALMOST AS THOUGH WE WERE ELOPING...
FINALLY, IT WAS AS THOUGH MY SOUL LEFT MY BODY AND FLEW OFF INTO THE BRIGHT BLUE SKY...
AHHH...!
WHOOSH
BUT I CAN'T REMEMBER ANY OF THE DETAILS...
WAHH
HMM...
DAMMIT, WHAT HAPPENED...?
TWIST TWIST
SKR
UM... IF YOU COULD...
YES?
I'D LIKE TO ASK FOR DIRECTIONS...
SLENDER

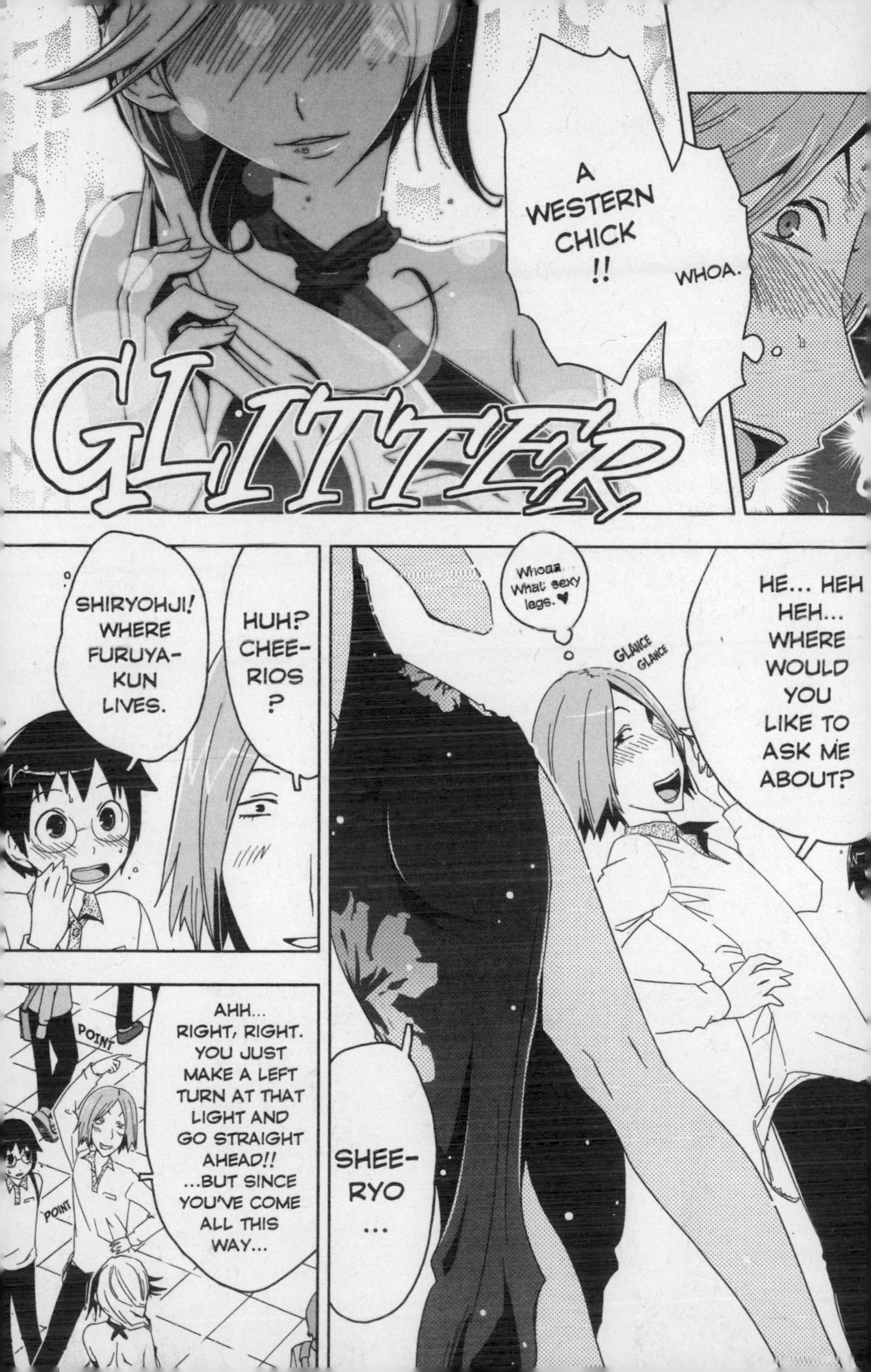
A WESTERN CHICK !!
WHOA.
GLITTER
HE... HEH HEH... WHERE WOULD YOU LIKE TO ASK ME ABOUT?
Whoaa. What sexy legs.♥
GLANCE GLANCE
SHEE-RYO ...
HUH? CHEE-RIOS ?
SHIRYOHJI! WHERE FURUYA-KUN LIVES.
AHH... RIGHT, RIGHT. YOU JUST MAKE A LEFT TURN AT THAT LIGHT AND GO STRAIGHT AHEAD!! ...BUT SINCE YOU'VE COME ALL THIS WAY...
POINT
POINT

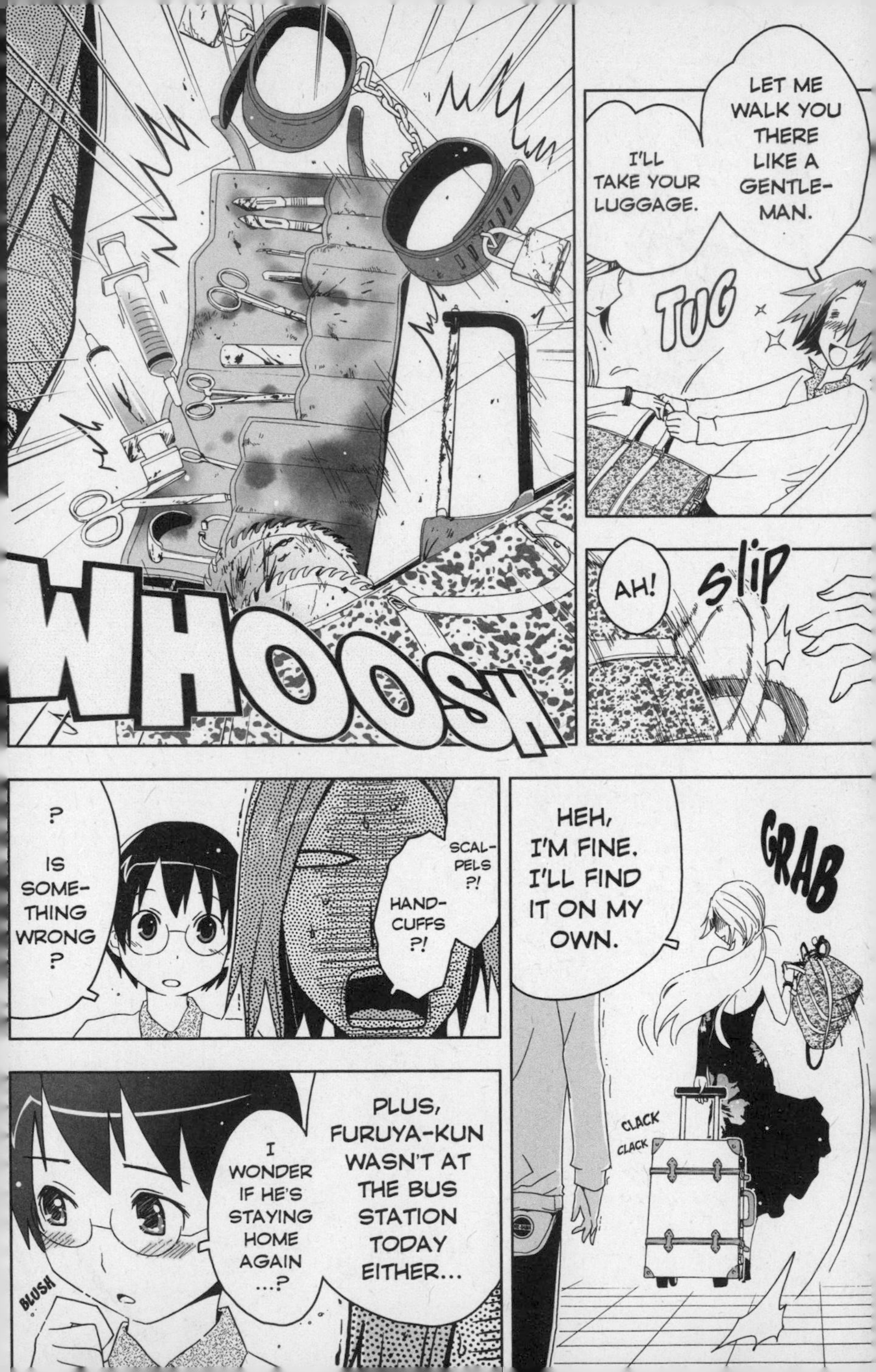
LET ME WALK YOU THERE LIKE A GENTLE-MAN.
I'LL TAKE YOUR LUGGAGE.
TUG
SLIP
AH!
WHOOSH
GRAB
HEH, I'M FINE. I'LL FIND IT ON MY OWN.
CLACK
CLACK
SCAL-PELS ?!
HAND-CUFFS ?!
? IS SOME-THING WRONG ?
PLUS, FURUYA-KUN WASN'T AT THE BUS STATION TODAY EITHER...
I WONDER IF HE'S STAYING HOME AGAIN ...?
BLUSH

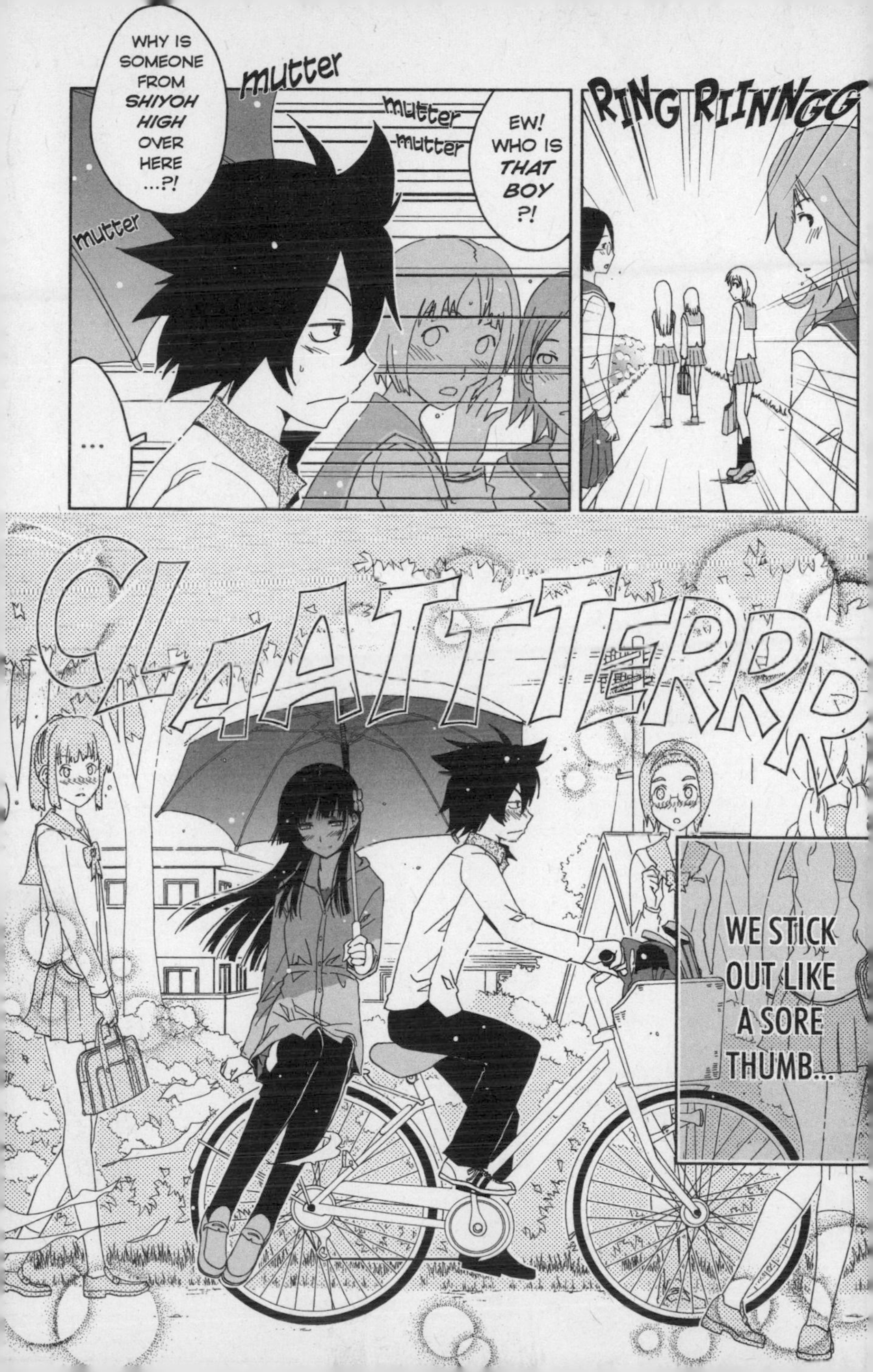
RING RIINNGG
mutter
mutter
mutter
EW! WHO IS THAT BOY?!
WHY IS SOMEONE FROM SHIYOH HIGH OVER HERE ...?!
mutter
...
CLATTERRR
WE STICK OUT LIKE A SORE THUMB...

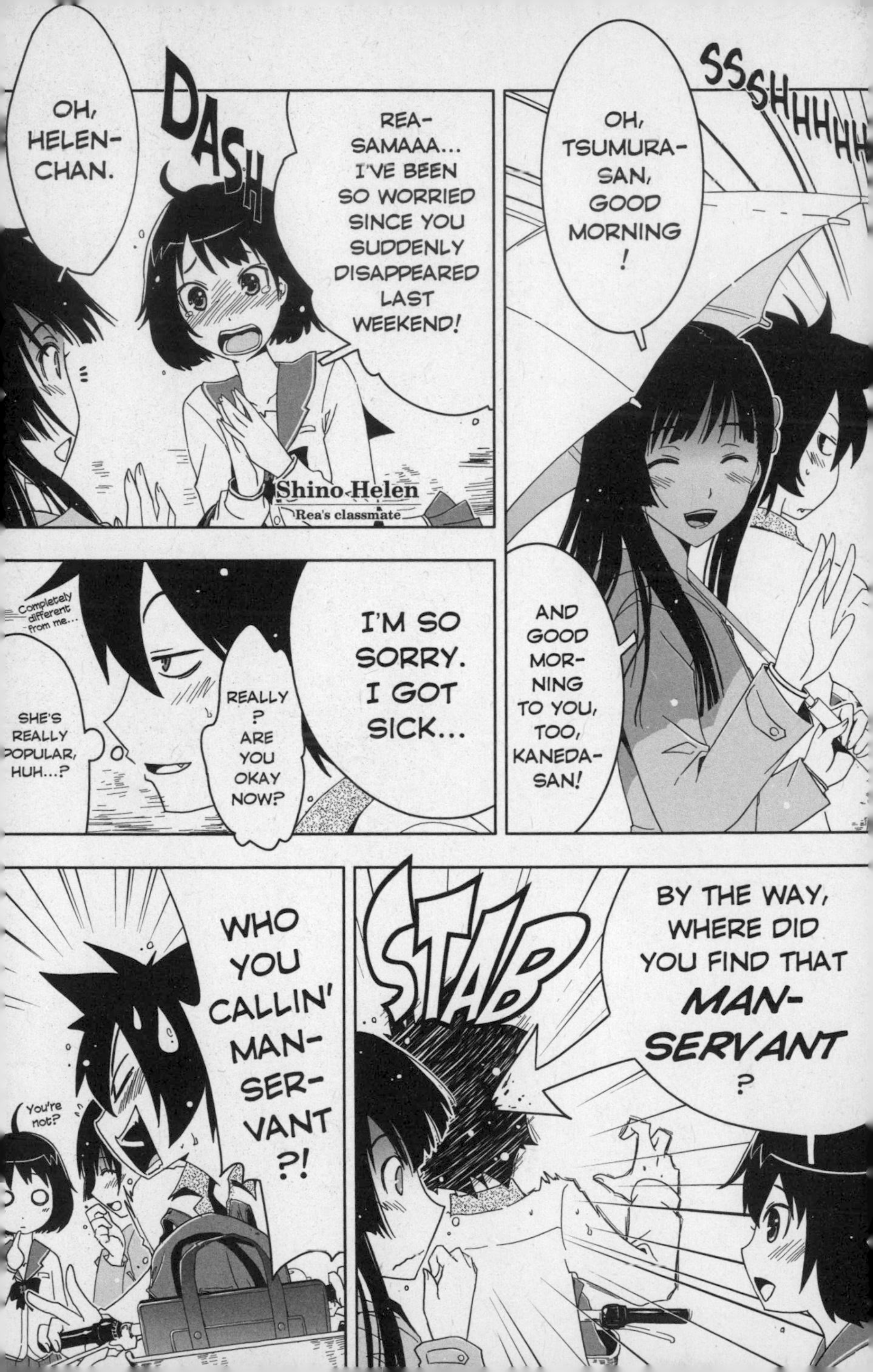
SSSHHHHH
OH, TSUMURA-SAN, GOOD MORNING!
AND GOOD MORNING TO YOU, TOO, KANEDA-SAN!
REA-SAMAAA... I'VE BEEN SO WORRIED SINCE YOU SUDDENLY DISAPPEARED LAST WEEKEND!
DASH
OH, HELEN-CHAN.
Shino Helen
Rea's classmate
I'M SO SORRY. I GOT SICK...
REALLY? ARE YOU OKAY NOW?
SHE'S REALLY POPULAR, HUH...?
Completely different from me...
BY THE WAY, WHERE DID YOU FIND THAT MAN-SERVANT?
STAB
WHO YOU CALLIN' MAN-SERVANT?!
You're not?

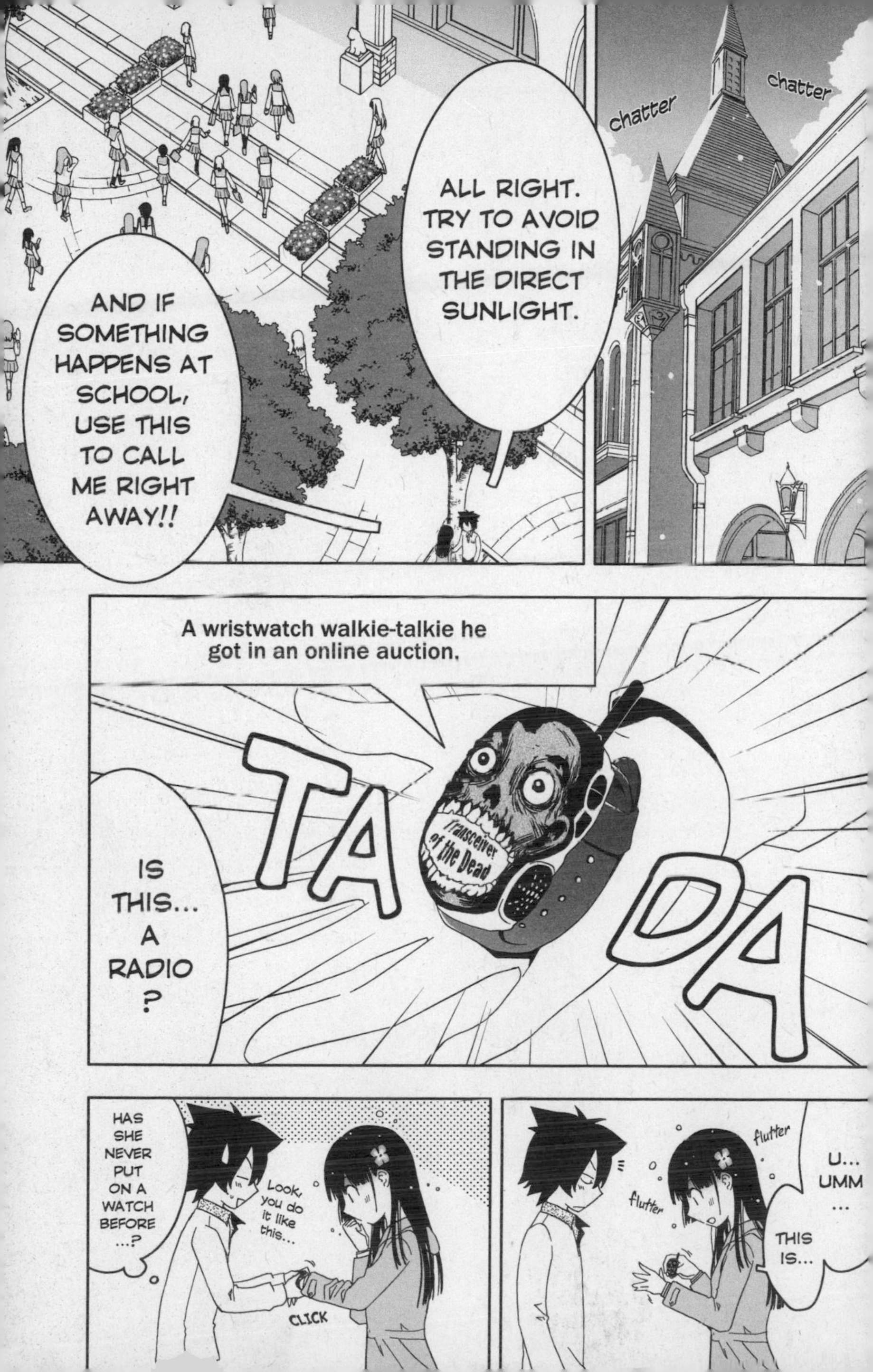
chatter
chatter
ALL RIGHT. TRY TO AVOID STANDING IN THE DIRECT SUNLIGHT.
AND IF SOMETHING HAPPENS AT SCHOOL, USE THIS TO CALL ME RIGHT AWAY!!
A wristwatch walkie-talkie he got in an online auction.
Transceiver of the Dead
TA DA
IS THIS... A RADIO ?
flutter
U... UMM ...
THIS IS...
flutter
HAS SHE NEVER PUT ON A WATCH BEFORE ...?
Look, you do it like this...
CLICK

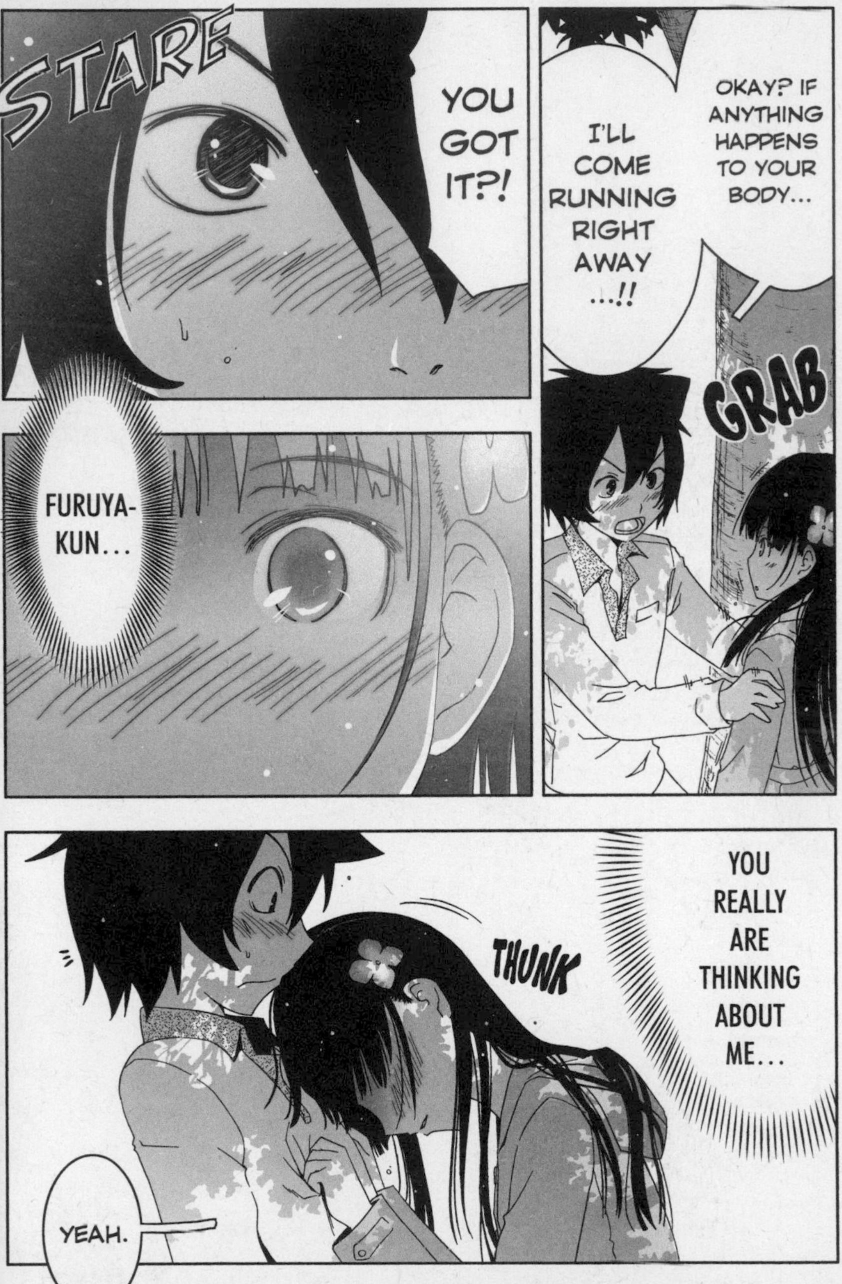
OKAY? IF ANYTHING HAPPENS TO YOUR BODY...
I'LL COME RUNNING RIGHT AWAY ...!!
GRAB
STARE
YOU GOT IT?!
FURUYA-KUN...
YOU REALLY ARE THINKING ABOUT ME...
THUNK
YEAH.

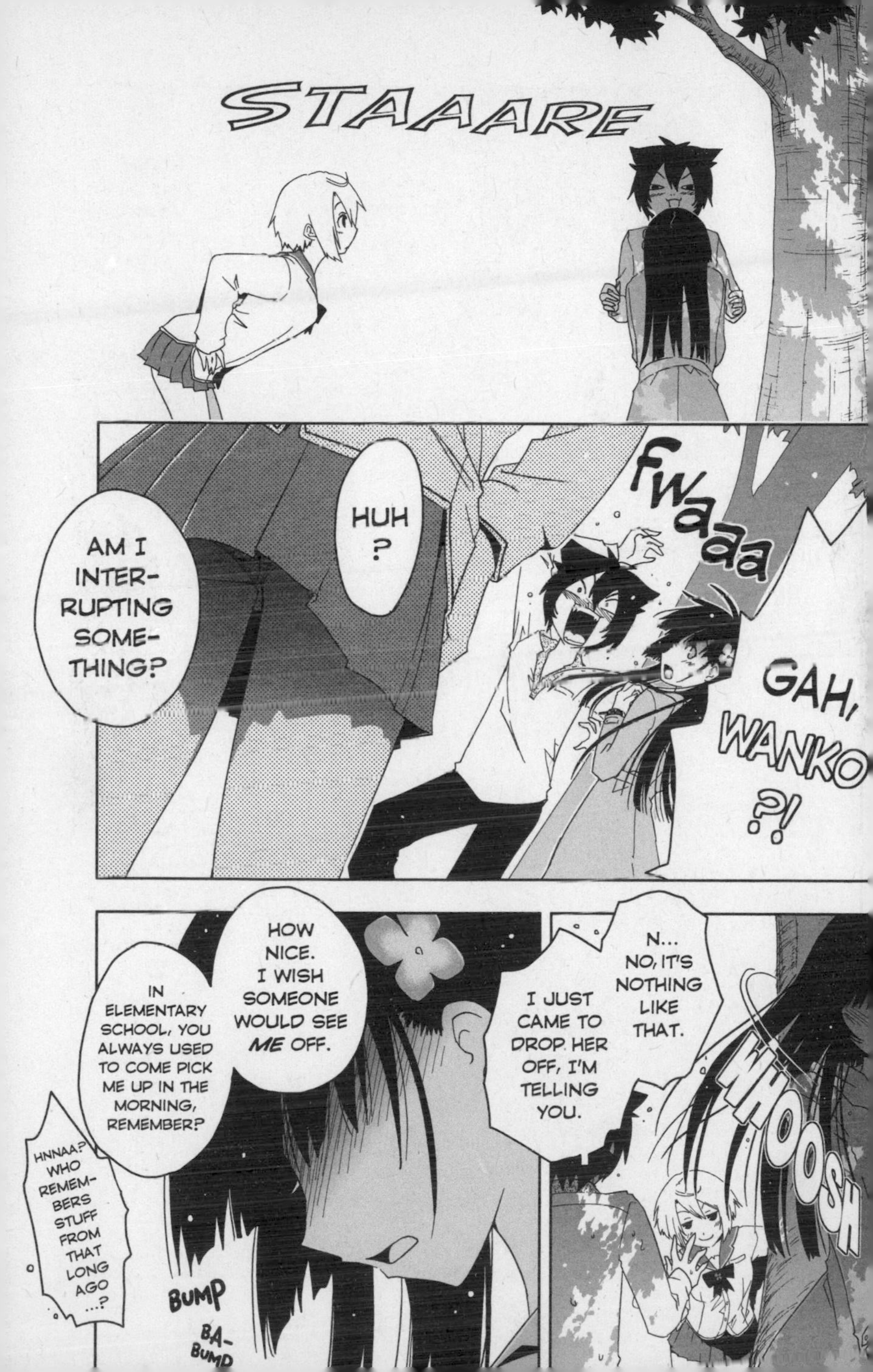
STAAARE
fwaaa
GAH, WANKO?!
HUH?
AM I INTERRUPTING SOMETHING?
N... NO, IT'S NOTHING LIKE THAT.
I JUST CAME TO DROP HER OFF, I'M TELLING YOU.
WHOOSH
HOW NICE. I WISH SOMEONE WOULD SEE *ME* OFF.
IN ELEMENTARY SCHOOL, YOU ALWAYS USED TO COME PICK ME UP IN THE MORNING, REMEMBER?
HNNAA? WHO REMEMBERS STUFF FROM THAT LONG AGO ...?
BUMP
BA-BUMP

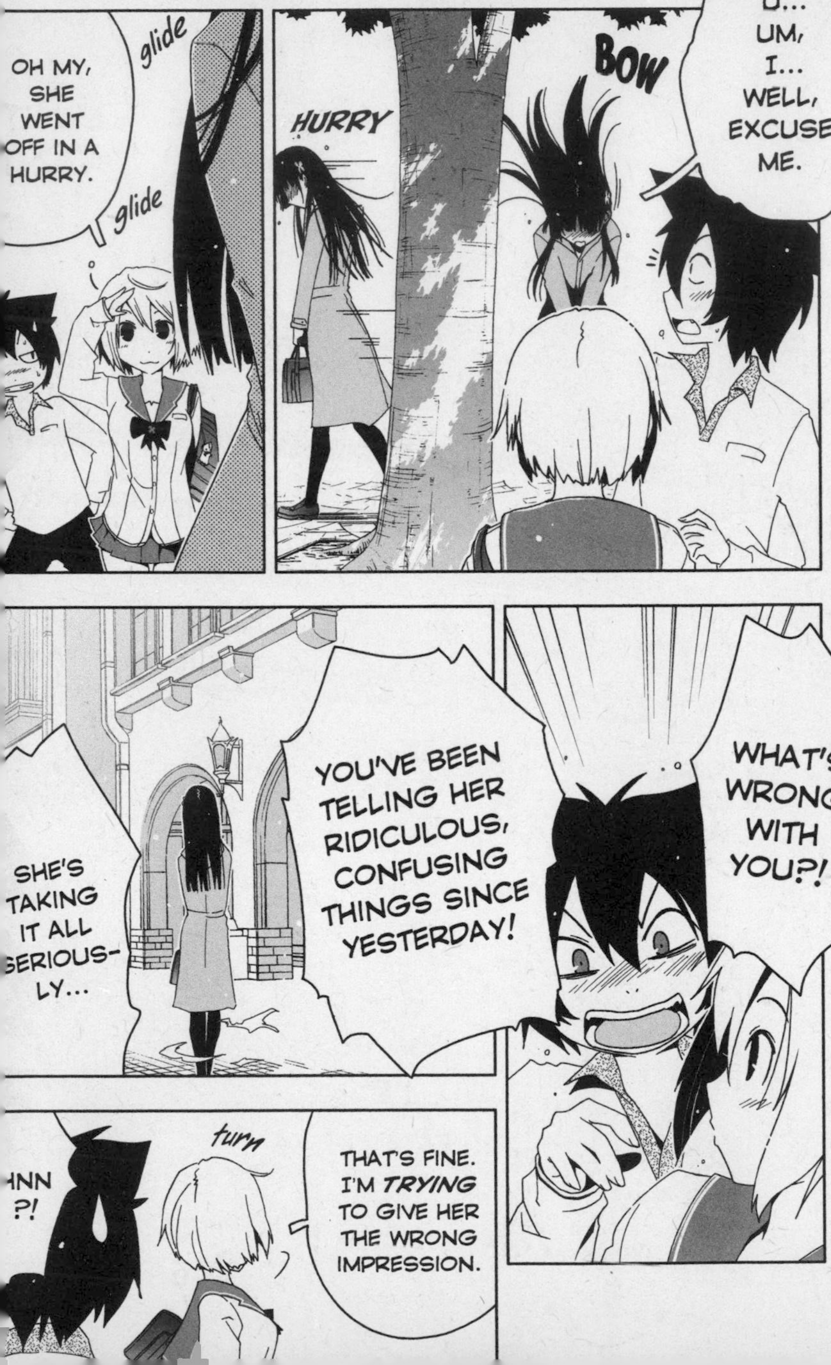
U... UM, I... WELL, EXCUSE ME.
BOW
HURRY
glide
OH MY, SHE WENT OFF IN A HURRY.
glide
WHAT'S WRONG WITH YOU?!
YOU'VE BEEN TELLING HER RIDICULOUS, CONFUSING THINGS SINCE YESTERDAY!
SHE'S TAKING IT ALL SERIOUSLY...
turn
THAT'S FINE. I'M *TRYING* TO GIVE HER THE WRONG IMPRESSION.
HNN ?!

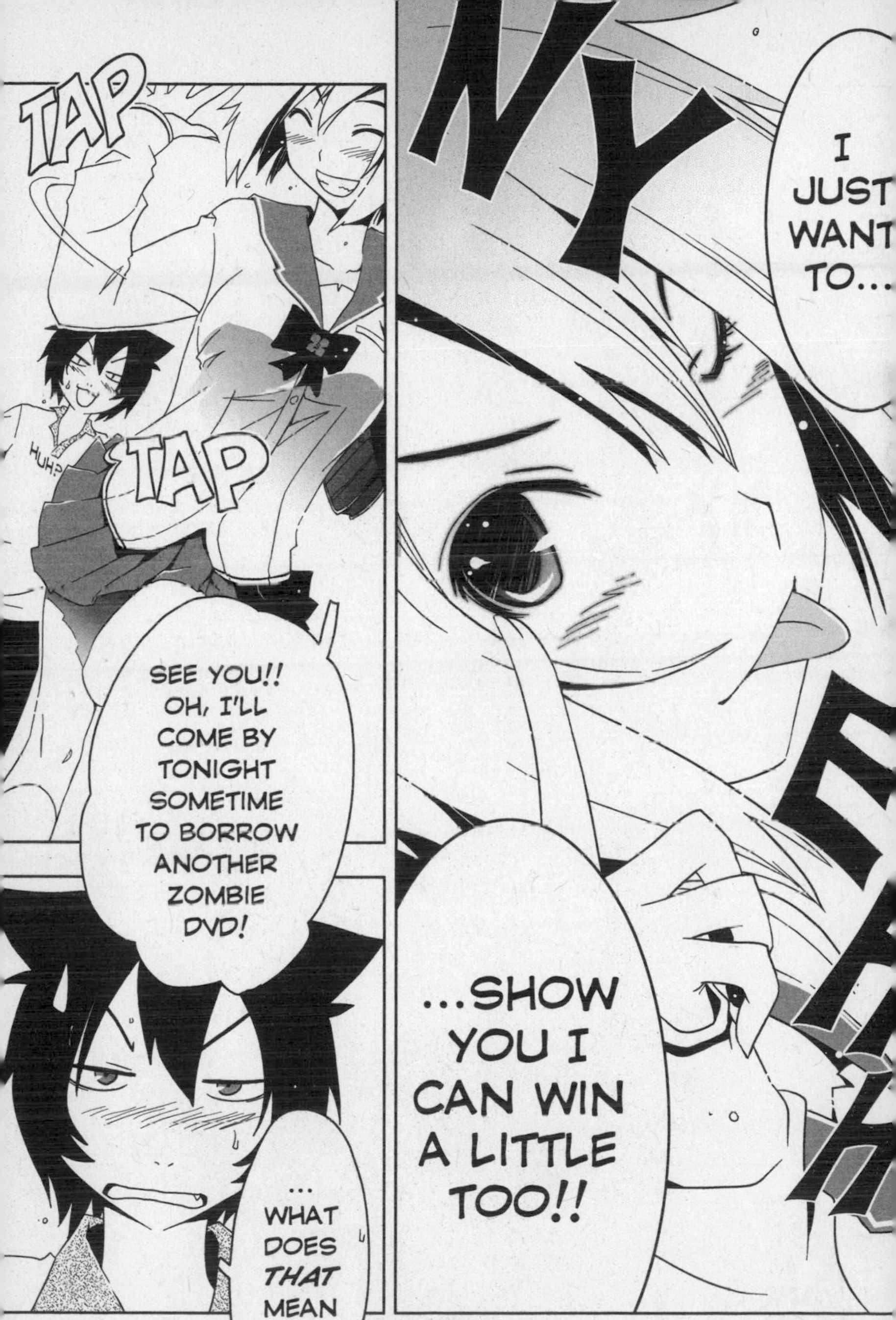
NY
I JUST WANT TO...
...SHOW YOU I CAN WIN A LITTLE TOO!!
TAP
TAP
HUH?
SEE YOU!! OH, I'LL COME BY TONIGHT SOMETIME TO BORROW ANOTHER ZOMBIE DVD!
... WHAT DOES *THAT* MEAN ?

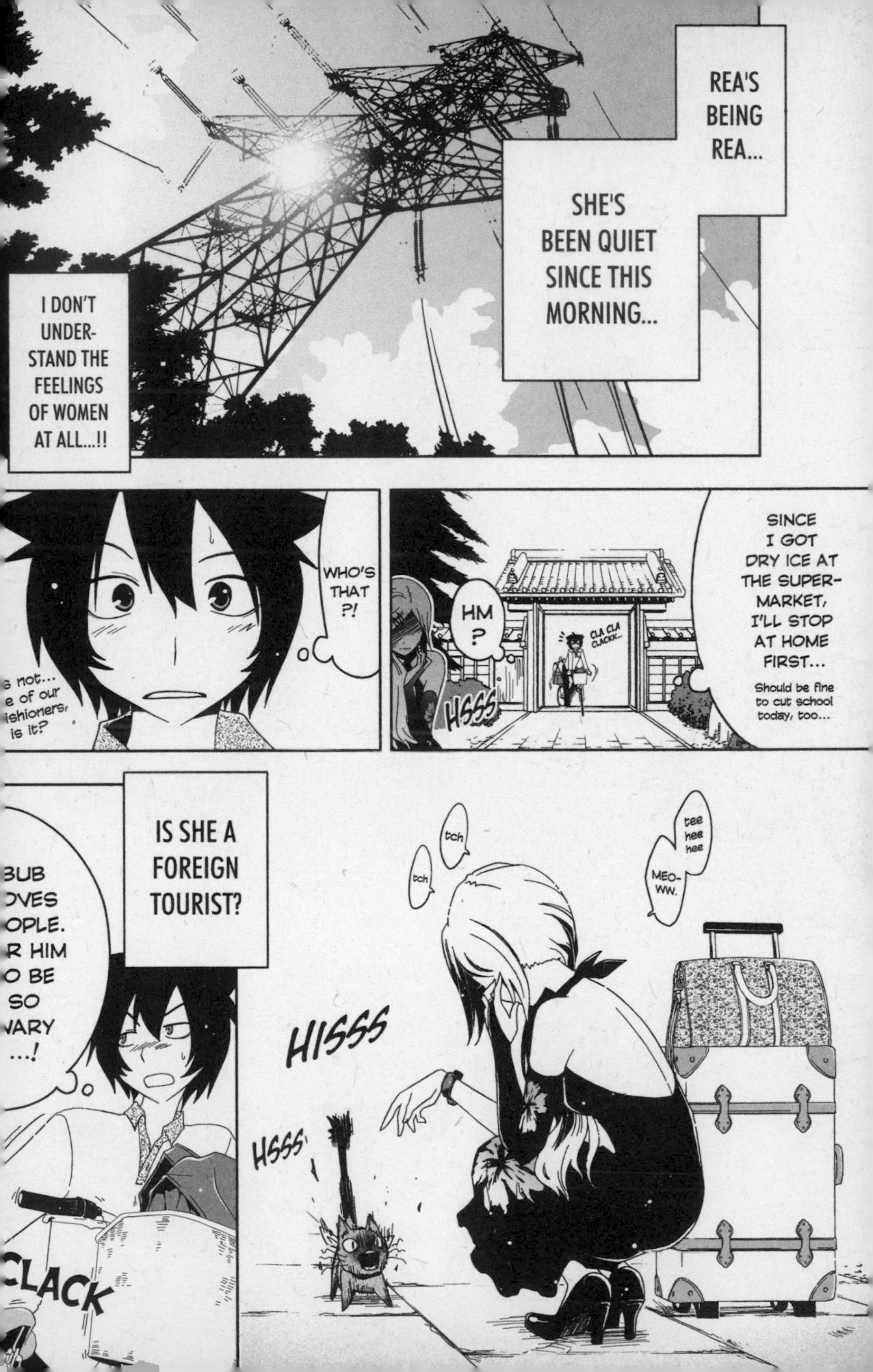
REA'S BEING REA...
SHE'S BEEN QUIET SINCE THIS MORNING...
I DON'T UNDER-STAND THE FEELINGS OF WOMEN AT ALL...!!
SINCE I GOT DRY ICE AT THE SUPER-MARKET, I'LL STOP AT HOME FIRST...
Should be fine to cut school today, too...
CLA CLA CLACKK...
HM ?
HSSS
WHO'S THAT ?!
s not... e of our ishioners, is it?
tee hee hee
MEO-WW.
tch
tch
HISSS
HSSS
IS SHE A FOREIGN TOURIST?
BUB OVES OPLE. R HIM O BE SO WARY ...!
CLACK

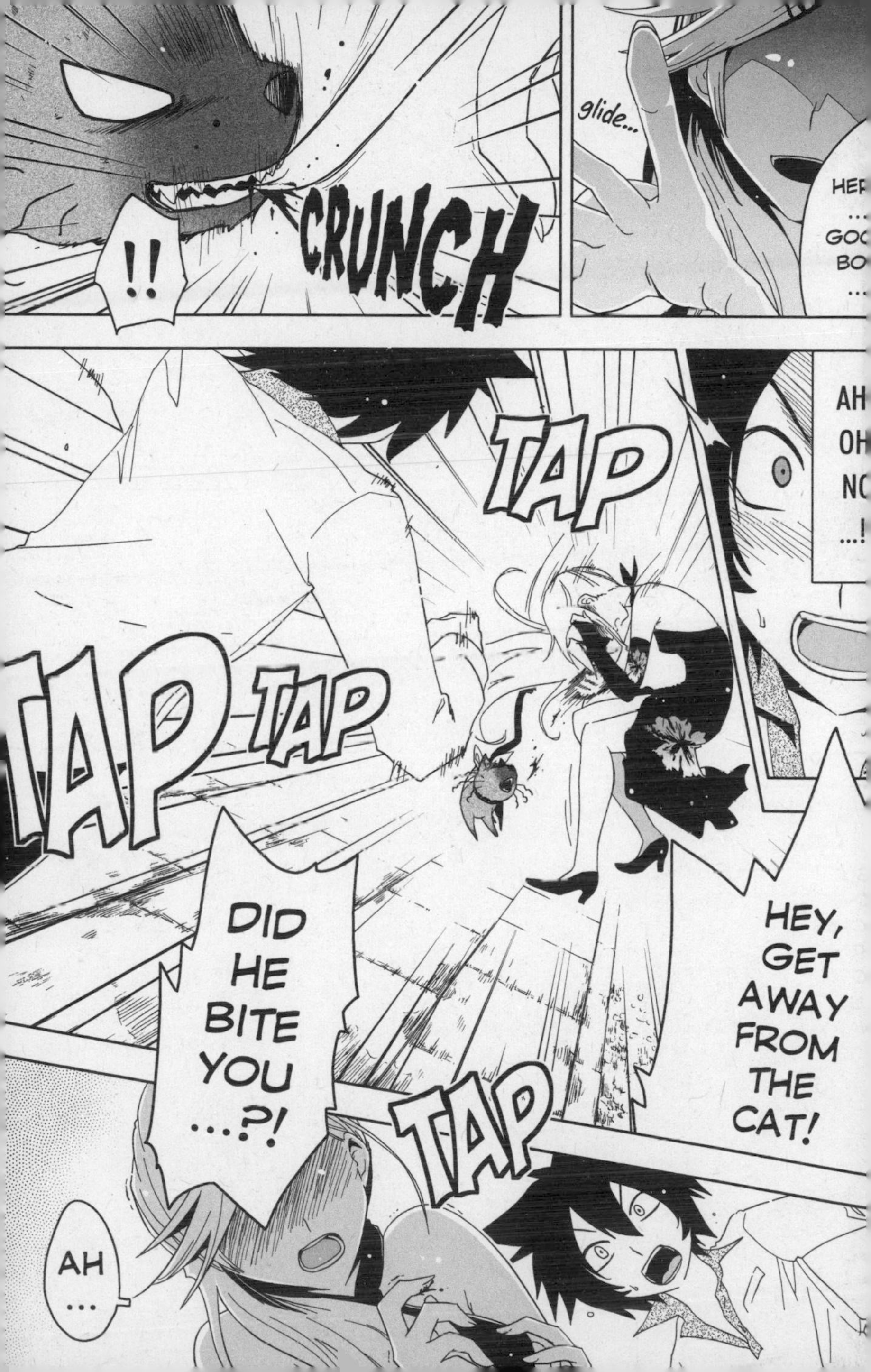
glide...
HER ... GOO BO ...
CRUNCH
!!
AH OH NO ...!
TAP
TAP
TAP
HEY, GET AWAY FROM THE CAT!
DID HE BITE YOU ...?!
TAP
AH ...

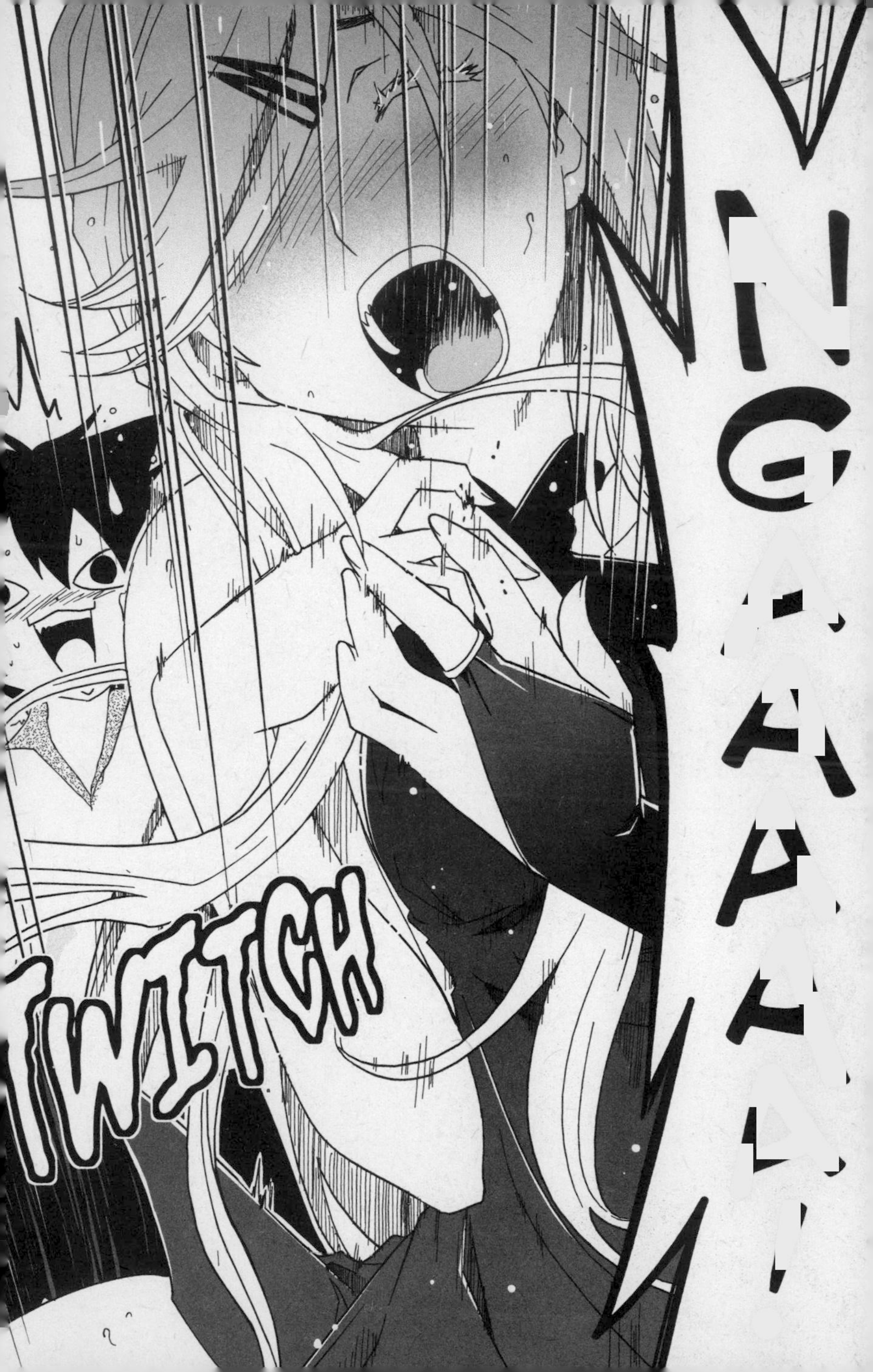
NGAAAAA!
TWITCH

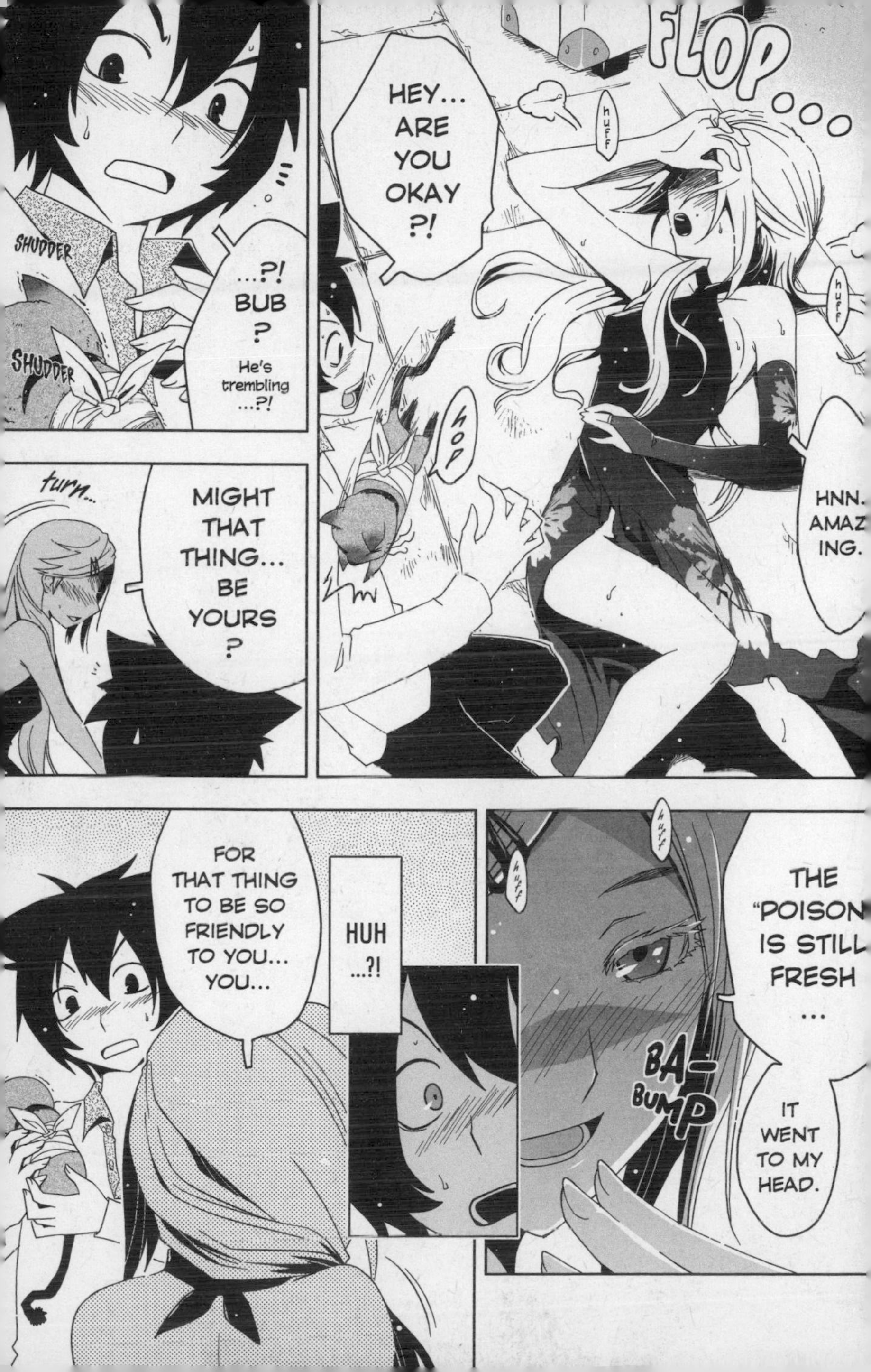
FLOP ooo
huff
HEY... ARE YOU OKAY?!
huff
HNN. AMAZING.
hop
SHUDDER
SHUDDER
...?! BUB?
He's trembling ...?!
turn...
MIGHT THAT THING... BE YOURS?
huff
huff
THE "POISON IS STILL FRESH...
BA-BUMP
IT WENT TO MY HEAD.
HUH ...?!
FOR THAT THING TO BE SO FRIENDLY TO YOU... YOU...

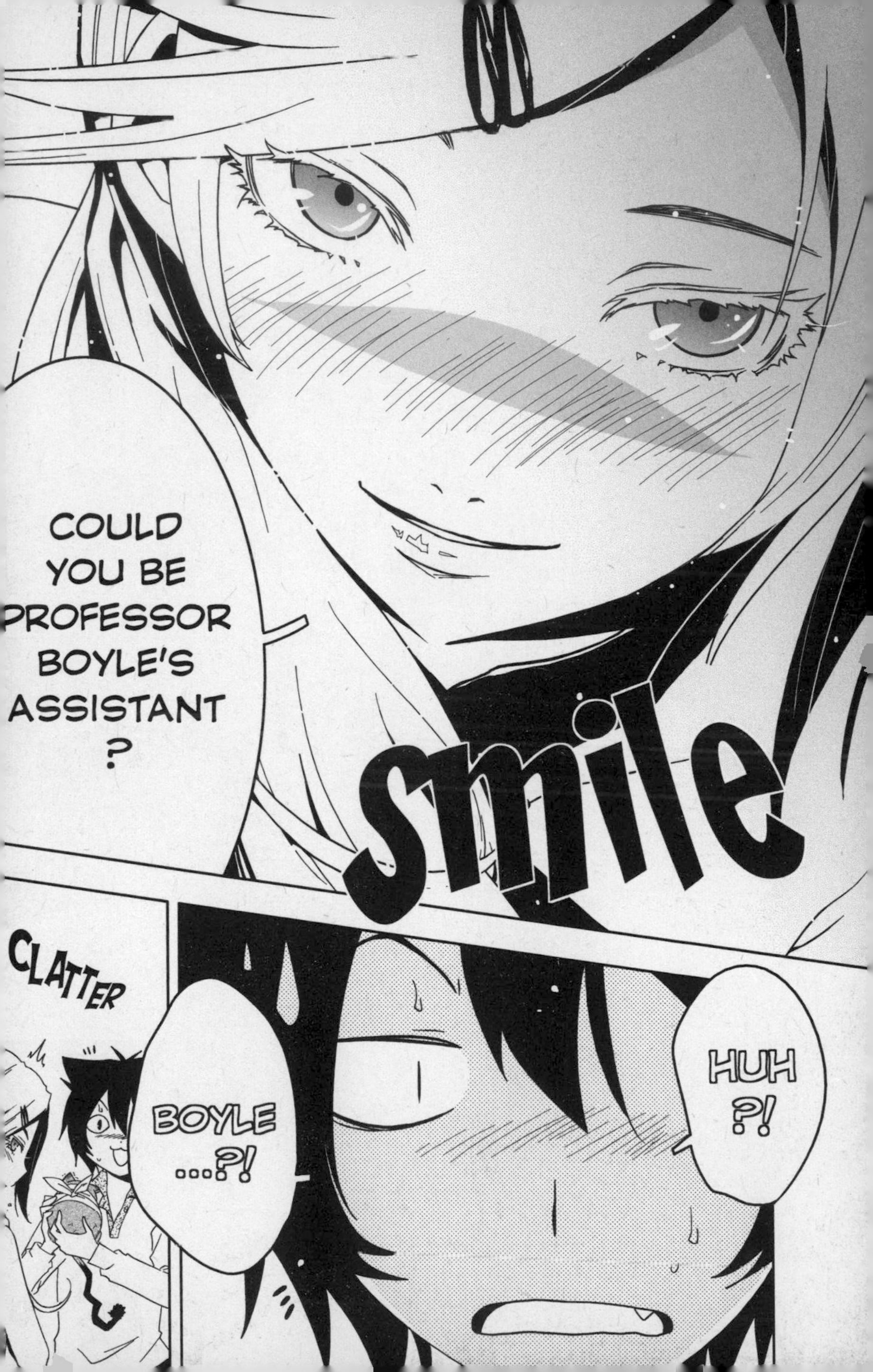
COULD YOU BE PROFESSOR BOYLE'S ASSISTANT ?
smile
HUH ?!
BOYLE ...?!
CLATTER

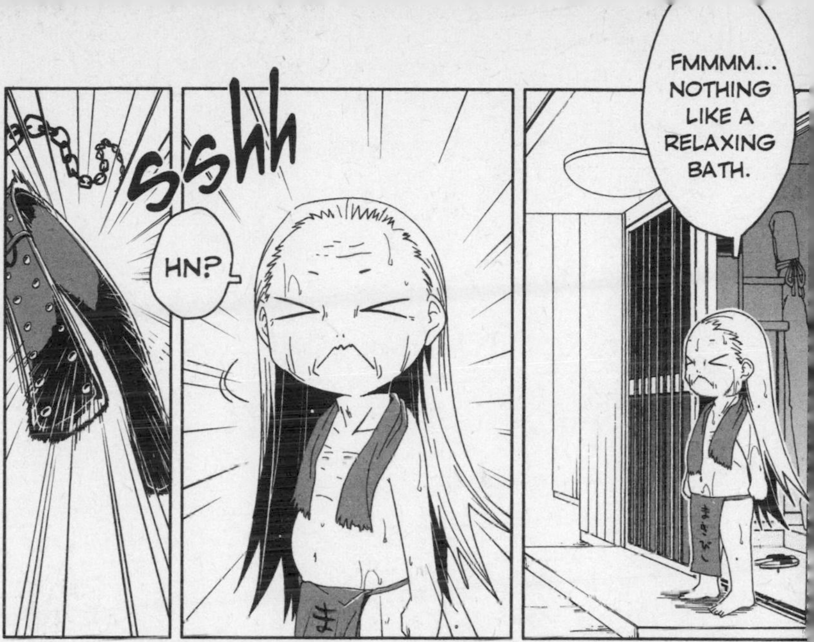
FMMMM... NOTHING LIKE A RELAXING BATH.
SSHH
HN?

LOINCLOTH: "Makibishi," A Japanese version of calt

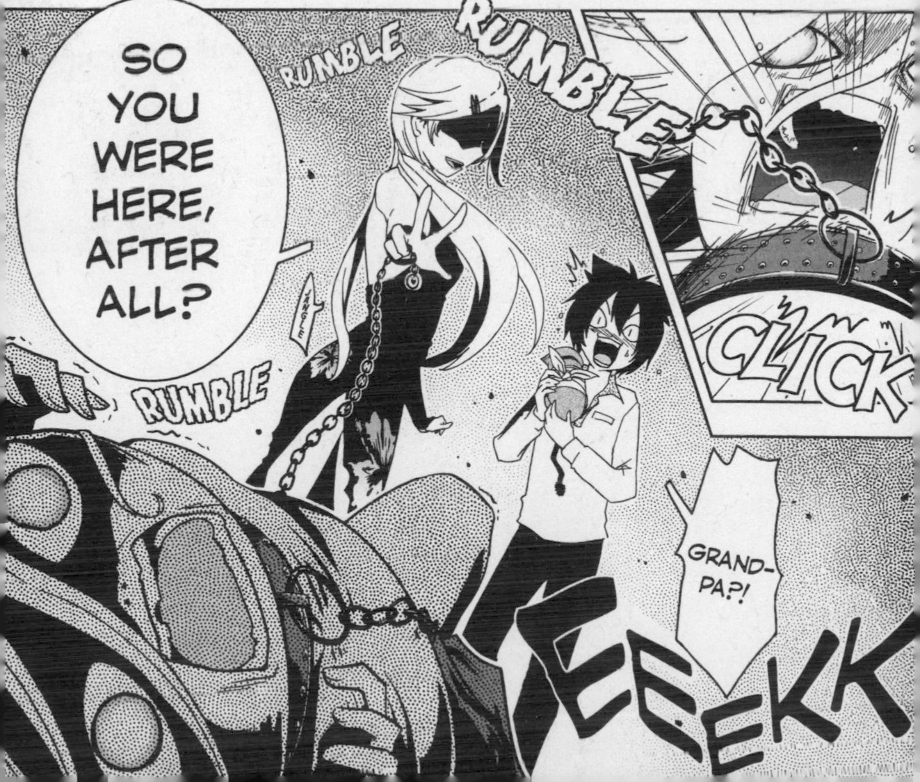
CLICK
RUMBLE
RUMBLE
SO YOU WERE HERE, AFTER ALL?
JANGLE
RUMBLE
GRAND-PA?!
EEEKK

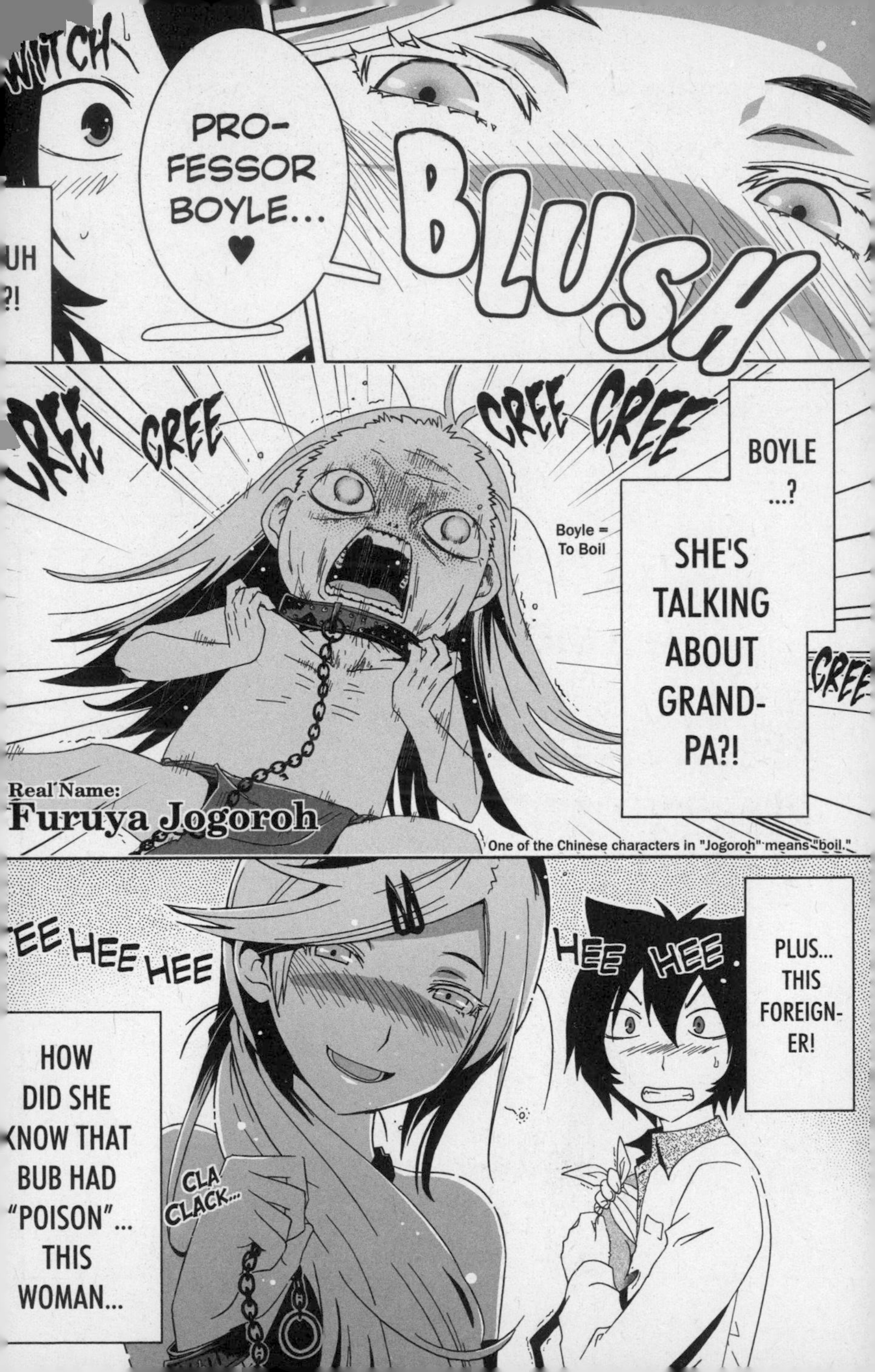

BLUSH
PRO-FESSOR BOYLE... ♥
WITCH
UH ?!
CREE CREE
BOYLE ...?
SHE'S TALKING ABOUT GRAND-PA?!
Boyle = To Boil
CREE
CREE CREE
Real Name: Furuya Jogoroh
One of the Chinese characters in "Jogoroh" means "boil."
PLUS... THIS FOREIGN-ER!
HEE HEE
CLA CLACK...
EE HEE HEE
HOW DID SHE NOW THAT BUB HAD "POISON"... THIS WOMAN...

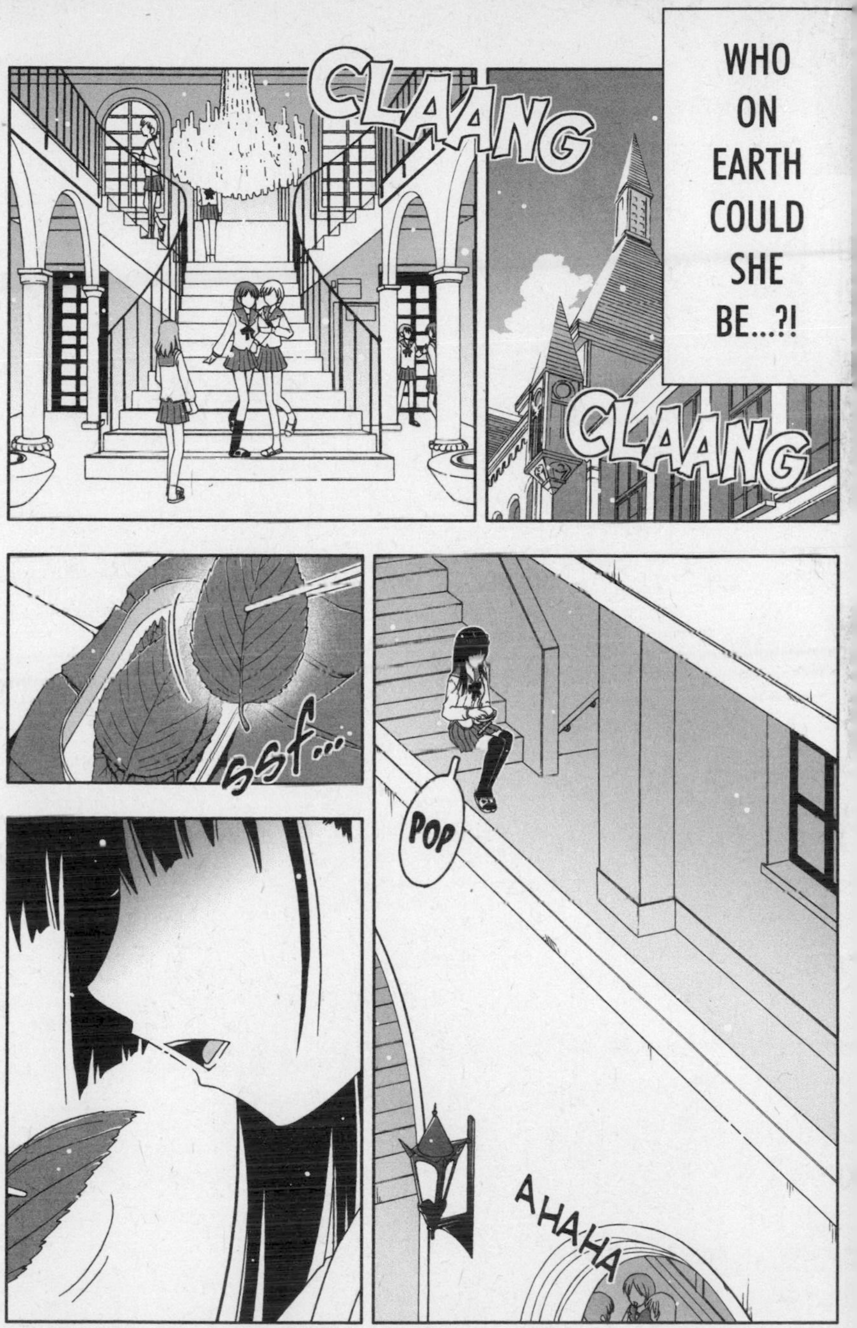
WHO ON EARTH COULD SHE BE...?!
CLAANG
CLAANG
POP
AHAHA
ssf...

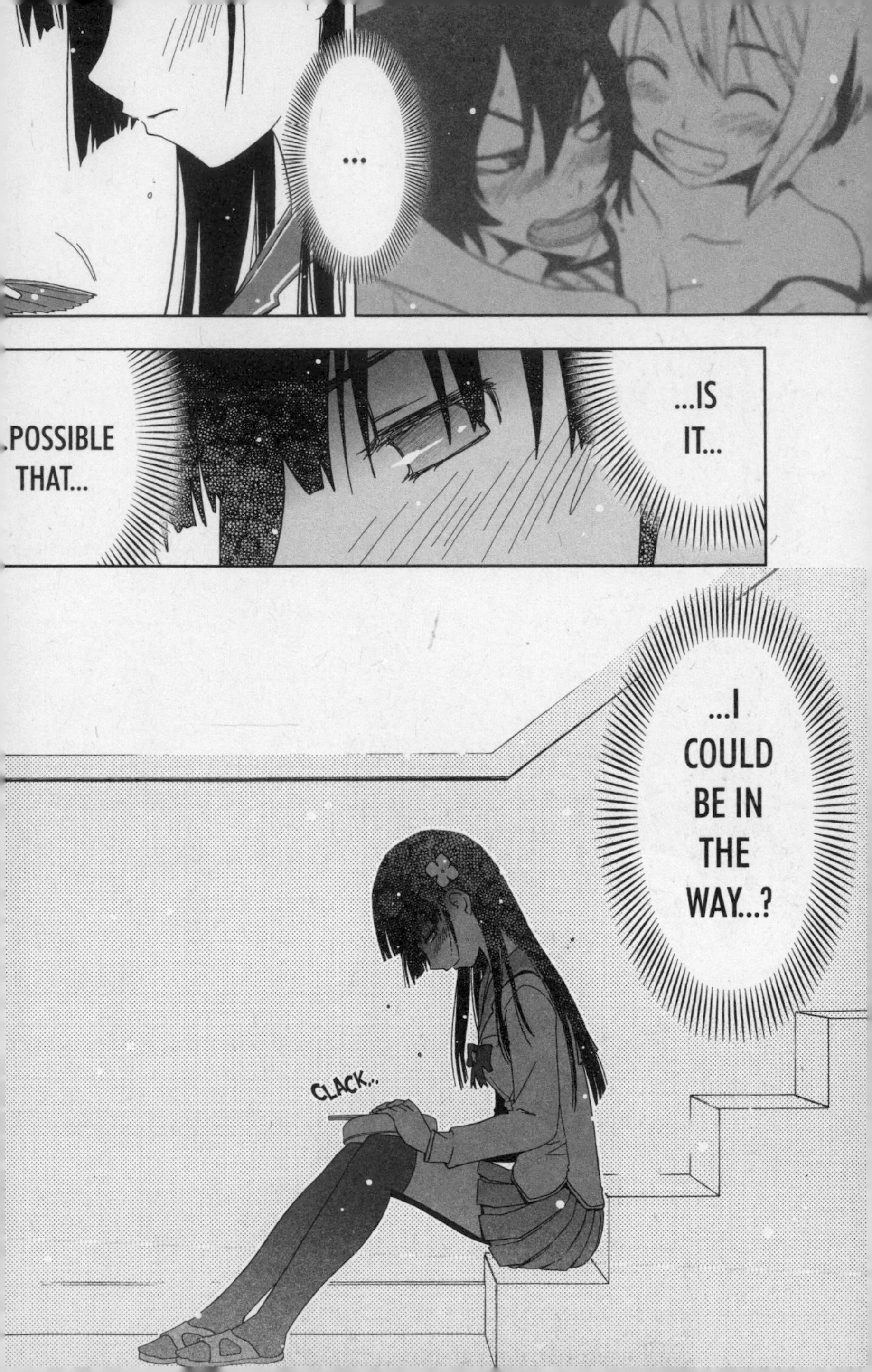
...
...IS IT...
.POSSIBLE THAT...
...I COULD BE IN THE WAY...?
CLACK..

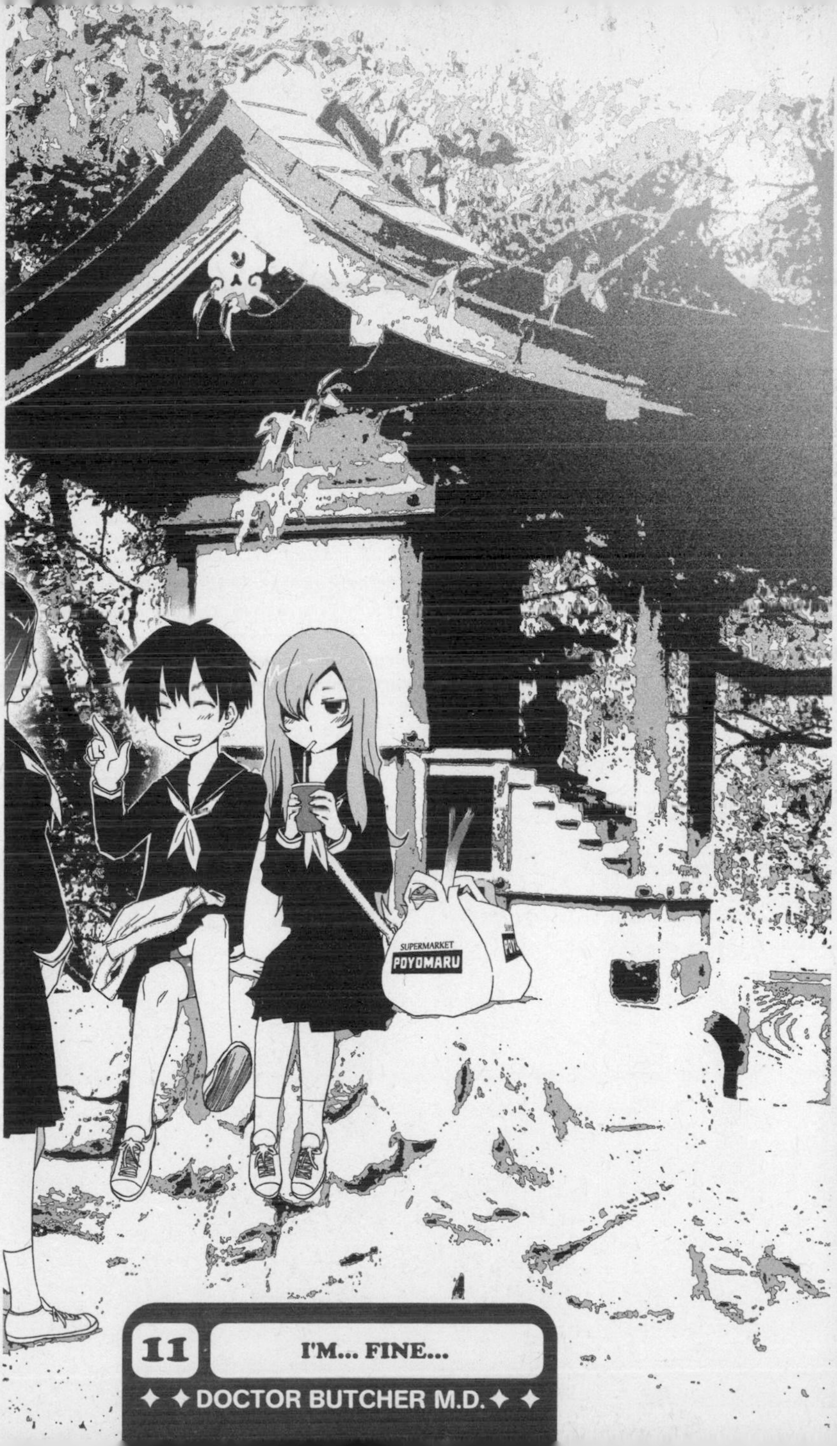
SUPERMARKET
POYOMARU
11
I'M... FINE...
DOCTOR BUTCHER M.D.

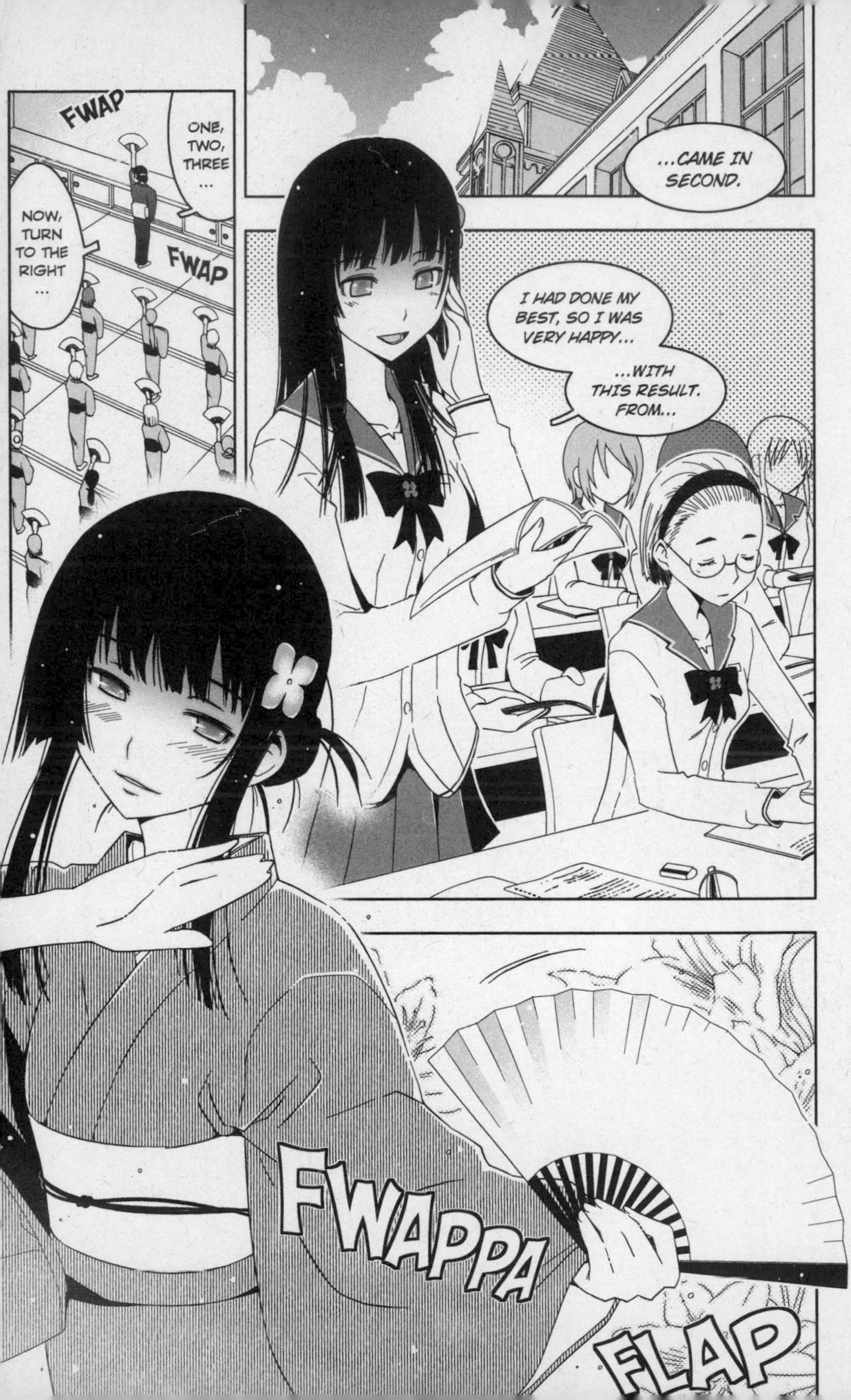
...CAME IN SECOND.
I HAD DONE MY BEST, SO I WAS VERY HAPPY...
...WITH THIS RESULT. FROM...
FWAP
ONE, TWO, THREE ...
NOW, TURN TO THE RIGHT ...
FWAP
FWAPPA
FLAP

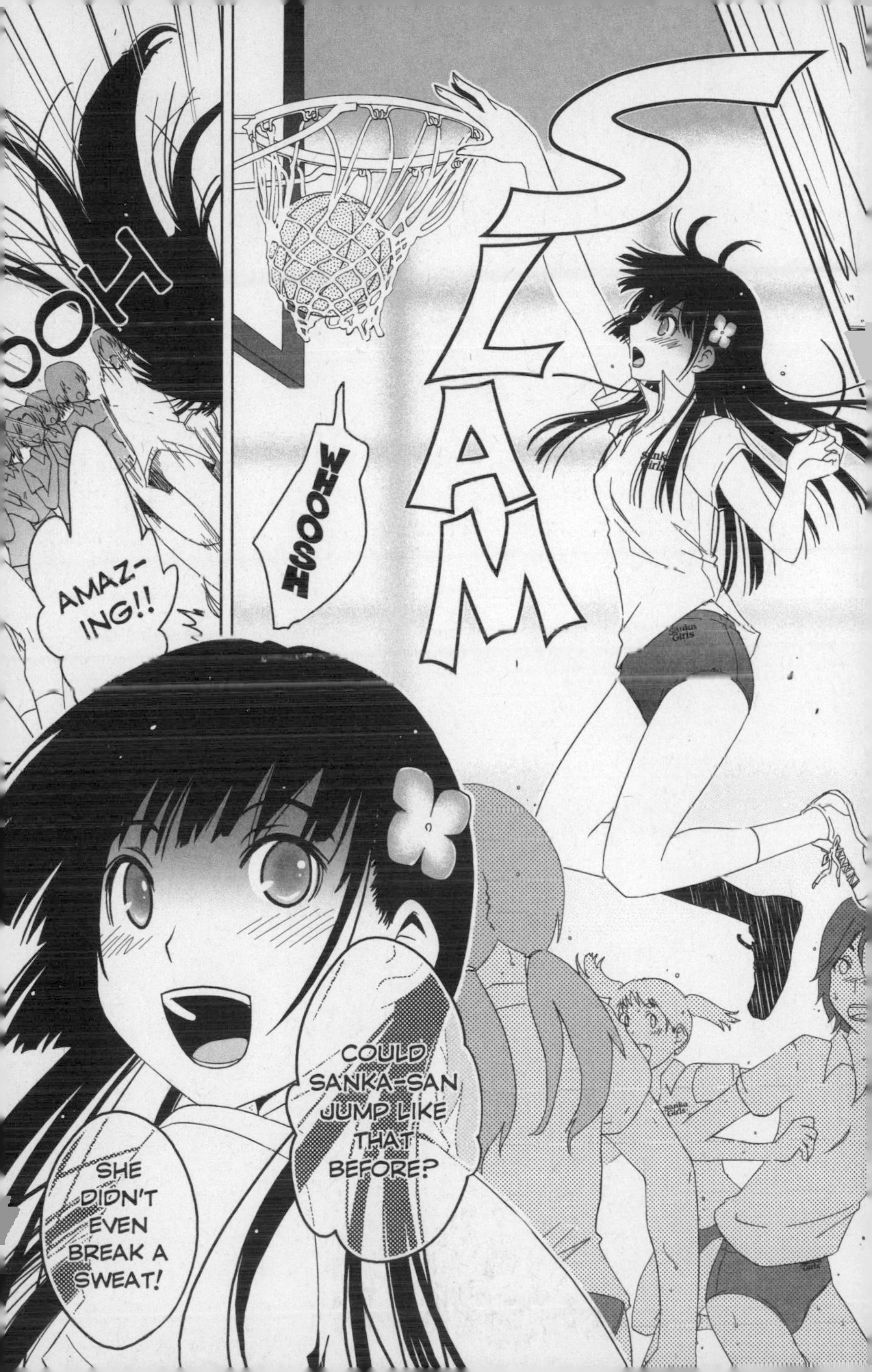
SLAM
WHOOSH
OOH
AMAZ-ING!!
COULD SANKA-SAN JUMP LIKE THAT BEFORE?
SHE DIDN'T EVEN BREAK A SWEAT!

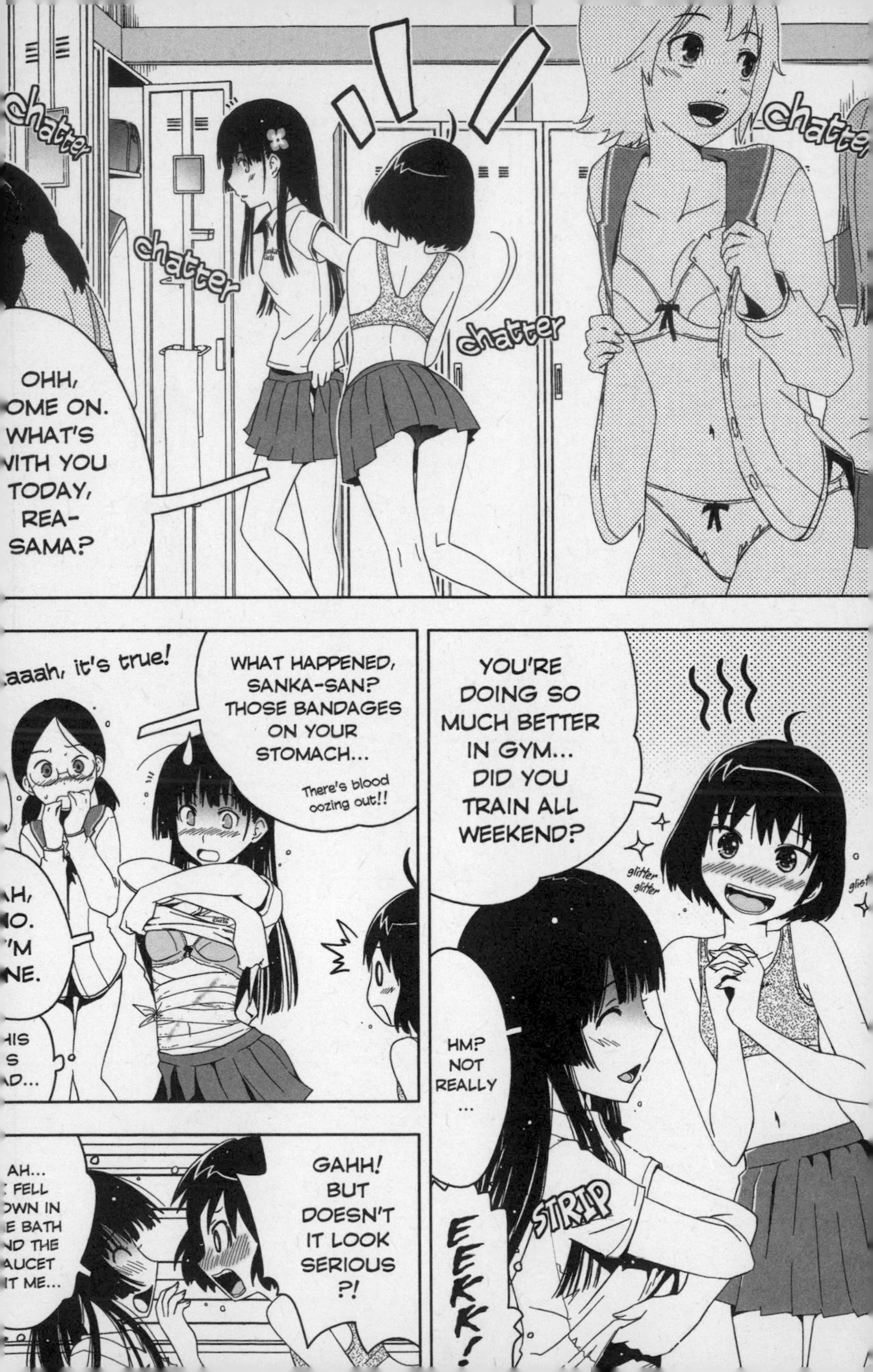
chatter
chatter
chatter
chatter
OHH, OME ON. WHAT'S VITH YOU TODAY, REA-SAMA?
YOU'RE DOING SO MUCH BETTER IN GYM... DID YOU TRAIN ALL WEEKEND?
glist
glitter glitter
HM? NOT REALLY ...
STRIP
EEEK!
WHAT HAPPENED, SANKA-SAN? THOSE BANDAGES ON YOUR STOMACH...
There's blood oozing out!!
aaah, it's true!
H, IO. 'M NE.
HIS S D...
GAHH! BUT DOESN'T IT LOOK SERIOUS ?!
AH... FELL OWN IN E BATH ND THE AUCET IT ME...

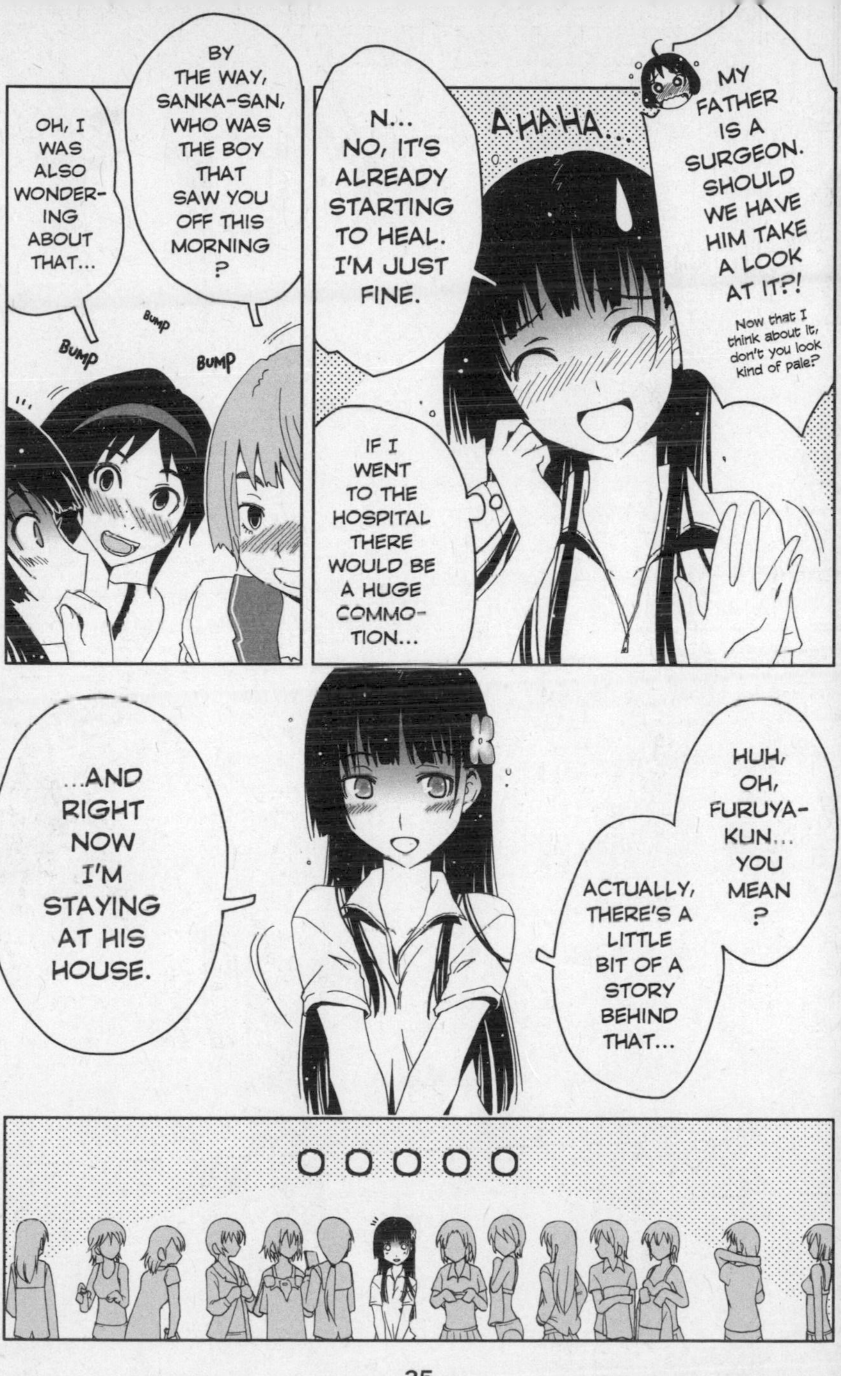
MY FATHER IS A SURGEON. SHOULD WE HAVE HIM TAKE A LOOK AT IT?!
Now that I think about it, don't you look kind of pale?
AHAHA...
N... NO, IT'S ALREADY STARTING TO HEAL. I'M JUST FINE.
IF I WENT TO THE HOSPITAL THERE WOULD BE A HUGE COMMOTION...
BY THE WAY, SANKA-SAN, WHO WAS THE BOY THAT SAW YOU OFF THIS MORNING?
OH, I WAS ALSO WONDERING ABOUT THAT...
BUMP
BUMP
BUMP
HUH, OH, FURUYA-KUN... YOU MEAN?
ACTUALLY, THERE'S A LITTLE BIT OF A STORY BEHIND THAT...
...AND RIGHT NOW I'M STAYING AT HIS HOUSE.
OOOOO

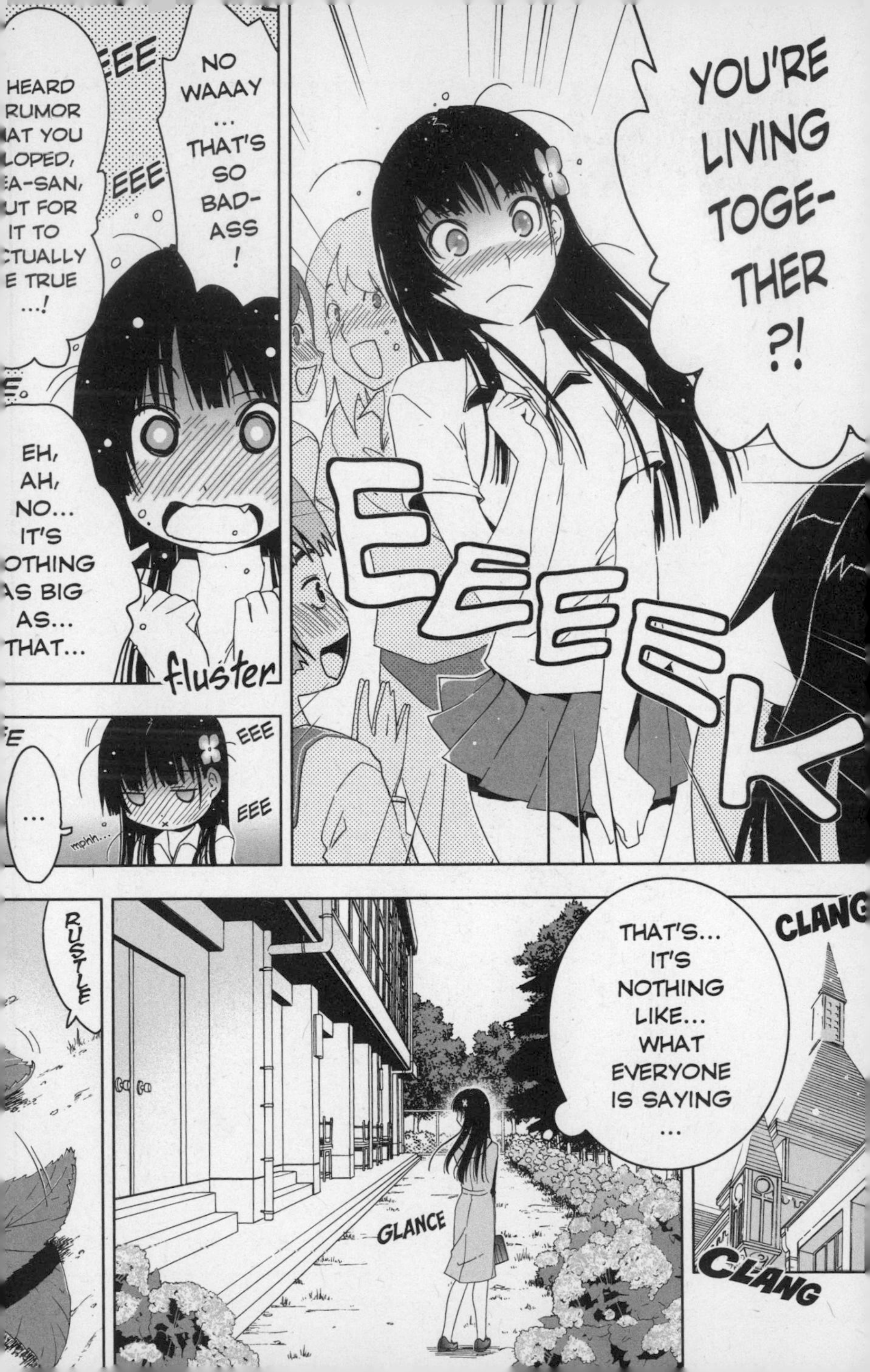
YOU'RE LIVING TOGE-THER ?!
EEEEEK
NO WAAAY ... THAT'S SO BAD-ASS !
EEE
EEE
HEARD RUMOR AT YOU LOPED, EA-SAN, UT FOR IT TO CTUALLY E TRUE ...!
EH, AH, NO... IT'S OTHING AS BIG AS... THAT...
fluster
EEE
EEE
mphh...
...
CLANG
CLANG
THAT'S... IT'S NOTHING LIKE... WHAT EVERYONE IS SAYING ...
GLANCE
RUSTLE

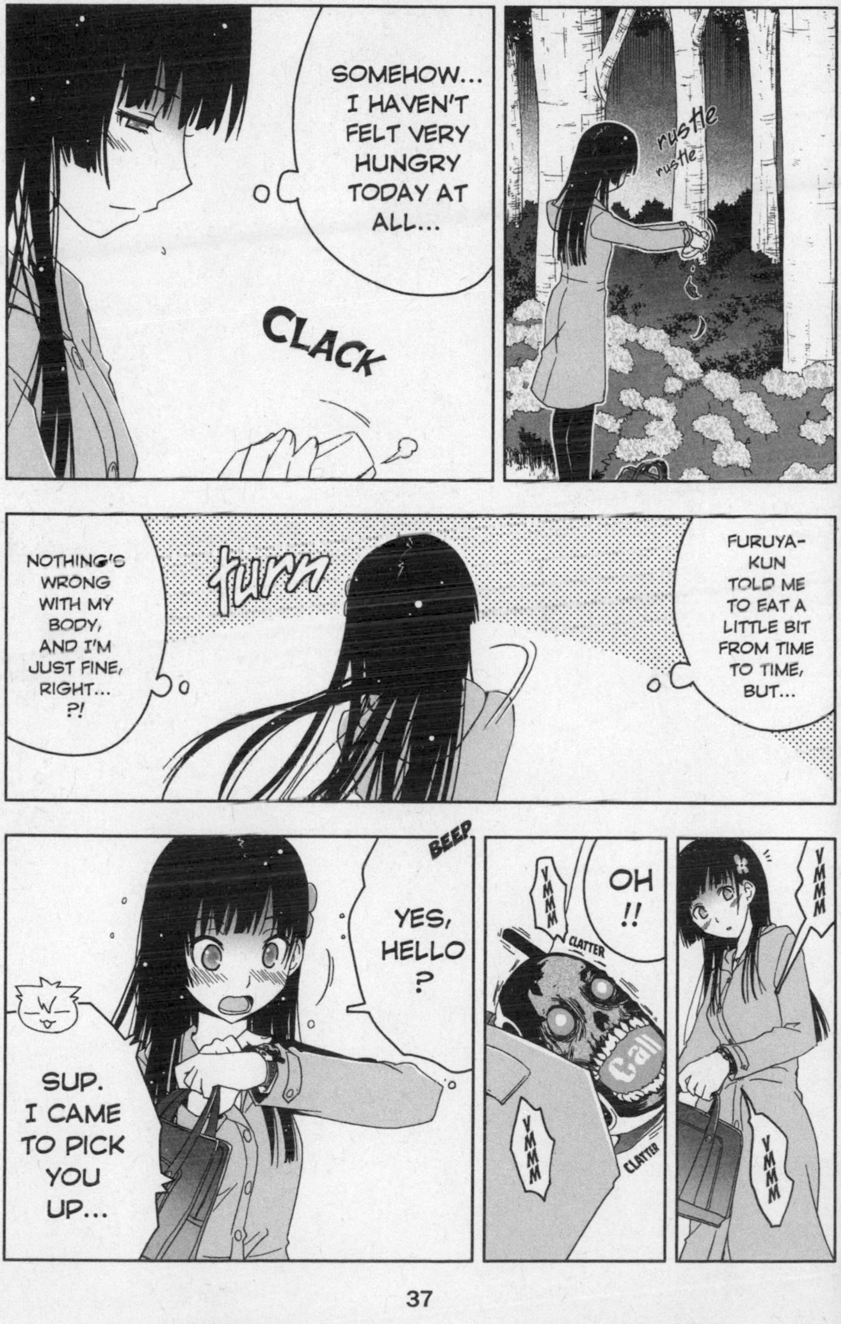
rustle
rustle
SOMEHOW... I HAVEN'T FELT VERY HUNGRY TODAY AT ALL...
CLACK
FURUYA-KUN TOLD ME TO EAT A LITTLE BIT FROM TIME TO TIME, BUT...
turn
NOTHING'S WRONG WITH MY BODY, AND I'M JUST FINE, RIGHT... ?!
VMMM
VMMM
OH !!
VMMM
CLATTER
Call
VMMM
CLATTER
BEEP
YES, HELLO ?
SUP. I CAME TO PICK YOU UP...

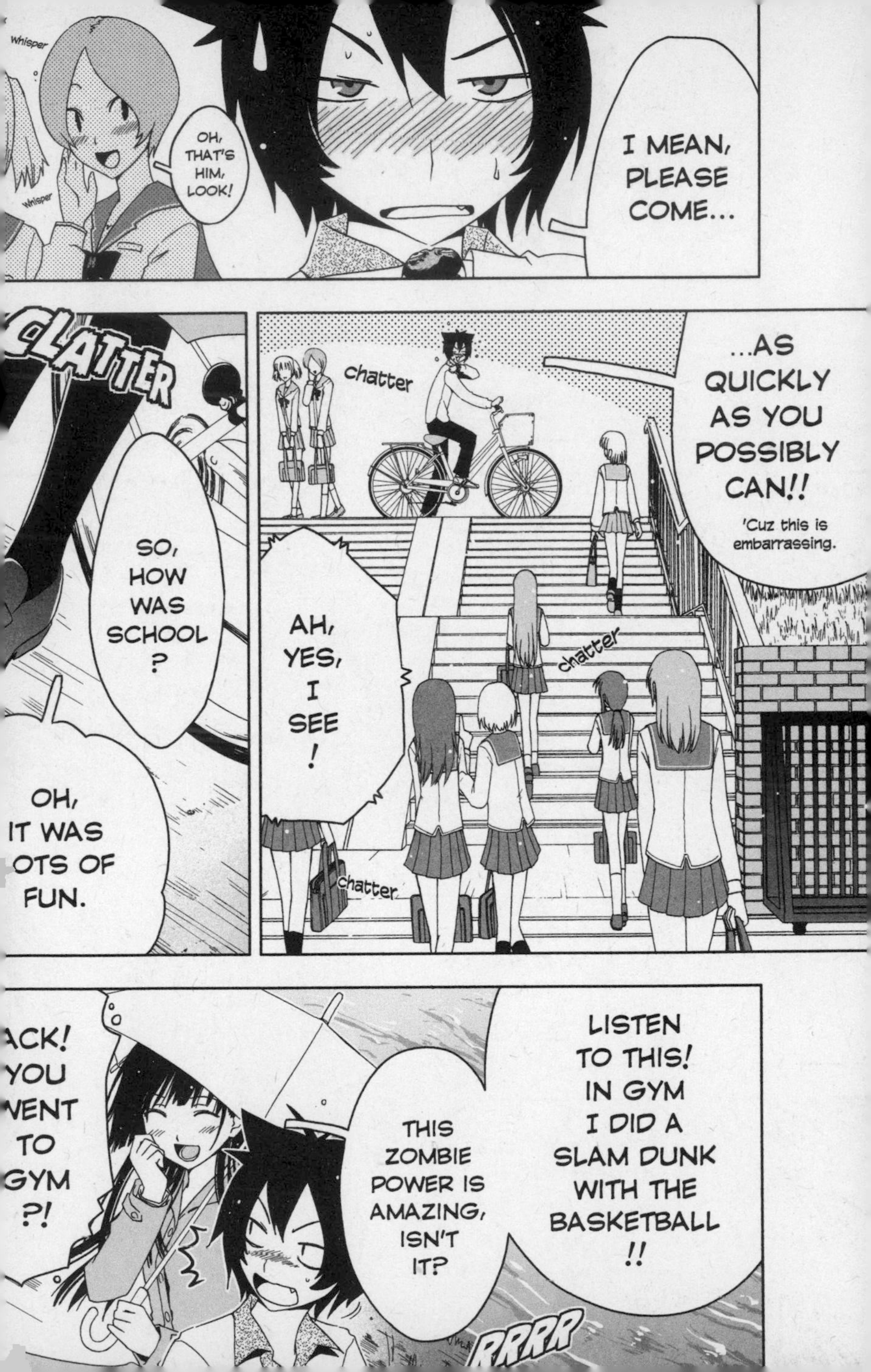
I MEAN, PLEASE COME...
OH, THAT'S HIM, LOOK!
Whisper
Whisper
...AS QUICKLY AS YOU POSSIBLY CAN!!
'Cuz this is embarrassing.
chatter
AH, YES, I SEE!
chatter
chatter
CLATTER
SO, HOW WAS SCHOOL?
OH, IT WAS OTS OF FUN.
LISTEN TO THIS! IN GYM I DID A SLAM DUNK WITH THE BASKETBALL!!
THIS ZOMBIE POWER IS AMAZING, ISN'T IT?
ACK! YOU WENT TO GYM?!
RRRR

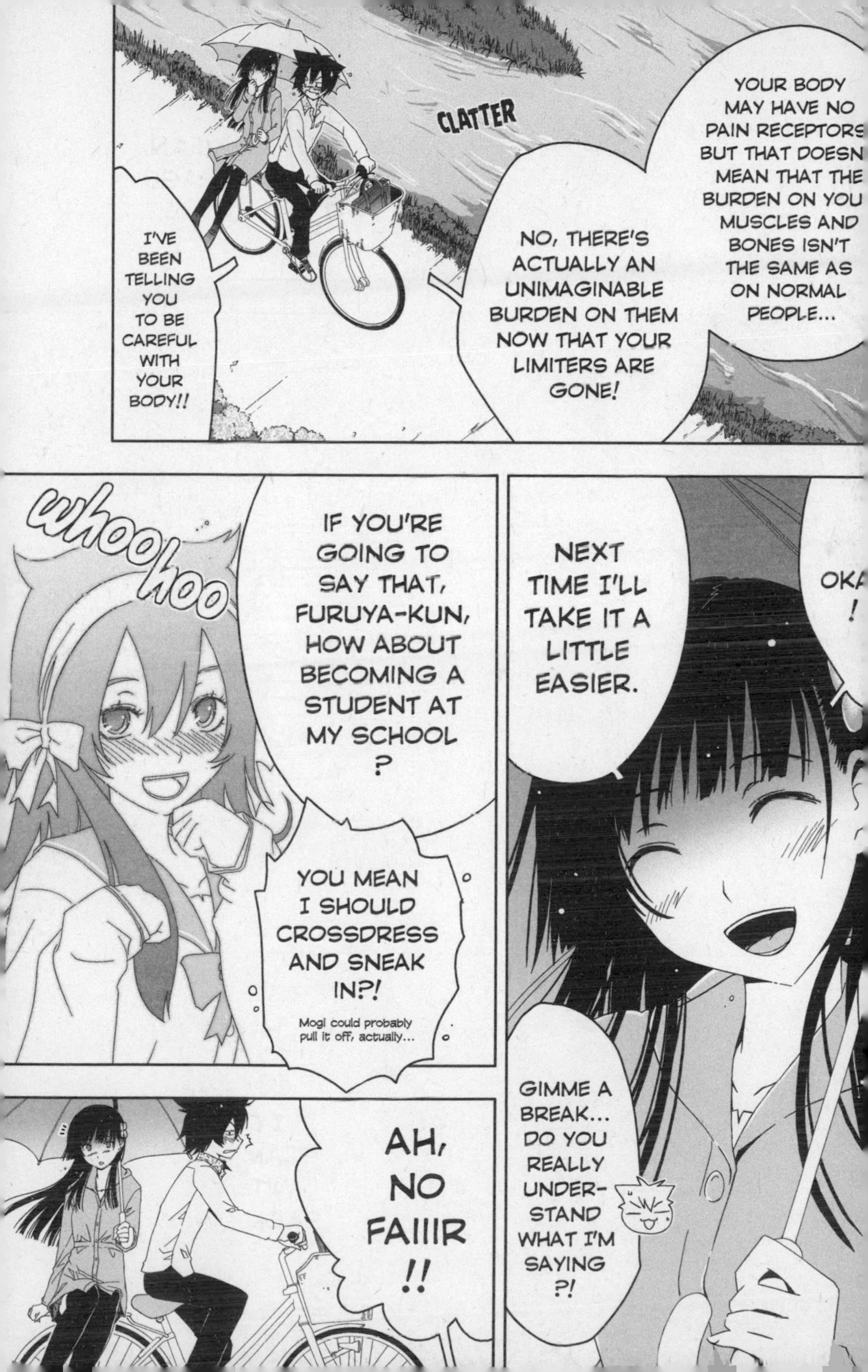
YOUR BODY MAY HAVE NO PAIN RECEPTORS BUT THAT DOESN MEAN THAT THE BURDEN ON YOU MUSCLES AND BONES ISN'T THE SAME AS ON NORMAL PEOPLE...
NO, THERE'S ACTUALLY AN UNIMAGINABLE BURDEN ON THEM NOW THAT YOUR LIMITERS ARE GONE!
CLATTER
I'VE BEEN TELLING YOU TO BE CAREFUL WITH YOUR BODY!!
OKA !
NEXT TIME I'LL TAKE IT A LITTLE EASIER.
GIMME A BREAK... DO YOU REALLY UNDER-STAND WHAT I'M SAYING?!
IF YOU'RE GOING TO SAY THAT, FURUYA-KUN, HOW ABOUT BECOMING A STUDENT AT MY SCHOOL?
whoohoo
YOU MEAN I SHOULD CROSSDRESS AND SNEAK IN?!
Mogi could probably pull it off, actually...
AH, NO FAIIIR!!

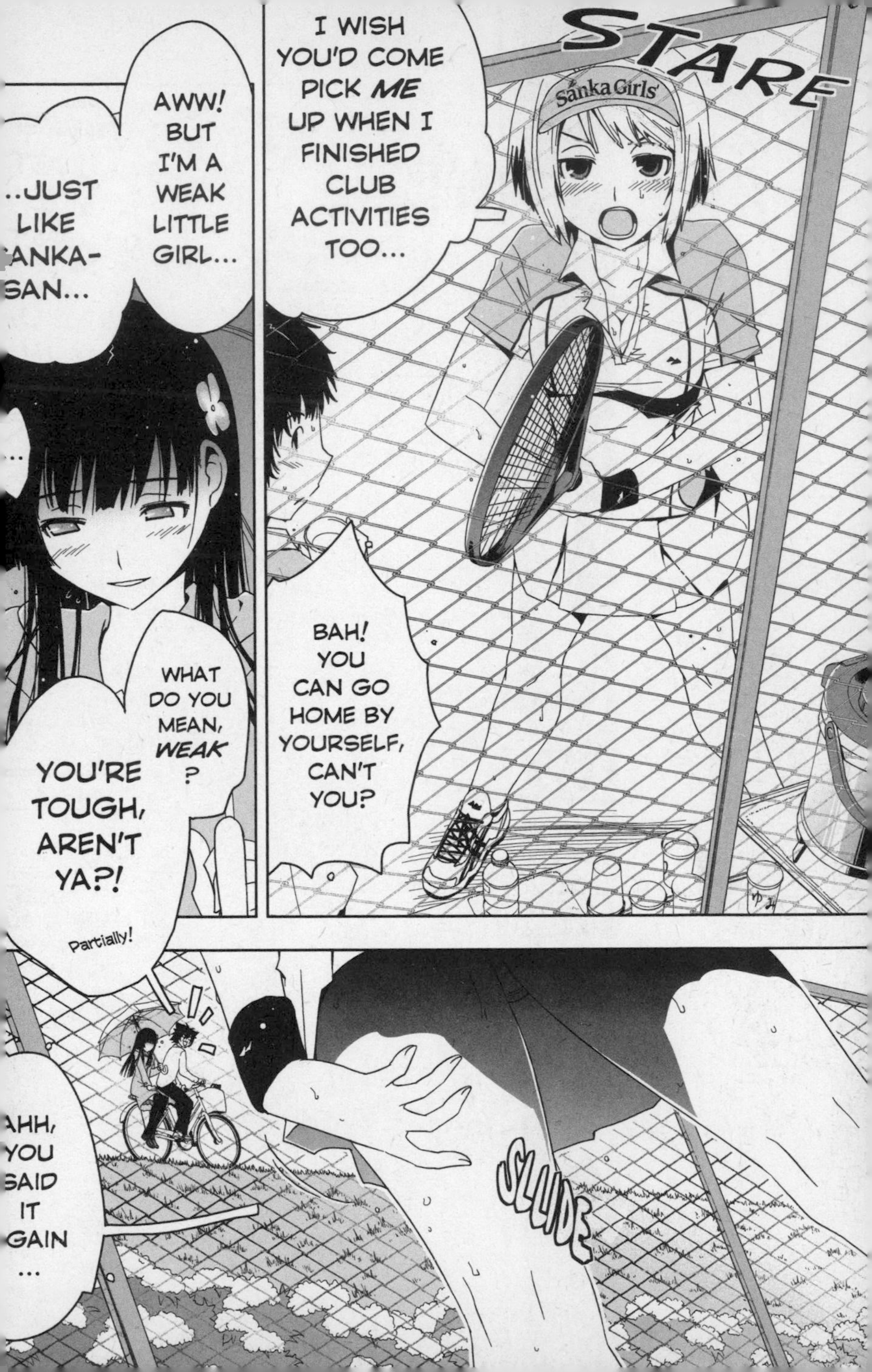
STARE
Sanka Girls'
I WISH YOU'D COME PICK ME UP WHEN I FINISHED CLUB ACTIVITIES TOO...
BAH! YOU CAN GO HOME BY YOURSELF, CAN'T YOU?
AWW! BUT I'M A WEAK LITTLE GIRL...
..JUST LIKE ANKA-SAN...
...
WHAT DO YOU MEAN, WEAK?
YOU'RE TOUGH, AREN'T YA?!
Partially!
SLIDE
AHH, YOU SAID IT GAIN ...

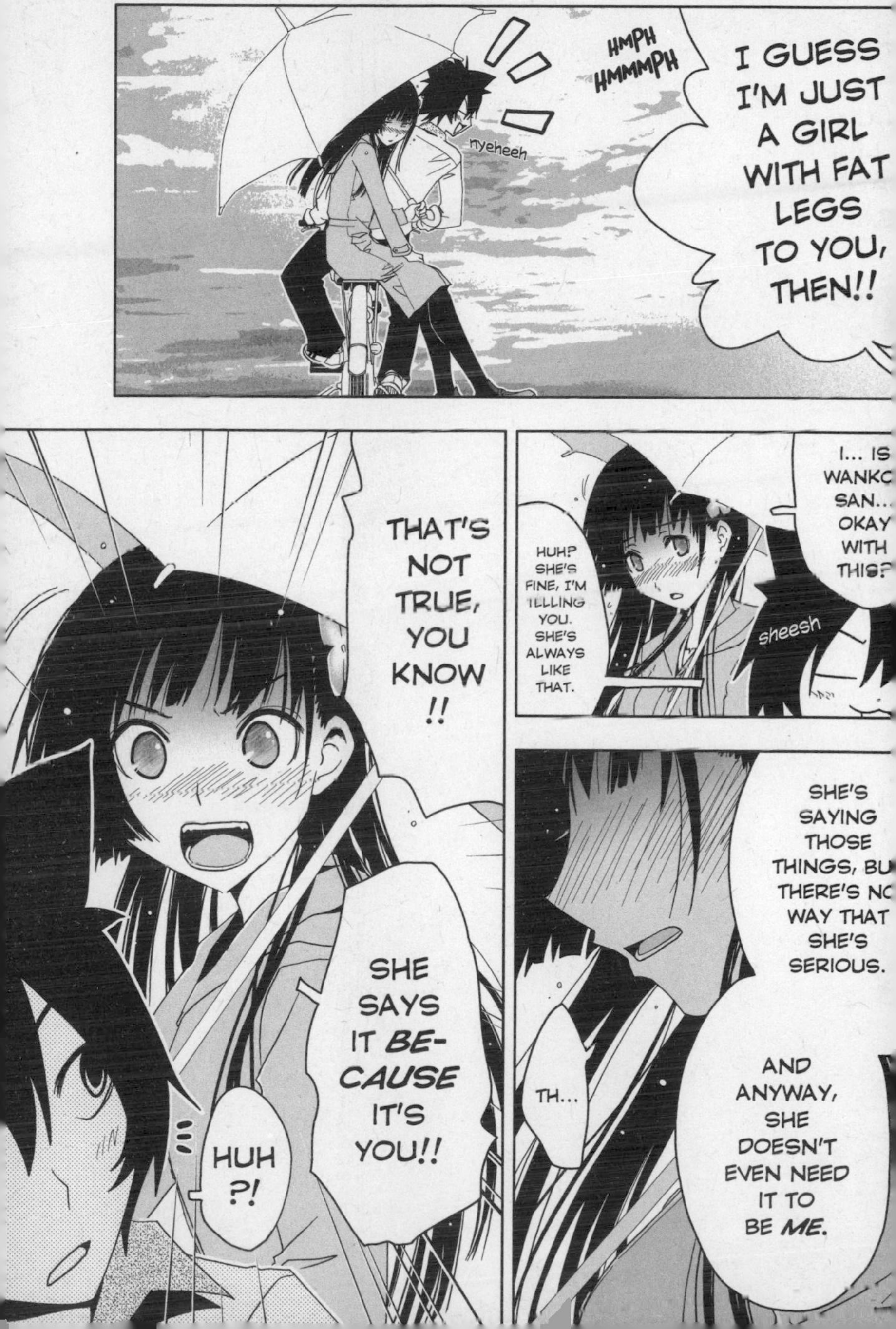
I GUESS I'M JUST A GIRL WITH FAT LEGS TO YOU, THEN!!
HMPH HMMMPH
nyeheeh
I... IS WANKO SAN... OKAY WITH THIS?
sheesh
HUH? SHE'S FINE, I'M TELLING YOU. SHE'S ALWAYS LIKE THAT.
SHE'S SAYING THOSE THINGS, BUT THERE'S NO WAY THAT SHE'S SERIOUS.
AND ANYWAY, SHE DOESN'T EVEN NEED IT TO BE *ME.*
TH...
THAT'S NOT TRUE, YOU KNOW!!
SHE SAYS IT *BE-CAUSE* IT'S YOU!!
HUH?!

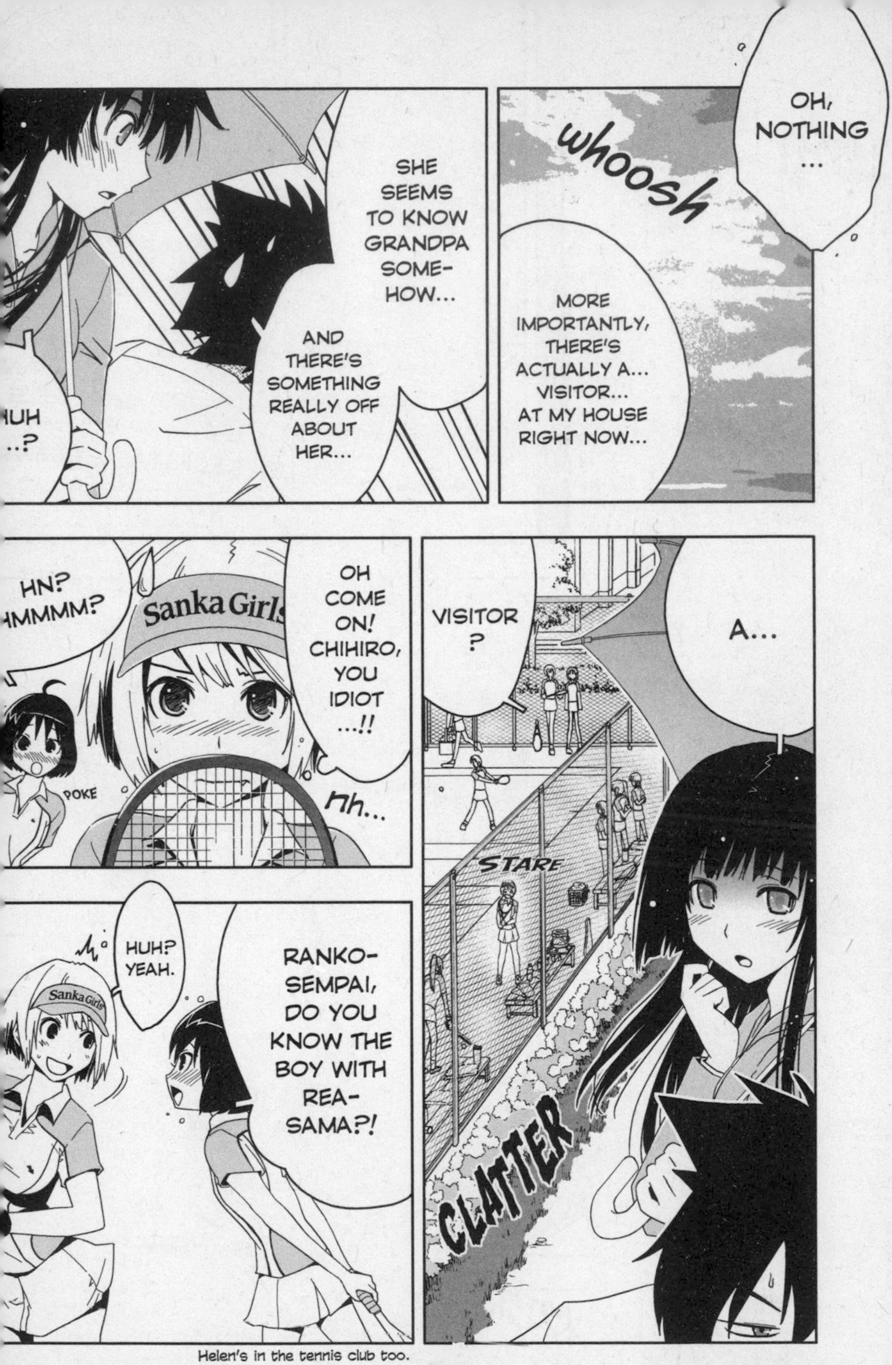
OH, NOTHING ...
whoosh
MORE IMPORTANTLY, THERE'S ACTUALLY A... VISITOR... AT MY HOUSE RIGHT NOW...
SHE SEEMS TO KNOW GRANDPA SOME-HOW...
AND THERE'S SOMETHING REALLY OFF ABOUT HER...
HUH ..?
A...
VISITOR ?
STARE
CLATTER
OH COME ON! CHIHIRO, YOU IDIOT ...!!
HN? HMMMM?
Sanka Girls
POKE
nh...
RANKO-SEMPAI, DO YOU KNOW THE BOY WITH REA-SAMA?!
HUH? YEAH.
Sanka Girls
Helen's in the tennis club too.

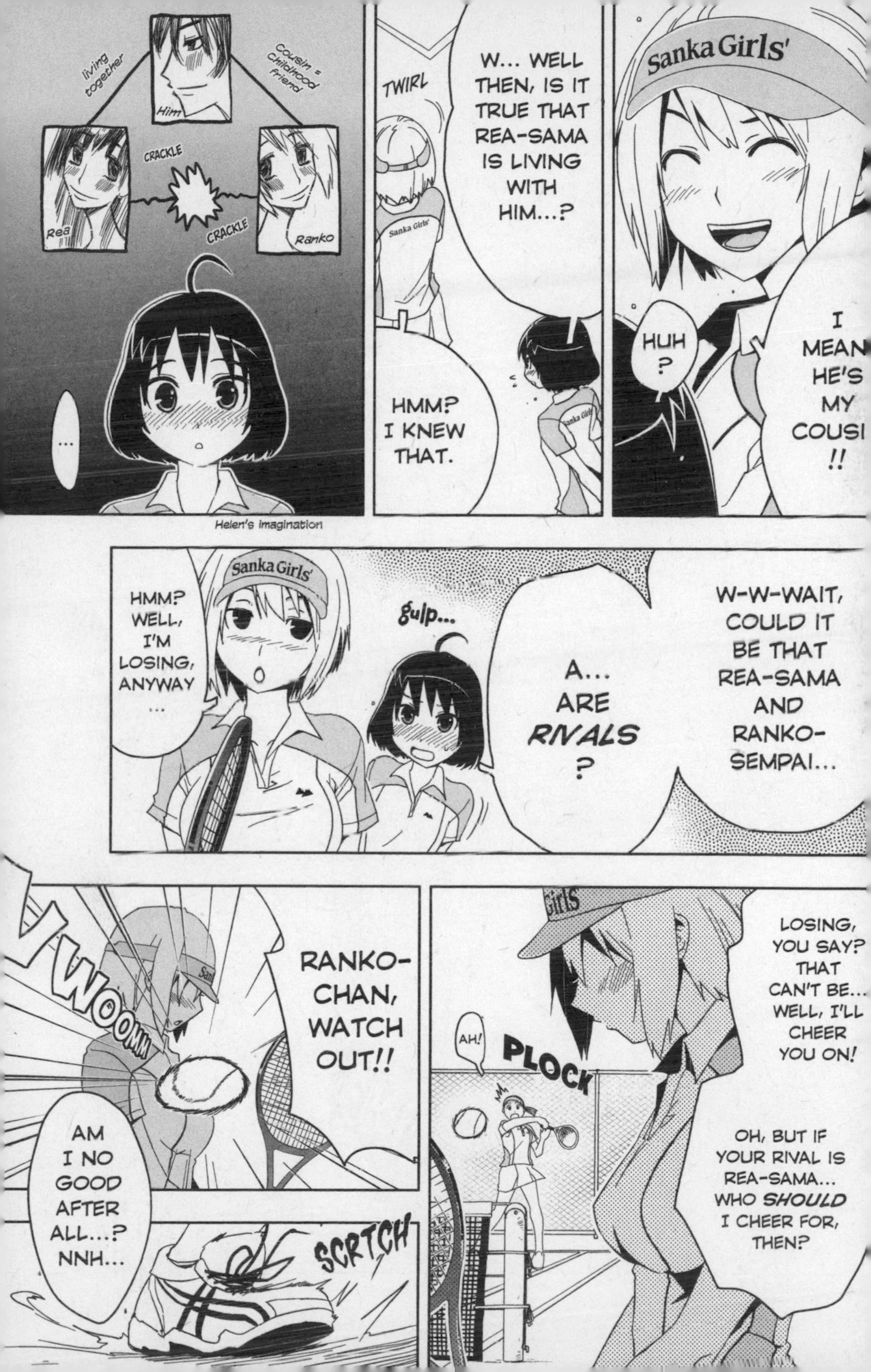
Sanka Girls'
I MEAN HE'S MY COUSI!!
HUH?
W... WELL THEN, IS IT TRUE THAT REA-SAMA IS LIVING WITH HIM...?
TWIRL
HMM? I KNEW THAT.
Cousin = Childhood friend
living together
Him
CRACKLE
Rea
CRACKLE
Ranko
...
Helen's imagination
W-W-WAIT, COULD IT BE THAT REA-SAMA AND RANKO-SEMPAI...
A... ARE *RIVALS*?
gulp...
HMM? WELL, I'M LOSING, ANYWAY...
LOSING, YOU SAY? THAT CAN'T BE... WELL, I'LL CHEER YOU ON!
OH, BUT IF YOUR RIVAL IS REA-SAMA... WHO *SHOULD* I CHEER FOR, THEN?
AH!
PLOCK
RANKO-CHAN, WATCH OUT!!
VWOOMM
AM I NO GOOD AFTER ALL...? NNH...
SCRTCH

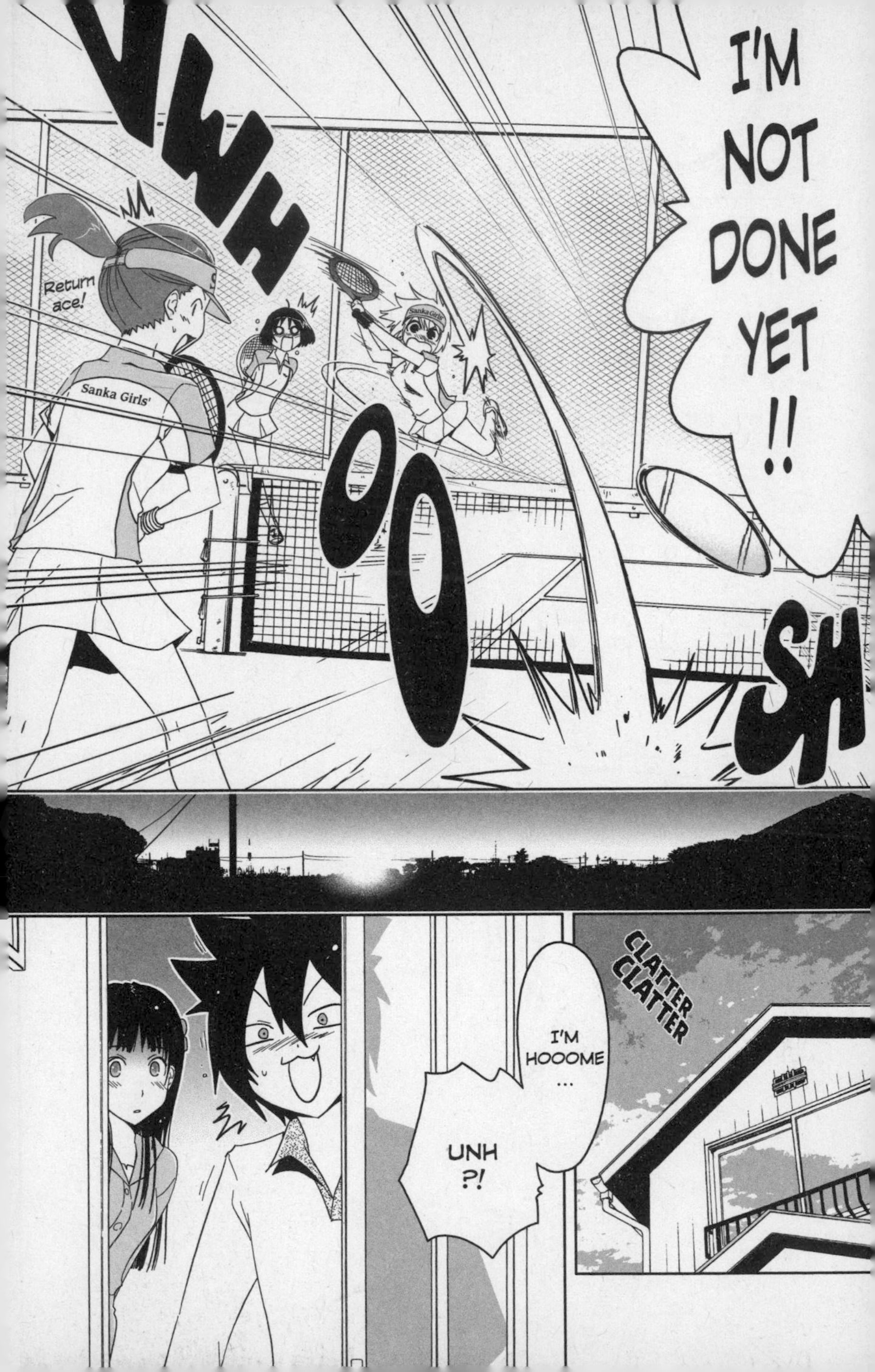
I'M NOT DONE YET!!
VWH
Return ace!
Sanka Girls'
Sanka Girls'
OO
SH
CLATTER CLATTER
I'M HOOOME ...
UNH ?!

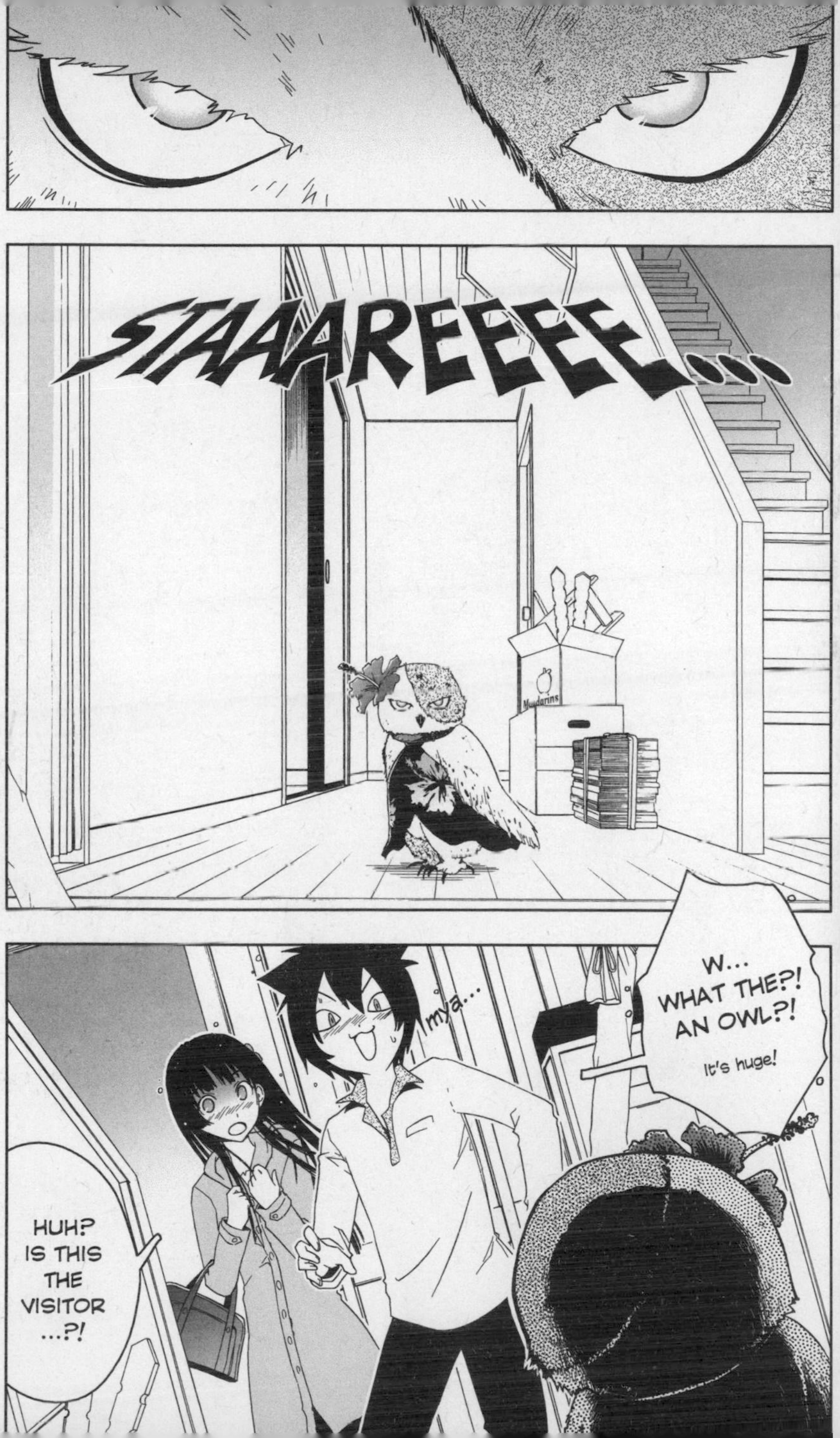
STAAAREEEE...
Mandarins
W... WHAT THE?! AN OWL?!
It's huge!
mya...
HUH? IS THIS THE VISITOR ...?!

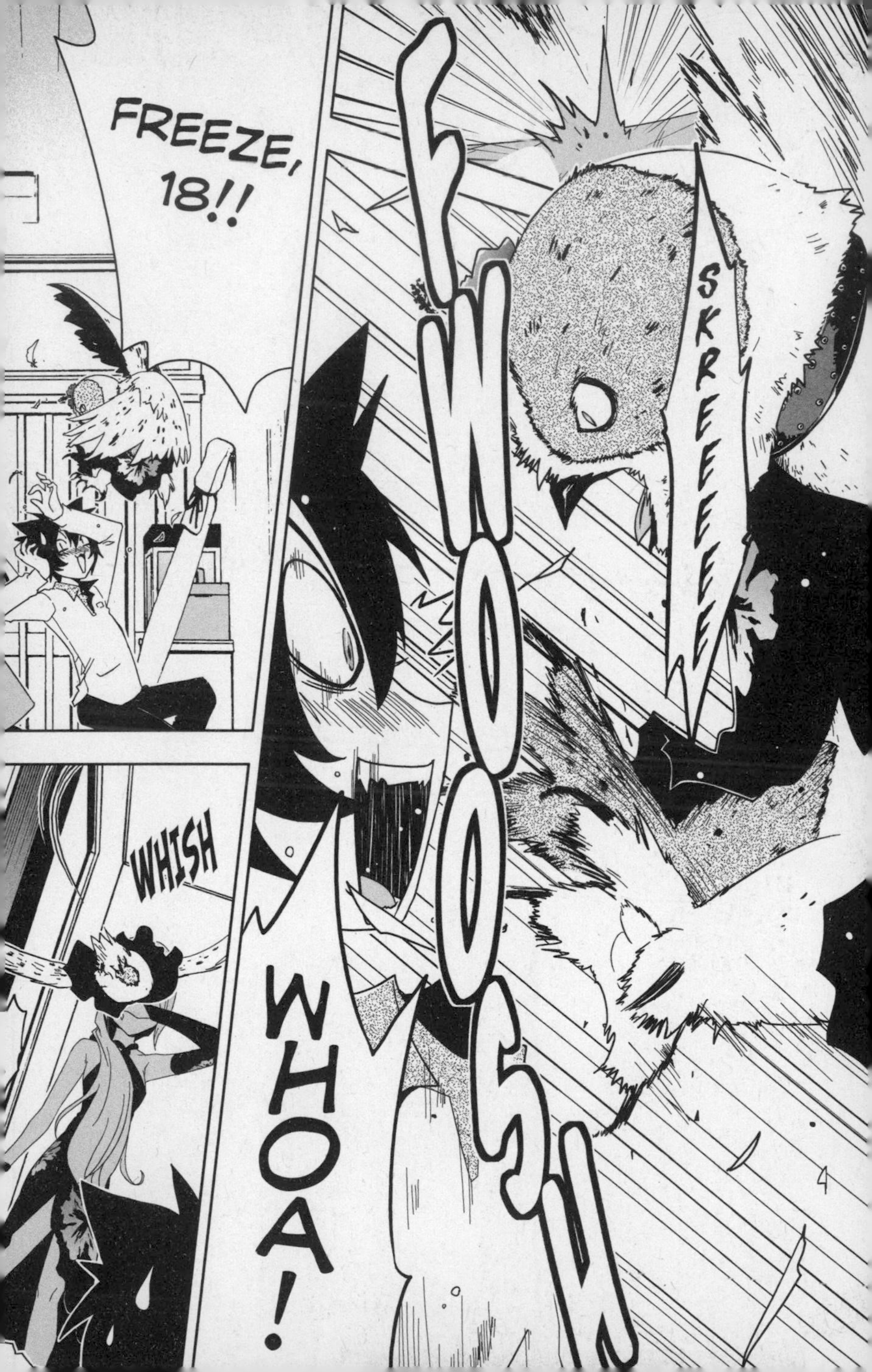
SKREEEE
WHOOOSH
WHOA!
FREEZE, 18!!
WHISH

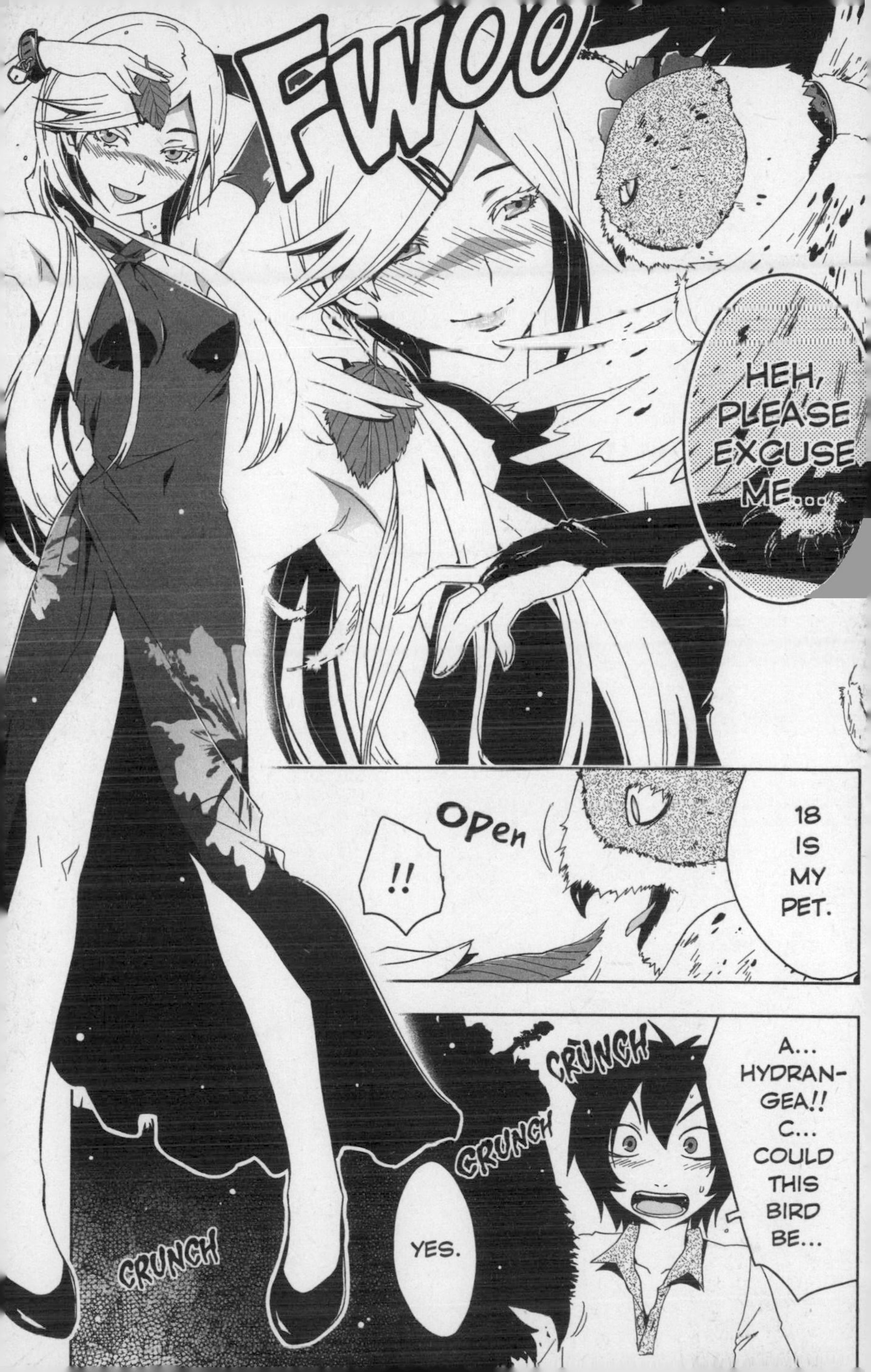
FWOO
HEH, PLEASE EXCUSE ME...
18 IS MY PET.
Open
!!
A... HYDRANGEA!! C... COULD THIS BIRD BE...
CRUNCH
CRUNCH
YES.
CRUNCH

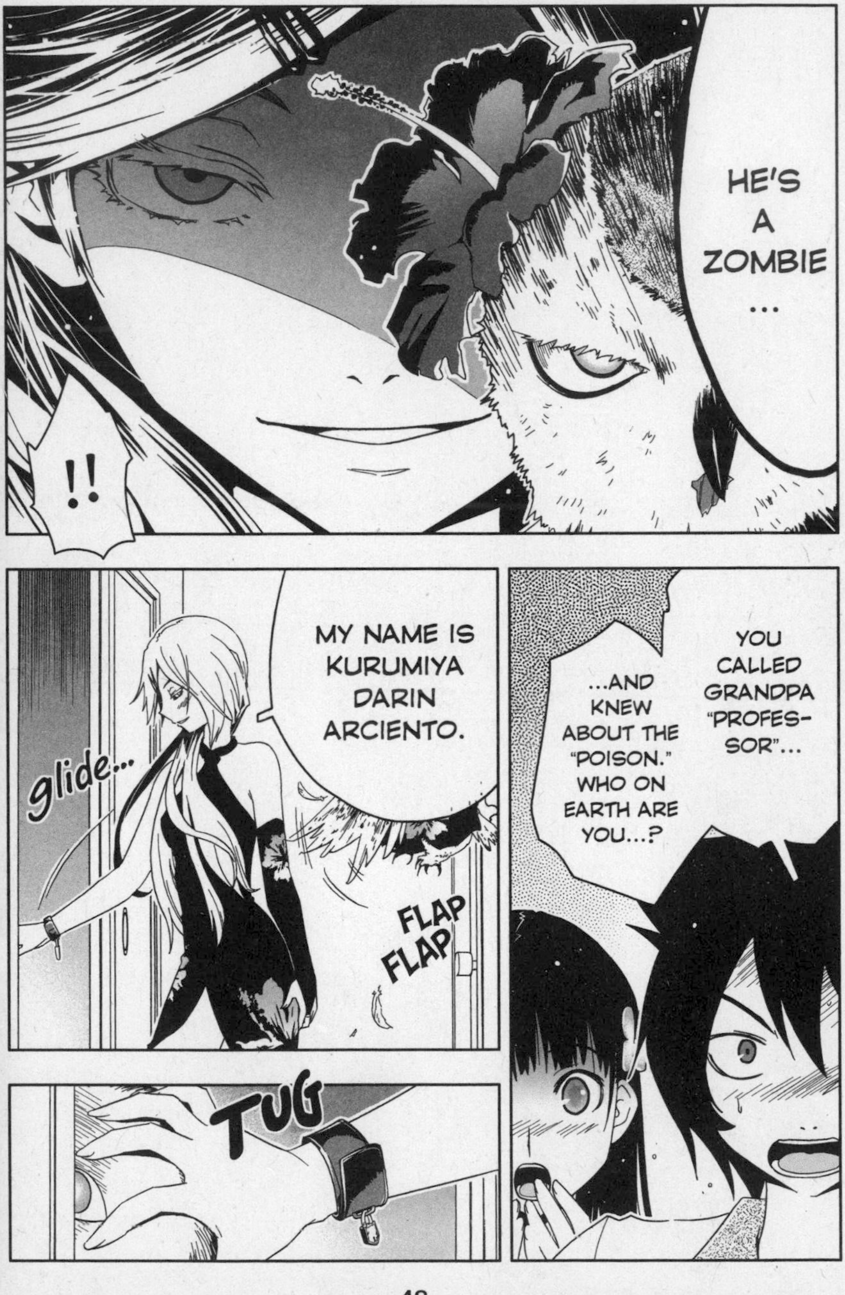
HE'S A ZOMBIE ...
!!
YOU CALLED GRANDPA "PROFES-SOR"...
...AND KNEW ABOUT THE "POISON." WHO ON EARTH ARE YOU...?
MY NAME IS KURUMIYA DARIN ARCIENTO.
glide...
FLAP FLAP
TUG

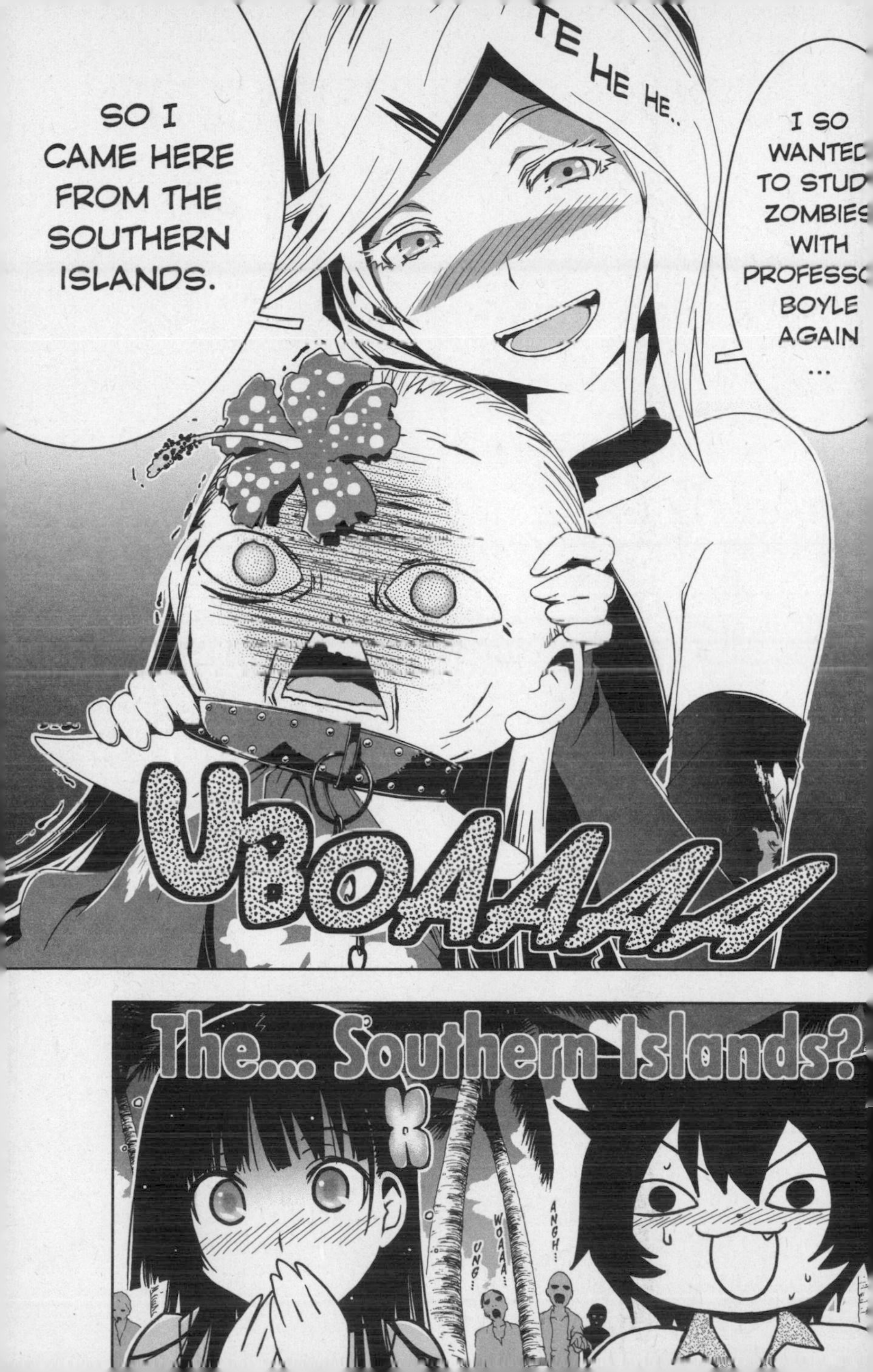
I SO WANTED TO STUD ZOMBIES WITH PROFESSO BOYLE AGAIN ...
TE HE HE..
SO I CAME HERE FROM THE SOUTHERN ISLANDS.
UBOAAAA
The... Southern Islands?
ANGH...
WOAAA...
UNG...

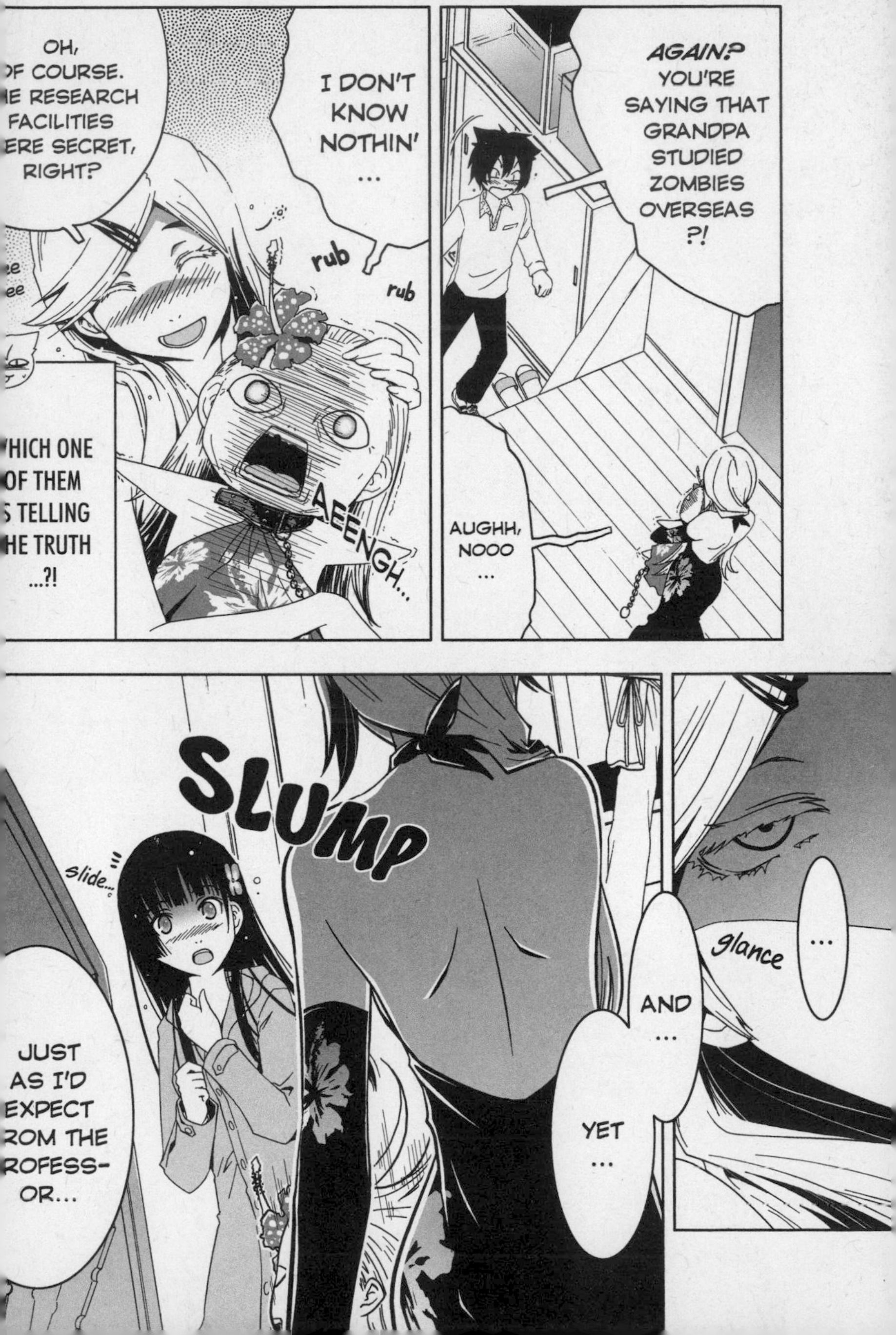
AGAIN?
YOU'RE SAYING THAT GRANDPA STUDIED ZOMBIES OVERSEAS ?!
AUGHH, NOOO ...
I DON'T KNOW NOTHIN' ...
rub
rub
AEENGH...
OH, OF COURSE. IE RESEARCH FACILITIES ERE SECRET, RIGHT?
HICH ONE OF THEM S TELLING HE TRUTH ...?!
glance
...
AND ...
YET ...
SLUMP
slide...
JUST AS I'D EXPECT ROM THE ROFESS- OR...

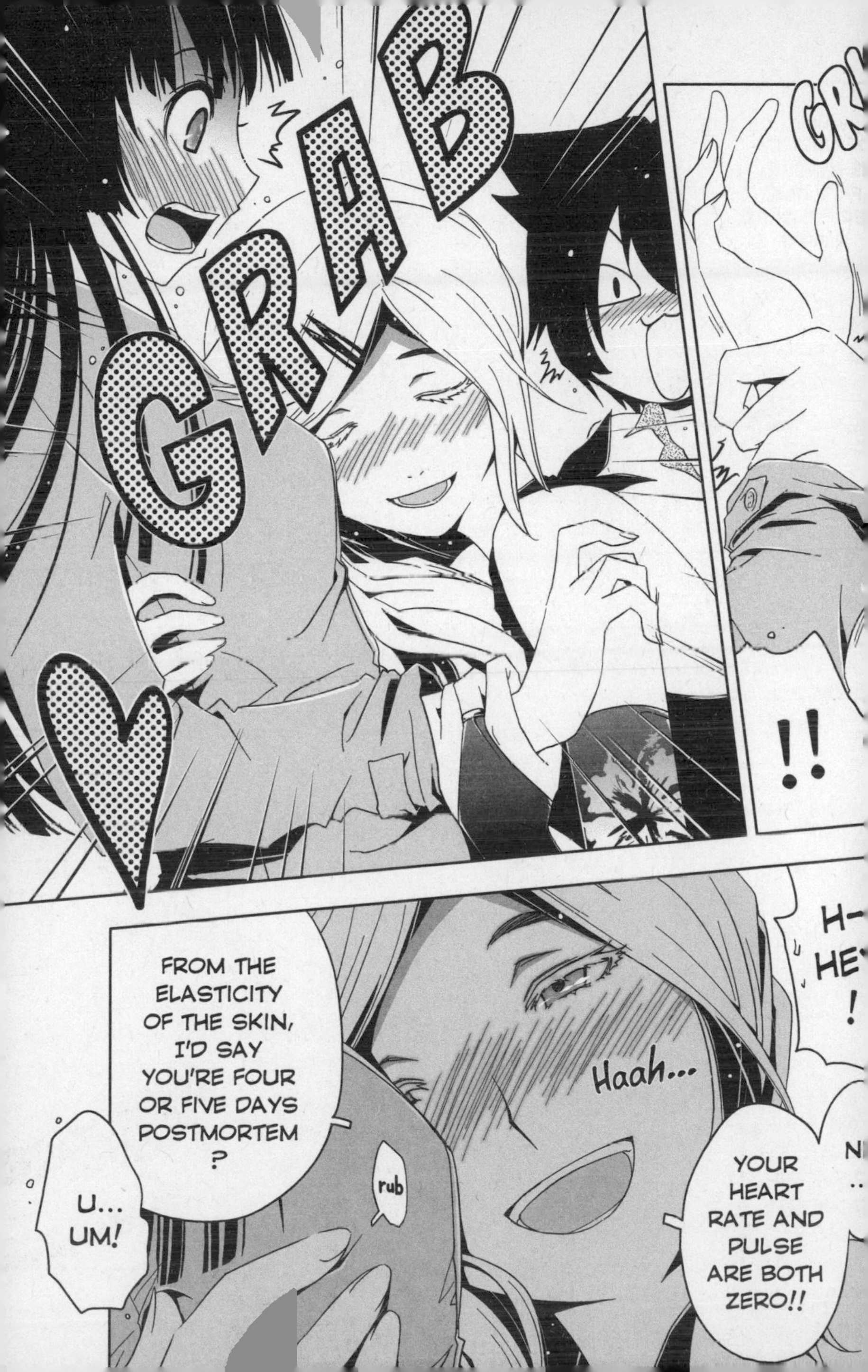
!!
GRAB
H– HE !
YOUR HEART RATE AND PULSE ARE BOTH ZERO!!
Haah...
FROM THE ELASTICITY OF THE SKIN, I'D SAY YOU'RE FOUR OR FIVE DAYS POSTMORTEM ?
rub
U... UM!

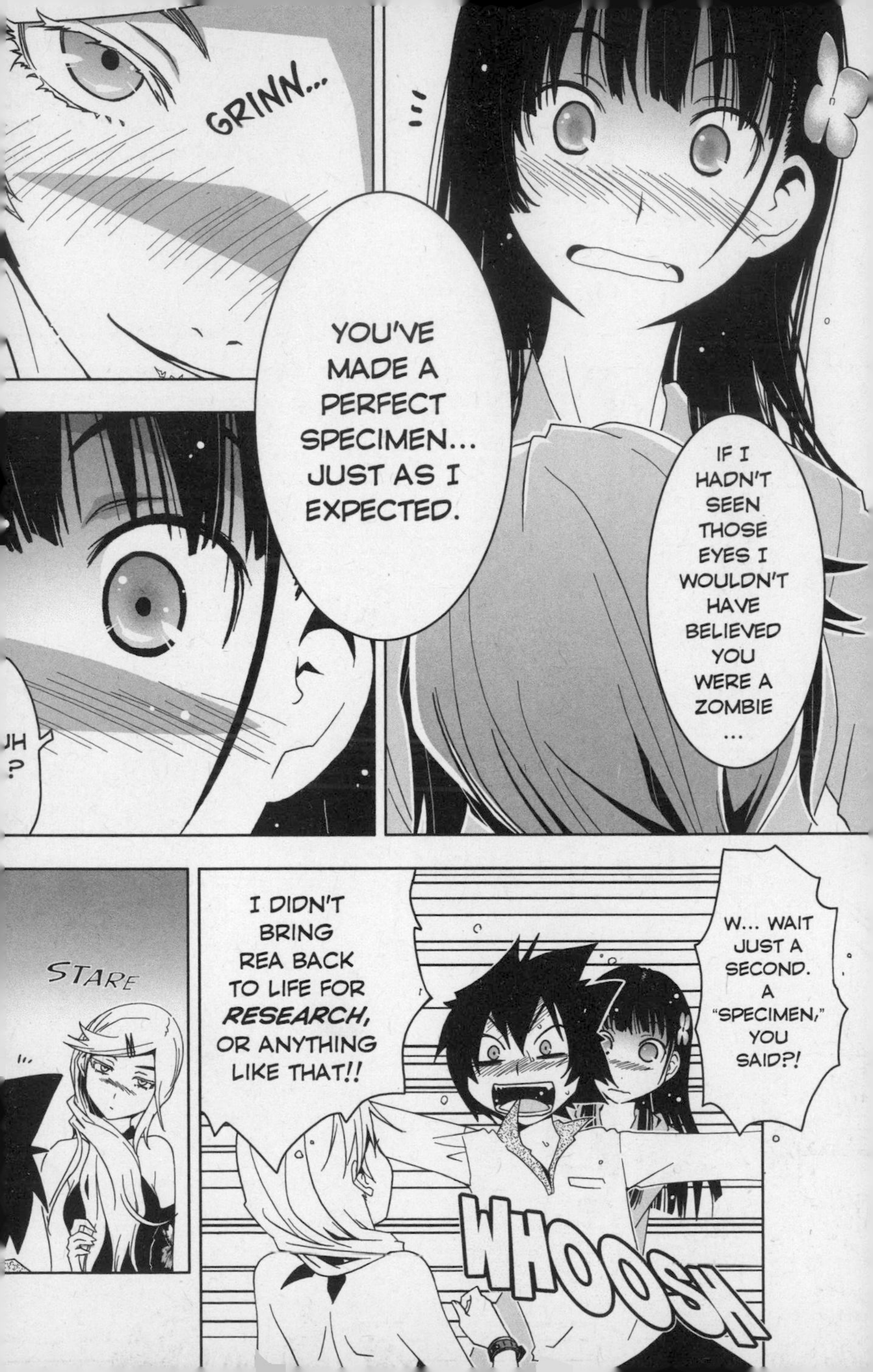
IF I HADN'T SEEN THOSE EYES I WOULDN'T HAVE BELIEVED YOU WERE A ZOMBIE ...
GRINN...
YOU'VE MADE A PERFECT SPECIMEN... JUST AS I EXPECTED.
W... WAIT JUST A SECOND. A "SPECIMEN," YOU SAID?!
I DIDN'T BRING REA BACK TO LIFE FOR *RESEARCH*, OR ANYTHING LIKE THAT!!
WHOOSH
STARE

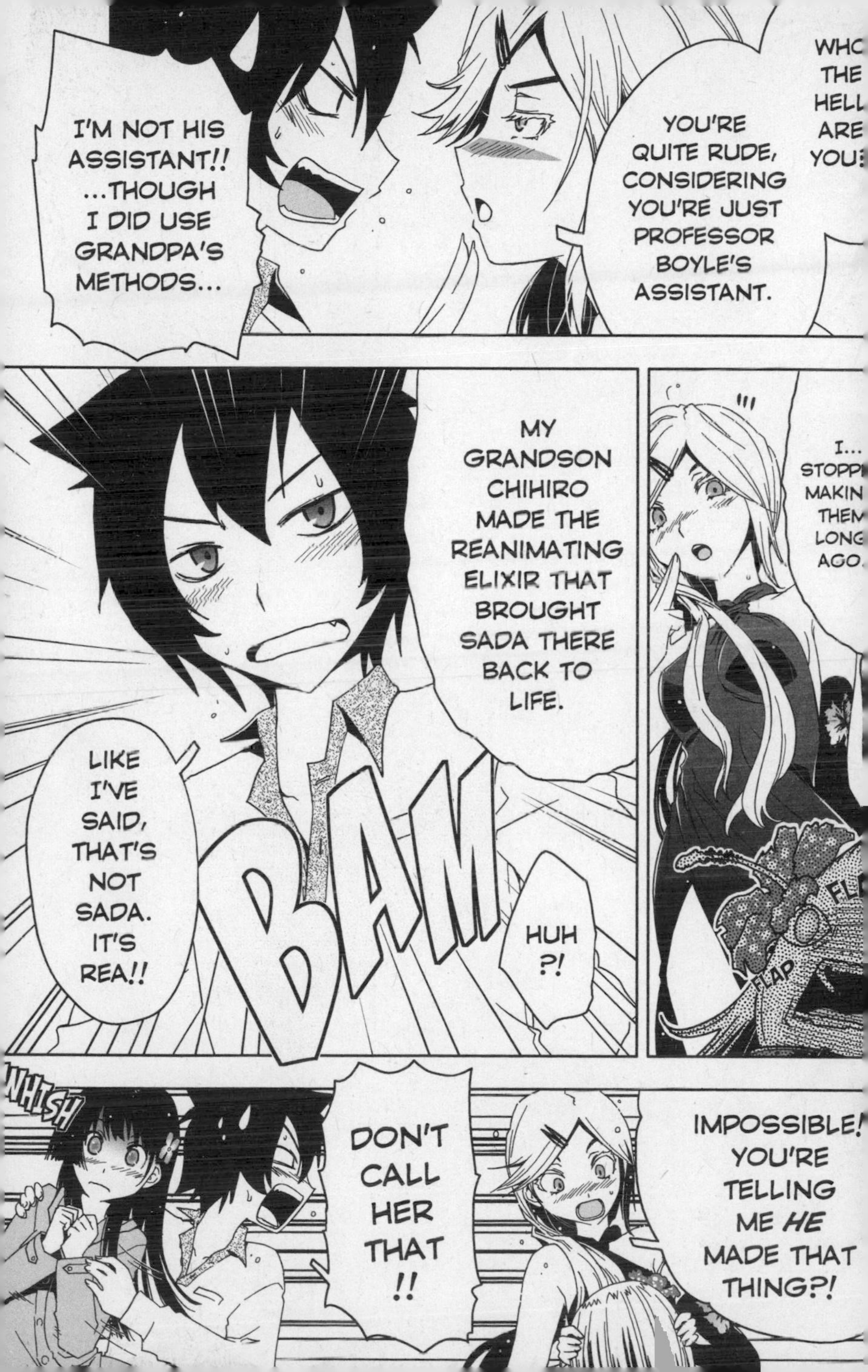
WHO THE HELL ARE YOU?
YOU'RE QUITE RUDE, CONSIDERING YOU'RE JUST PROFESSOR BOYLE'S ASSISTANT.
I'M NOT HIS ASSISTANT!! ...THOUGH I DID USE GRANDPA'S METHODS...
I... STOPP MAKIN THEM LONG AGO.
FLAP
MY GRANDSON CHIHIRO MADE THE REANIMATING ELIXIR THAT BROUGHT SADA THERE BACK TO LIFE.
HUH ?!
BAM
LIKE I'VE SAID, THAT'S NOT SADA. IT'S REA!!
IMPOSSIBLE! YOU'RE TELLING ME *HE* MADE THAT THING?!
DON'T CALL HER THAT !!
WHISH

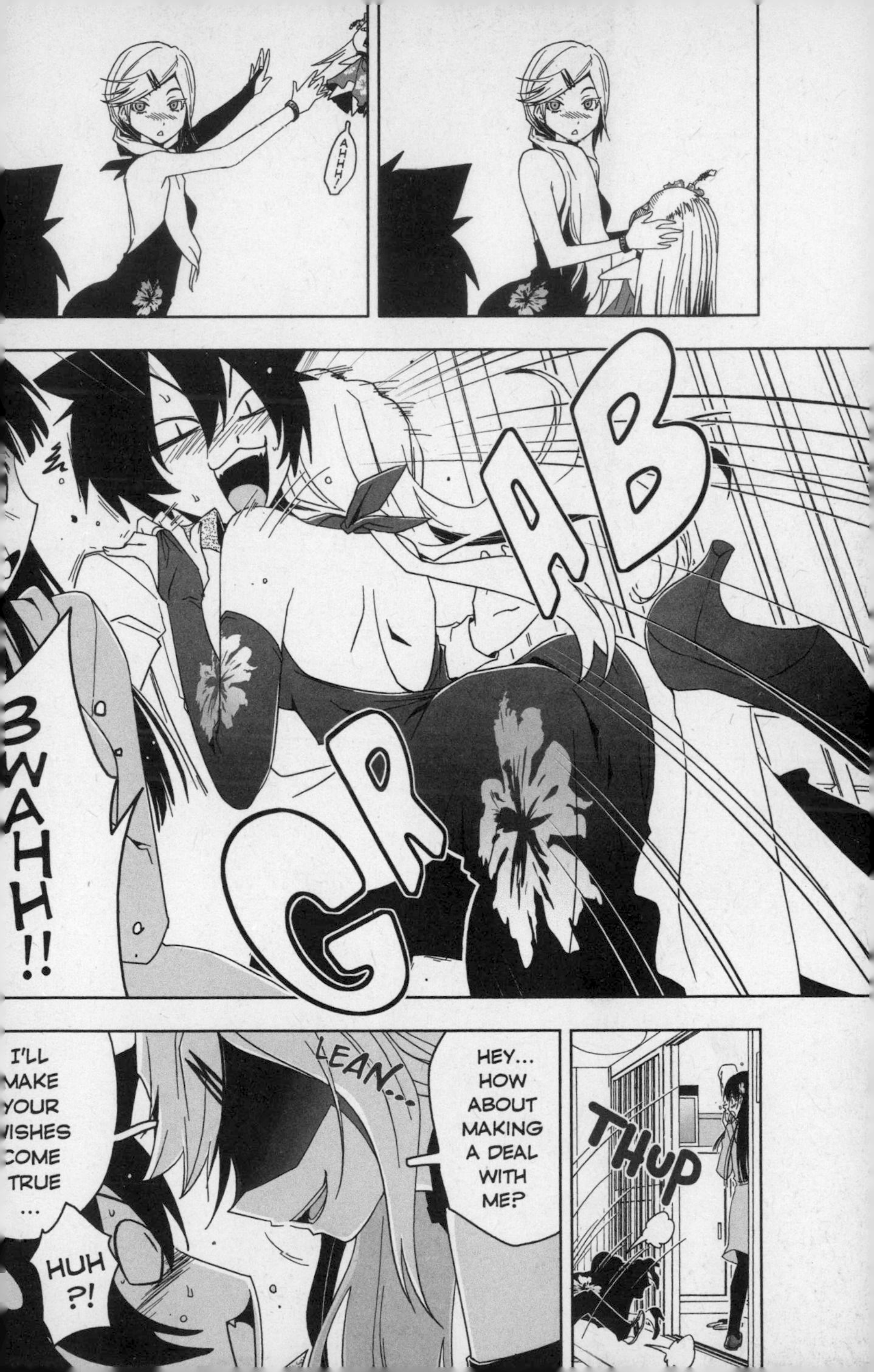
AHHH!
GRAB
BWAHH!!
THUP
HEY... HOW ABOUT MAKING A DEAL WITH ME?
LEAN...
I'LL MAKE YOUR WISHES COME TRUE ...
HUH ?!

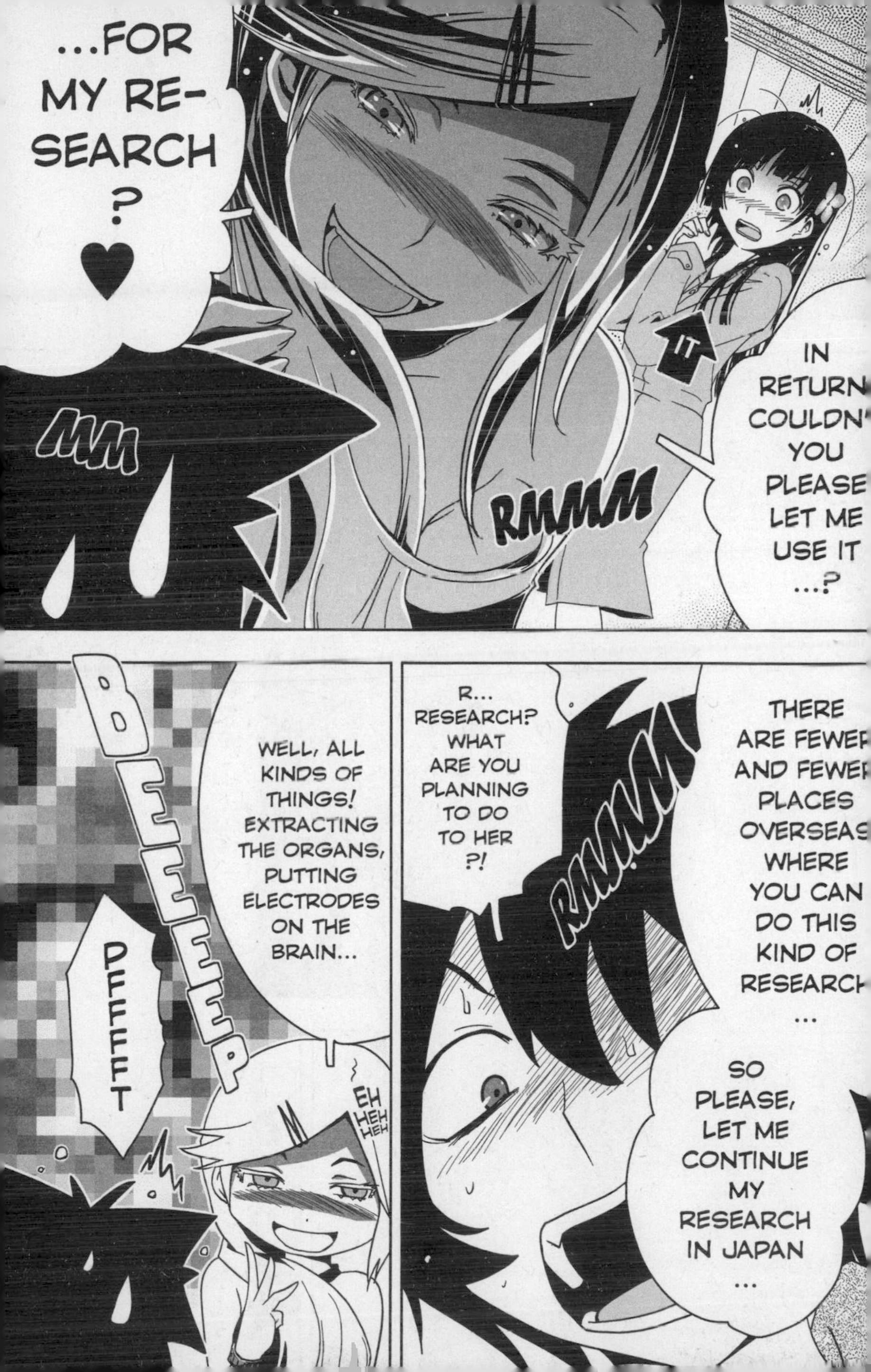
IN RETURN COULDN'T YOU PLEASE LET ME USE IT ...?
IT
RMMM
...FOR MY RE-SEARCH?♥
MM
THERE ARE FEWER AND FEWER PLACES OVERSEAS WHERE YOU CAN DO THIS KIND OF RESEARCH ...
SO PLEASE, LET ME CONTINUE MY RESEARCH IN JAPAN ...
R... RESEARCH? WHAT ARE YOU PLANNING TO DO TO HER ?!
WELL, ALL KINDS OF THINGS! EXTRACTING THE ORGANS, PUTTING ELECTRODES ON THE BRAIN...
BEEEEEP
PFFFFT
EH HEH HEH

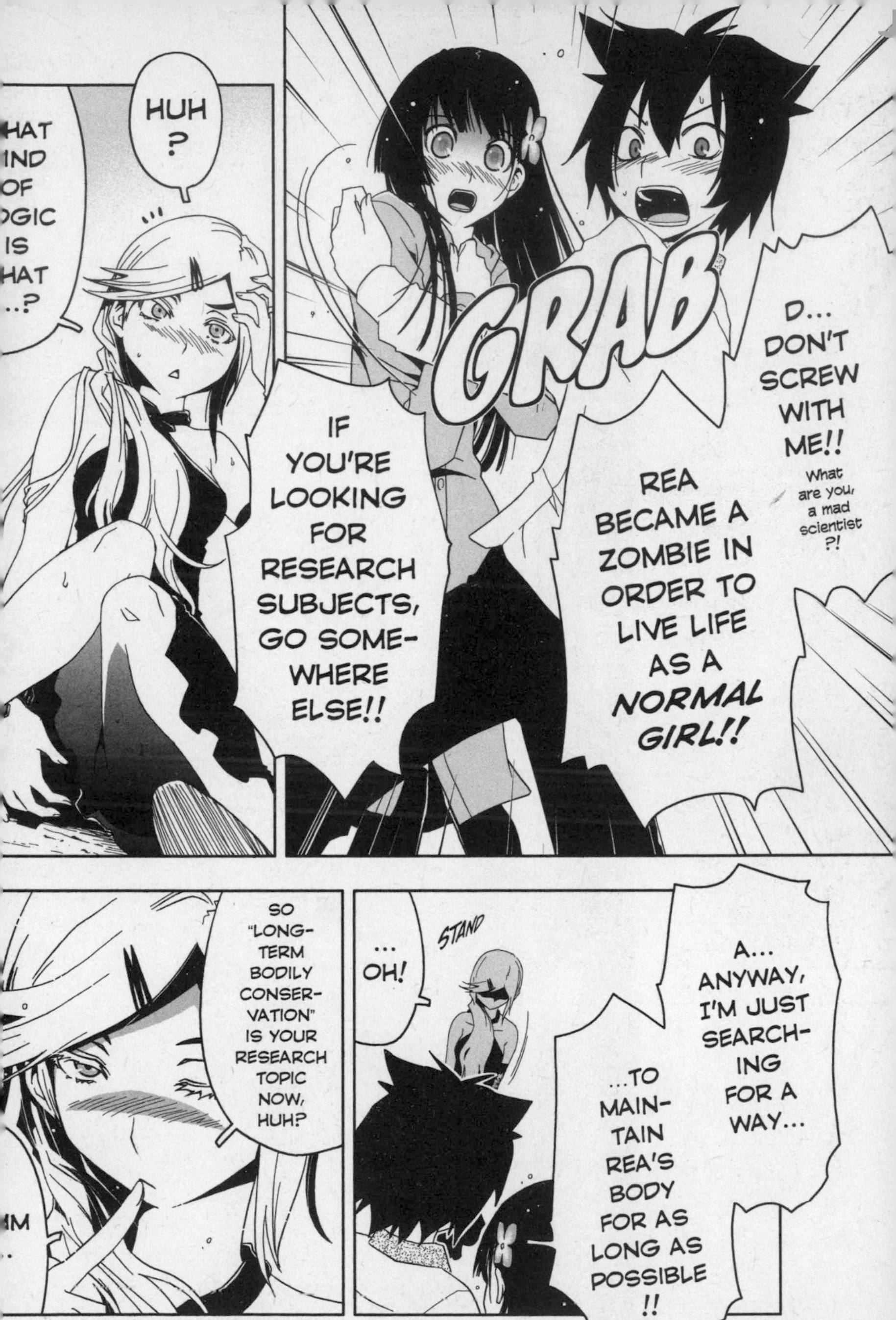
D... DON'T SCREW WITH ME!!
What are you, a mad scientist?!
GRAB
REA BECAME A ZOMBIE IN ORDER TO LIVE LIFE AS A NORMAL GIRL!!
IF YOU'RE LOOKING FOR RESEARCH SUBJECTS, GO SOME-WHERE ELSE!!
HUH?
HAT IND OF OGIC IS HAT ..?
A... ANYWAY, I'M JUST SEARCH-ING FOR A WAY...
...TO MAIN-TAIN REA'S BODY FOR AS LONG AS POSSIBLE!!
STAND
... OH!
SO "LONG-TERM BODILY CONSER-VATION" IS YOUR RESEARCH TOPIC NOW, HUH?
IM .

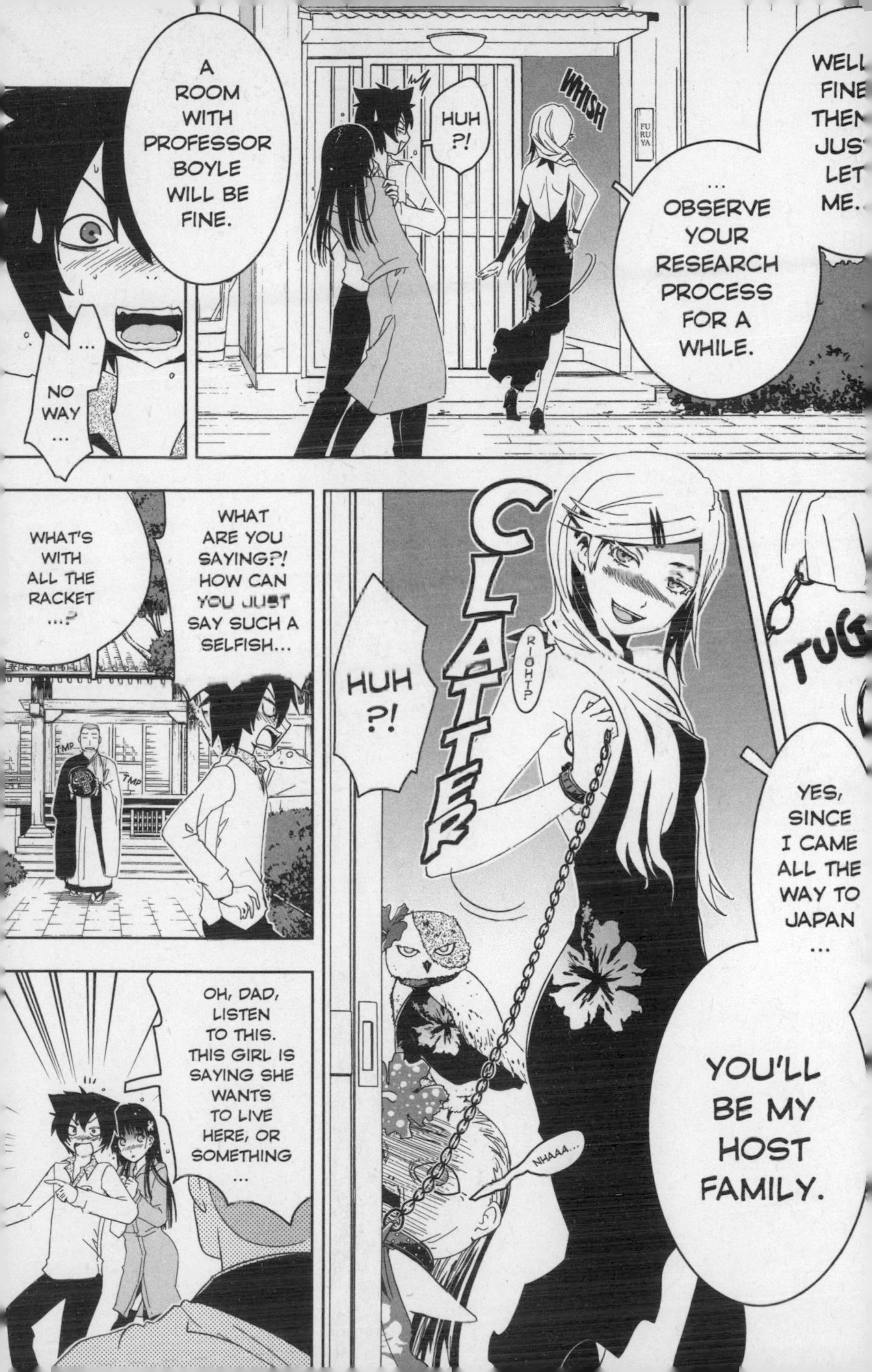

WELL FINE THEN JUST LET ME...
... OBSERVE YOUR RESEARCH PROCESS FOR A WHILE.
WHISH
HUH ?!
FU RU YA
A ROOM WITH PROFESSOR BOYLE WILL BE FINE.
... NO WAY ...
TUG
YES, SINCE I CAME ALL THE WAY TO JAPAN ...
YOU'LL BE MY HOST FAMILY.
CLATTER
RIGHT?
HUH ?!
NHAAA...
WHAT ARE YOU SAYING?! HOW CAN YOU JUST SAY SUCH A SELFISH...
WHAT'S WITH ALL THE RACKET ...?
TMP
TMP
OH, DAD, LISTEN TO THIS. THIS GIRL IS SAYING SHE WANTS TO LIVE HERE, OR SOMETHING ...

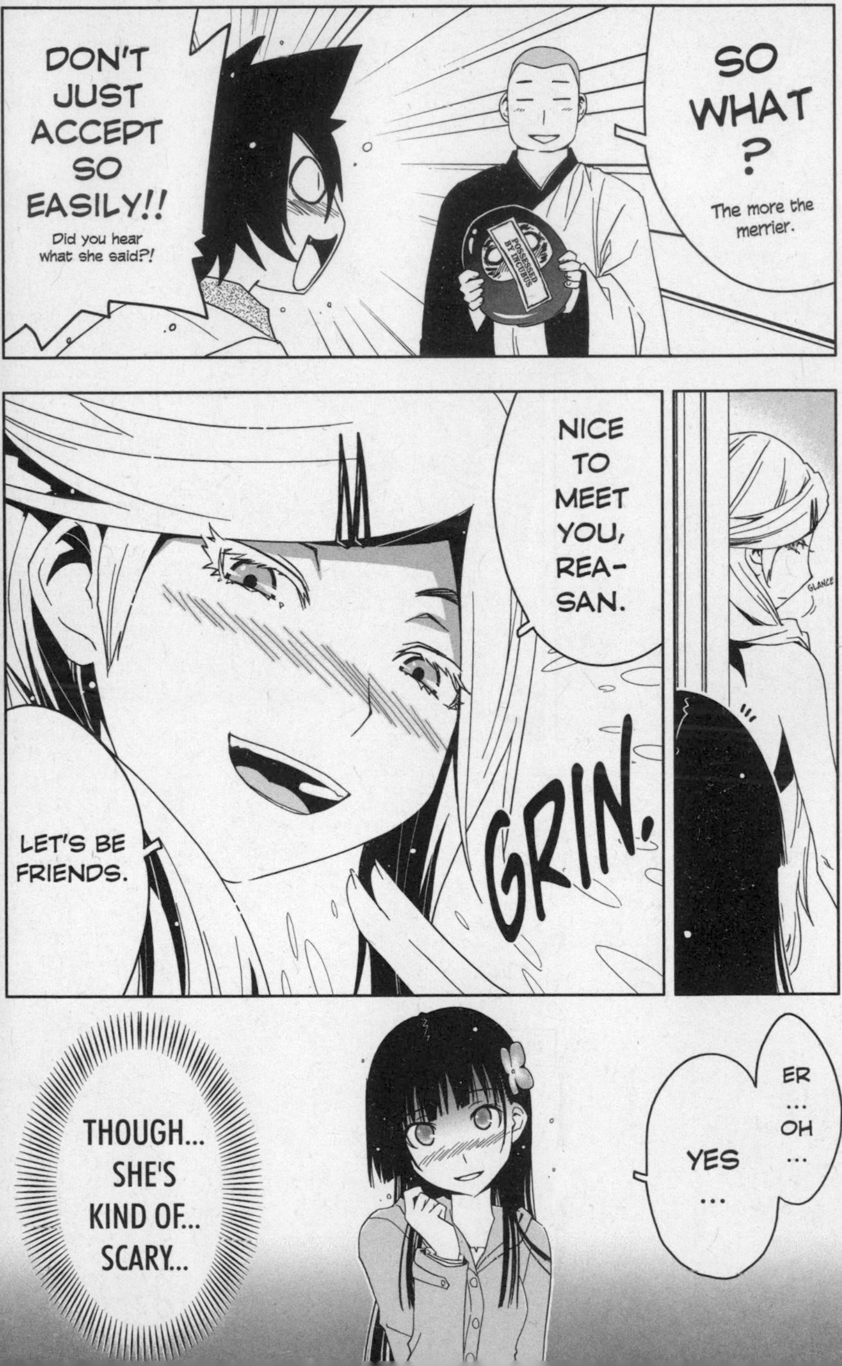
SO WHAT?
The more the merrier.
POSSESSED BY INCUBUS
DON'T JUST ACCEPT SO EASILY!!
Did you hear what she said?!
GLANCE
NICE TO MEET YOU, REA-SAN.
GRIN.
LET'S BE FRIENDS.
ER... OH... YES...
THOUGH... SHE'S KIND OF... SCARY...

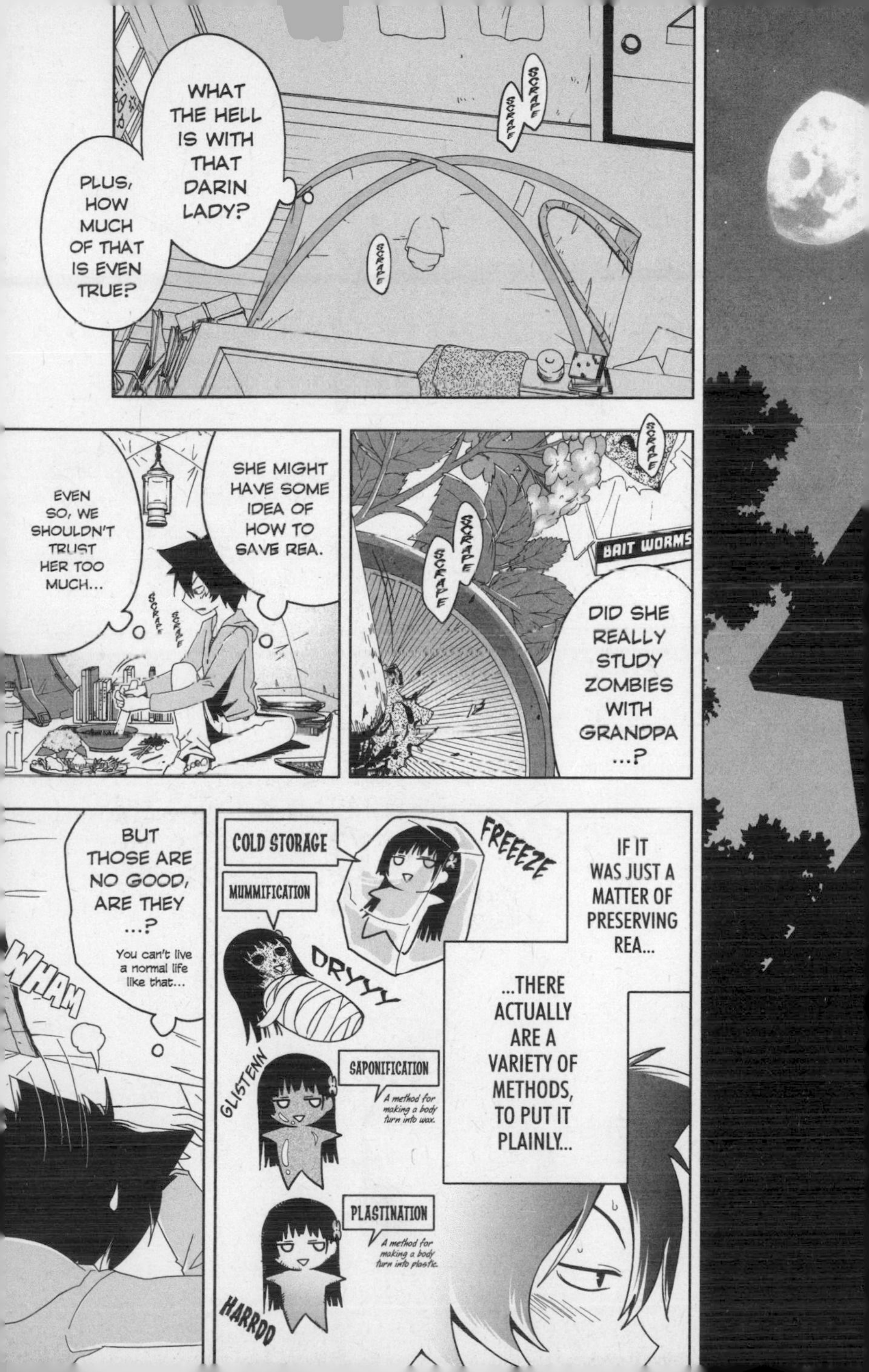
WHAT THE HELL IS WITH THAT DARIN LADY?
PLUS, HOW MUCH OF THAT IS EVEN TRUE?
SCRAPE SCRAPE
SCRAPE
SCRAPE
BAIT WORMS
SCRAPE SCRAPE
DID SHE REALLY STUDY ZOMBIES WITH GRANDPA ...?
SHE MIGHT HAVE SOME IDEA OF HOW TO SAVE REA.
EVEN SO, WE SHOULDN'T TRUST HER TOO MUCH...
SCRAPE SCRAPE
IF IT WAS JUST A MATTER OF PRESERVING REA...
...THERE ACTUALLY ARE A VARIETY OF METHODS, TO PUT IT PLAINLY...
COLD STORAGE
FREEEZE
MUMMIFICATION
DRYYY
SAPONIFICATION
GLISTENN
A method for making a body turn into wax.
PLASTINATION
A method for making a body turn into plastic.
HARRDD
BUT THOSE ARE NO GOOD, ARE THEY ...?
You can't live a normal life like that...
WHAM

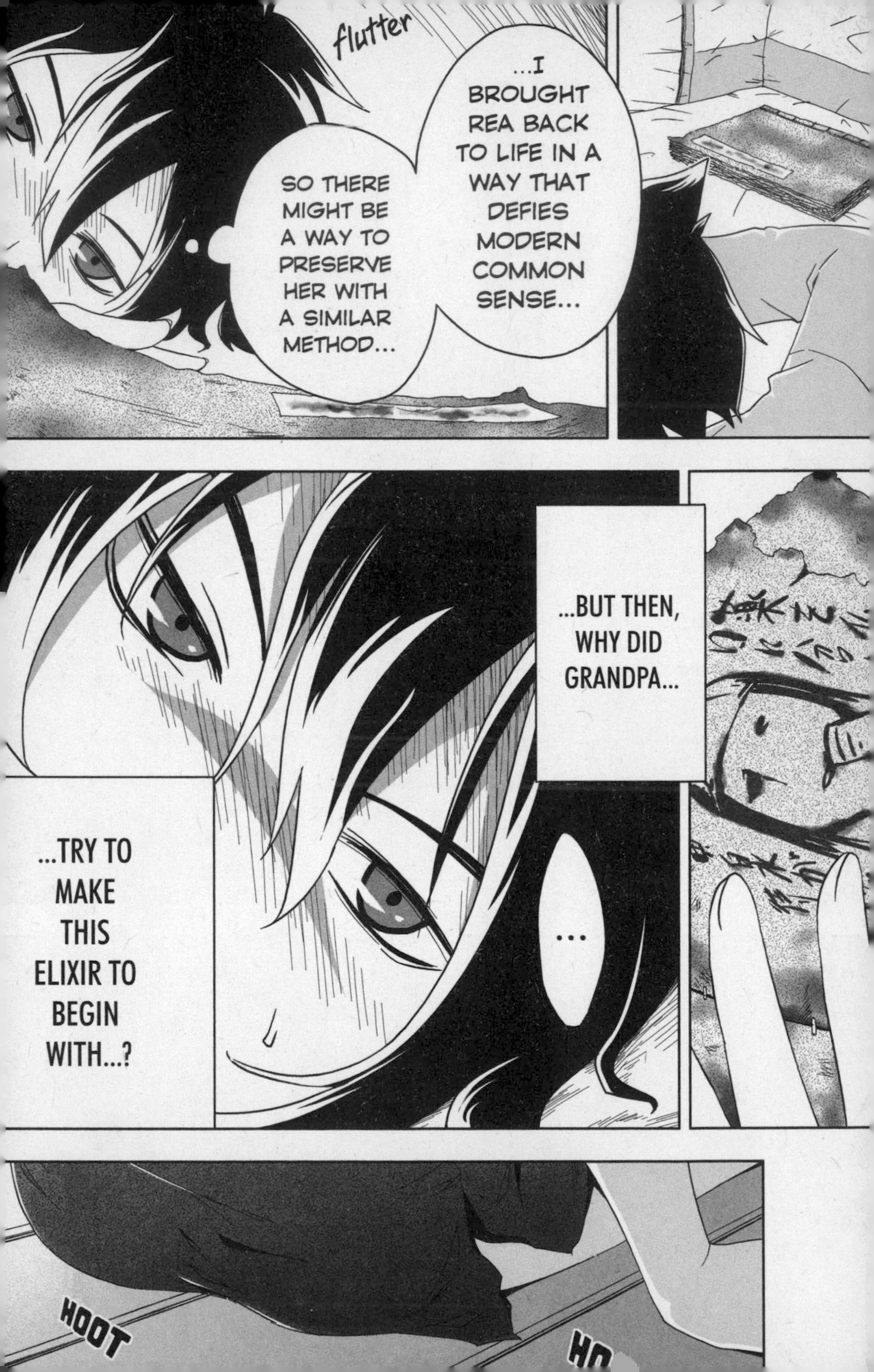
flutter
...I BROUGHT REA BACK TO LIFE IN A WAY THAT DEFIES MODERN COMMON SENSE...
SO THERE MIGHT BE A WAY TO PRESERVE HER WITH A SIMILAR METHOD...
...BUT THEN, WHY DID GRANDPA...
...
...TRY TO MAKE THIS ELIXIR TO BEGIN WITH...?
HOOT
HO

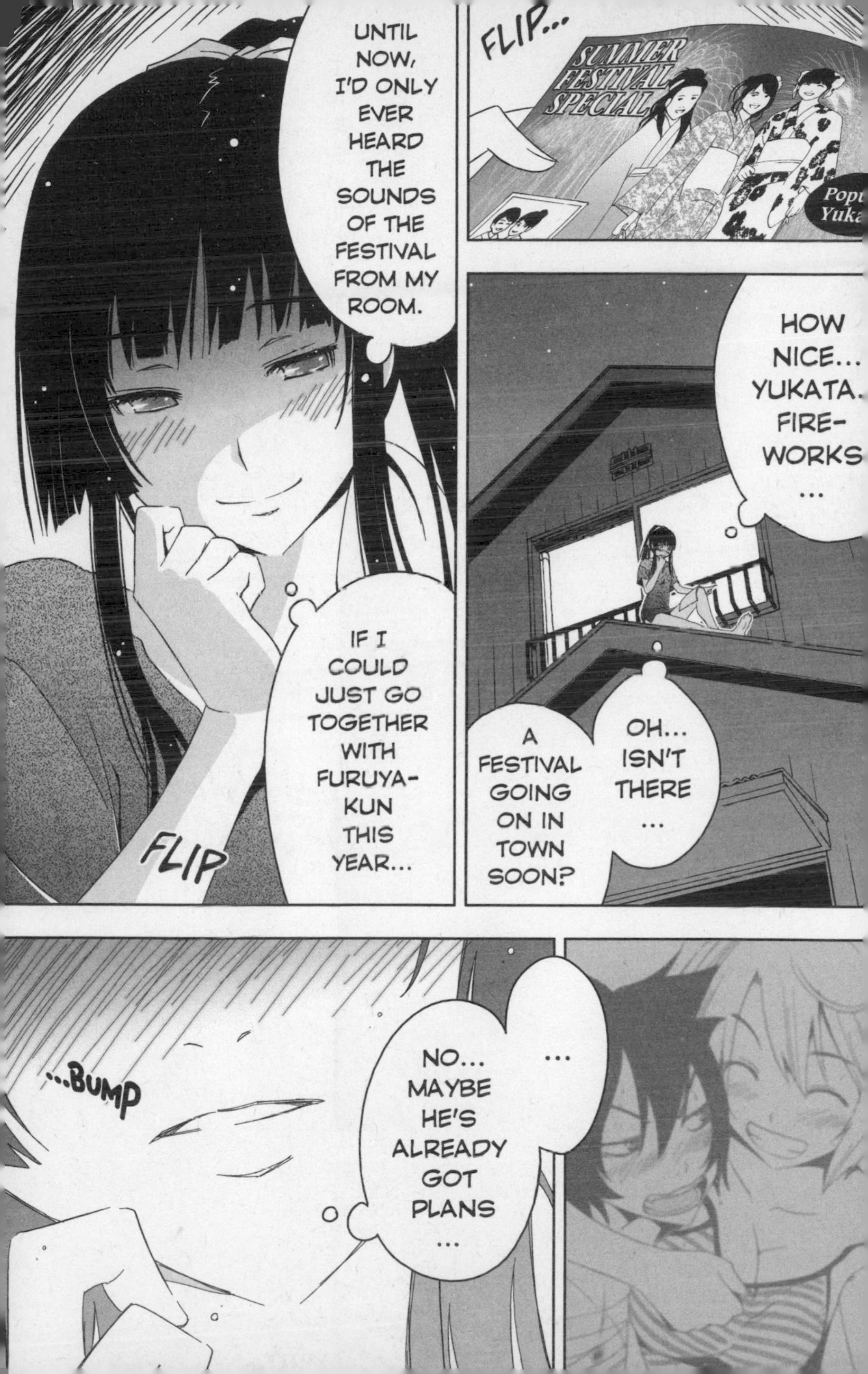
FLIP...
SUMMER FESTIVAL SPECIAL
HOW NICE... YUKATA... FIRE-WORKS ...
OH... ISN'T THERE ...
A FESTIVAL GOING ON IN TOWN SOON?
UNTIL NOW, I'D ONLY EVER HEARD THE SOUNDS OF THE FESTIVAL FROM MY ROOM.
IF I COULD JUST GO TOGETHER WITH FURUYA-KUN THIS YEAR...
FLIP
...
NO... MAYBE HE'S ALREADY GOT PLANS ...
...BUMP

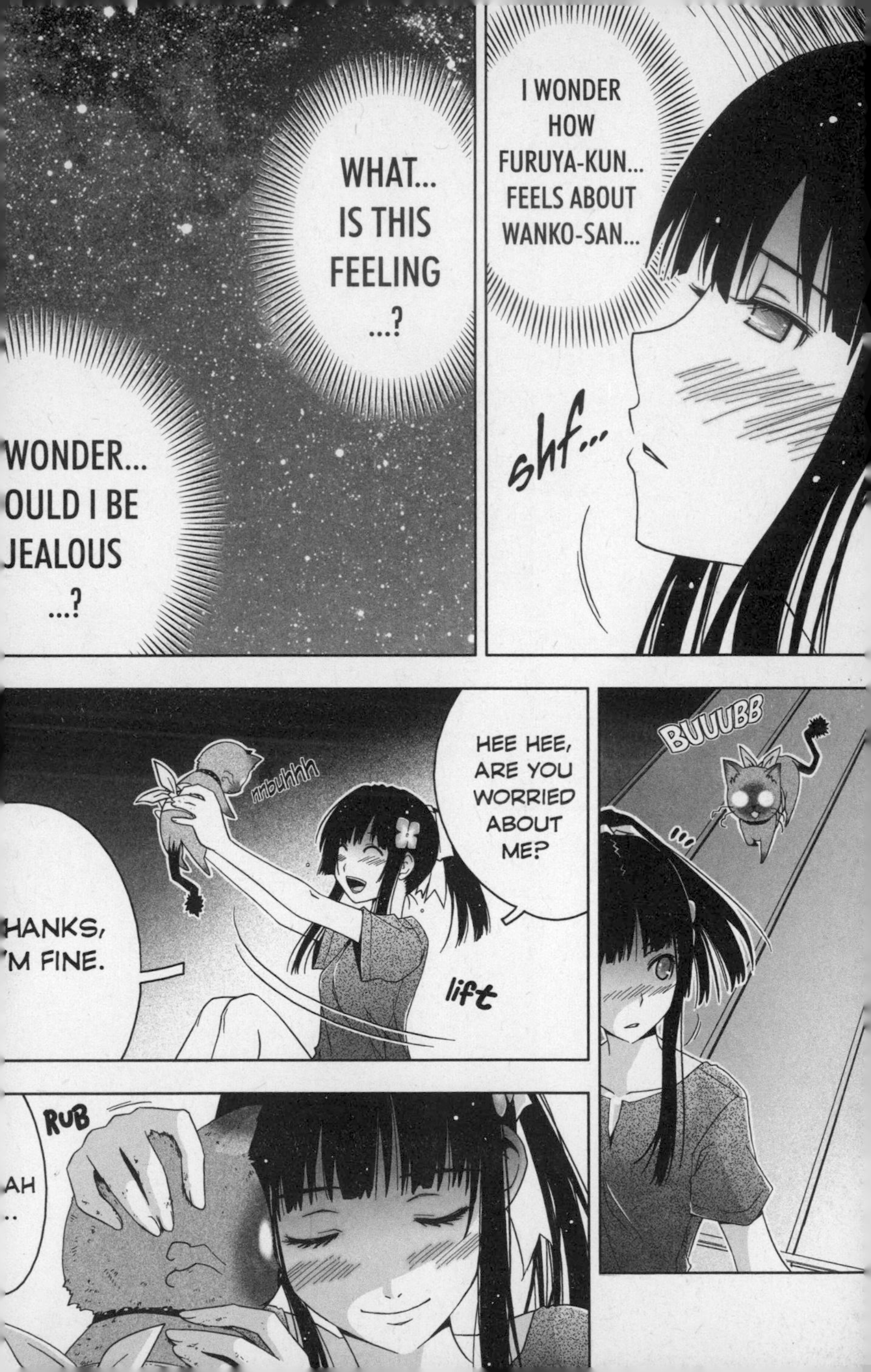
I WONDER HOW FURUYA-KUN... FEELS ABOUT WANKO-SAN...
shf...
WHAT... IS THIS FEELING ...?
WONDER... OULD I BE JEALOUS ...?
BUUUBB
...
HEE HEE, ARE YOU WORRIED ABOUT ME?
nnbuhhh
lift
HANKS, 'M FINE.
RUB
AH ..

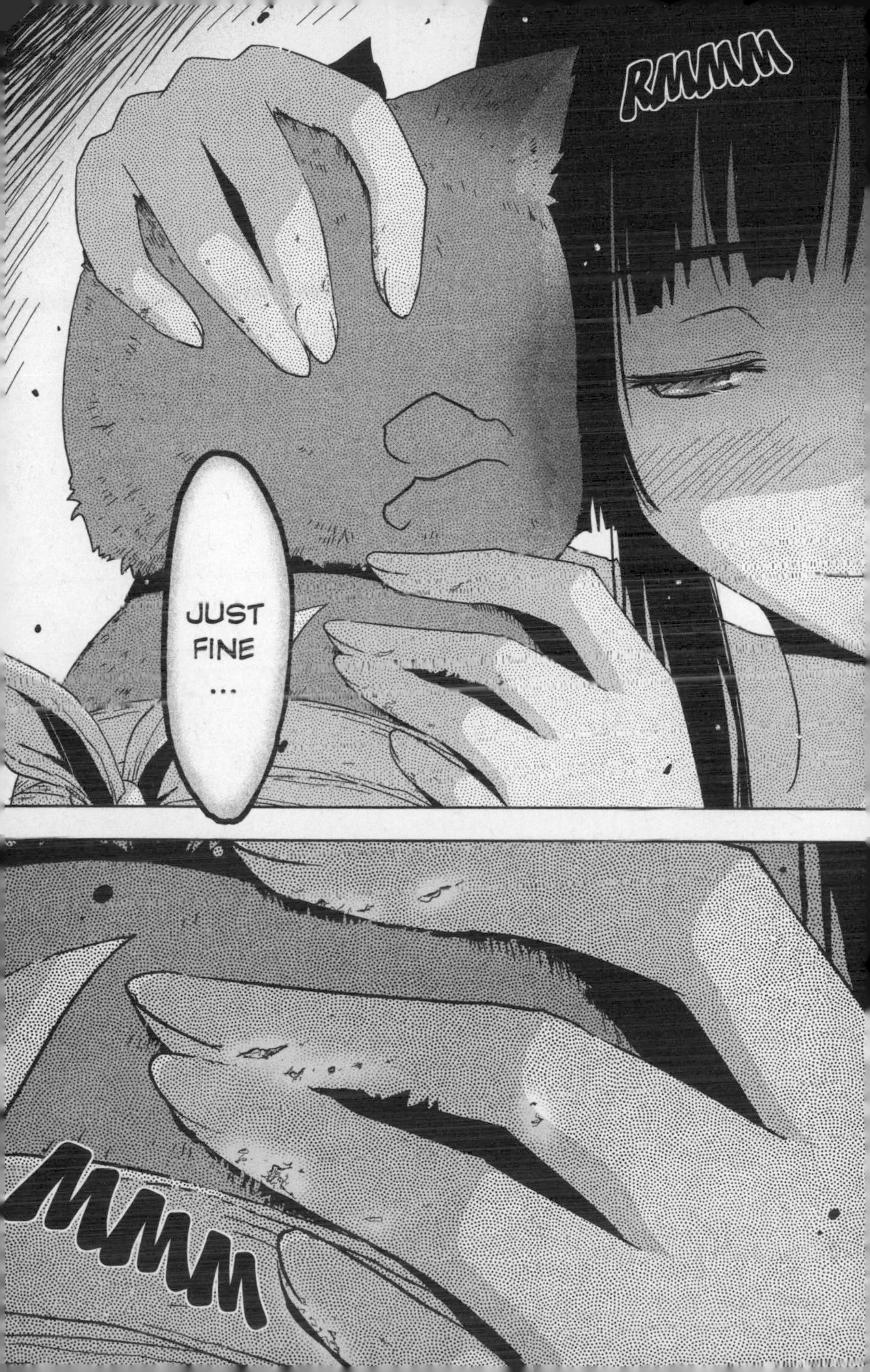
RMMMM
JUST FINE ...
MMMM

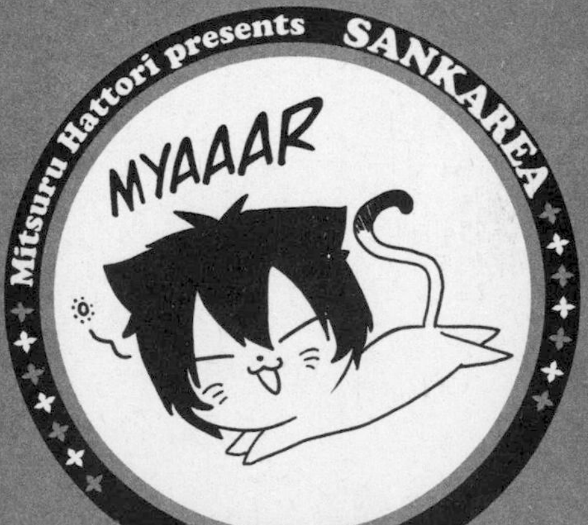
Mitsuru Hattori presents
SANKAREA
MYAAAR

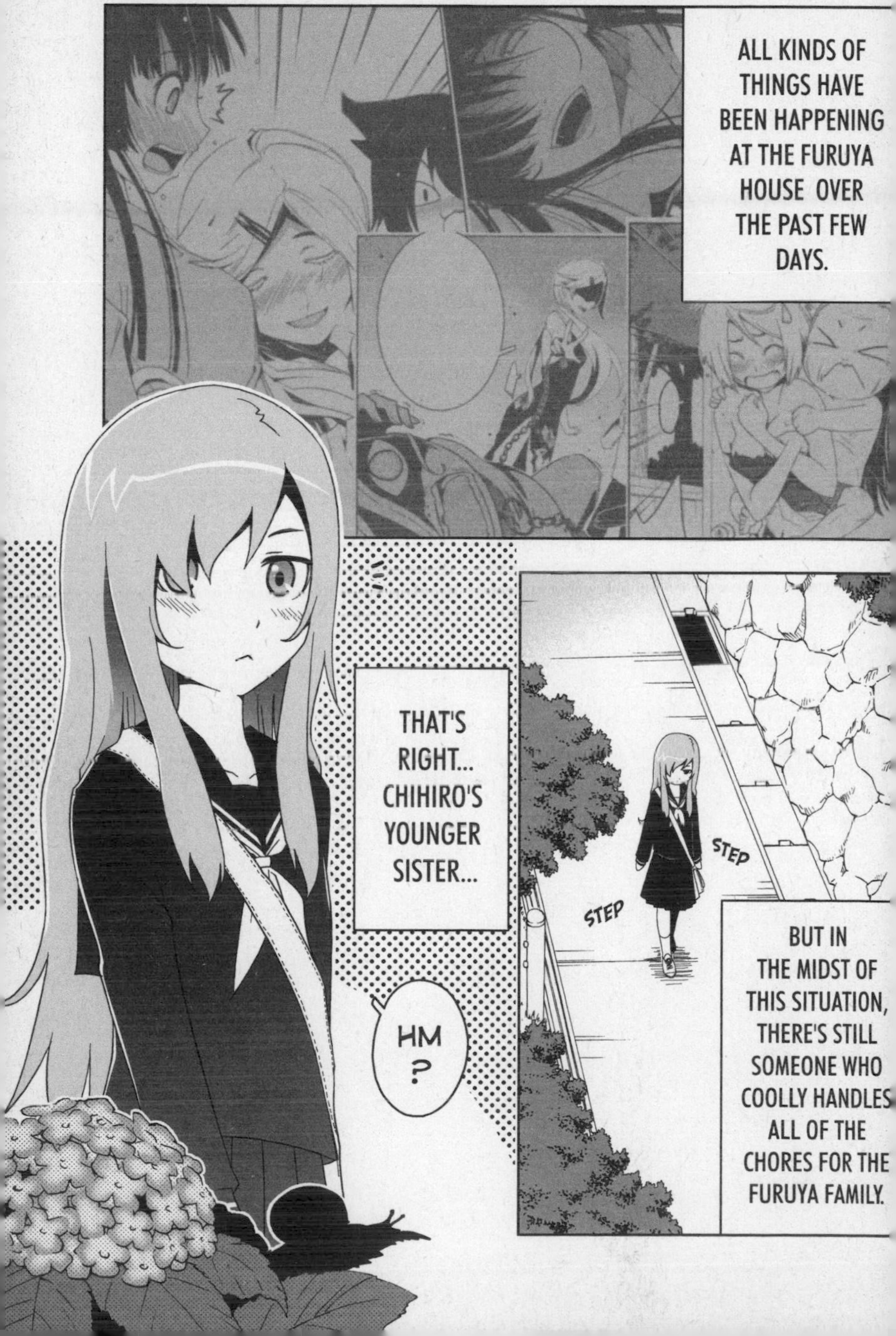
ALL KINDS OF THINGS HAVE BEEN HAPPENING AT THE FURUYA HOUSE OVER THE PAST FEW DAYS.
STEP
STEP
BUT IN THE MIDST OF THIS SITUATION, THERE'S STILL SOMEONE WHO COOLLY HANDLES ALL OF THE CHORES FOR THE FURUYA FAMILY.
THAT'S RIGHT... CHIHIRO'S YOUNGER SISTER...
HM?

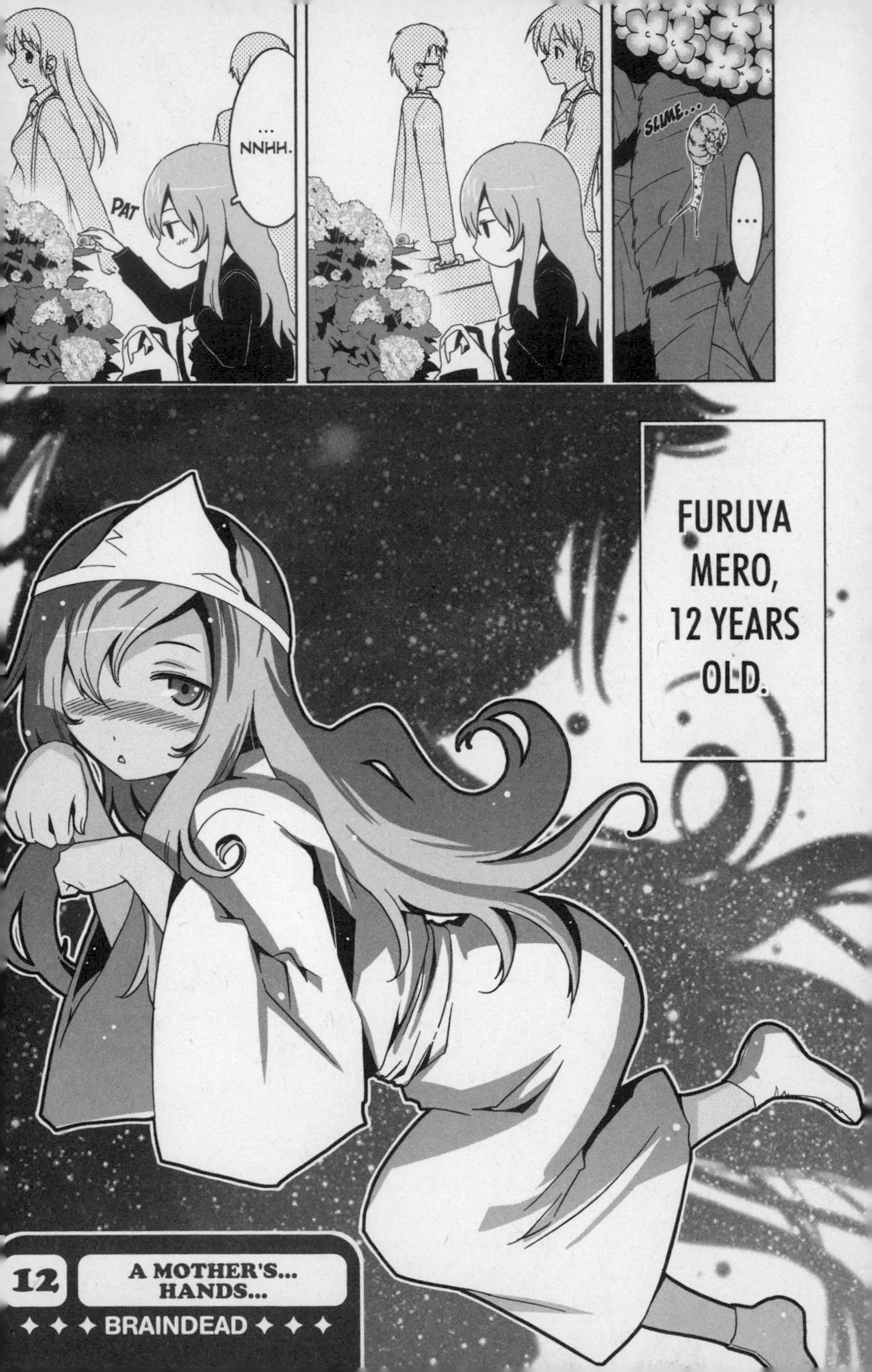
SLIME...
...
... NNHH.
PAT
FURUYA MERO, 12 YEARS OLD.
12
A MOTHER'S... HANDS...
BRAINDEAD

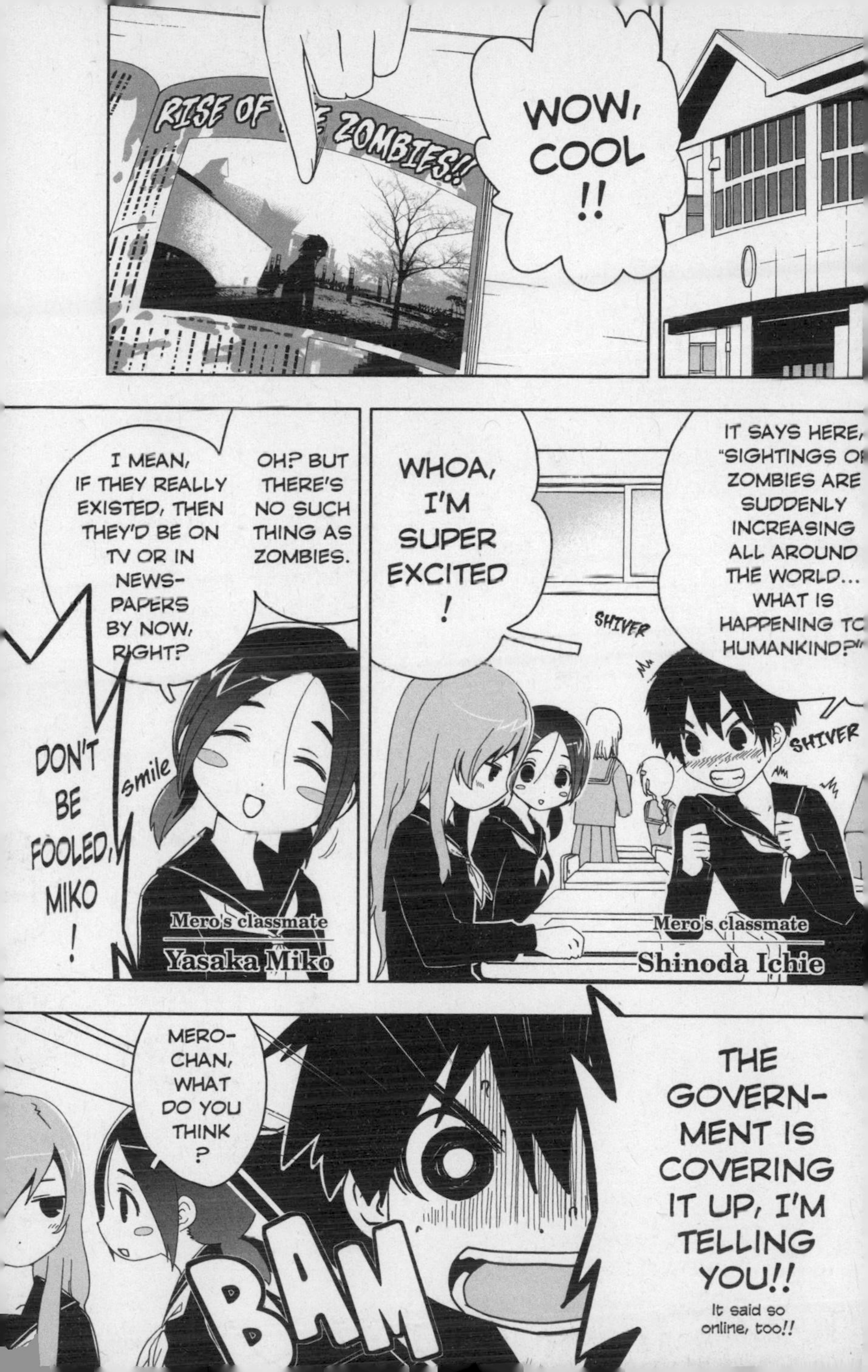
WOW, COOL!!
RISE OF
E ZOMBIES!!
IT SAYS HERE, "SIGHTINGS OF ZOMBIES ARE SUDDENLY INCREASING ALL AROUND THE WORLD... WHAT IS HAPPENING TO HUMANKIND?"
SHIVER
SHIVER
WHOA, I'M SUPER EXCITED!
Mero's classmate
Shinoda Ichie
OH? BUT THERE'S NO SUCH THING AS ZOMBIES.
I MEAN, IF THEY REALLY EXISTED, THEN THEY'D BE ON TV OR IN NEWS-PAPERS BY NOW, RIGHT?
DON'T BE FOOLED, MIKO!
smile
Mero's classmate
Yasaka Miko
THE GOVERN-MENT IS COVERING IT UP, I'M TELLING YOU!!
It said so online, too!!
BAM
MERO-CHAN, WHAT DO YOU THINK?

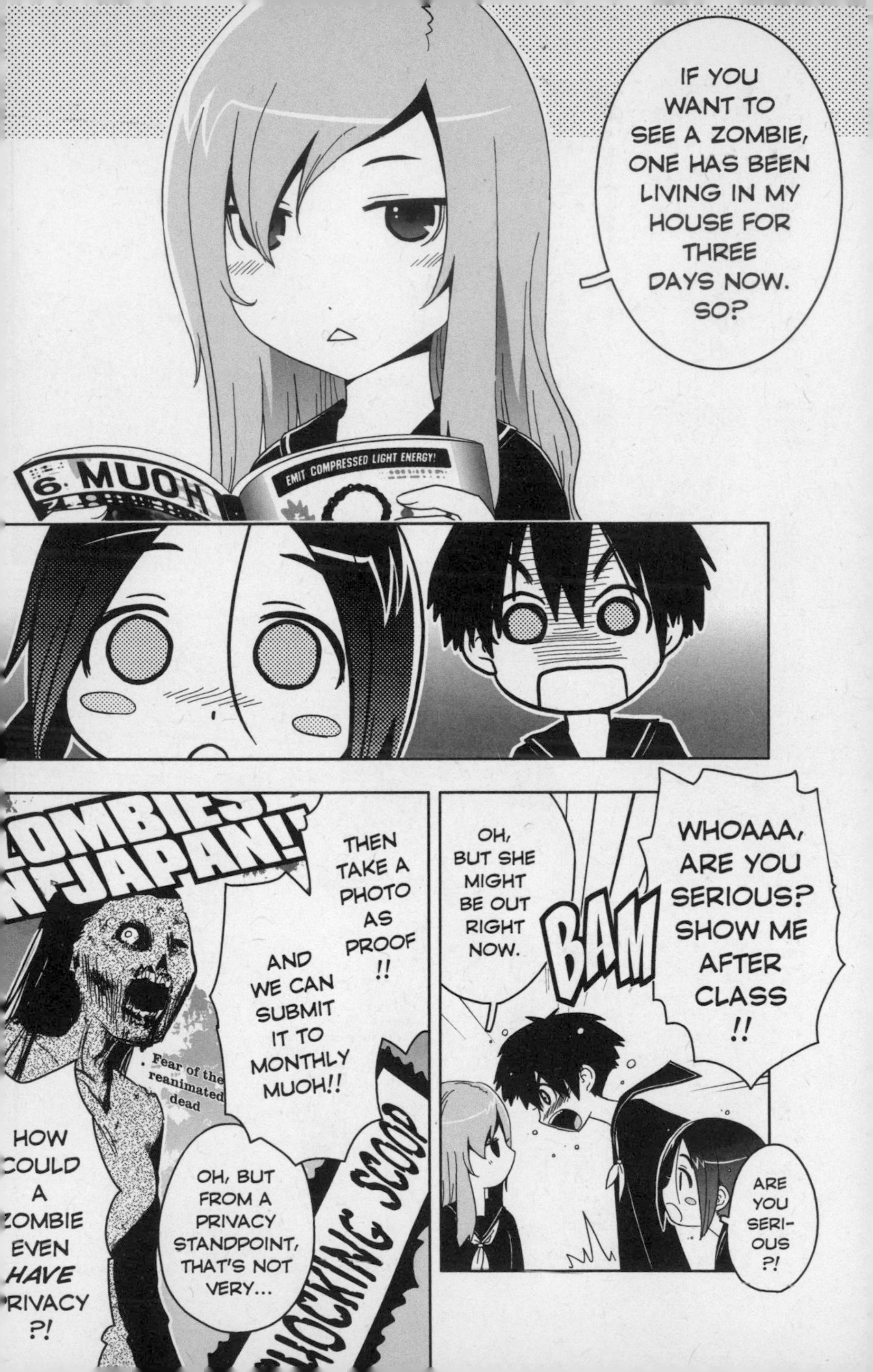
IF YOU WANT TO SEE A ZOMBIE, ONE HAS BEEN LIVING IN MY HOUSE FOR THREE DAYS NOW. SO?
EMIT COMPRESSED LIGHT ENERGY!
MUOH
WHOAAA, ARE YOU SERIOUS? SHOW ME AFTER CLASS!!
BAM
OH, BUT SHE MIGHT BE OUT RIGHT NOW.
ARE YOU SERI-OUS?!
THEN TAKE A PHOTO AS PROOF!!
AND WE CAN SUBMIT IT TO MONTHLY MUOH!!
Fear of the reanimated dead
OH, BUT FROM A PRIVACY STANDPOINT, THAT'S NOT VERY...
HOW COULD A ZOMBIE EVEN HAVE PRIVACY?!

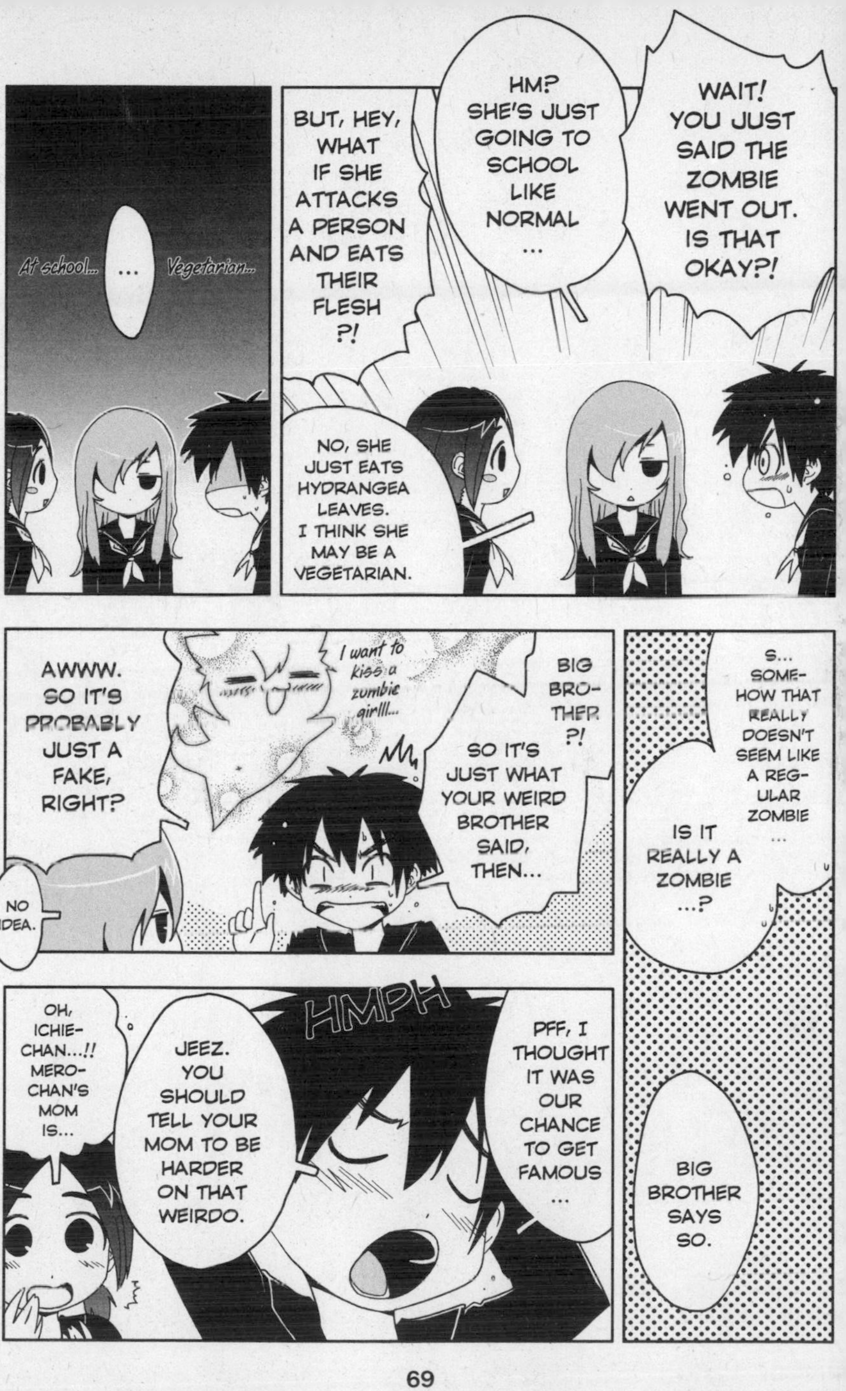
WAIT! YOU JUST SAID THE ZOMBIE WENT OUT. IS THAT OKAY?!
HM? SHE'S JUST GOING TO SCHOOL LIKE NORMAL ...
BUT, HEY, WHAT IF SHE ATTACKS A PERSON AND EATS THEIR FLESH ?!
NO, SHE JUST EATS HYDRANGEA LEAVES. I THINK SHE MAY BE A VEGETARIAN.
Vegetarian...
...
At school...
S... SOME-HOW THAT REALLY DOESN'T SEEM LIKE A REG-ULAR ZOMBIE ...
IS IT REALLY A ZOMBIE ...?
BIG BROTHER SAYS SO.
BIG BRO-THER ?!
SO IT'S JUST WHAT YOUR WEIRD BROTHER SAID, THEN...
I want to kiss a zombie girllll...
AWWW. SO IT'S PROBABLY JUST A FAKE, RIGHT?
NO IDEA.
PFF, I THOUGHT IT WAS OUR CHANCE TO GET FAMOUS ...
HMPH
JEEZ. YOU SHOULD TELL YOUR MOM TO BE HARDER ON THAT WEIRDO.
OH, ICHIE-CHAN...!! MERO-CHAN'S MOM IS...

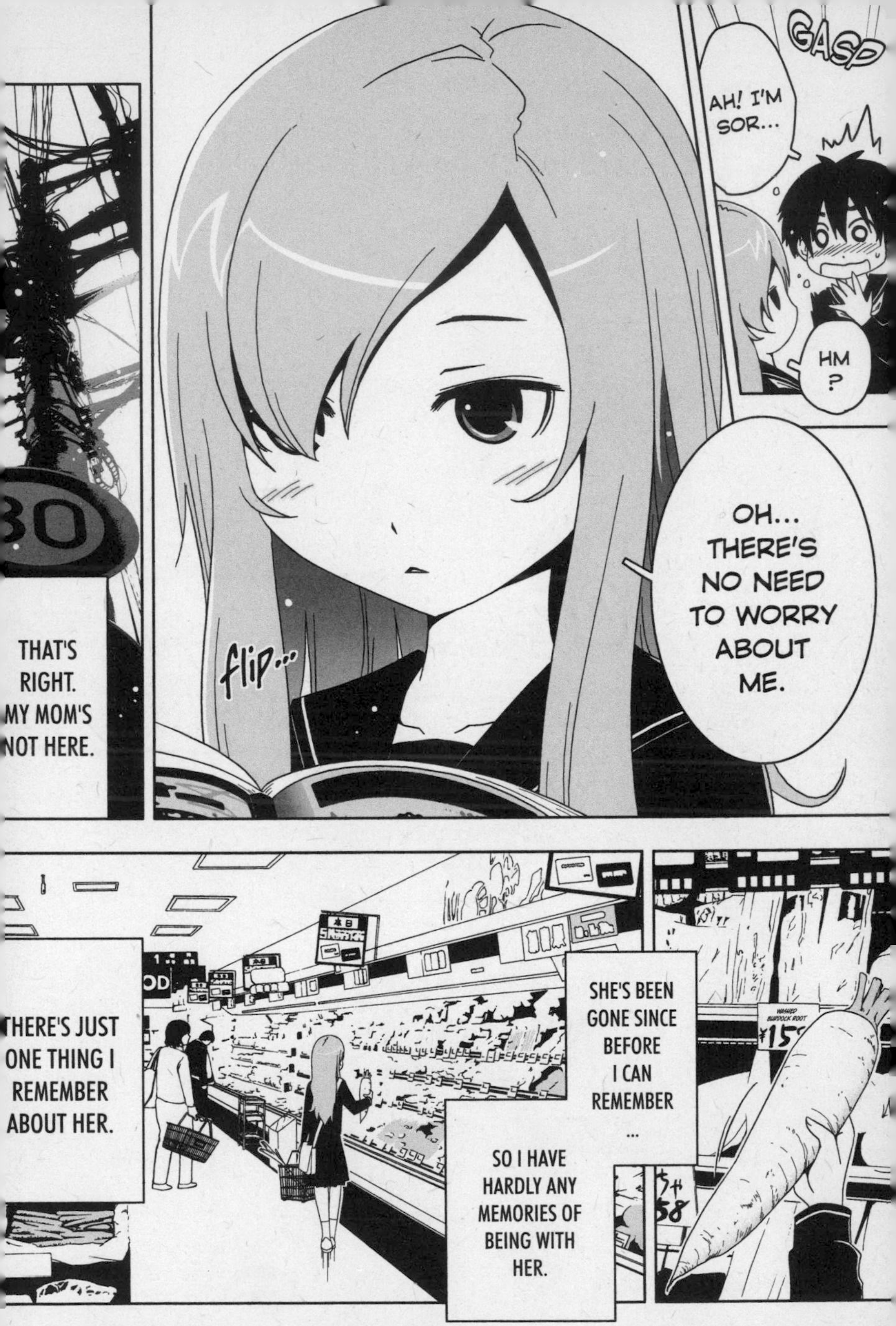
GASP
AH! I'M SOR...
HM?
OH... THERE'S NO NEED TO WORRY ABOUT ME.
flip...
THAT'S RIGHT. MY MOM'S NOT HERE.
SHE'S BEEN GONE SINCE BEFORE I CAN REMEMBER ...
SO I HAVE HARDLY ANY MEMORIES OF BEING WITH HER.
THERE'S JUST ONE THING I REMEMBER ABOUT HER.

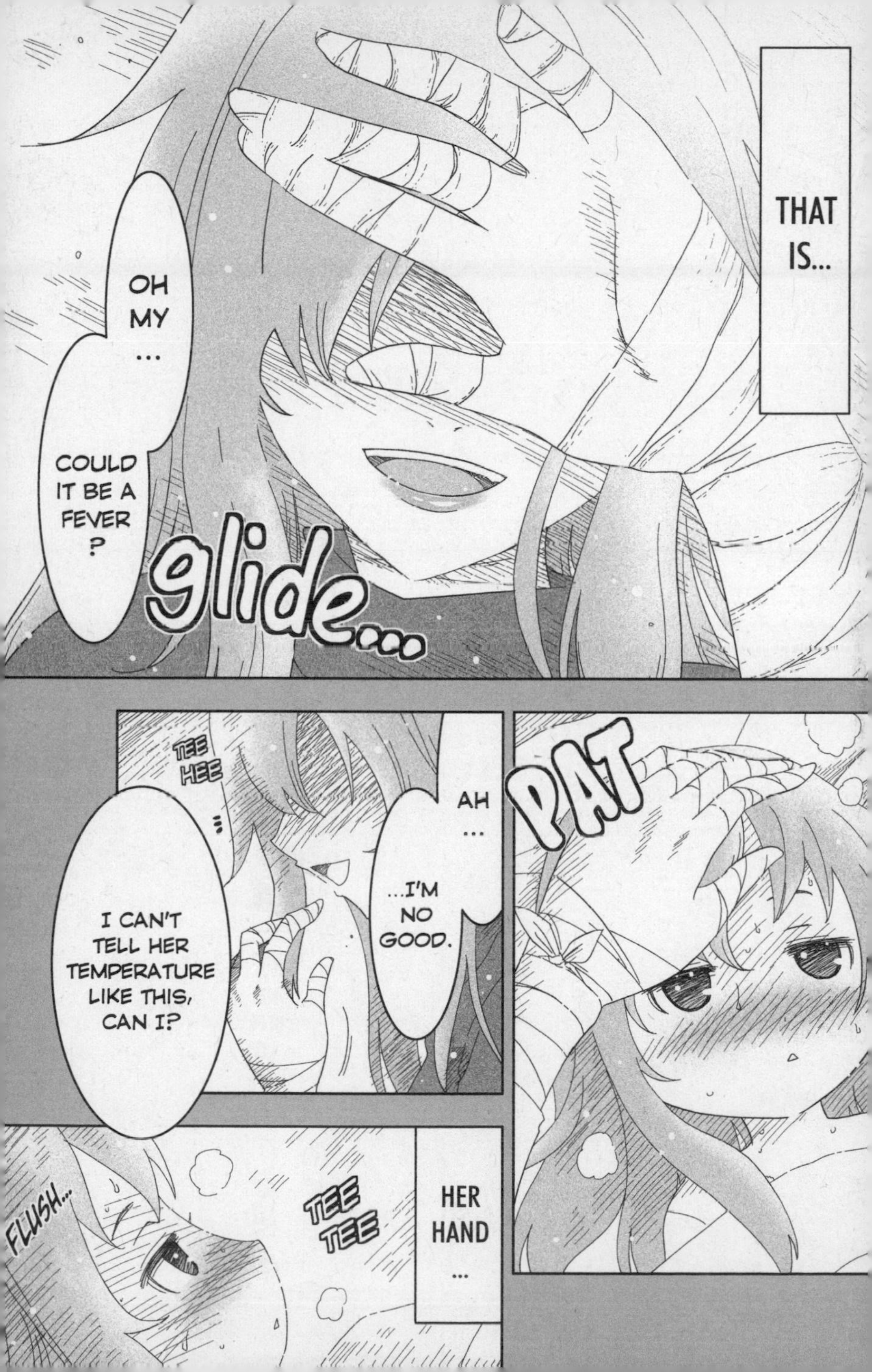
THAT IS...
OH MY ... COULD IT BE A FEVER?
glide...
PAT
AH ... ...I'M NO GOOD.
TEE HEE
I CAN'T TELL HER TEMPERATURE LIKE THIS, CAN I?
HER HAND ...
TEE TEE
FLUSH...

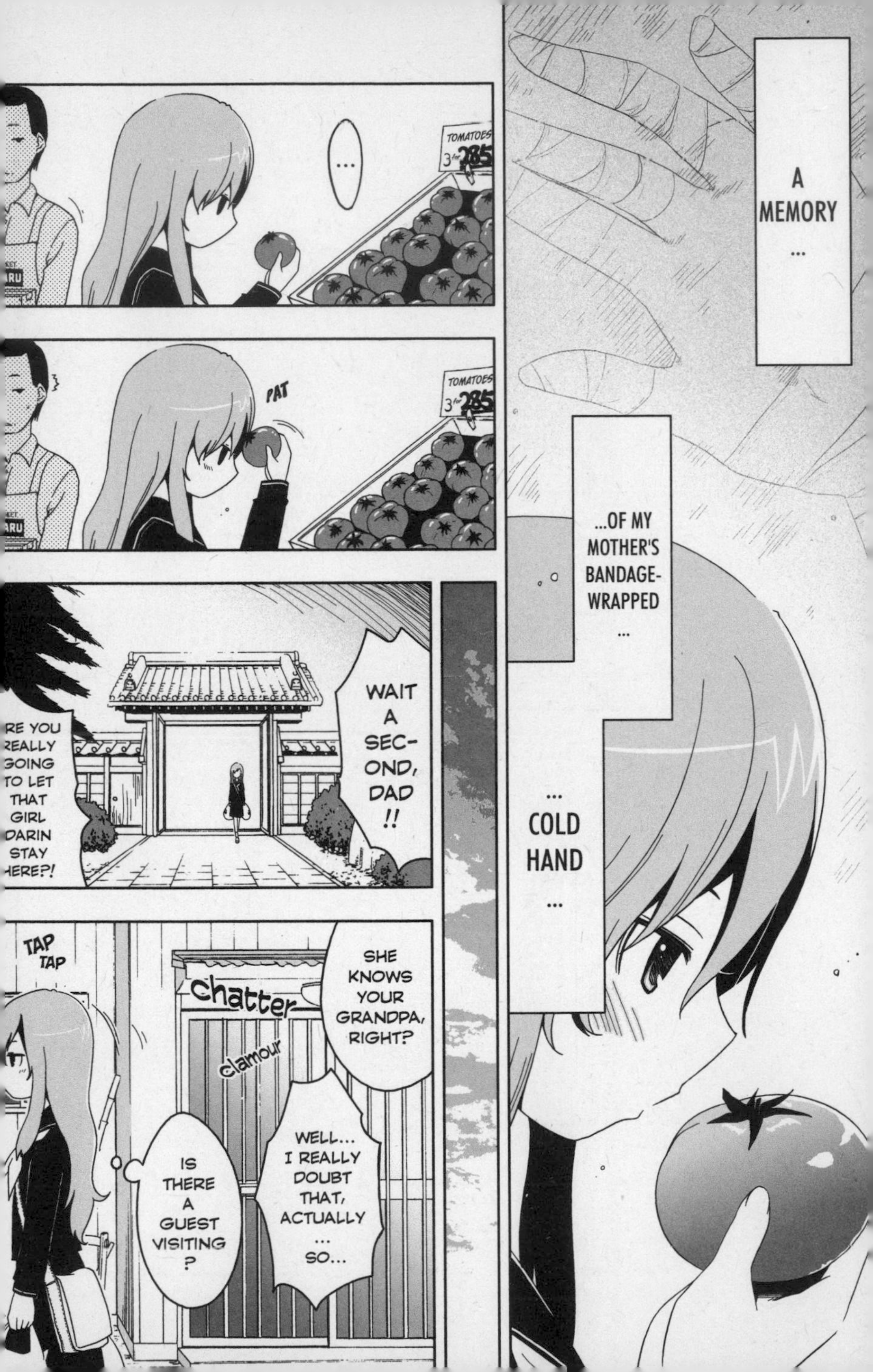

A MEMORY ...
...OF MY MOTHER'S BANDAGE-WRAPPED ...
... COLD HAND ...
...
TOMATOES 3 for 285
PAT
TOMATOES 3 for 285
WAIT A SEC- OND, DAD !!
RE YOU EALLY GOING TO LET THAT GIRL DARIN STAY ERE?!
SHE KNOWS YOUR GRANDPA, RIGHT?
chatter
clamour
WELL... I REALLY DOUBT THAT, ACTUALLY ... SO...
TAP TAP
IS THERE A GUEST VISITING ?

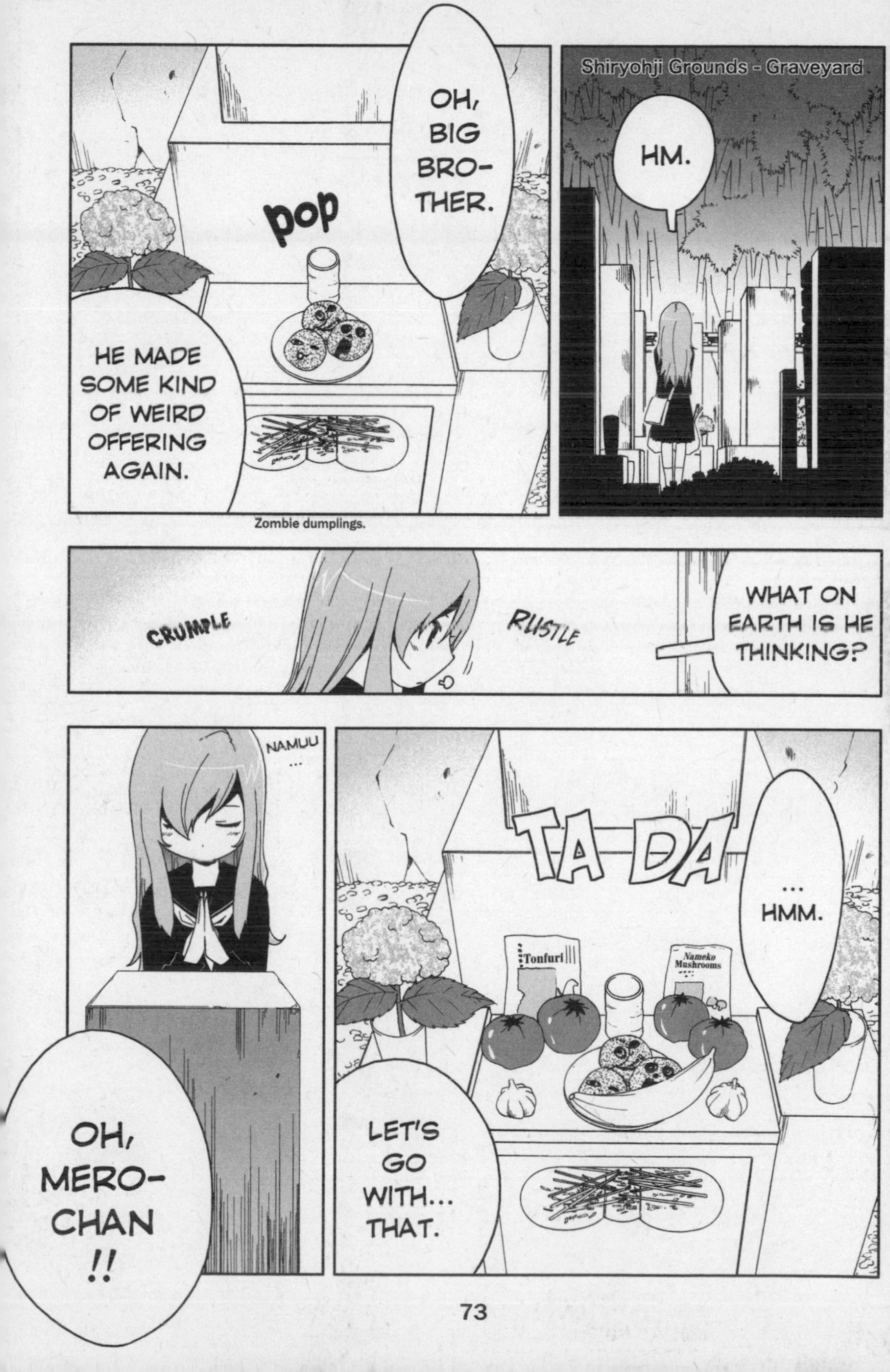
Shiryohji Grounds - Graveyard
HM.
OH, BIG BROTHER.
pop
HE MADE SOME KIND OF WEIRD OFFERING AGAIN.
Zombie dumplings.
WHAT ON EARTH IS HE THINKING?
RUSTLE
CRUMPLE
TA DA
... HMM.
Nameko Mushrooms
Tonfuri
LET'S GO WITH... THAT.
NAMUU ...
OH, MERO-CHAN !!

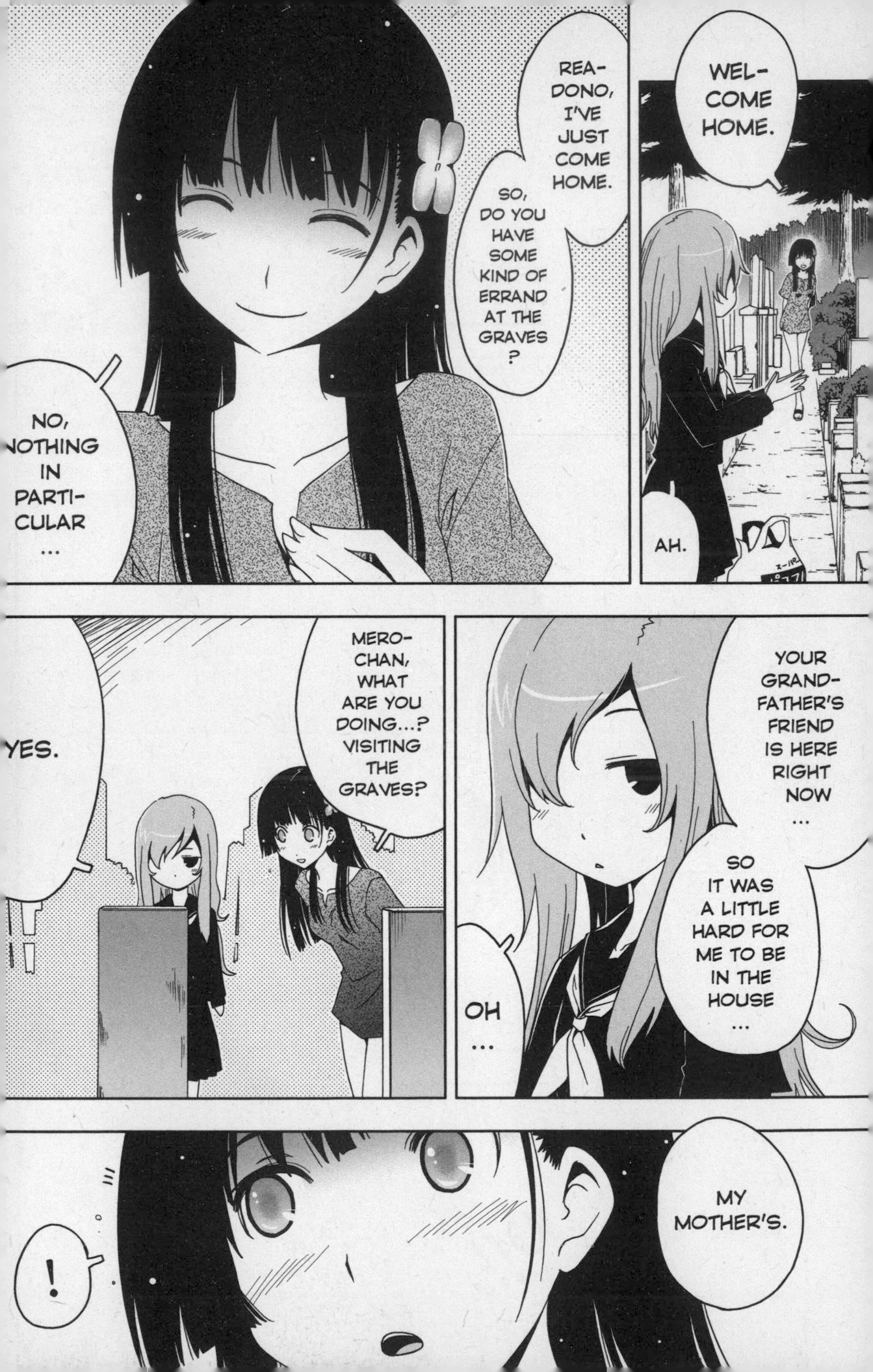
WELCOME HOME.
AH.
REA-DONO, I'VE JUST COME HOME.
SO, DO YOU HAVE SOME KIND OF ERRAND AT THE GRAVES?
NO, NOTHING IN PARTICULAR...
YOUR GRANDFATHER'S FRIEND IS HERE RIGHT NOW...
SO IT WAS A LITTLE HARD FOR ME TO BE IN THE HOUSE...
OH...
MERO-CHAN, WHAT ARE YOU DOING...? VISITING THE GRAVES?
YES.
MY MOTHER'S.
!

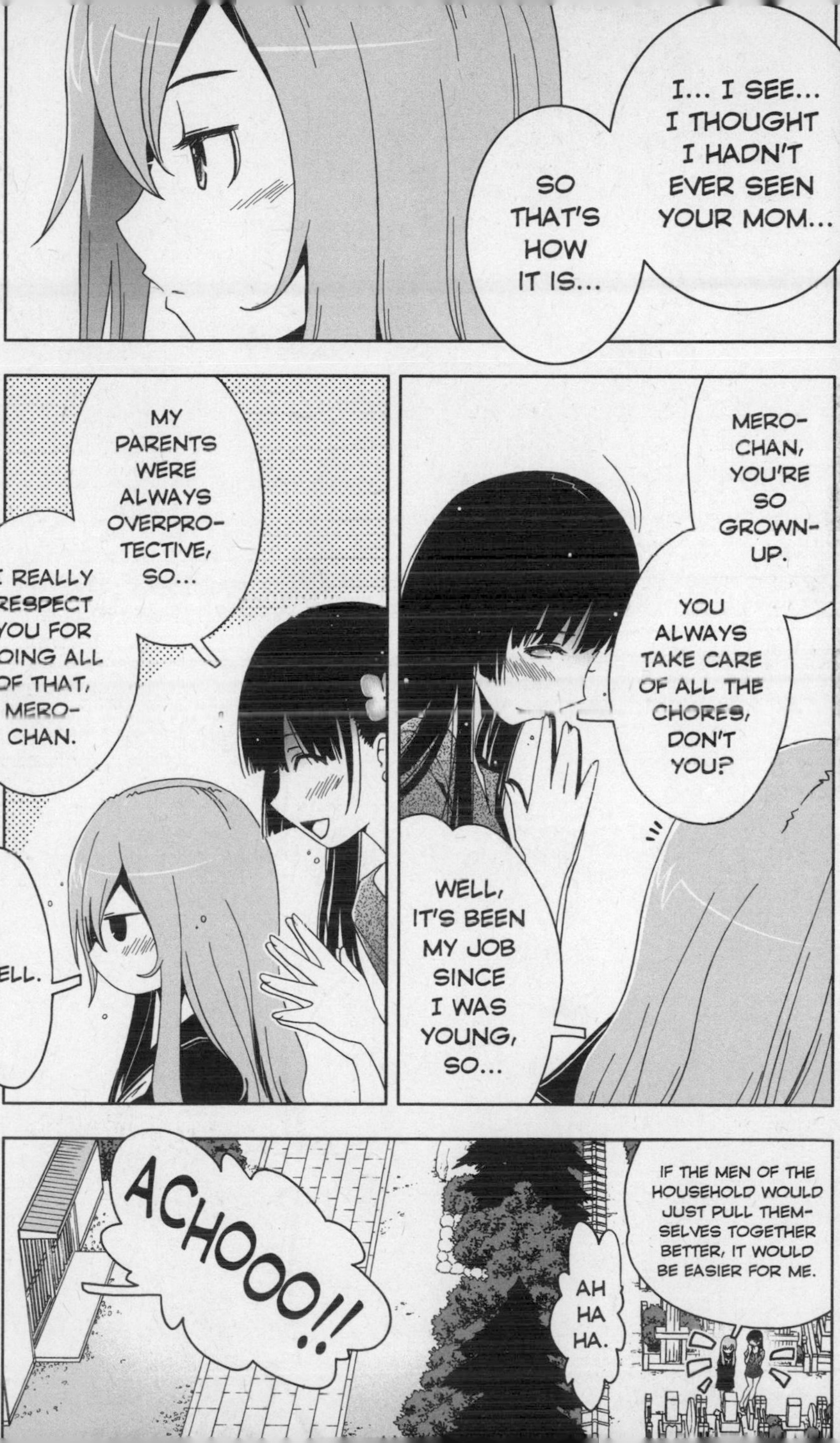
I... I SEE... I THOUGHT I HADN'T EVER SEEN YOUR MOM...
SO THAT'S HOW IT IS...
MERO-CHAN, YOU'RE SO GROWN-UP.
YOU ALWAYS TAKE CARE OF ALL THE CHORES, DON'T YOU?
WELL, IT'S BEEN MY JOB SINCE I WAS YOUNG, SO...
MY PARENTS WERE ALWAYS OVERPROTECTIVE, SO...
I REALLY RESPECT YOU FOR DOING ALL OF THAT, MERO-CHAN.
WELL.
IF THE MEN OF THE HOUSEHOLD WOULD JUST PULL THEMSELVES TOGETHER BETTER, IT WOULD BE EASIER FOR ME.
AH HA HA.
ACHOOO!!

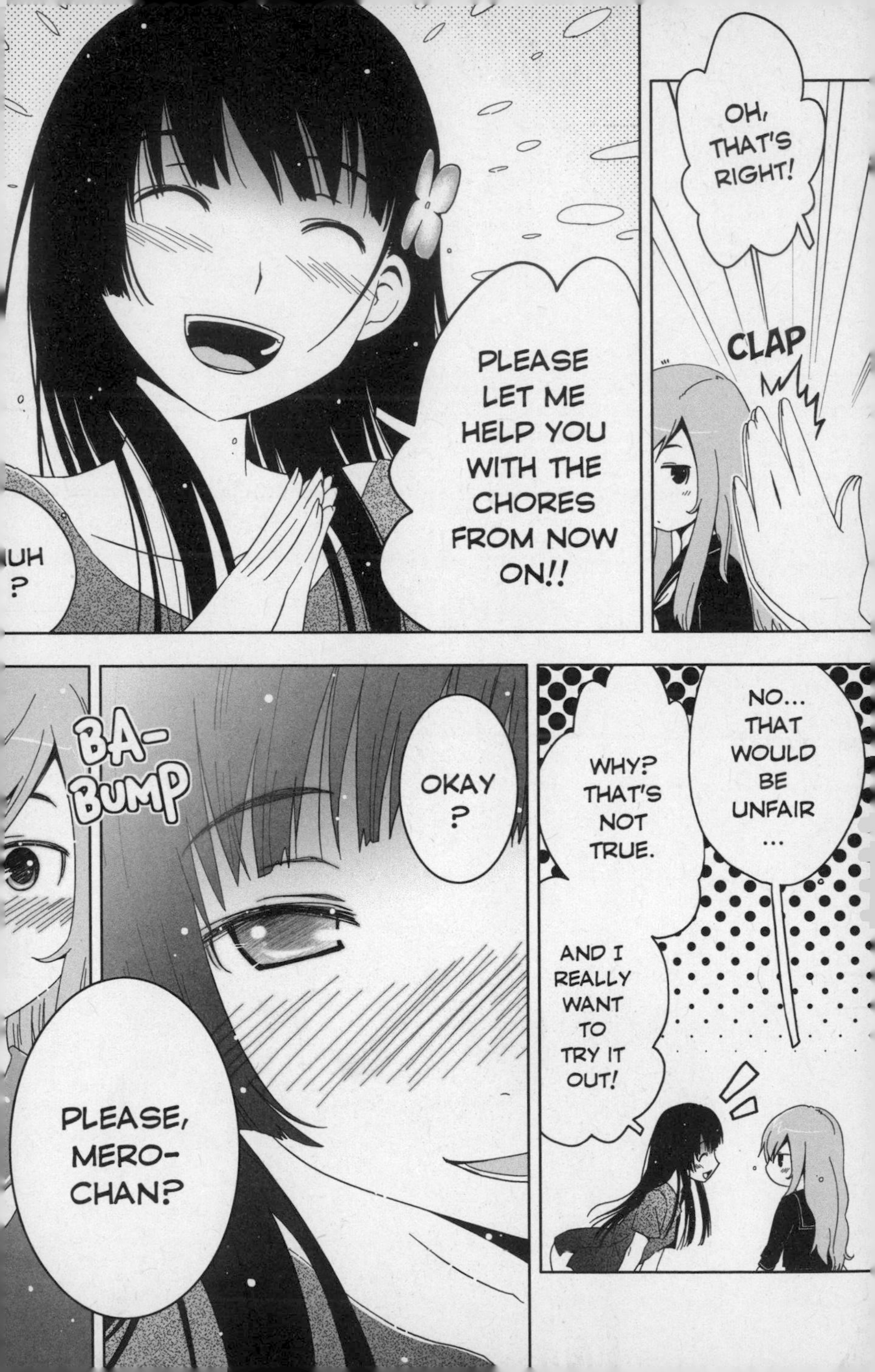
OH, THAT'S RIGHT!
CLAP
PLEASE LET ME HELP YOU WITH THE CHORES FROM NOW ON!!
UH ?
NO... THAT WOULD BE UNFAIR ...
WHY? THAT'S NOT TRUE.
AND I REALLY WANT TO TRY IT OUT!
OKAY ?
PLEASE, MERO-CHAN?
BA-BUMP

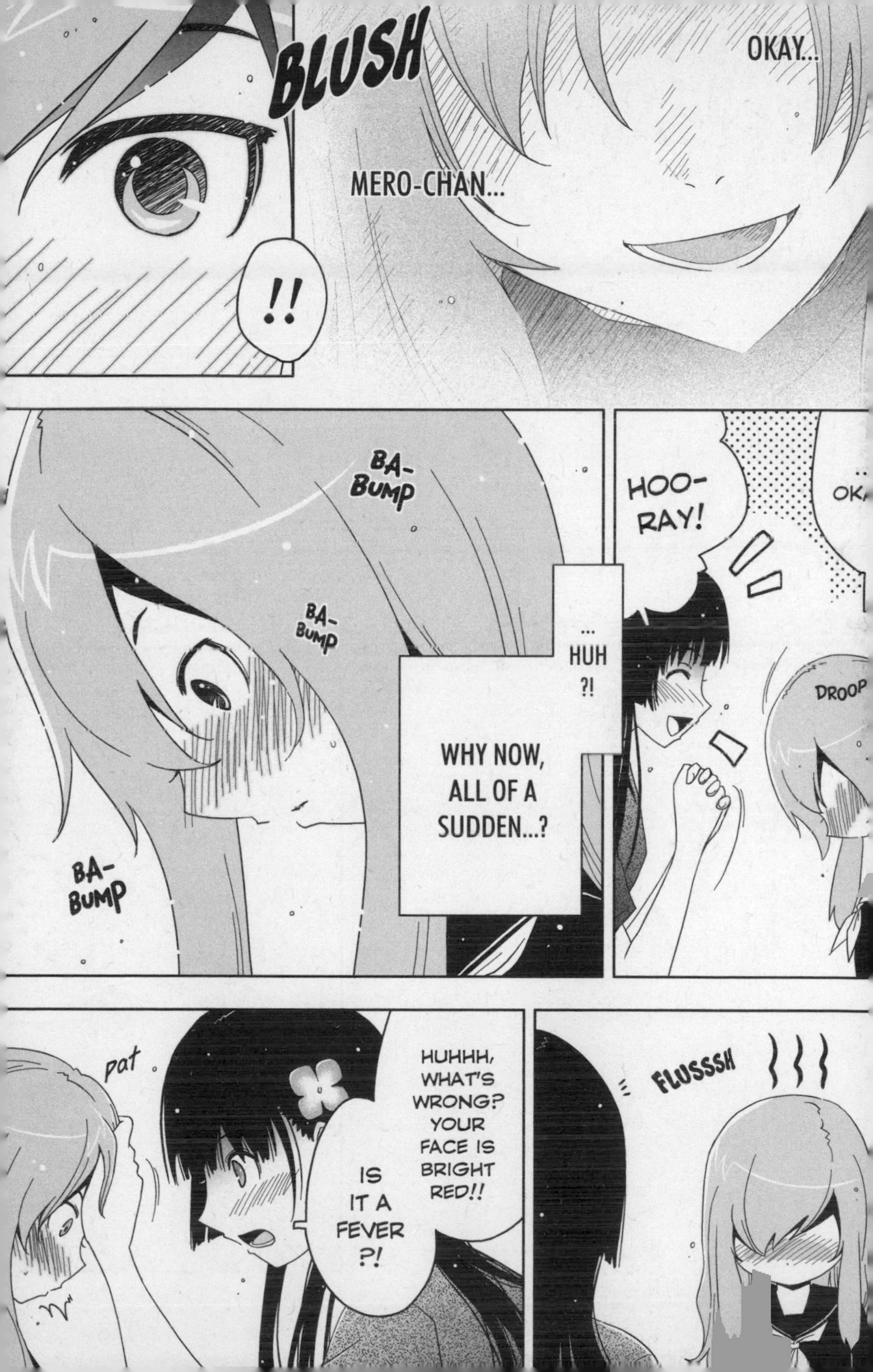
OKAY...
MERO-CHAN...
BLUSH
!!
... OKA
HOO-RAY!
DROOP
... HUH ?!
BA-BUMP
BA-BUMP
BA-BUMP
WHY NOW, ALL OF A SUDDEN...?
FLUSSSH
pat
HUHHH, WHAT'S WRONG? YOUR FACE IS BRIGHT RED!!
IS IT A FEVER ?!

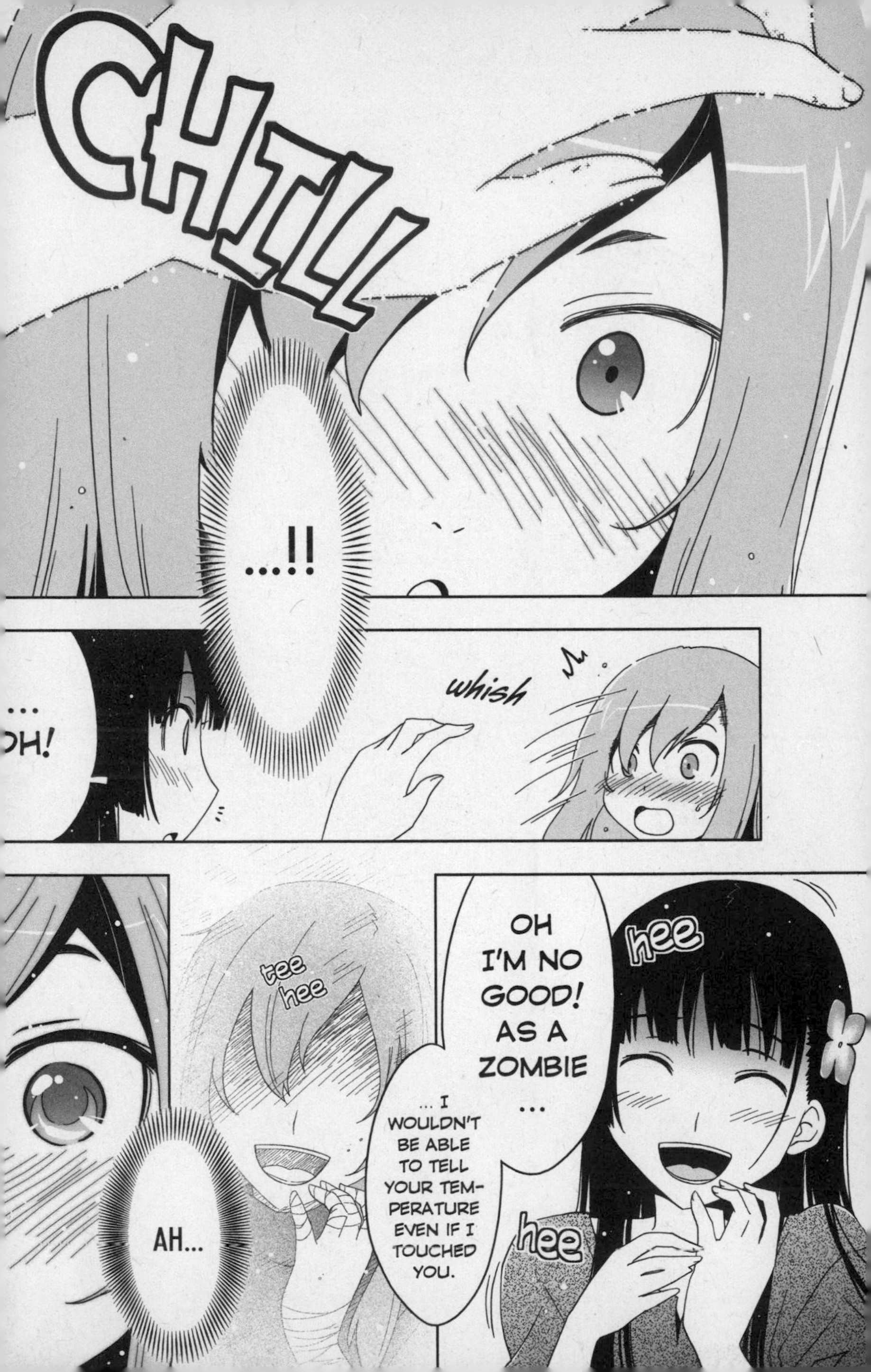
CHILL
...!!
whish
... OH!
hee
OH I'M NO GOOD! AS A ZOMBIE ...
tee hee
... I WOULDN'T BE ABLE TO TELL YOUR TEM-PERATURE EVEN IF I TOUCHED YOU.
hee
AH...

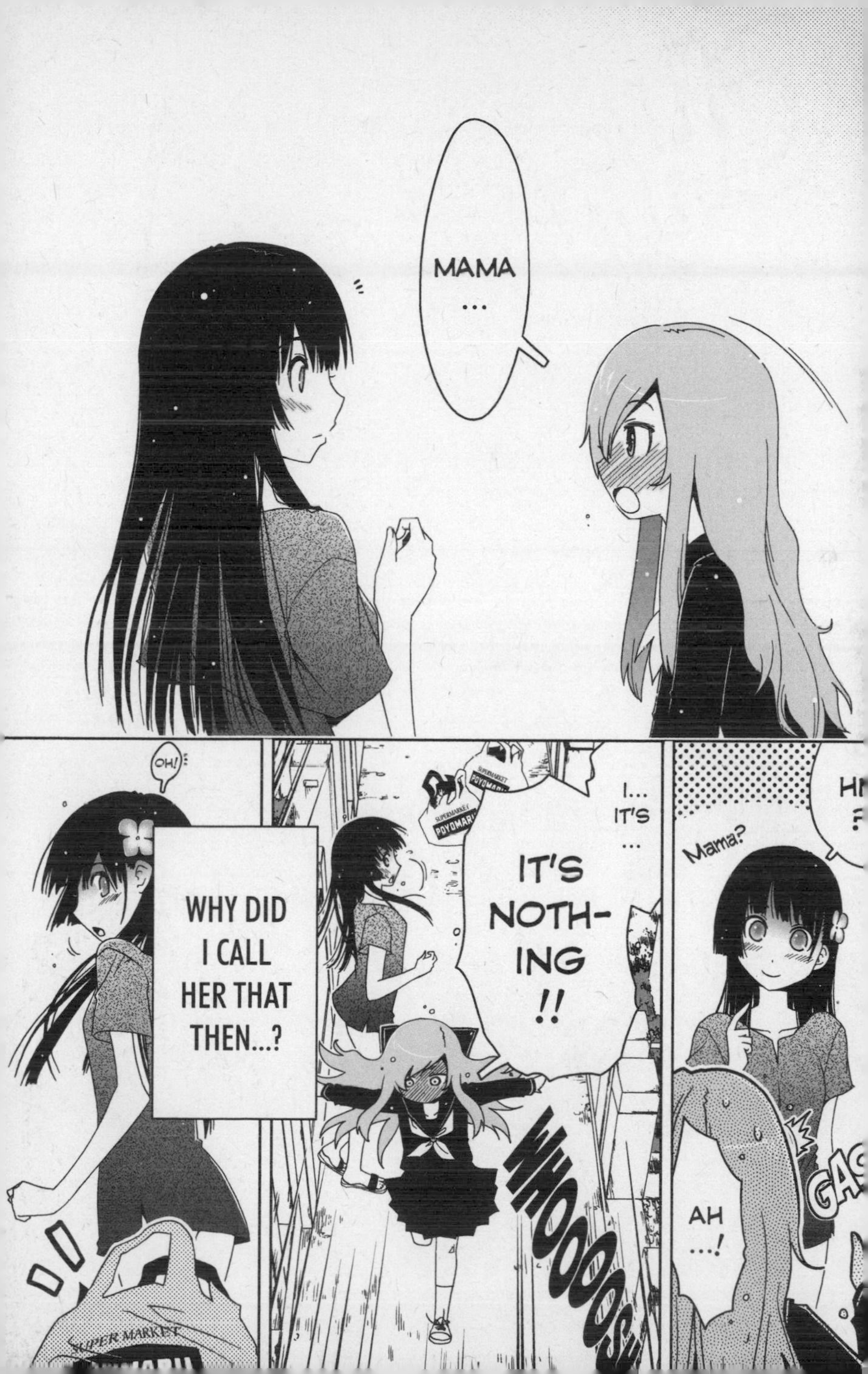
MAMA ...
Mama?
AH ...!
I... IT'S ...
IT'S NOTHING!!
SUPERMARKET POYOMARU
OH!
WHY DID I CALL HER THAT THEN...?

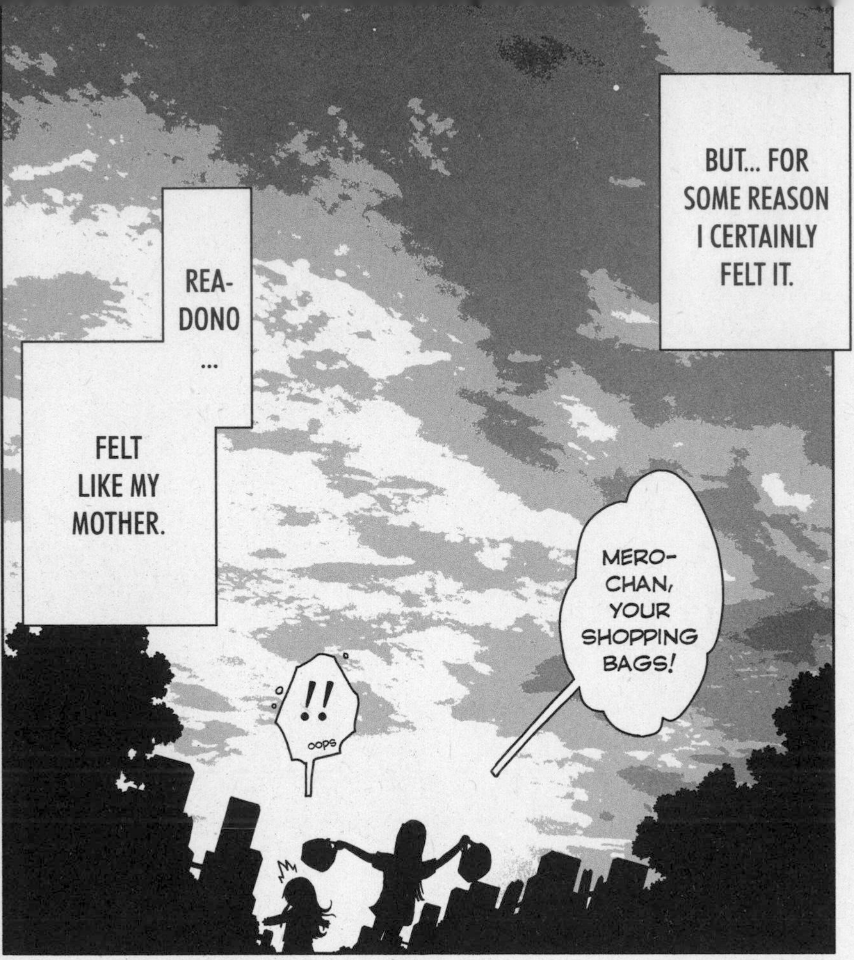
BUT... FOR SOME REASON I CERTAINLY FELT IT.
REA-DONO ...
FELT LIKE MY MOTHER.
MERO-CHAN, YOUR SHOPPING BAGS!
!! oops

Afterwards, we made dinner together...

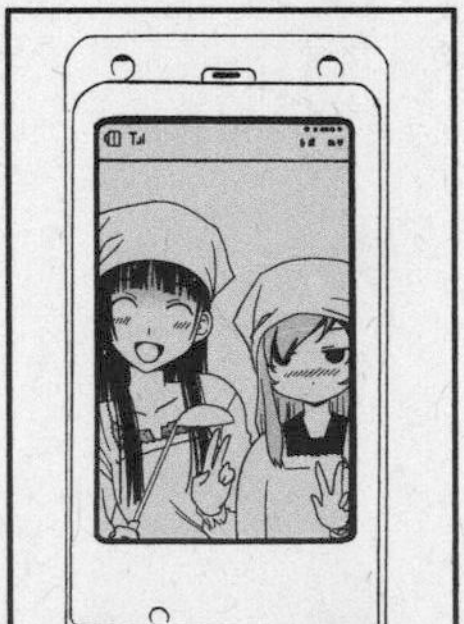

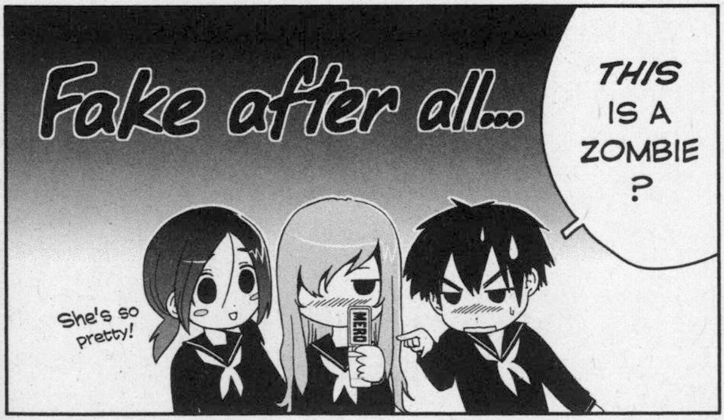
THIS IS A ZOMBIE ?
Fake after all...
MERO
She's so pretty!

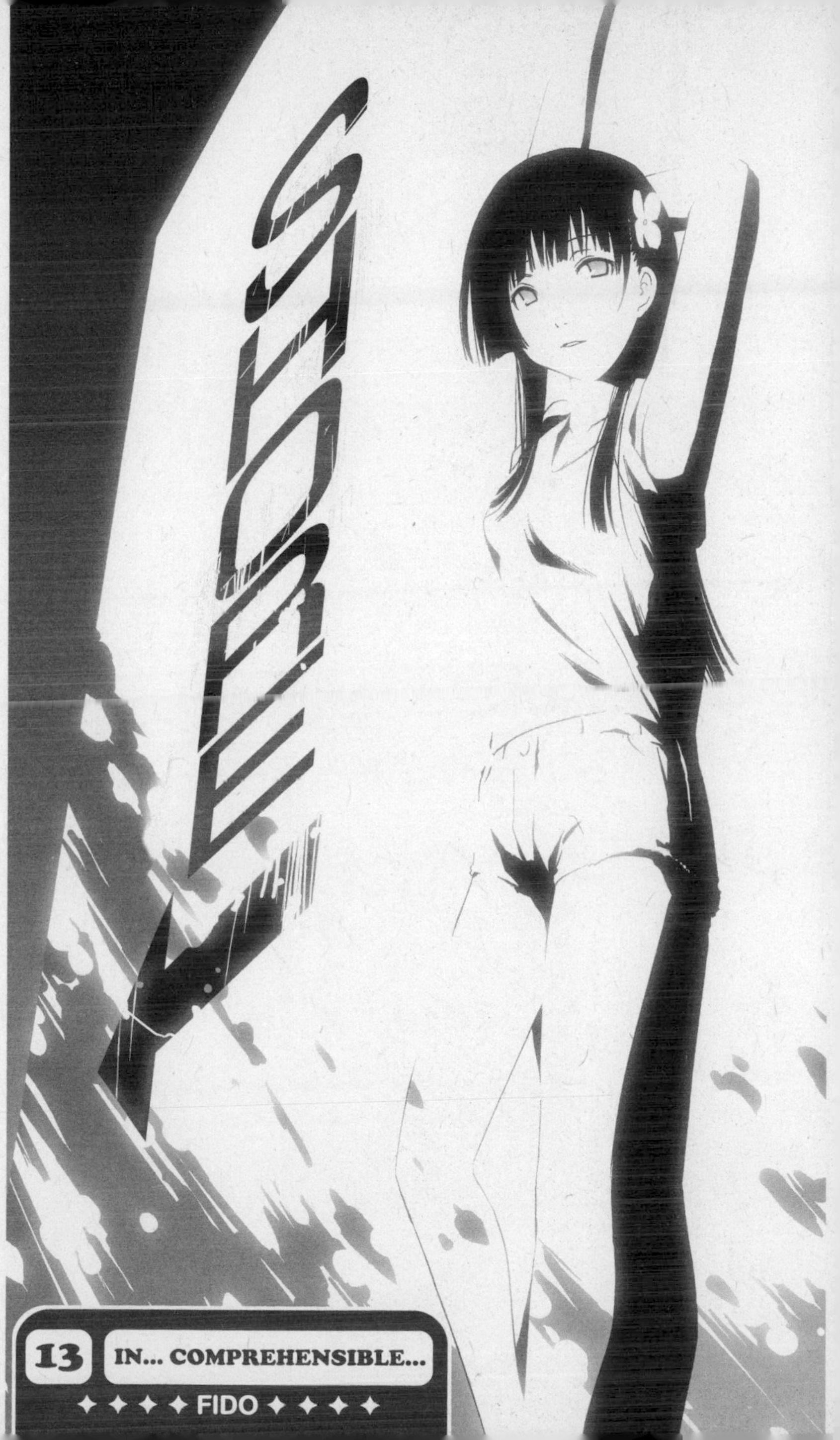
13
IN... COMPREHENSIBLE...
✦ ✦ ✦ ✦ FIDO ✦ ✦ ✦ ✦

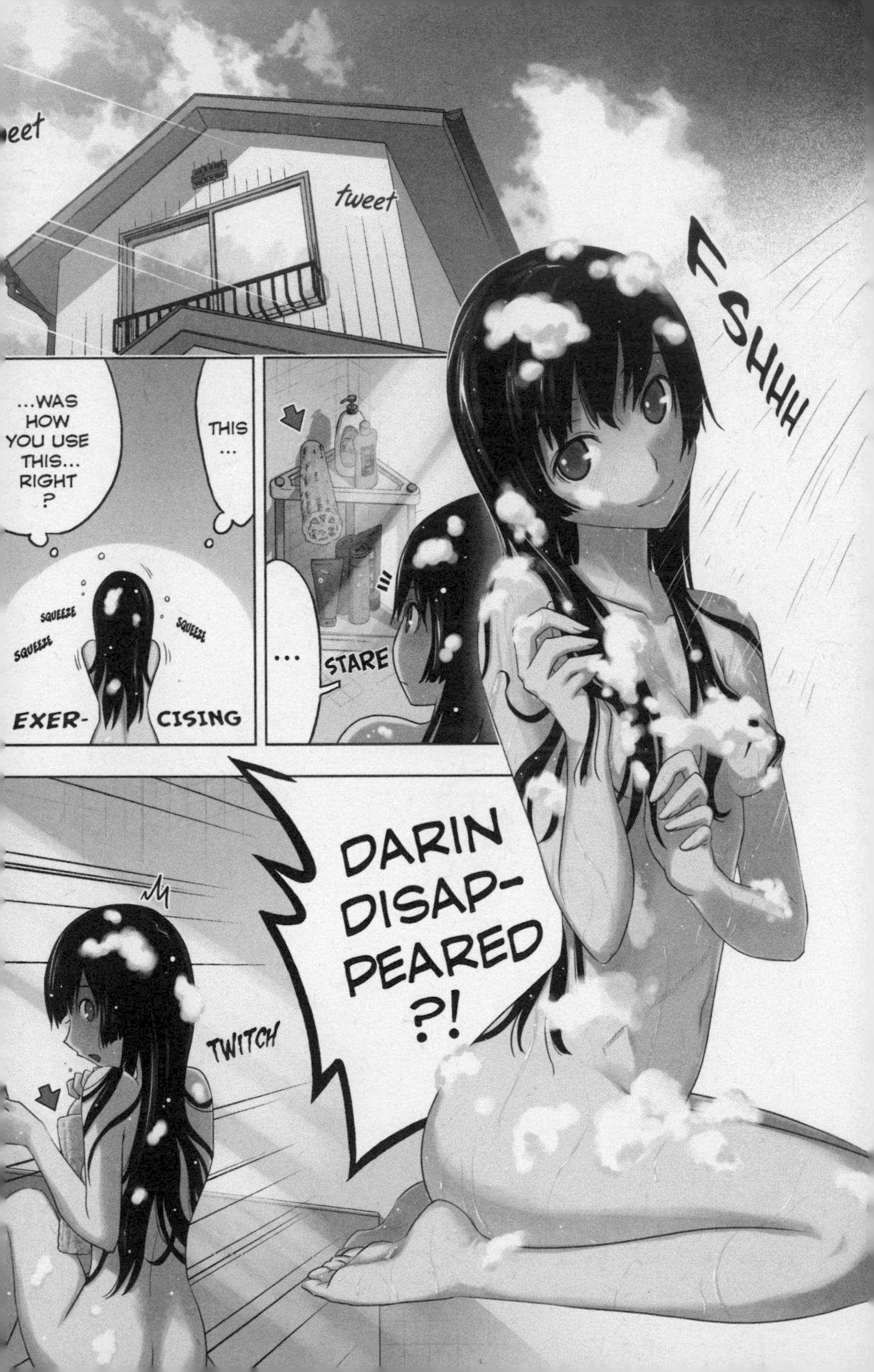

tweet
eet
FSHHH
STARE
...
THIS ...
...WAS HOW YOU USE THIS... RIGHT ?
SQUEEZE
SQUEEZE
SQUEEZE
EXER- CISING
DARIN DISAP- PEARED ?!
TWITCH

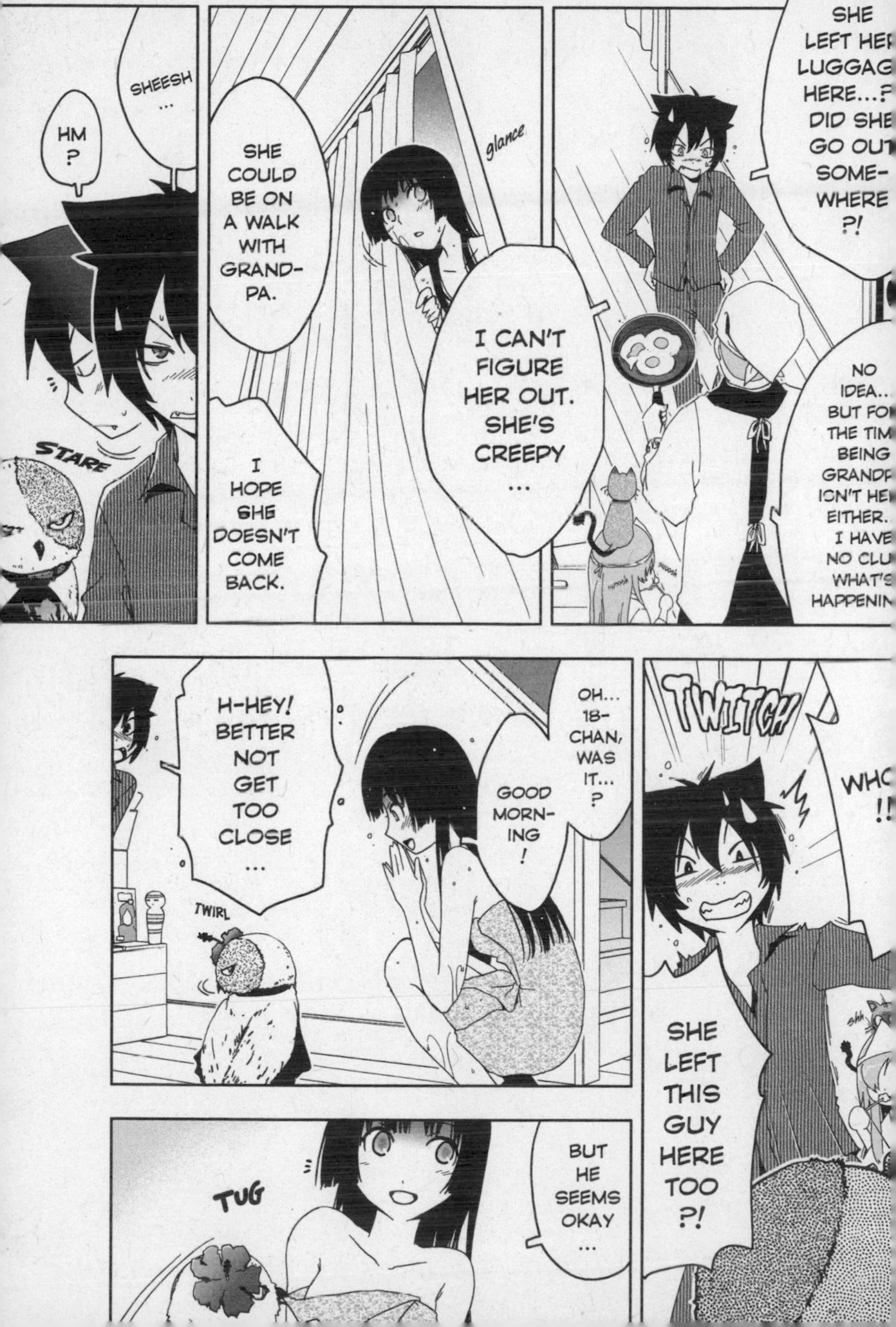
SHE LEFT HE LUGGAG HERE...? DID SHE GO OUT SOME-WHERE ?!
NO IDEA... BUT FO THE TIM BEING GRANDP ISN'T HE EITHER... I HAVE NO CLU WHAT'S HAPPENIN
glance
I CAN'T FIGURE HER OUT. SHE'S CREEPY ...
SHE COULD BE ON A WALK WITH GRAND-PA.
I HOPE SHE DOESN'T COME BACK.
SHEESH ...
HM ?
STARE
TWITCH
WHO !!
SHE LEFT THIS GUY HERE TOO ?!
OH... 18-CHAN, WAS IT... ?
GOOD MORN-ING !
H-HEY! BETTER NOT GET TOO CLOSE ...
TWIRL
BUT HE SEEMS OKAY ...
TUG

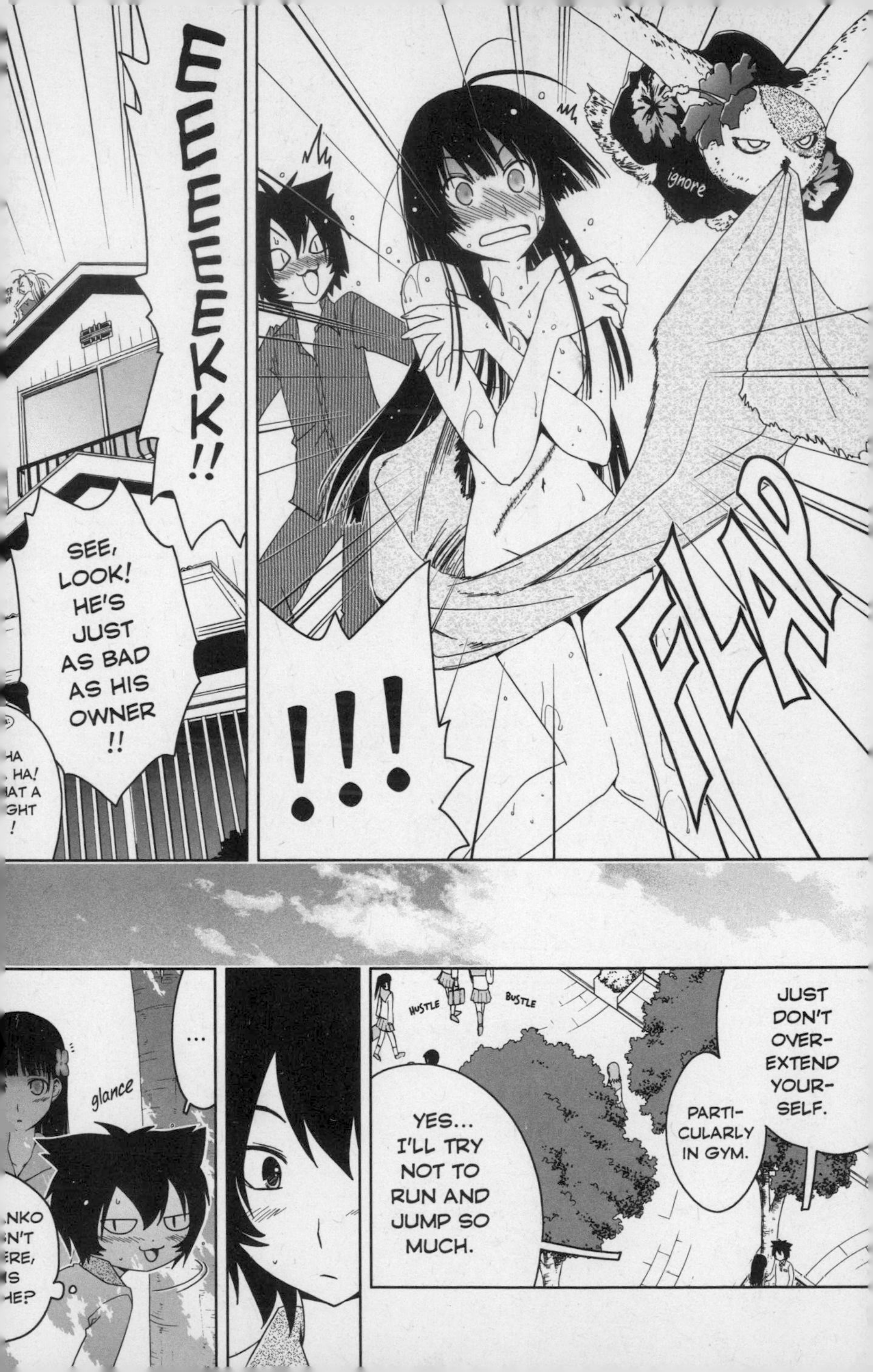
ignore
FLAP
!!!
EEEEEKK!!
SEE, LOOK! HE'S JUST AS BAD AS HIS OWNER!!
HA HA! HAT A GHT!
JUST DON'T OVER-EXTEND YOURSELF.
PARTI-CULARLY IN GYM.
HUSTLE BUSTLE
YES... I'LL TRY NOT TO RUN AND JUMP SO MUCH.
...
glance
NKO SN'T ERE, S HE?

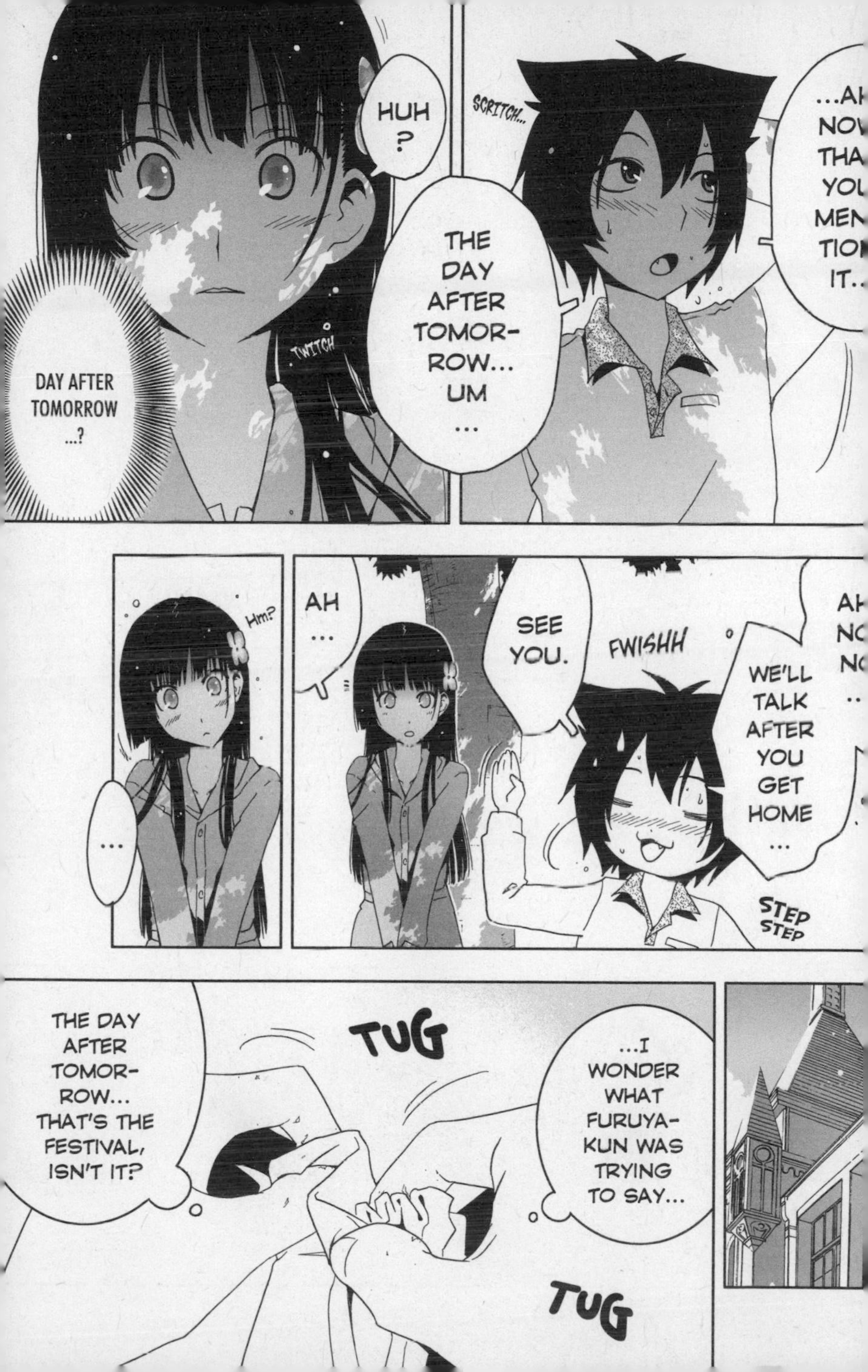
SCRITCH...
THE DAY AFTER TOMORROW... UM...
HUH?
TWITCH
DAY AFTER TOMORROW...?
WE'LL TALK AFTER YOU GET HOME...
STEP STEP
FWISHH
SEE YOU.
AH...
Hm?
...
...I WONDER WHAT FURUYA-KUN WAS TRYING TO SAY...
TUG
THE DAY AFTER TOMORROW... THAT'S THE FESTIVAL, ISN'T IT?
TUG

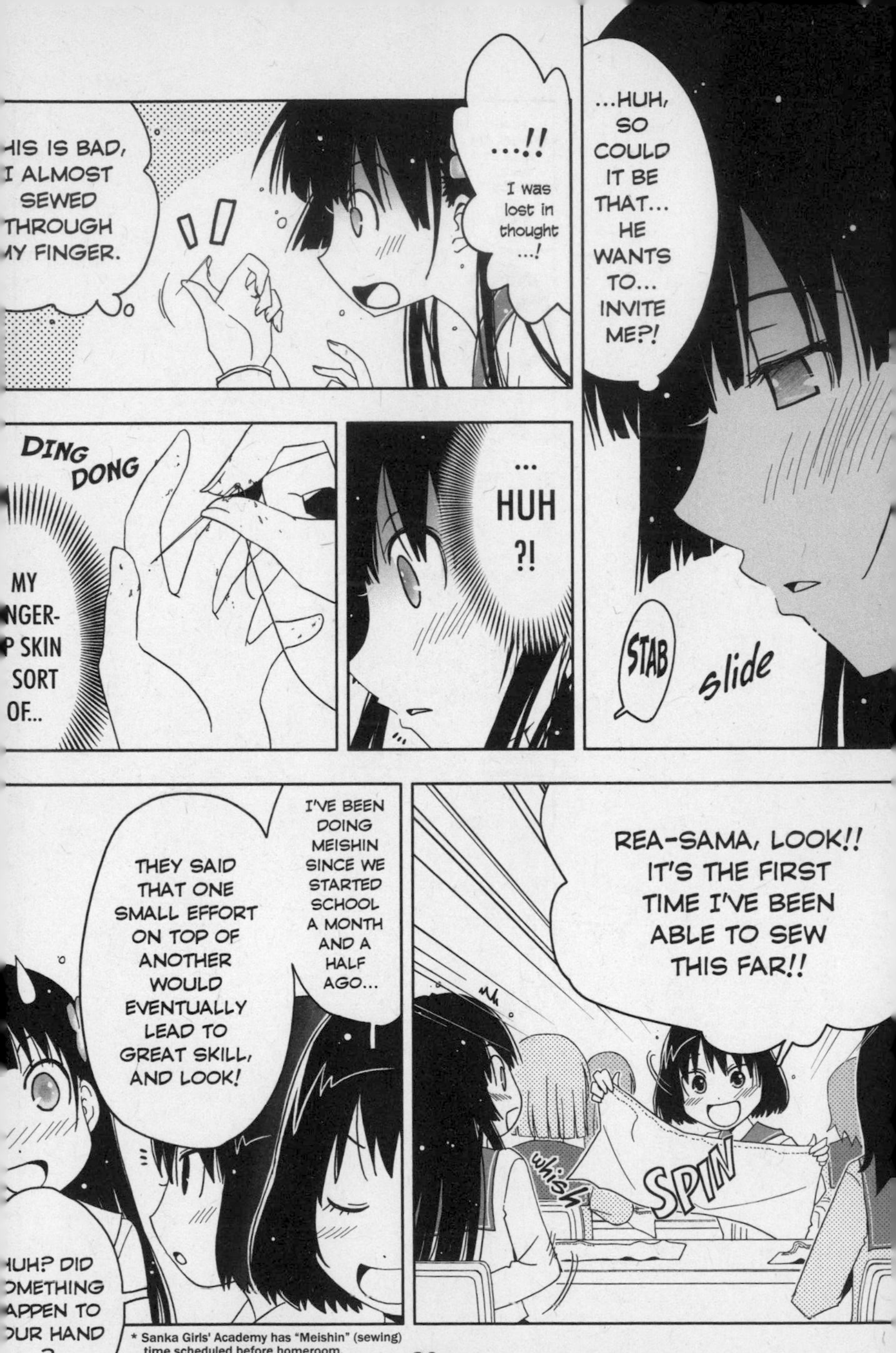

...HUH, SO COULD IT BE THAT... HE WANTS TO... INVITE ME?!
STAB
slide
...!!
I was lost in thought ...!
HIS IS BAD, I ALMOST SEWED THROUGH MY FINGER.
... HUH ?!
DING DONG
MY NGER-P SKIN SORT OF...
REA-SAMA, LOOK!! IT'S THE FIRST TIME I'VE BEEN ABLE TO SEW THIS FAR!!
whish
SPIN
I'VE BEEN DOING MEISHIN SINCE WE STARTED SCHOOL A MONTH AND A HALF AGO...
THEY SAID THAT ONE SMALL EFFORT ON TOP OF ANOTHER WOULD EVENTUALLY LEAD TO GREAT SKILL, AND LOOK!
HUH? DID OMETHING APPEN TO OUR HAND ?

* Sanka Girls' Academy has "Meishin" (sewing) time scheduled before homeroom.

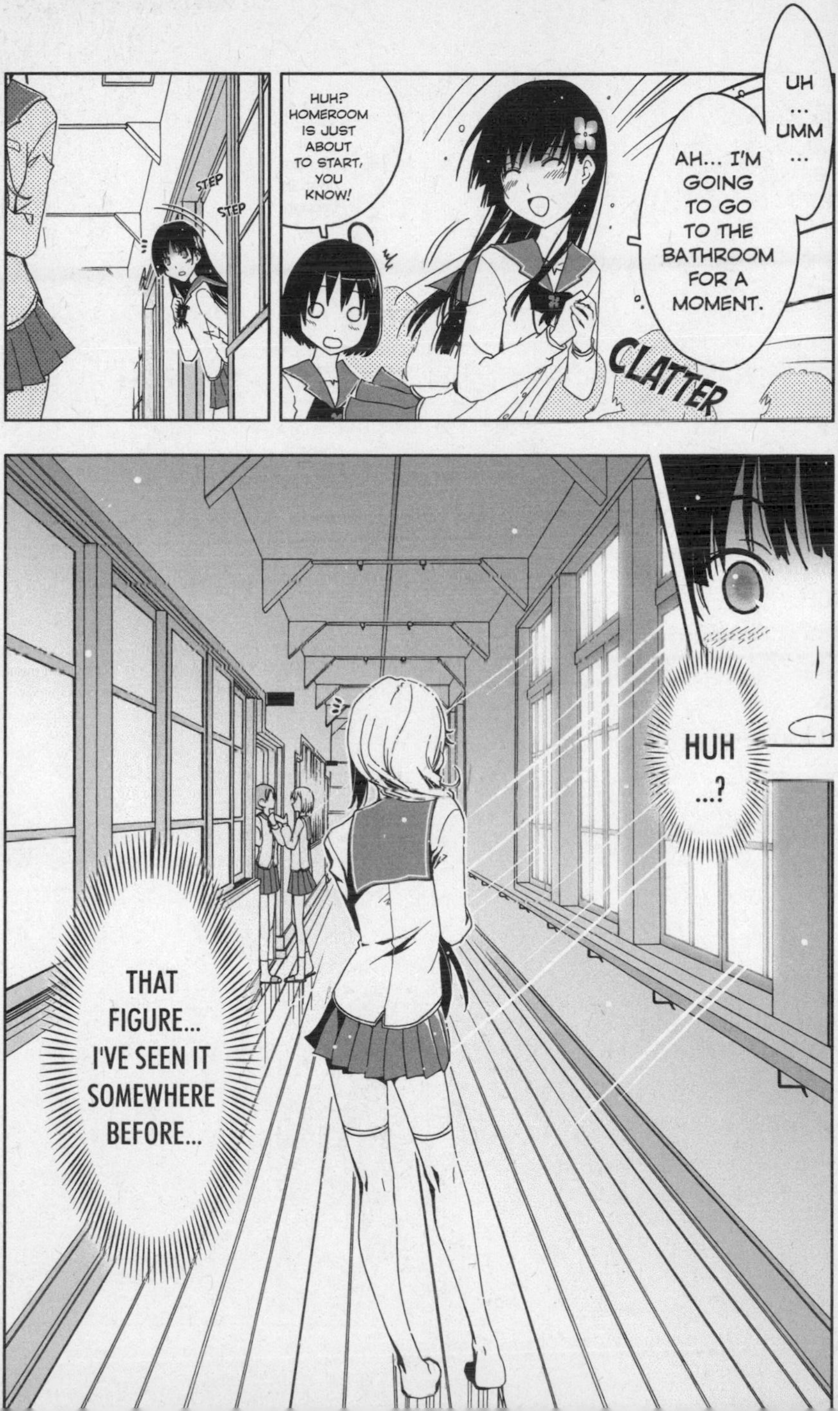
UH ... UMM ...
AH... I'M GOING TO GO TO THE BATHROOM FOR A MOMENT.
CLATTER
HUH? HOMEROOM IS JUST ABOUT TO START, YOU KNOW!
STEP
STEP
HUH ...?
THAT FIGURE... I'VE SEEN IT SOMEWHERE BEFORE...

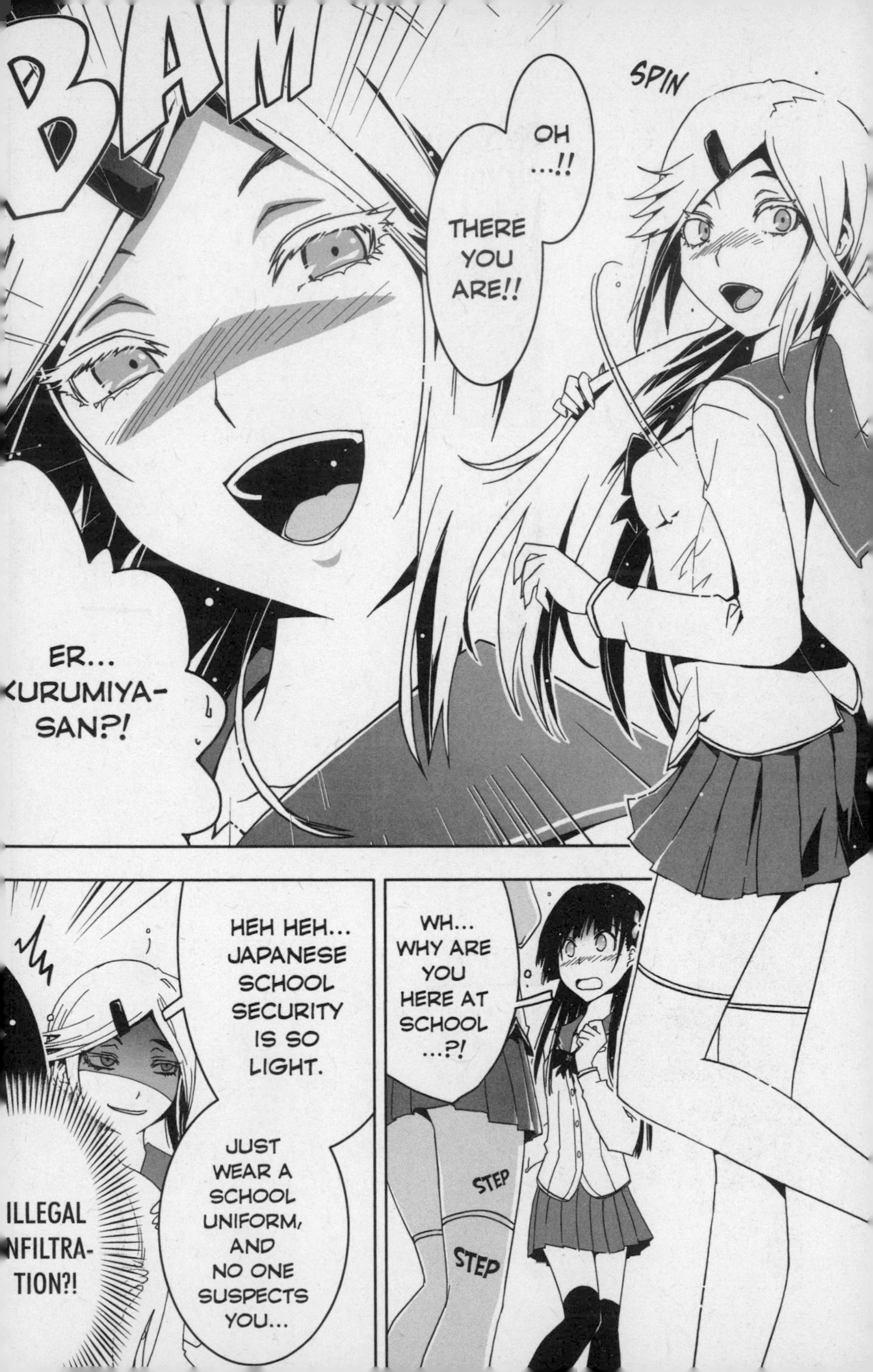
SPIN
OH ...!!
THERE YOU ARE!!
BAM
ER... KURUMIYA-SAN?!
WH... WHY ARE YOU HERE AT SCHOOL ...?!
STEP
STEP
HEH HEH... JAPANESE SCHOOL SECURITY IS SO LIGHT.
JUST WEAR A SCHOOL UNIFORM, AND NO ONE SUSPECTS YOU...
ILLEGAL INFILTRATION?!

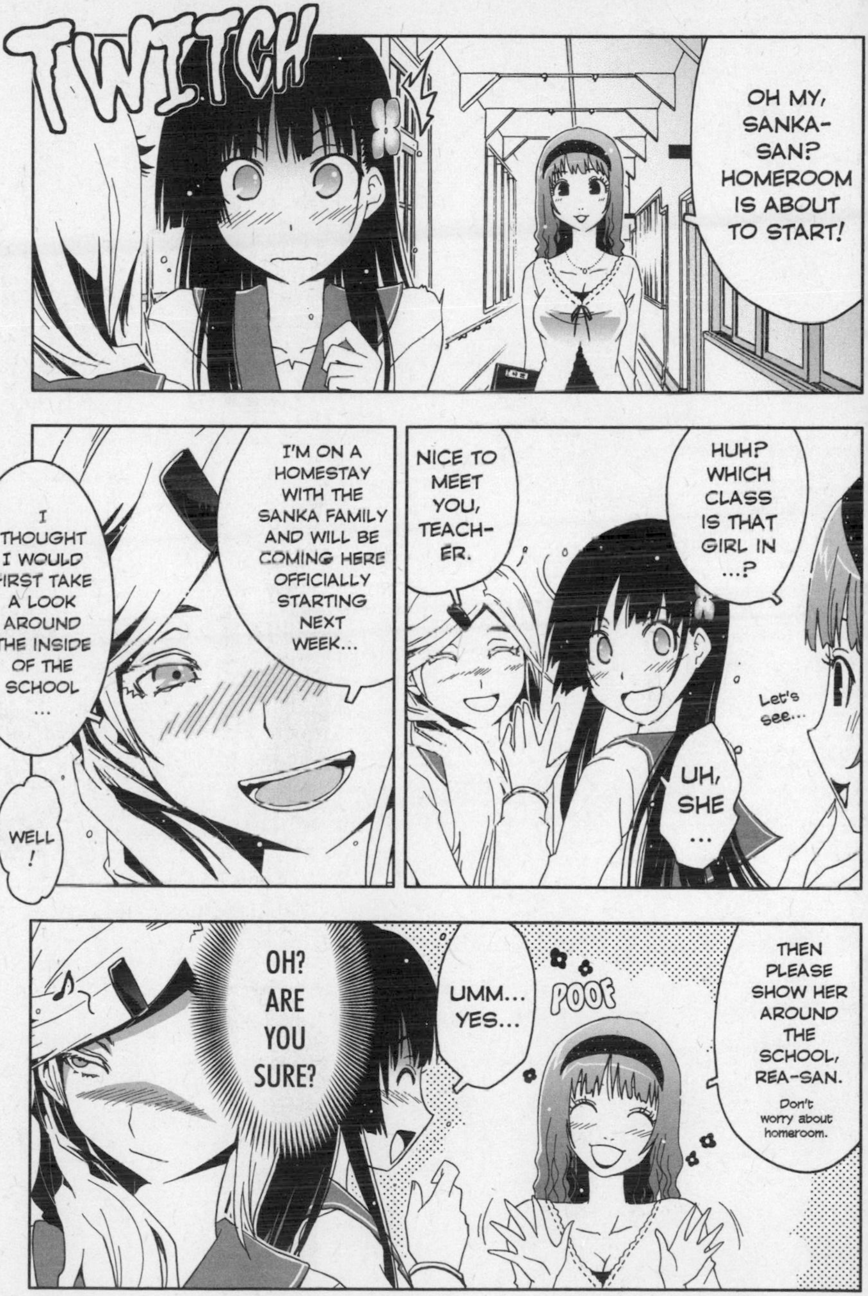
OH MY, SANKA-SAN? HOMEROOM IS ABOUT TO START!
TWITCH
HUH? WHICH CLASS IS THAT GIRL IN ...?
NICE TO MEET YOU, TEACHER.
Let's see...
UH, SHE ...
I'M ON A HOMESTAY WITH THE SANKA FAMILY AND WILL BE COMING HERE OFFICIALLY STARTING NEXT WEEK...
I THOUGHT I WOULD FIRST TAKE A LOOK AROUND THE INSIDE OF THE SCHOOL ...
WELL!
THEN PLEASE SHOW HER AROUND THE SCHOOL, REA-SAN.
Don't worry about homeroom.
POOF
UMM... YES...
OH? ARE YOU SURE?

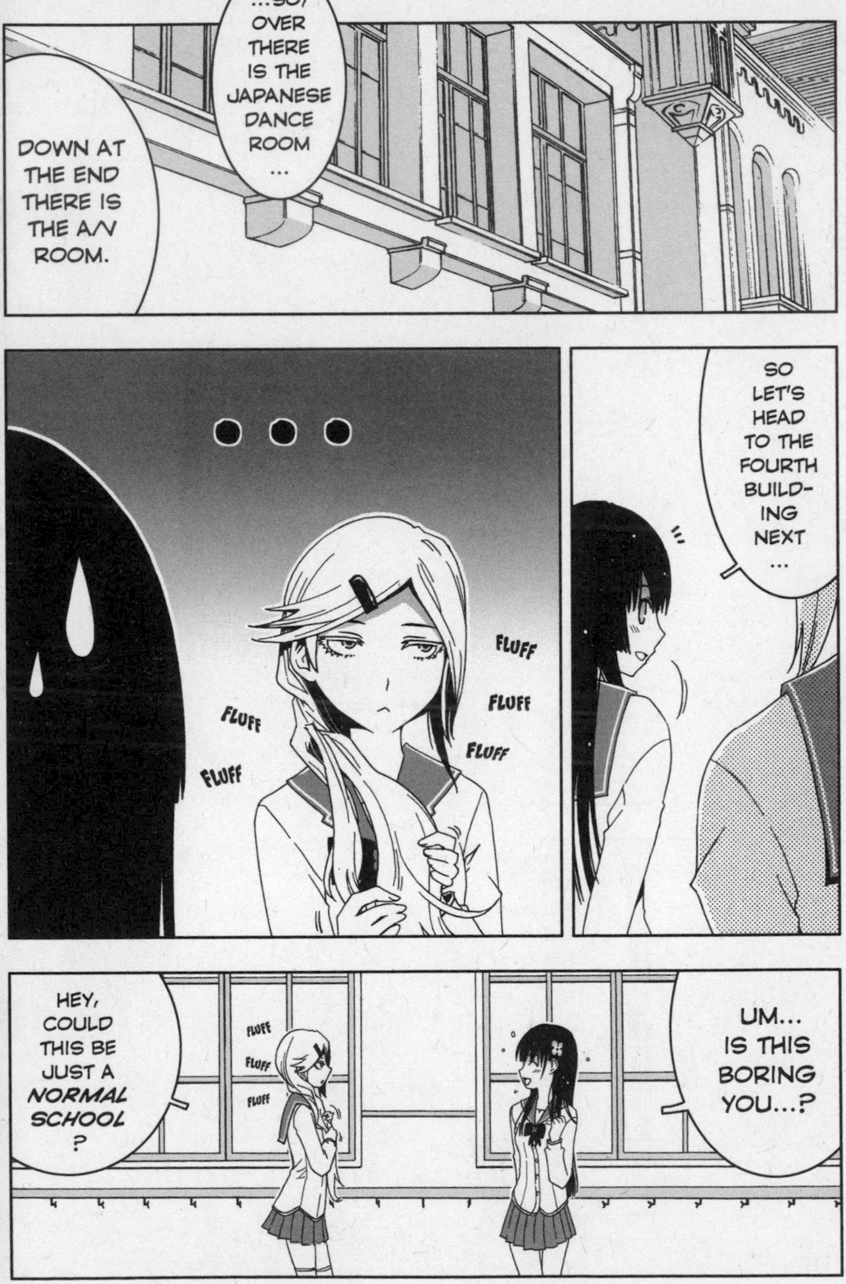
...SO, OVER THERE IS THE JAPANESE DANCE ROOM ...
DOWN AT THE END THERE IS THE A/V ROOM.
SO LET'S HEAD TO THE FOURTH BUILDING NEXT ...
FLUFF
FLUFF
FLUFF
FLUFF
FLUFF
UM... IS THIS BORING YOU...?
FLUFF
FLUFF
FLUFF
HEY, COULD THIS BE JUST A *NORMAL SCHOOL* ?

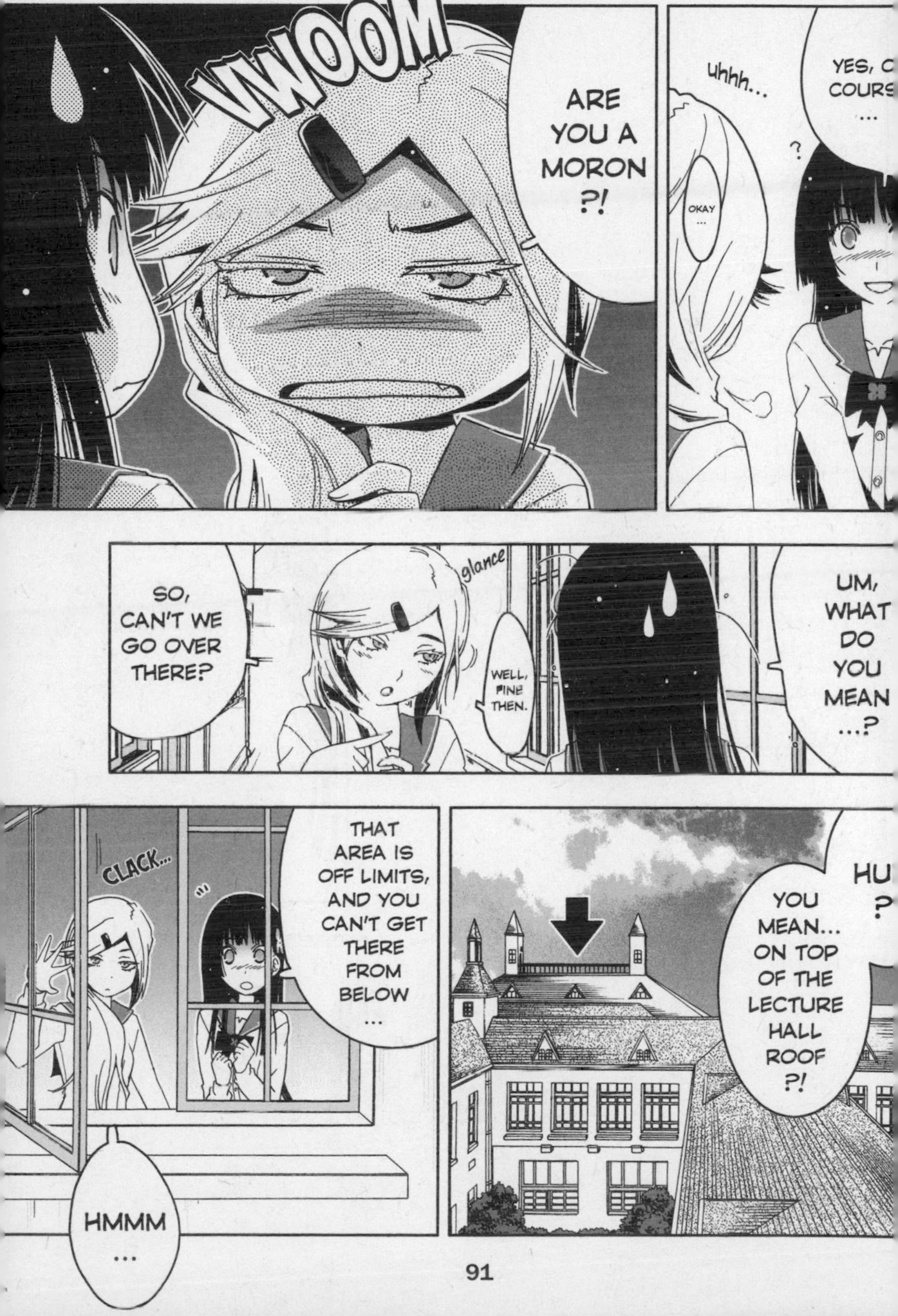
YES, C COURS ...
uhhh...
?
OKAY ...
ARE YOU A MORON ?!
VWOOM
UM, WHAT DO YOU MEAN ...?
WELL, FINE THEN.
glance
SO, CAN'T WE GO OVER THERE?
HU ?
YOU MEAN... ON TOP OF THE LECTURE HALL ROOF ?!
THAT AREA IS OFF LIMITS, AND YOU CAN'T GET THERE FROM BELOW ...
CLACK...
HMMM ...

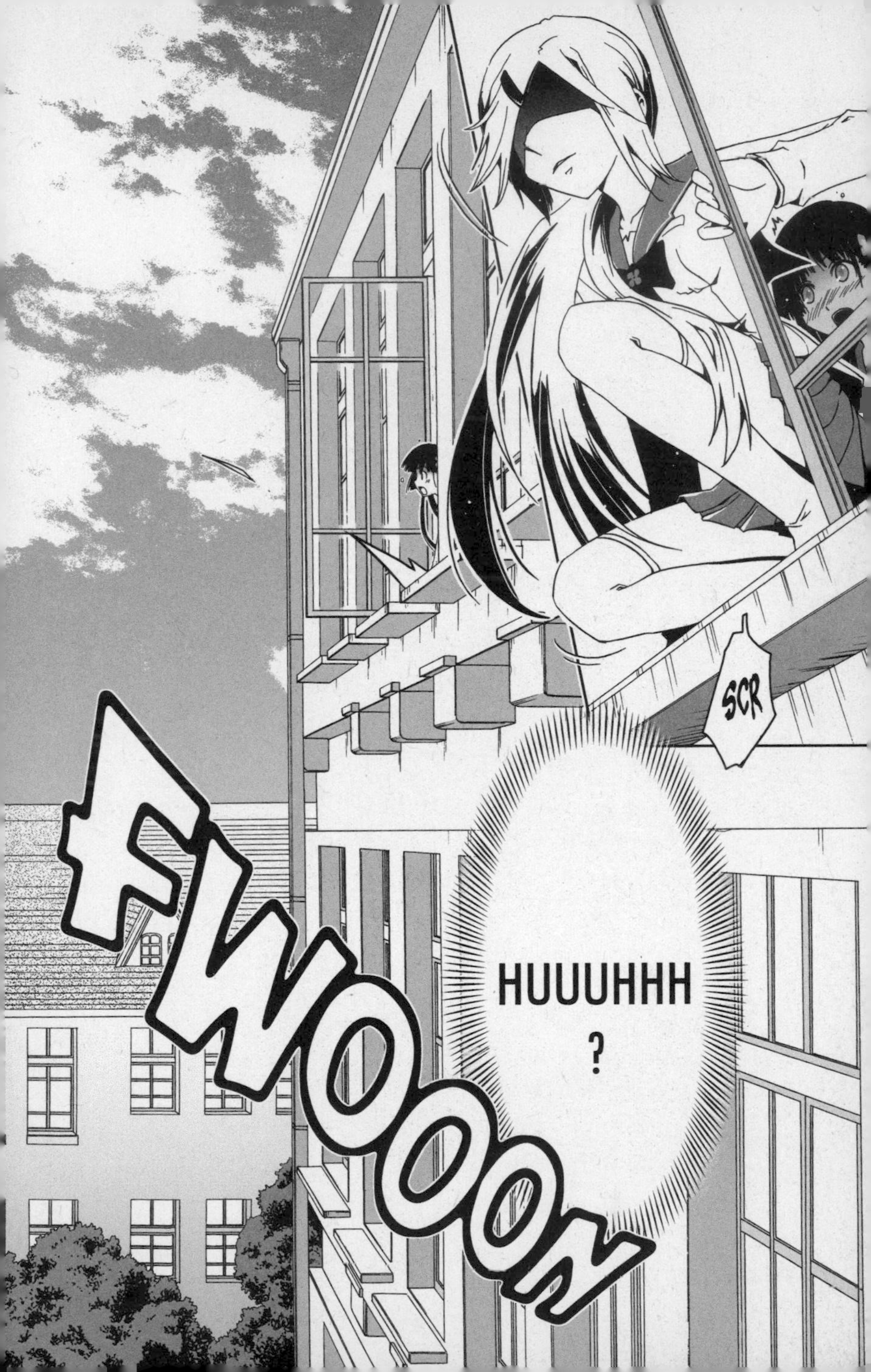
SCR
HUUUHHH ?
FWOOOOM

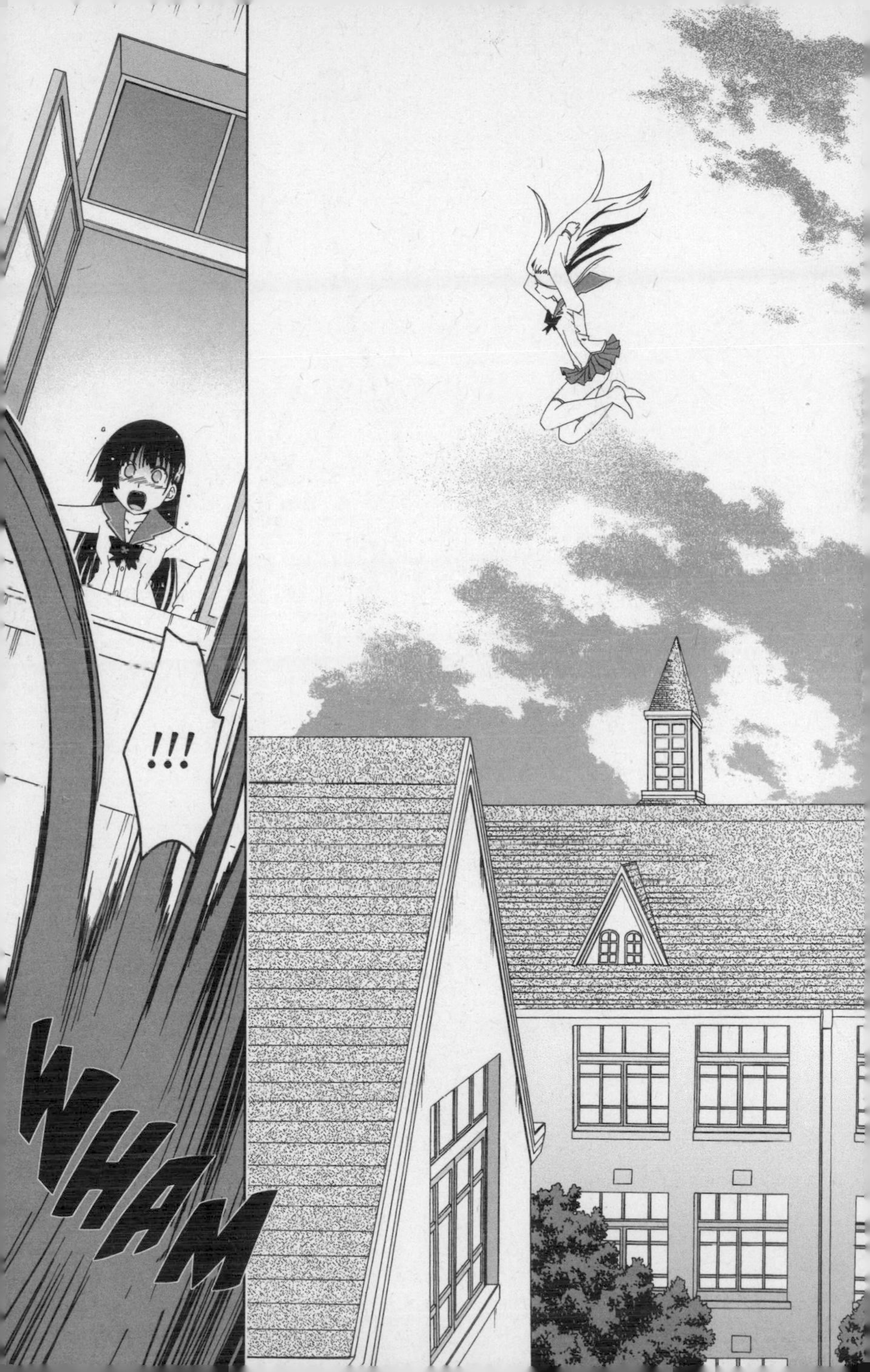
!!!
WHAM

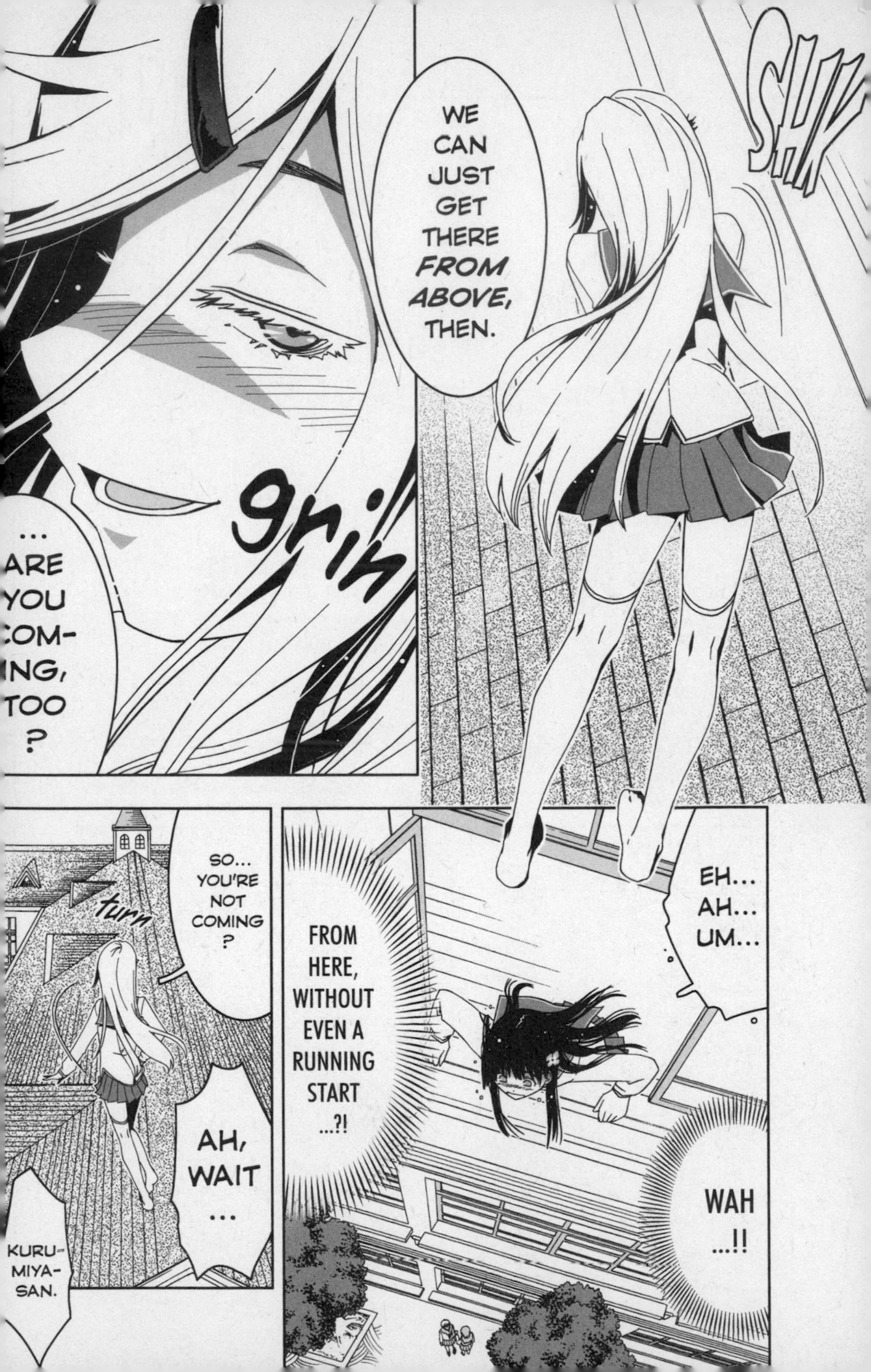
SHK
WE CAN JUST GET THERE FROM ABOVE, THEN.
grin
... ARE YOU COMING, TOO?
EH... AH... UM...
FROM HERE, WITHOUT EVEN A RUNNING START ...?!
WAH ...!!
SO... YOU'RE NOT COMING?
turn
AH, WAIT ...
KURU-MIYA-SAN.

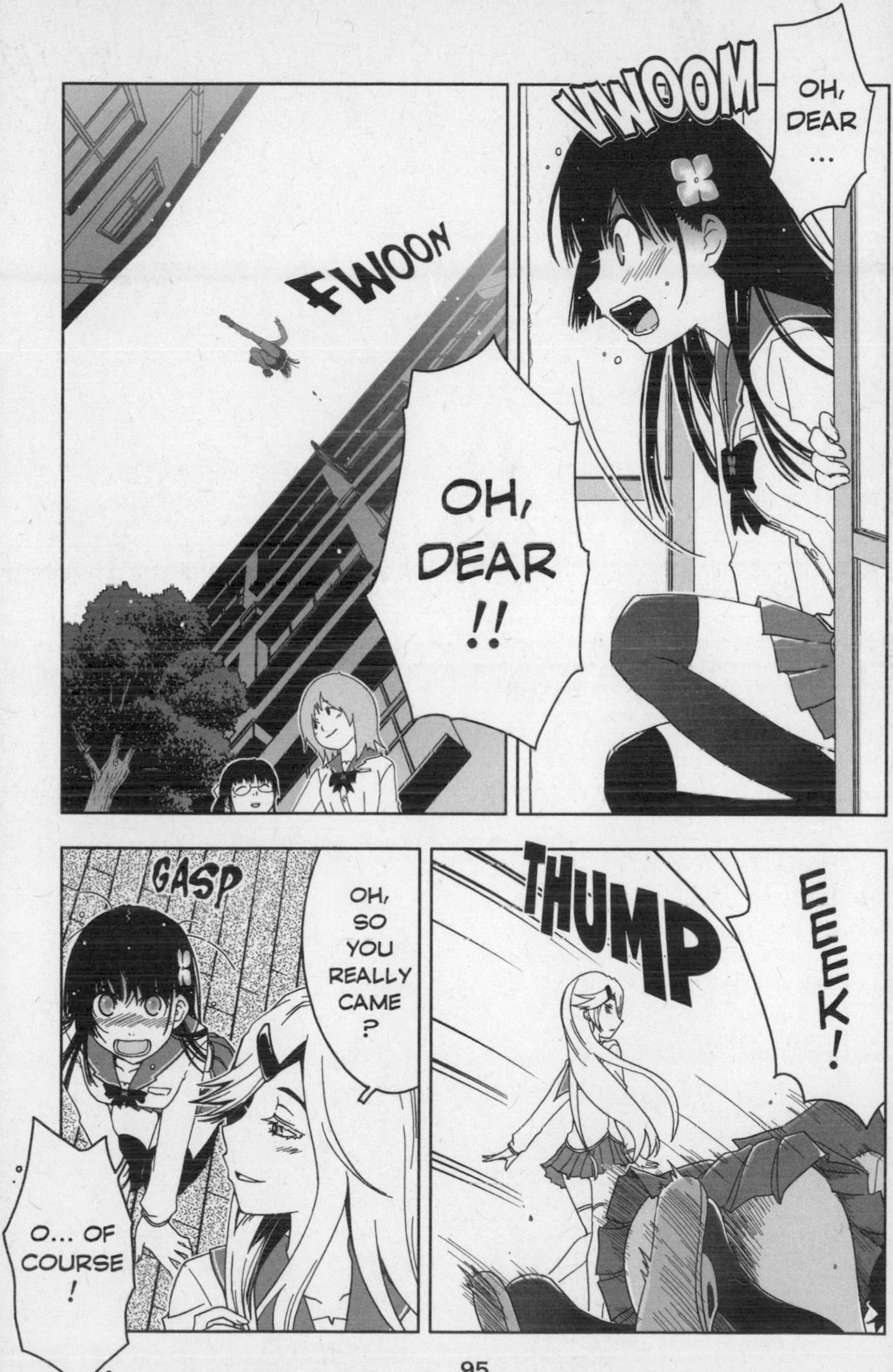
VWOOM
OH, DEAR ...
OH, DEAR !!
FWOON
THUMP
EEEK!
GASP
OH, SO YOU REALLY CAME ?
O... OF COURSE !

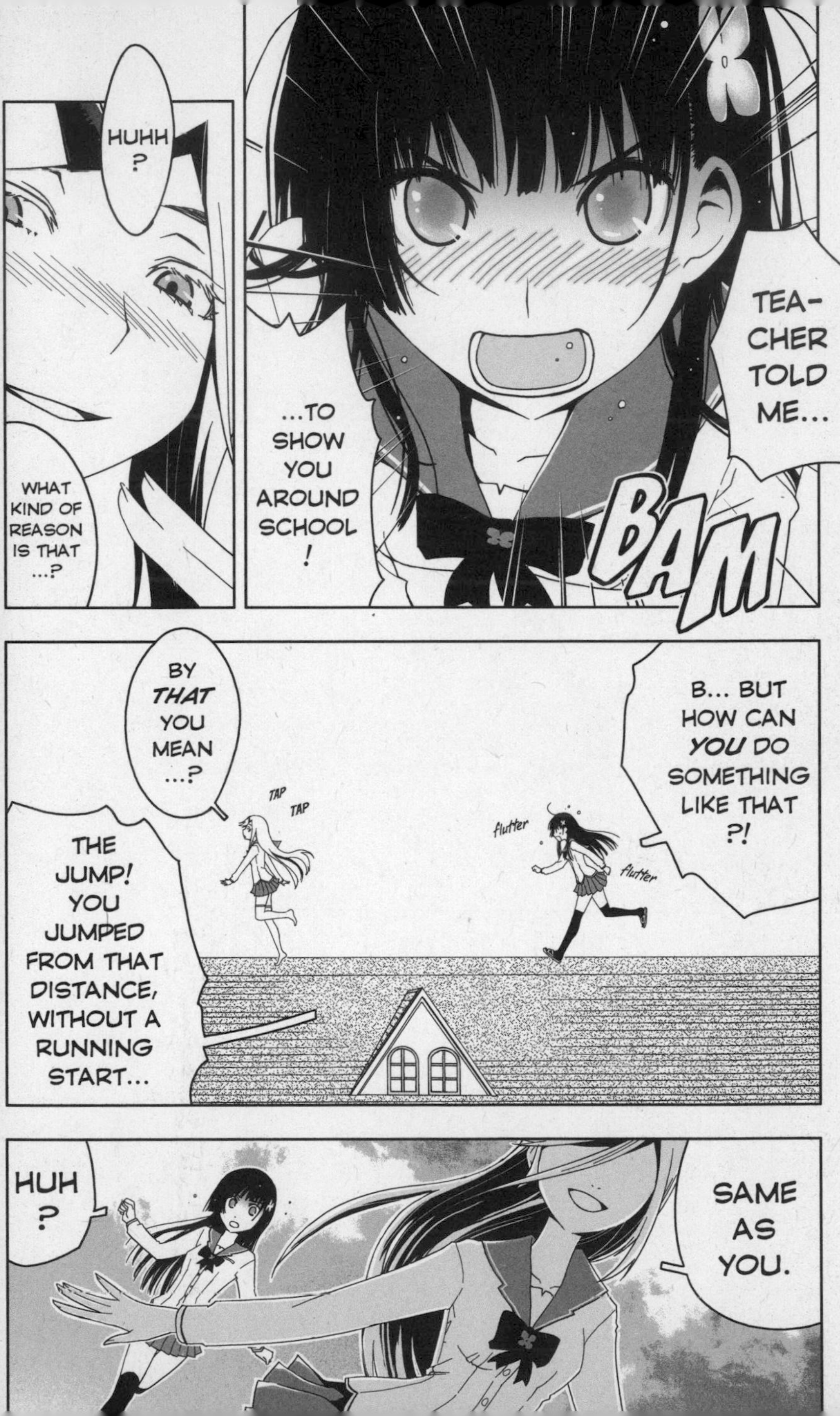
TEA-CHER TOLD ME...
...TO SHOW YOU AROUND SCHOOL!
BAM
HUHH?
WHAT KIND OF REASON IS THAT...?
B... BUT HOW CAN *YOU* DO SOMETHING LIKE THAT?!
flutter
flutter
TAP
TAP
BY *THAT* YOU MEAN...?
THE JUMP! YOU JUMPED FROM THAT DISTANCE, WITHOUT A RUNNING START...
SAME AS YOU.
HUH?

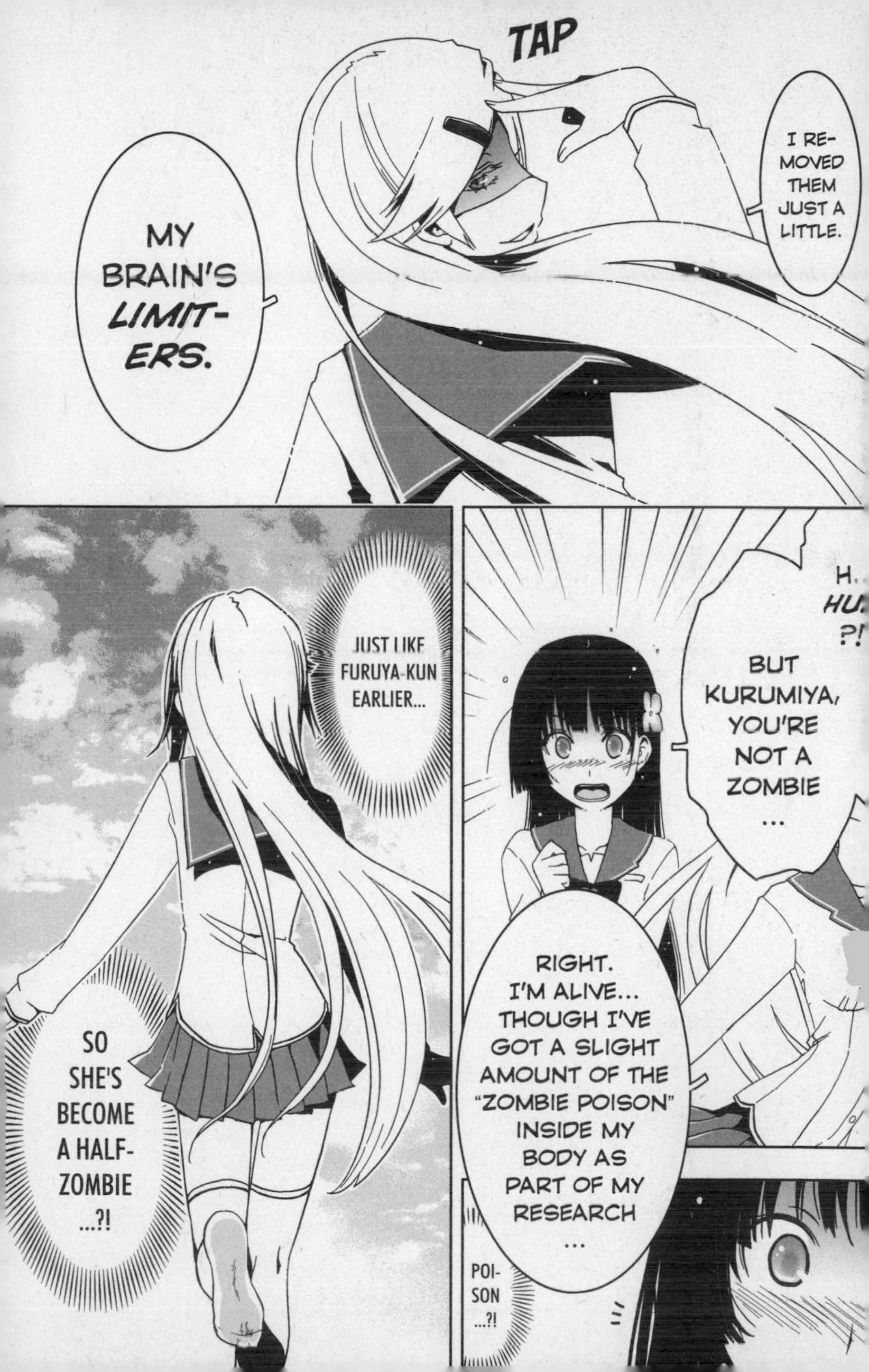
TAP
I RE-MOVED THEM JUST A LITTLE.
MY BRAIN'S *LIMIT-ERS.*
H. *HU.* ?!
BUT KURUMIYA, YOU'RE NOT A ZOMBIE ...
RIGHT. I'M ALIVE... THOUGH I'VE GOT A SLIGHT AMOUNT OF THE "ZOMBIE POISON" INSIDE MY BODY AS PART OF MY RESEARCH ...
POI-SON ...?!
JUST LIKE FURUYA-KUN EARLIER...
SO SHE'S BECOME A HALF-ZOMBIE ...?!

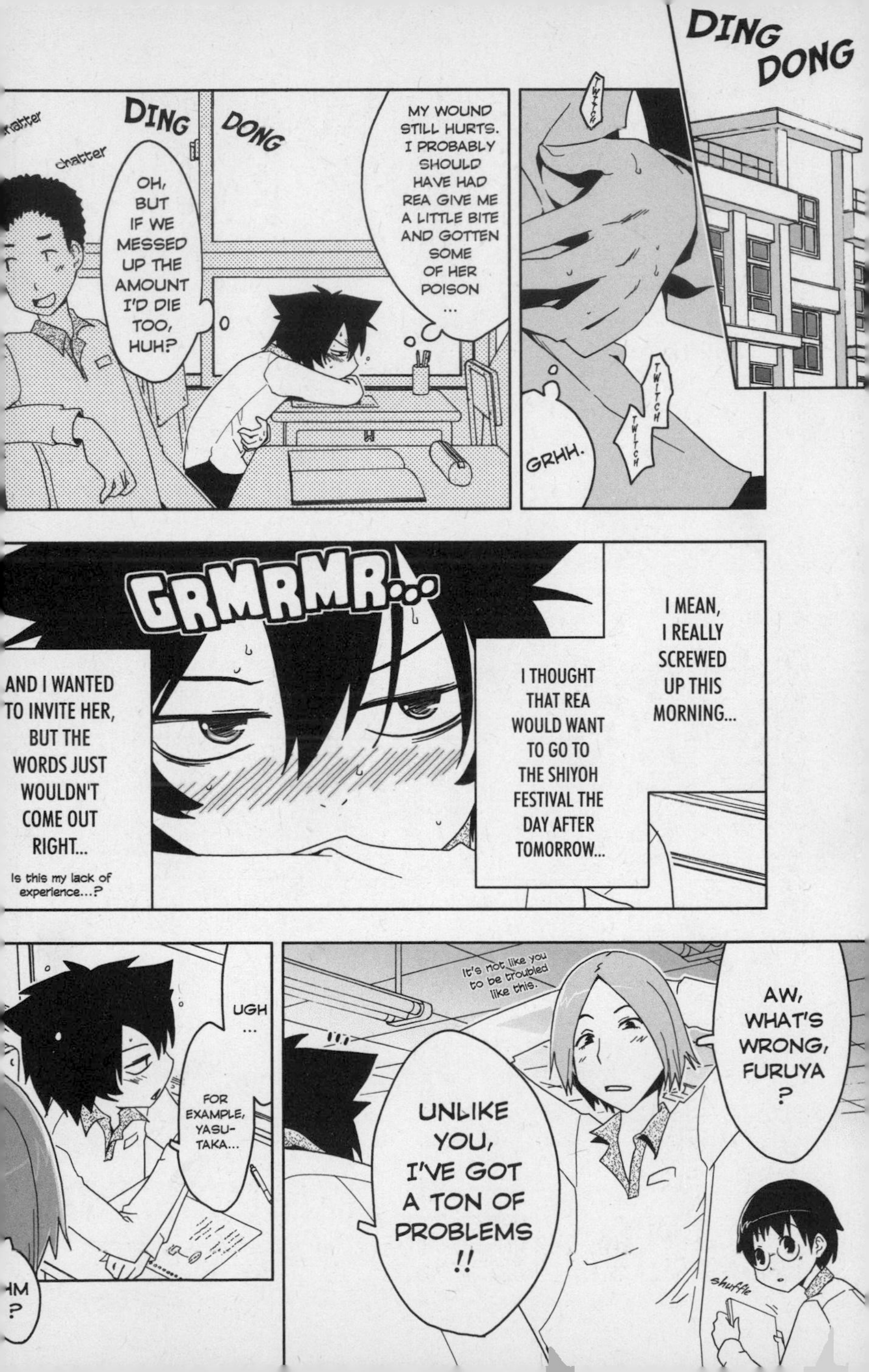
DING DONG
TWITCH
TWITCH
TWITCH
GRHH.
DONG
MY WOUND STILL HURTS. I PROBABLY SHOULD HAVE HAD REA GIVE ME A LITTLE BITE AND GOTTEN SOME OF HER POISON ...
DING
chatter
chatter
OH, BUT IF WE MESSED UP THE AMOUNT I'D DIE TOO, HUH?
I MEAN, I REALLY SCREWED UP THIS MORNING...
I THOUGHT THAT REA WOULD WANT TO GO TO THE SHIYOH FESTIVAL THE DAY AFTER TOMORROW...
GRMRMR...
AND I WANTED TO INVITE HER, BUT THE WORDS JUST WOULDN'T COME OUT RIGHT...
Is this my lack of experience...?
AW, WHAT'S WRONG, FURUYA ?
It's not like you to be troubled like this.
UNLIKE YOU, I'VE GOT A TON OF PROBLEMS !!
shuffle
UGH ...
FOR EXAMPLE, YASU-TAKA...
HM ?

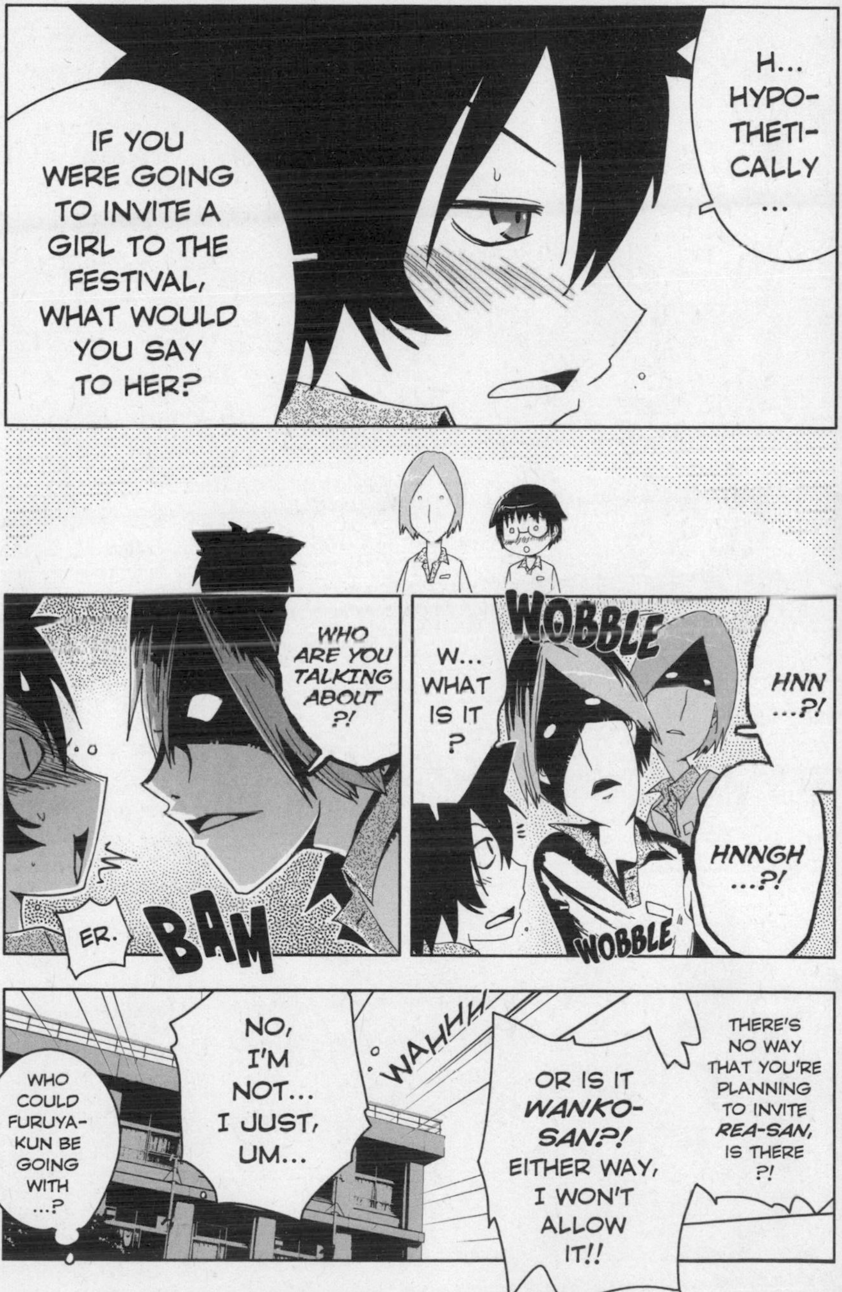
H... HYPO-THETI-CALLY ...
IF YOU WERE GOING TO INVITE A GIRL TO THE FESTIVAL, WHAT WOULD YOU SAY TO HER?
HNN ...?!
WOBBLE
W... WHAT IS IT ?
HNNGH ...?!
WOBBLE
WHO ARE YOU TALKING ABOUT ?!
ER.
BAM
THERE'S NO WAY THAT YOU'RE PLANNING TO INVITE REA-SAN, IS THERE ?!
OR IS IT WANKO-SAN?! EITHER WAY, I WON'T ALLOW IT!!
WAHHH
NO, I'M NOT... I JUST, UM...
WHO COULD FURUYA-KUN BE GOING WITH ...?
OWW...

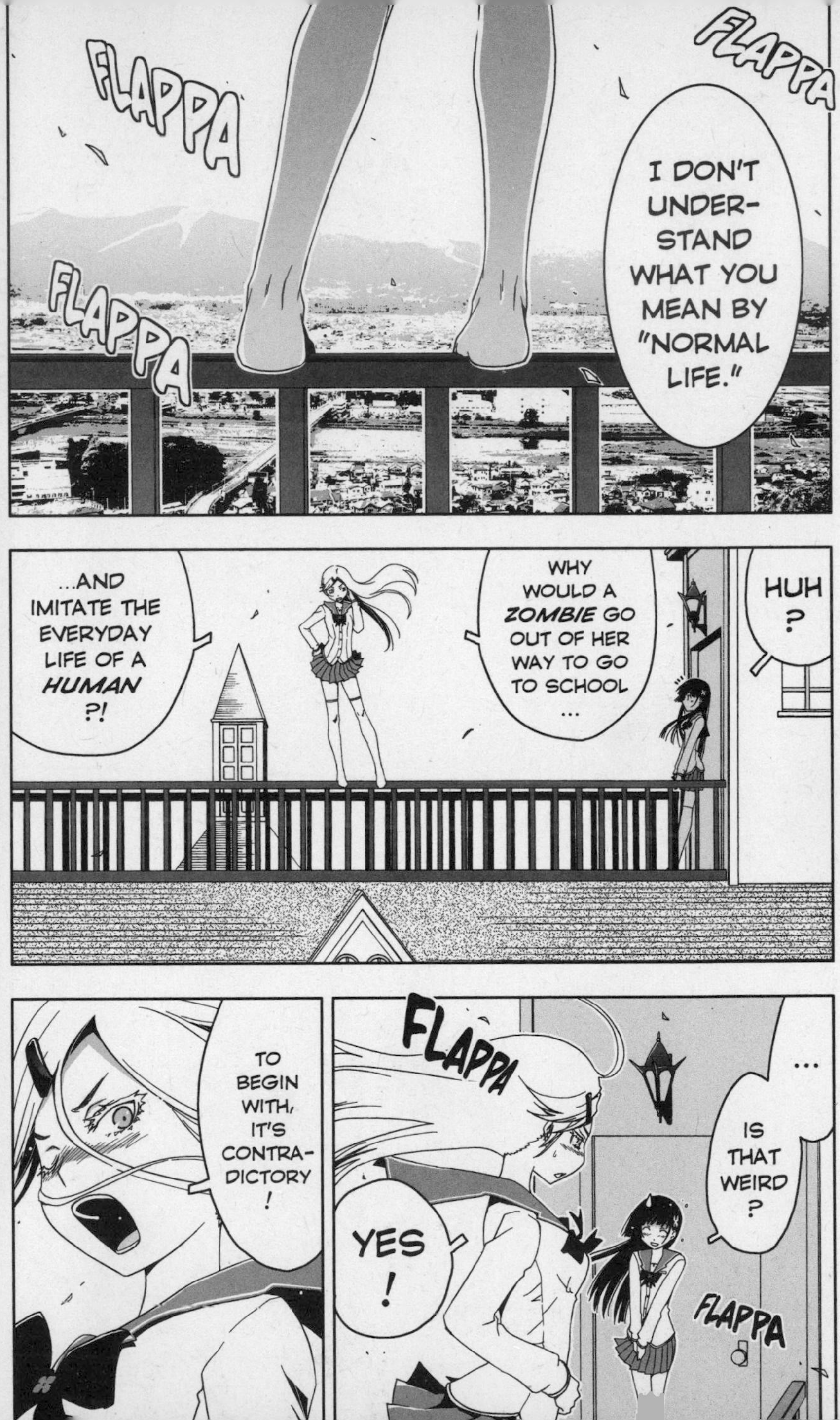
FLAPPA
I DON'T UNDERSTAND WHAT YOU MEAN BY "NORMAL LIFE."
FLAPPA
FLAPPA
HUH ?
WHY WOULD A *ZOMBIE* GO OUT OF HER WAY TO GO TO SCHOOL ...
...AND IMITATE THE EVERYDAY LIFE OF A *HUMAN* ?!
...
IS THAT WEIRD ?
FLAPPA
YES !
FLAPPA
TO BEGIN WITH, IT'S CONTRADICTORY !

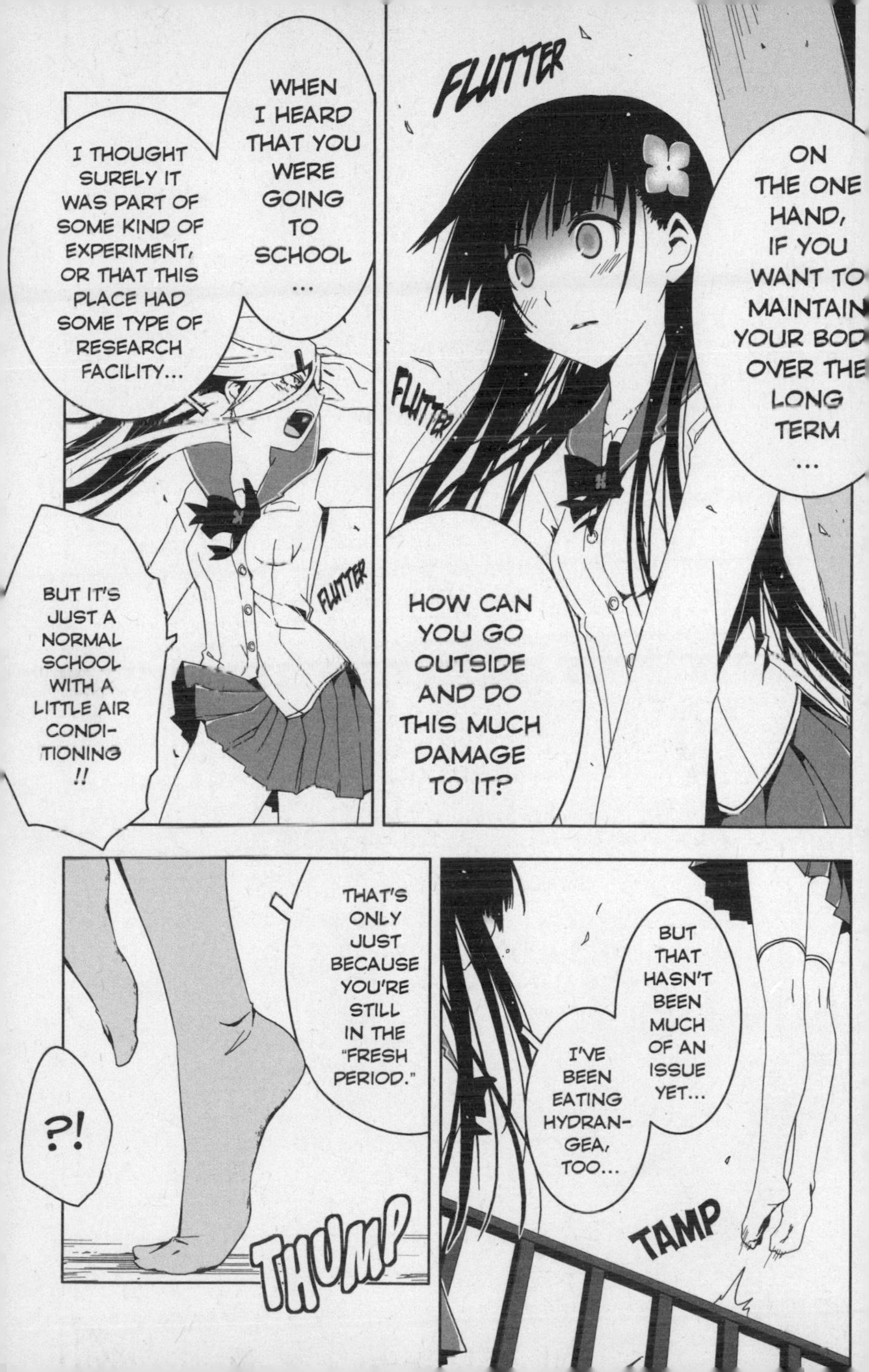
ON THE ONE HAND, IF YOU WANT TO MAINTAIN YOUR BOD OVER THE LONG TERM ...
FLUTTER
FLUTTER
HOW CAN YOU GO OUTSIDE AND DO THIS MUCH DAMAGE TO IT?
WHEN I HEARD THAT YOU WERE GOING TO SCHOOL ...
I THOUGHT SURELY IT WAS PART OF SOME KIND OF EXPERIMENT, OR THAT THIS PLACE HAD SOME TYPE OF RESEARCH FACILITY...
FLUTTER
BUT IT'S JUST A NORMAL SCHOOL WITH A LITTLE AIR CONDI-TIONING !!
BUT THAT HASN'T BEEN MUCH OF AN ISSUE YET...
I'VE BEEN EATING HYDRAN-GEA, TOO...
TAMP
THAT'S ONLY JUST BECAUSE YOU'RE STILL IN THE "FRESH PERIOD."
THUMP
?!

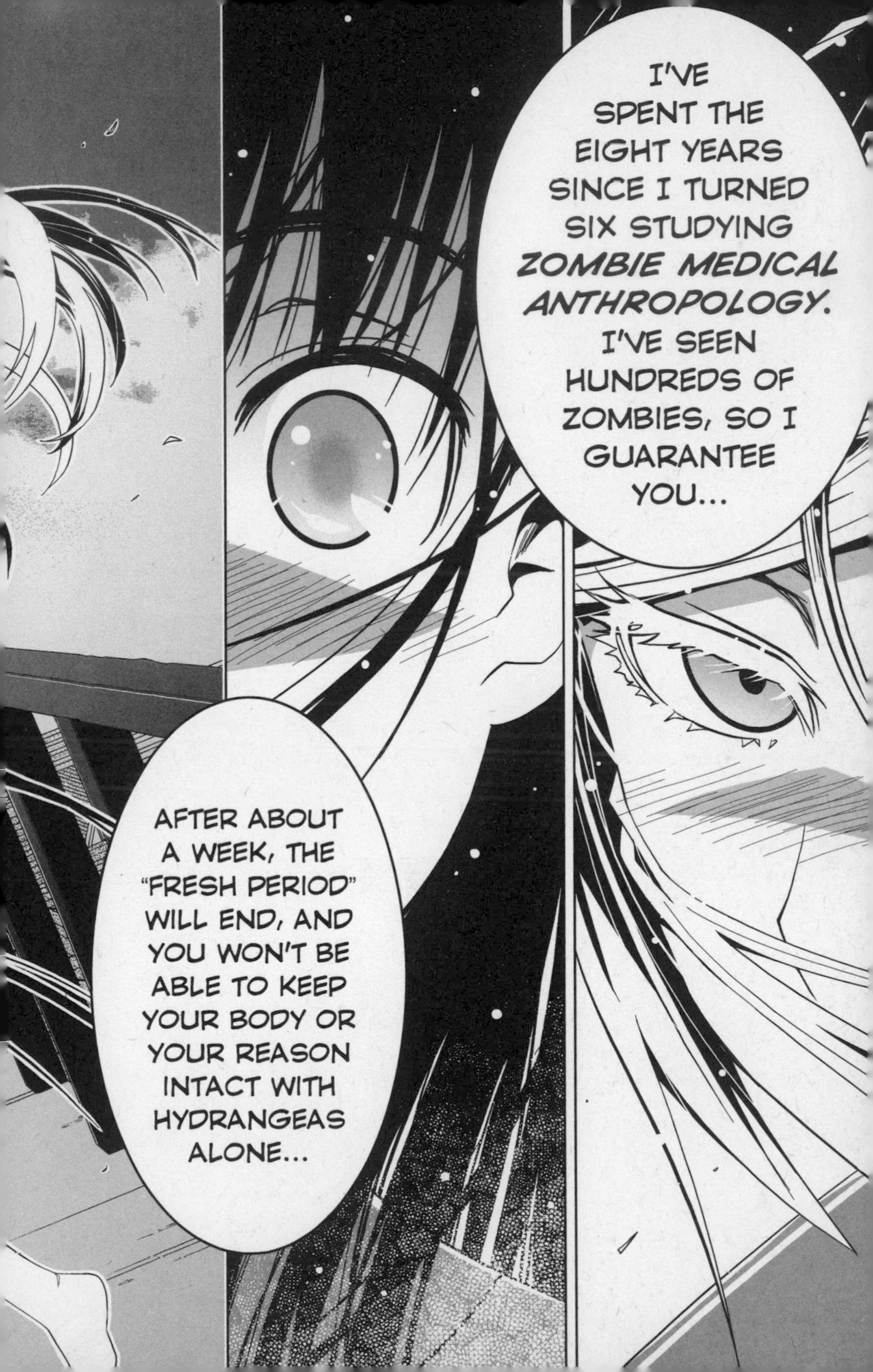
I'VE SPENT THE EIGHT YEARS SINCE I TURNED SIX STUDYING *ZOMBIE MEDICAL ANTHROPOLOGY.* I'VE SEEN HUNDREDS OF ZOMBIES, SO I GUARANTEE YOU...
AFTER ABOUT A WEEK, THE "FRESH PERIOD" WILL END, AND YOU WON'T BE ABLE TO KEEP YOUR BODY OR YOUR REASON INTACT WITH HYDRANGEAS ALONE...

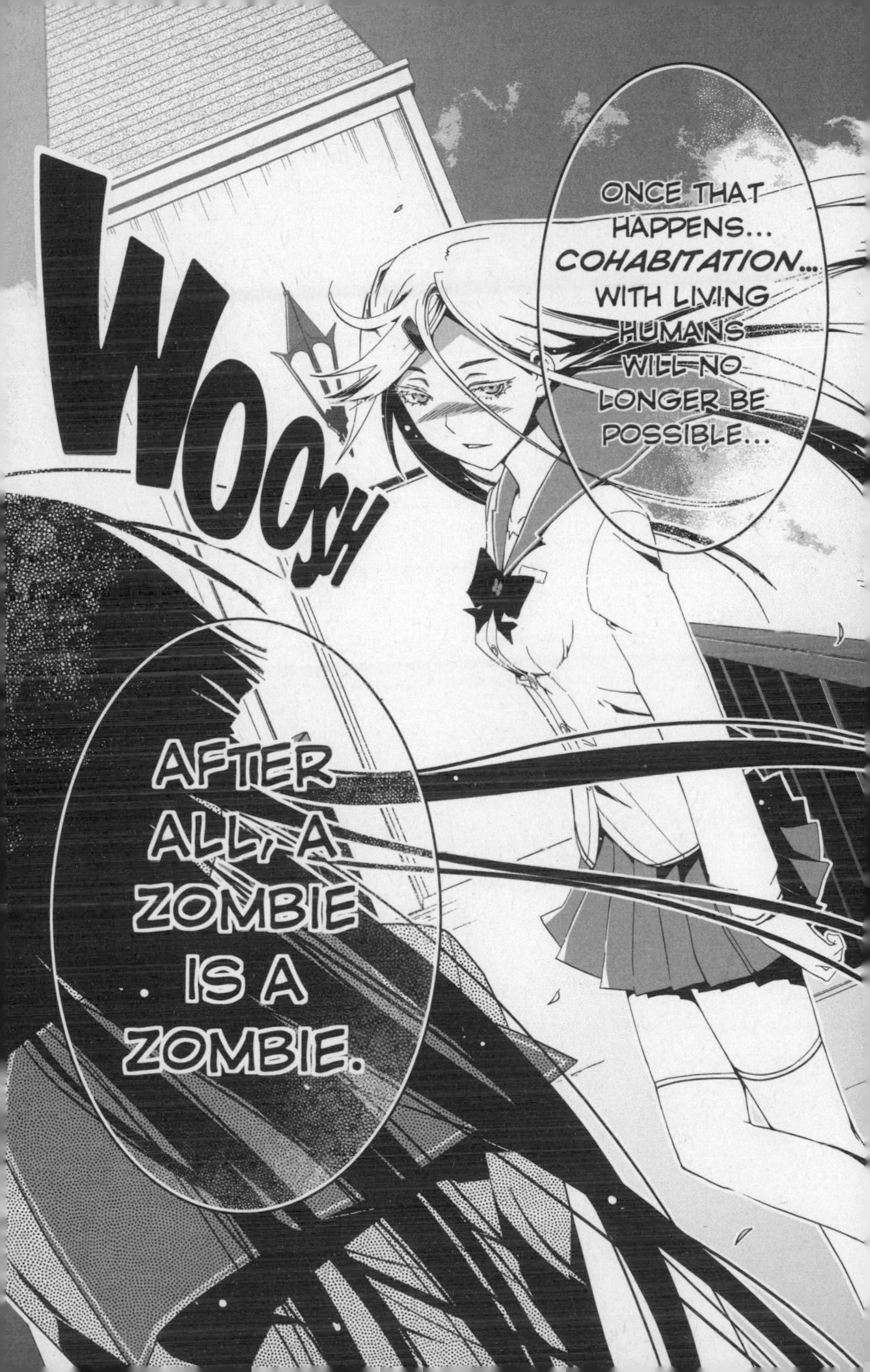
ONCE THAT HAPPENS... *COHABITATION*... WITH LIVING HUMANS WILL NO LONGER BE POSSIBLE...
WOOSH
AFTER ALL, A ZOMBIE IS A ZOMBIE.

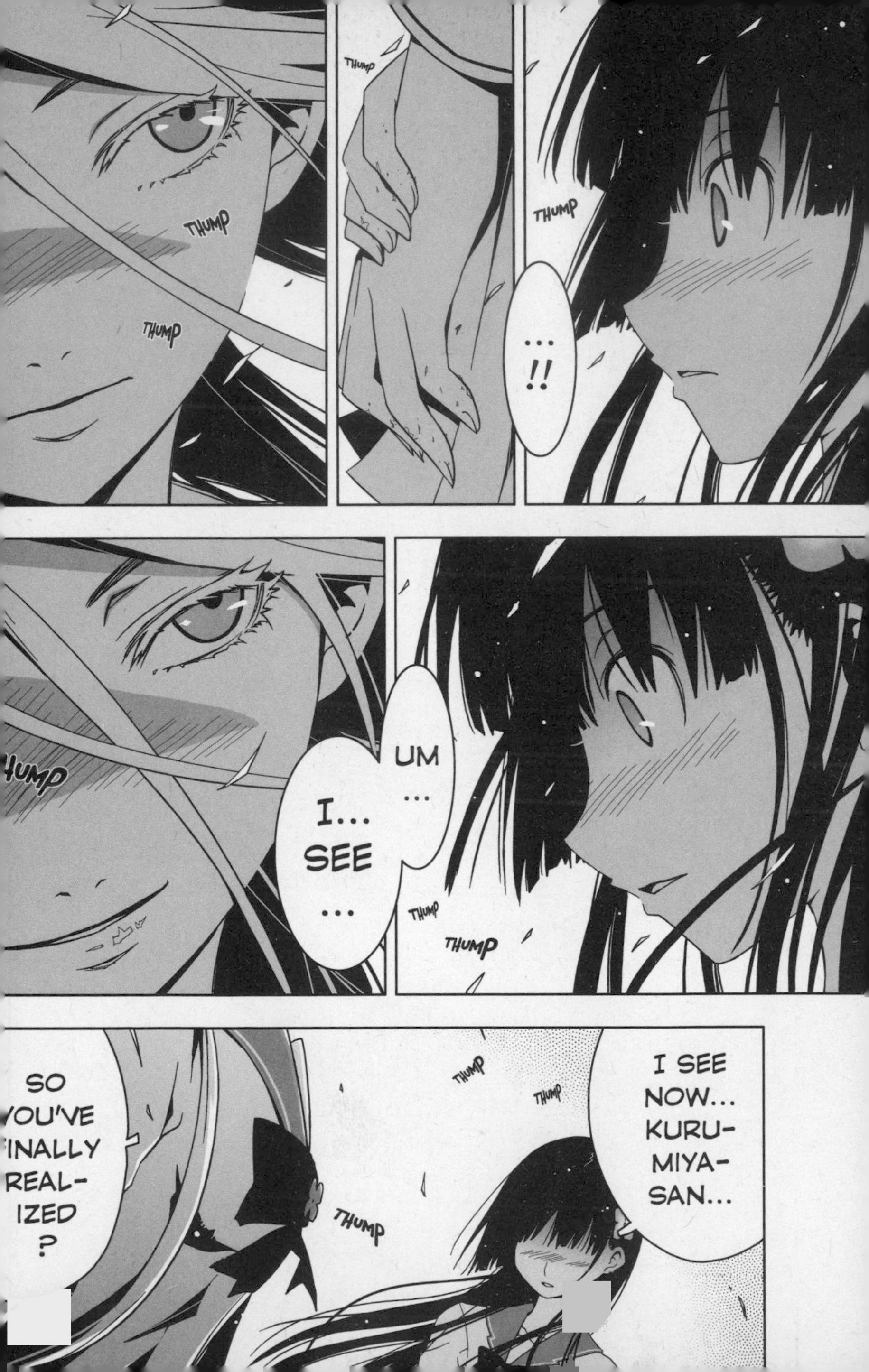
THUMP
...!!
THUMP
THUMP
THUMP
UM...
I... SEE...
THUMP
THUMP
HUMP
I SEE NOW... KURU-MIYA-SAN...
THUMP
THUMP
THUMP
SO YOU'VE FINALLY REAL-IZED?

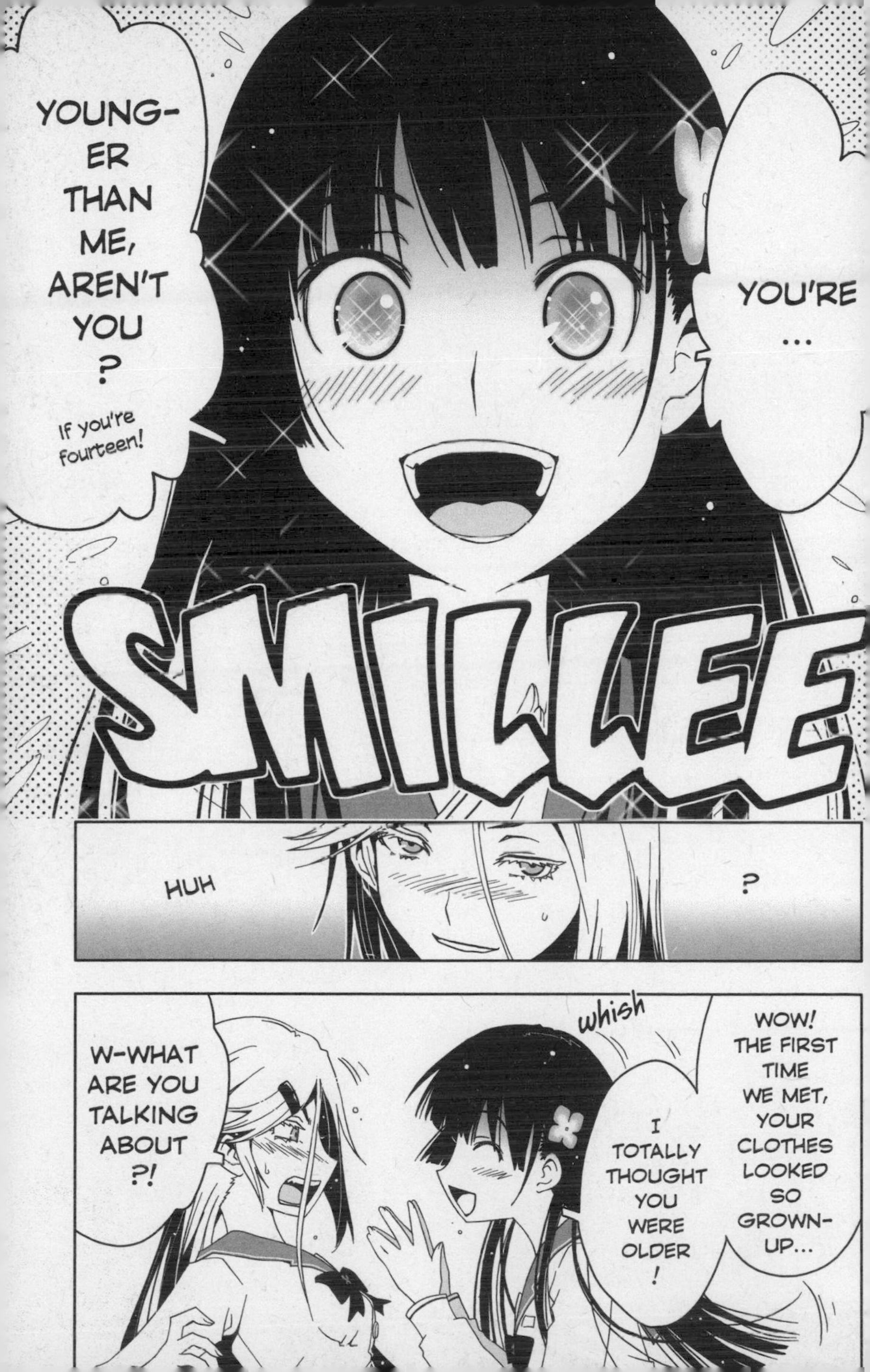
YOU'RE ...
YOUNG-ER THAN ME, AREN'T YOU?
If you're fourteen!
SMILLEE
HUH ?
whish
WOW! THE FIRST TIME WE MET, YOUR CLOTHES LOOKED SO GROWN-UP...
I TOTALLY THOUGHT YOU WERE OLDER!
W-WHAT ARE YOU TALKING ABOUT?!

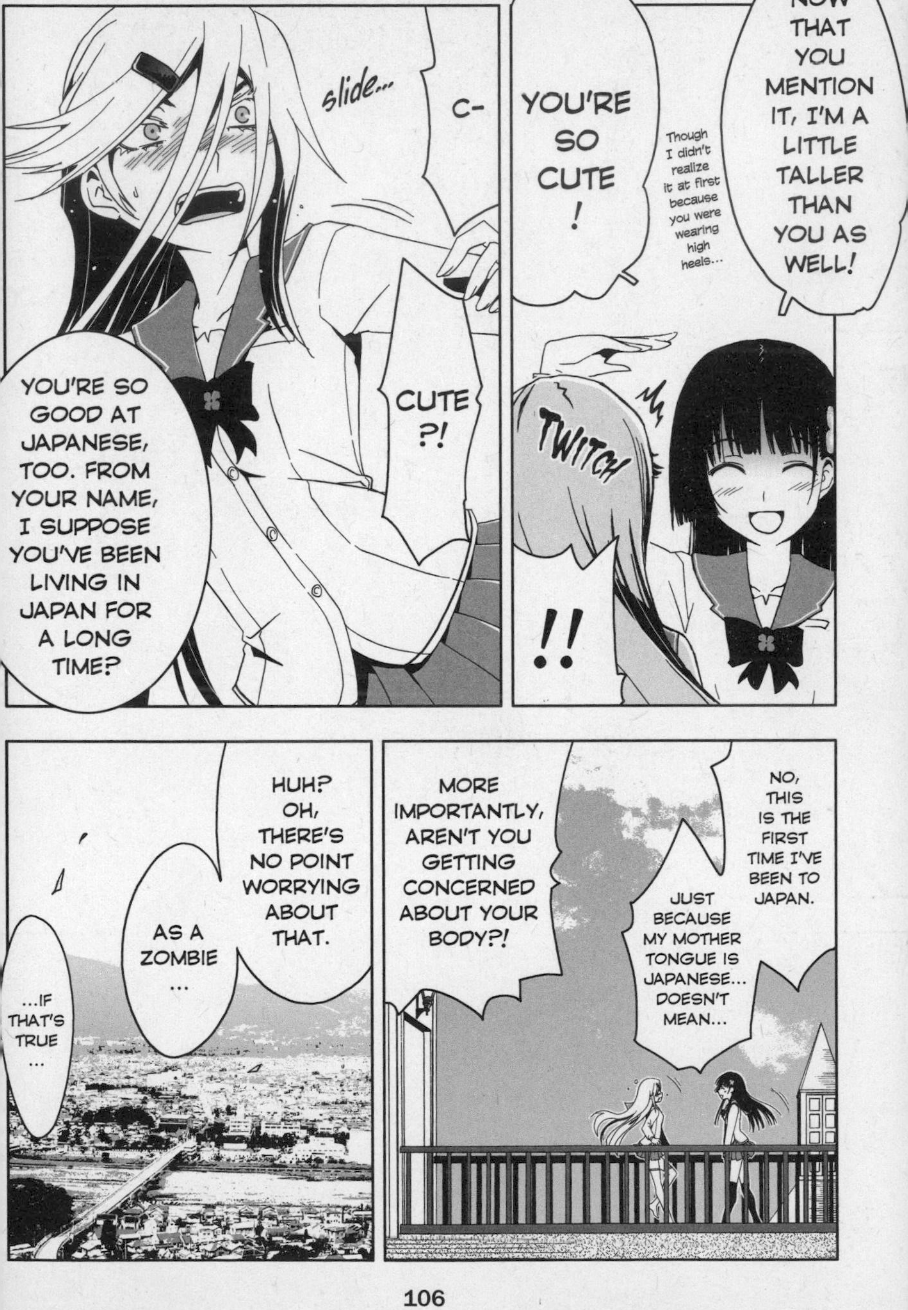
NOW THAT YOU MENTION IT, I'M A LITTLE TALLER THAN YOU AS WELL!
Though I didn't realize it at first because you were wearing high heels...
YOU'RE SO CUTE!
TWITCH
!!
C-
slide...
CUTE?!
YOU'RE SO GOOD AT JAPANESE, TOO. FROM YOUR NAME, I SUPPOSE YOU'VE BEEN LIVING IN JAPAN FOR A LONG TIME?
NO, THIS IS THE FIRST TIME I'VE BEEN TO JAPAN.
JUST BECAUSE MY MOTHER TONGUE IS JAPANESE... DOESN'T MEAN...
MORE IMPORTANTLY, AREN'T YOU GETTING CONCERNED ABOUT YOUR BODY?!
HUH? OH, THERE'S NO POINT WORRYING ABOUT THAT.
AS A ZOMBIE...
...IF THAT'S TRUE...

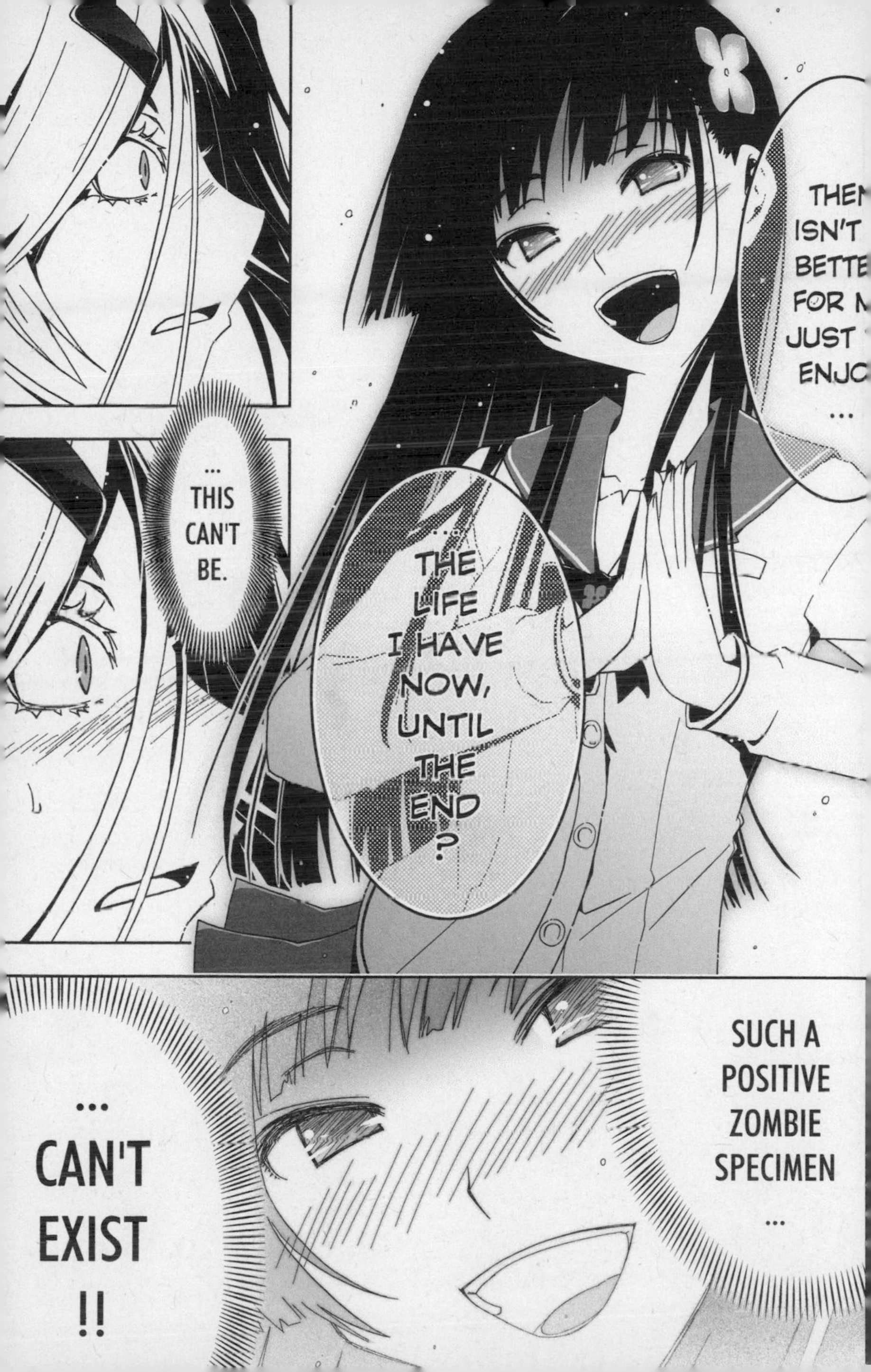
THEN ISN'T BETTE FOR M JUST ENJO ...
... THE LIFE I HAVE NOW, UNTIL THE END?
... THIS CAN'T BE.
SUCH A POSITIVE ZOMBIE SPECIMEN ...
... CAN'T EXIST !!

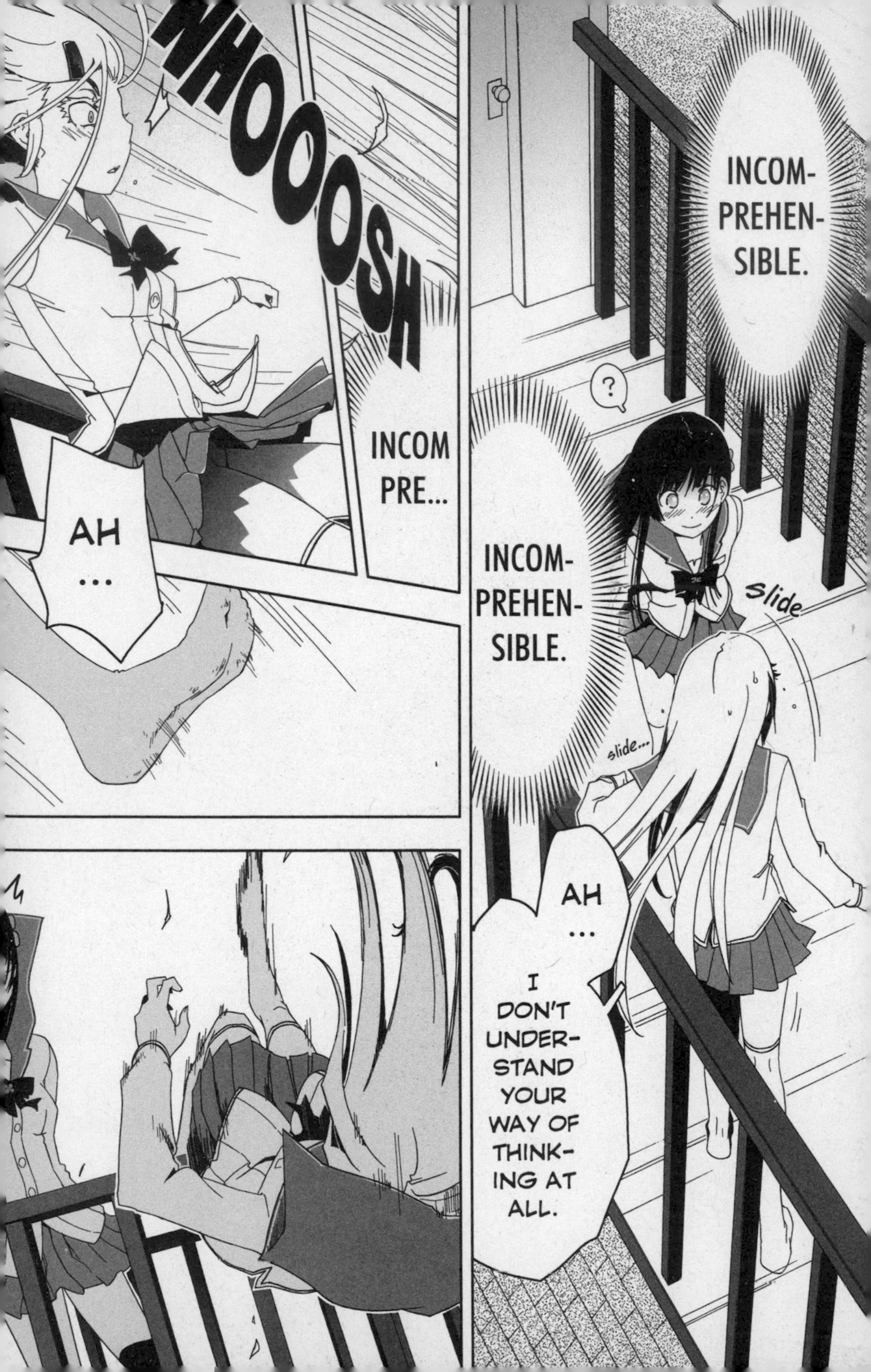
INCOM-PREHEN-SIBLE.
?
INCOM-PREHEN-SIBLE.
Slide
slide...
AH ... I DON'T UNDER-STAND YOUR WAY OF THINK-ING AT ALL.
INCOM PRE...
WHOOOSH
AH ...

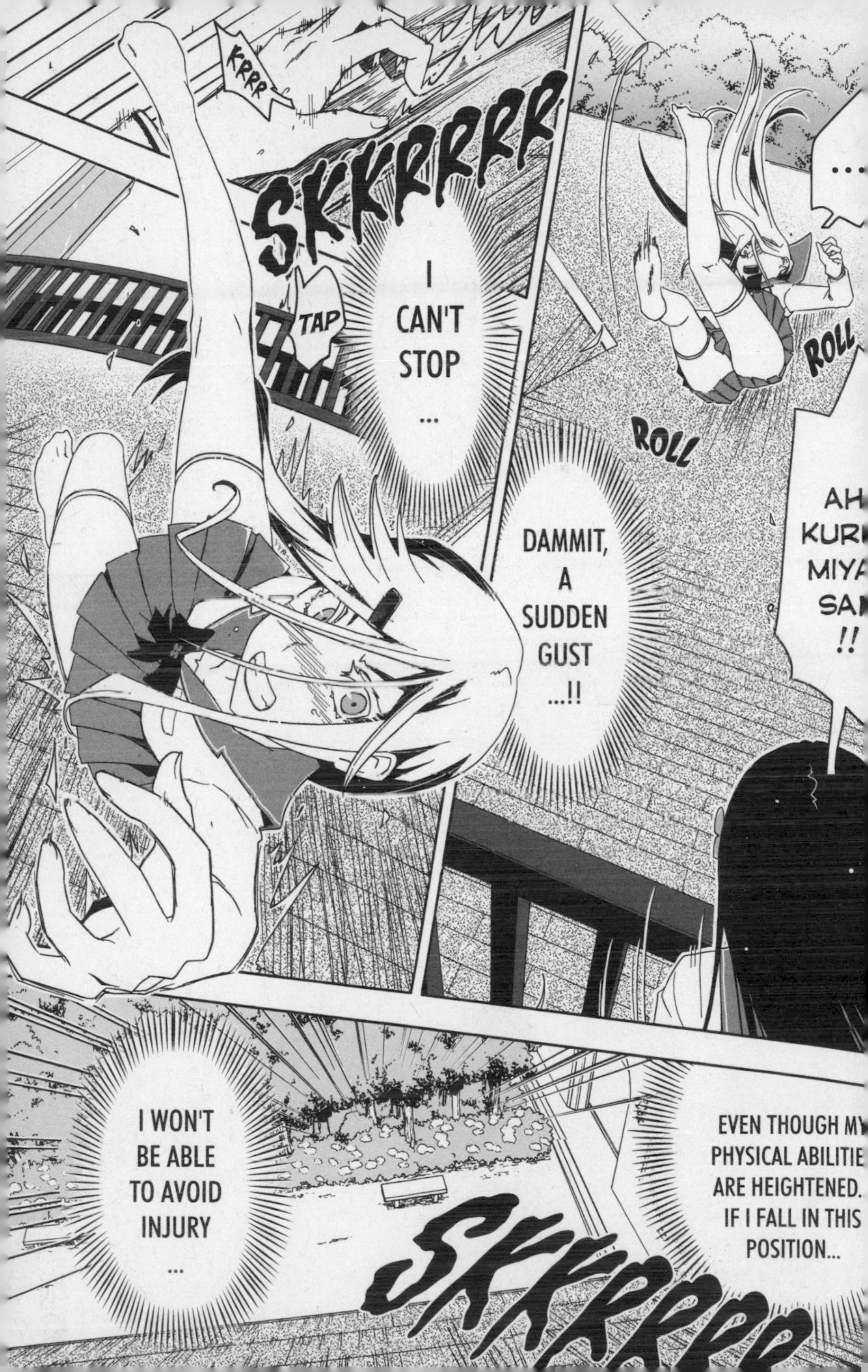
...
ROLL
ROLL
AH KUR MIYA SA !!
DAMMIT, A SUDDEN GUST ...!!
KRRR
SKKRRRRR
TAP
I CAN'T STOP ...
EVEN THOUGH MY PHYSICAL ABILITIE ARE HEIGHTENED. IF I FALL IN THIS POSITION...
SKKRRRRR
I WON'T BE ABLE TO AVOID INJURY ...

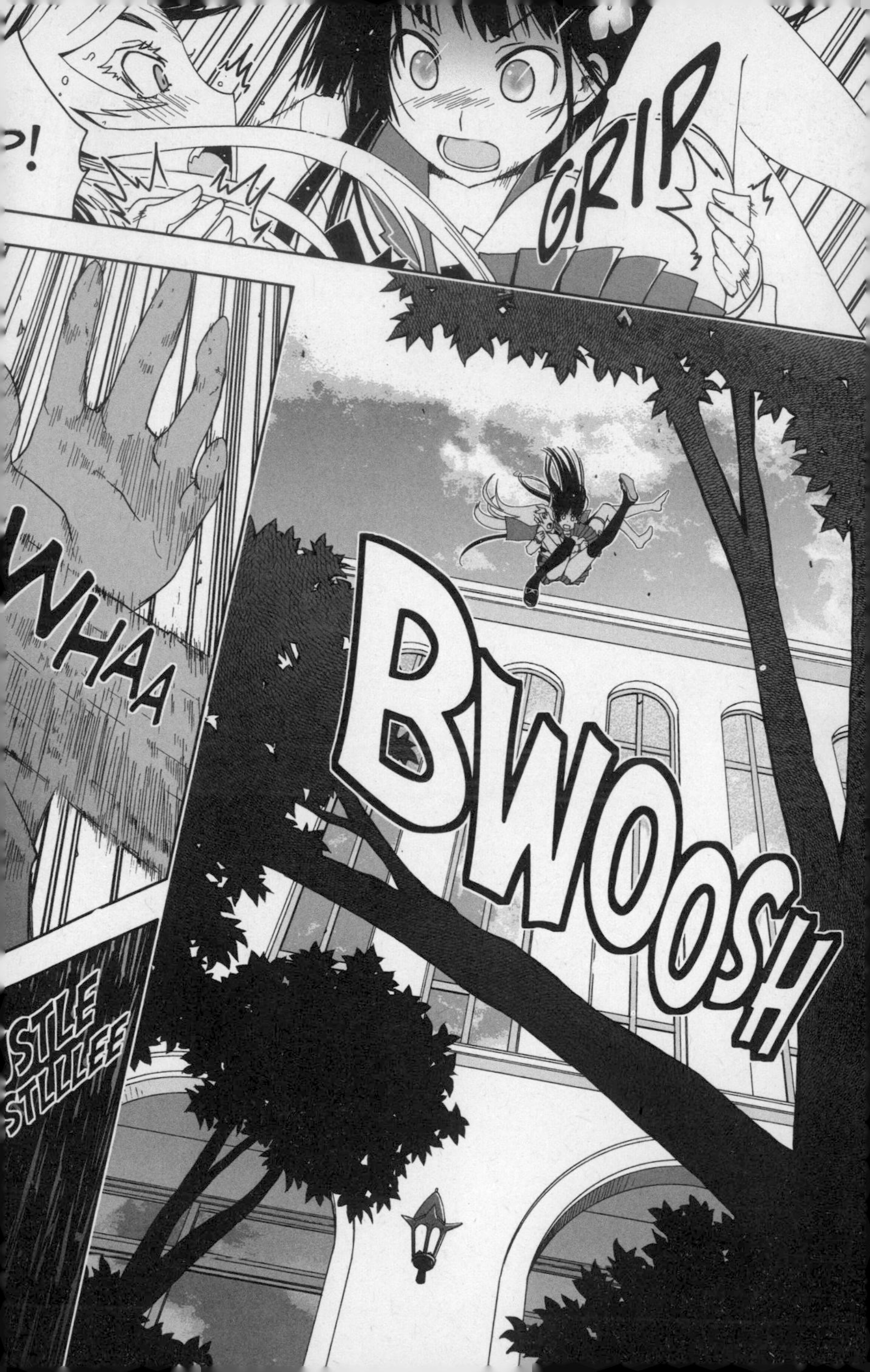
GRIP
?!
BWOOSH
WHAA
STLE
STLLLEE

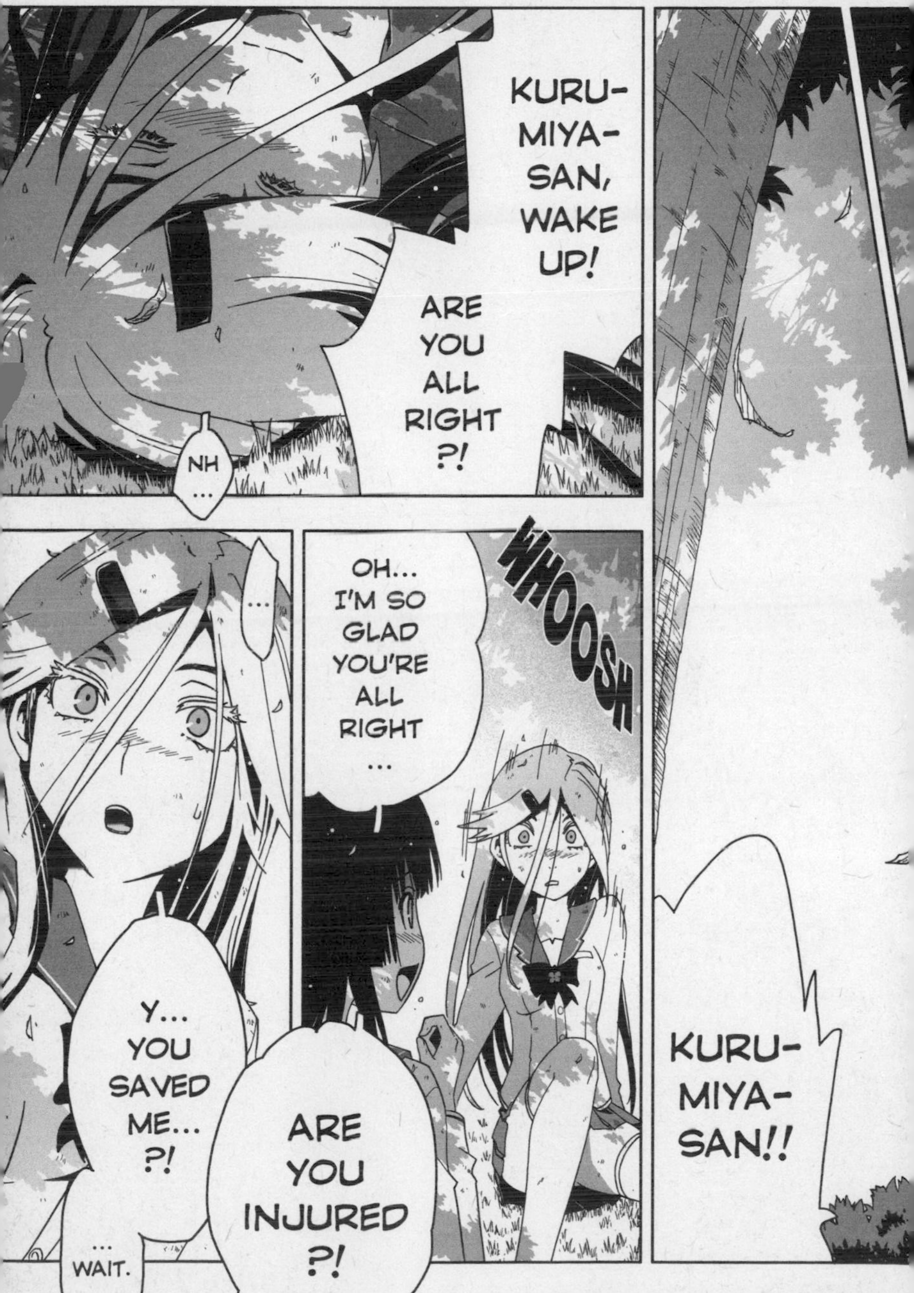
KURU-MIYA-SAN!!
KURU-MIYA-SAN, WAKE UP!
ARE YOU ALL RIGHT?!
NH...
WHOOSH
OH... I'M SO GLAD YOU'RE ALL RIGHT...
ARE YOU INJURED?!
...
Y... YOU SAVED ME...?!
...WAIT.

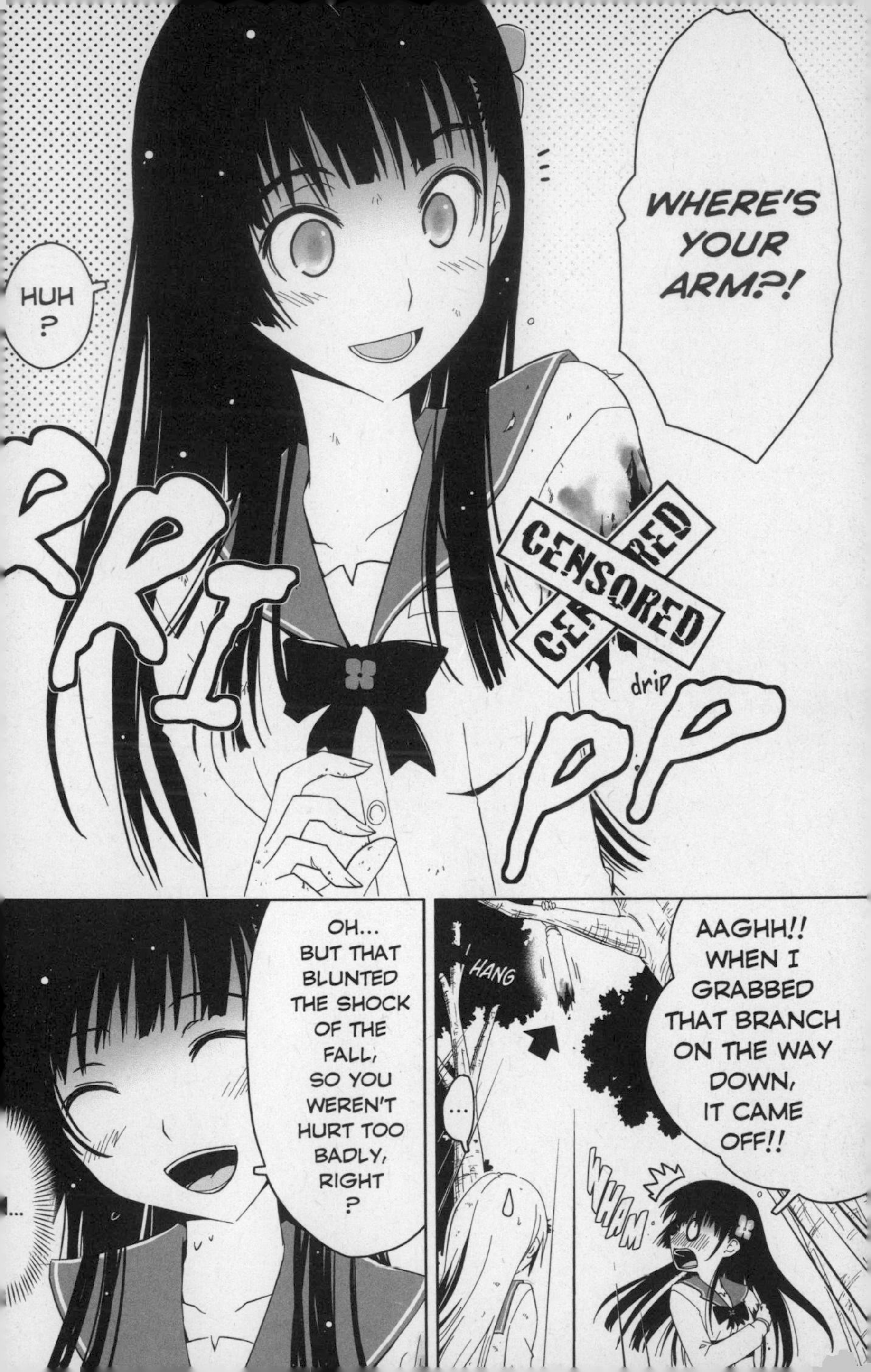
WHERE'S YOUR ARM?!
CENSORED
CENSORED
drip
HUH?
AAGHH!! WHEN I GRABBED THAT BRANCH ON THE WAY DOWN, IT CAME OFF!!
HANG
WHAM
...
OH... BUT THAT BLUNTED THE SHOCK OF THE FALL, SO YOU WEREN'T HURT TOO BADLY, RIGHT?
...

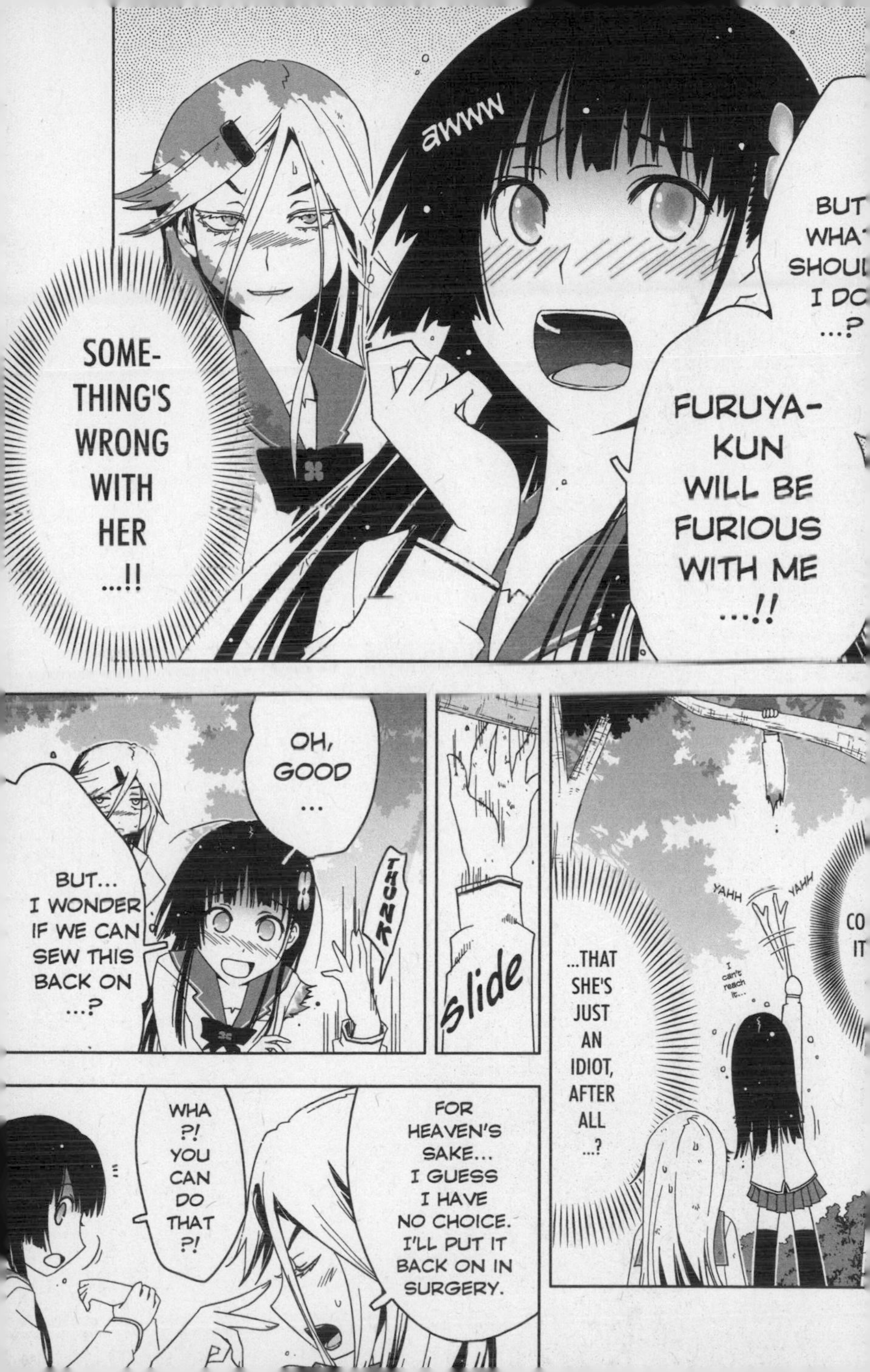
BUT WHA SHOU I DO ...?
awww
FURUYA-KUN WILL BE FURIOUS WITH ME ...!!
SOME-THING'S WRONG WITH HER ...!!
CO IT
YAHH YAHH
I can't reach it...
...THAT SHE'S JUST AN IDIOT, AFTER ALL ...?
slide
OH, GOOD ...
THUNK
BUT... I WONDER IF WE CAN SEW THIS BACK ON ...?
FOR HEAVEN'S SAKE... I GUESS I HAVE NO CHOICE. I'LL PUT IT BACK ON IN SURGERY.
WHA?! YOU CAN DO THAT?!

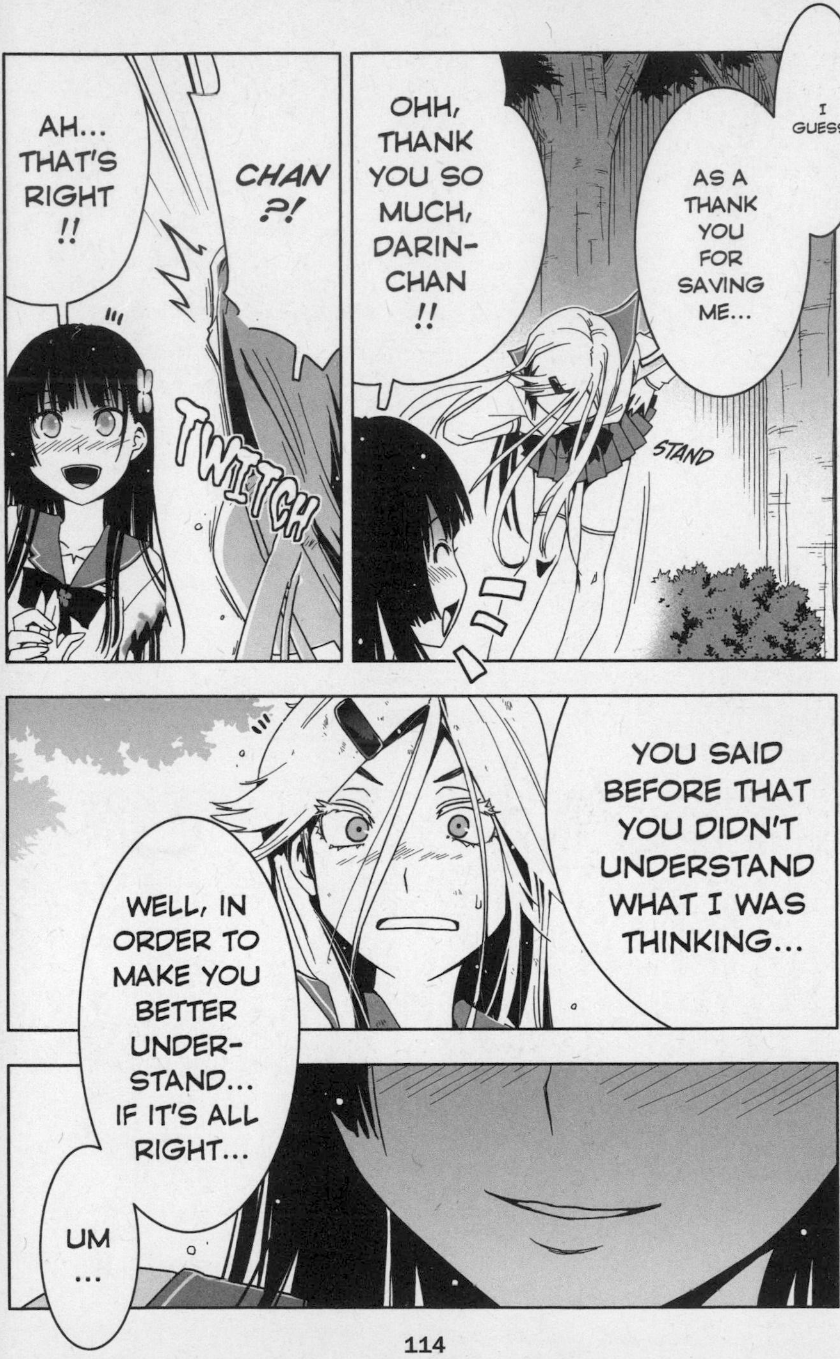
I GUESS.
AS A THANK YOU FOR SAVING ME...
OHH, THANK YOU SO MUCH, DARIN-CHAN!!
STAND
CHAN?!
TWITCH
AH... THAT'S RIGHT!!
YOU SAID BEFORE THAT YOU DIDN'T UNDERSTAND WHAT I WAS THINKING...
WELL, IN ORDER TO MAKE YOU BETTER UNDER-STAND... IF IT'S ALL RIGHT...
UM...

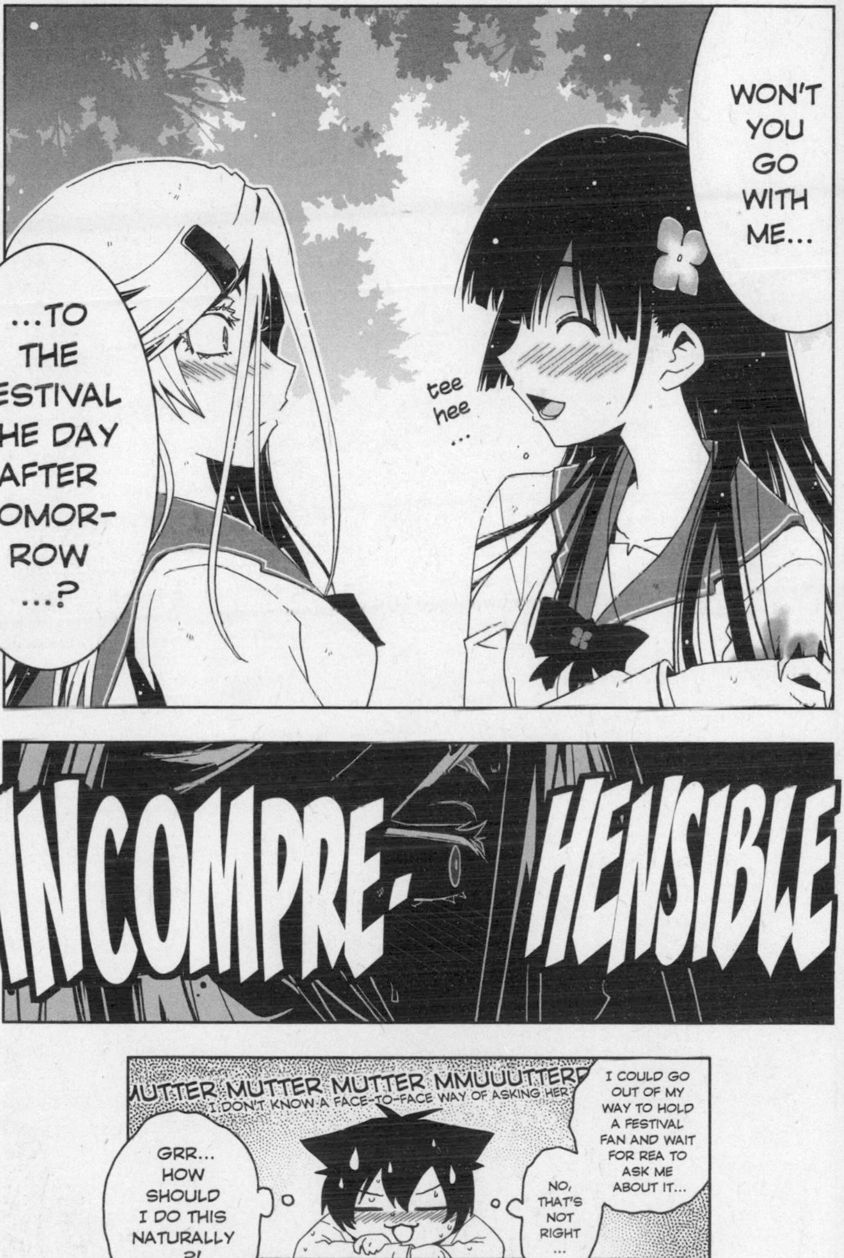
WON'T YOU GO WITH ME...
tee hee ...
...TO THE FESTIVAL THE DAY AFTER TOMORROW ...?
TOTALLY INCOMPRE-HENSIBLE
I COULD GO OUT OF MY WAY TO HOLD A FESTIVAL FAN AND WAIT FOR REA TO ASK ME ABOUT IT...
MUTTER MUTTER MUTTER MMUUUTTER
I DON'T KNOW A FACE-TO-FACE WAY OF ASKING HER
NO, THAT'S NOT RIGHT ...
GRR... HOW SHOULD I DO THIS NATURALLY ...?!

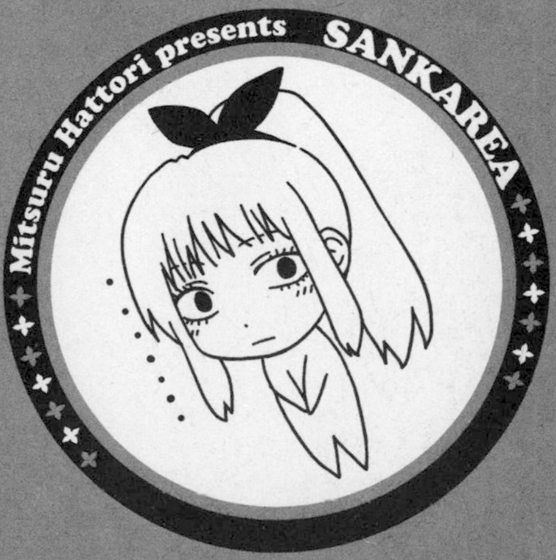
Mitsuru Hattori presents
SANKAREA

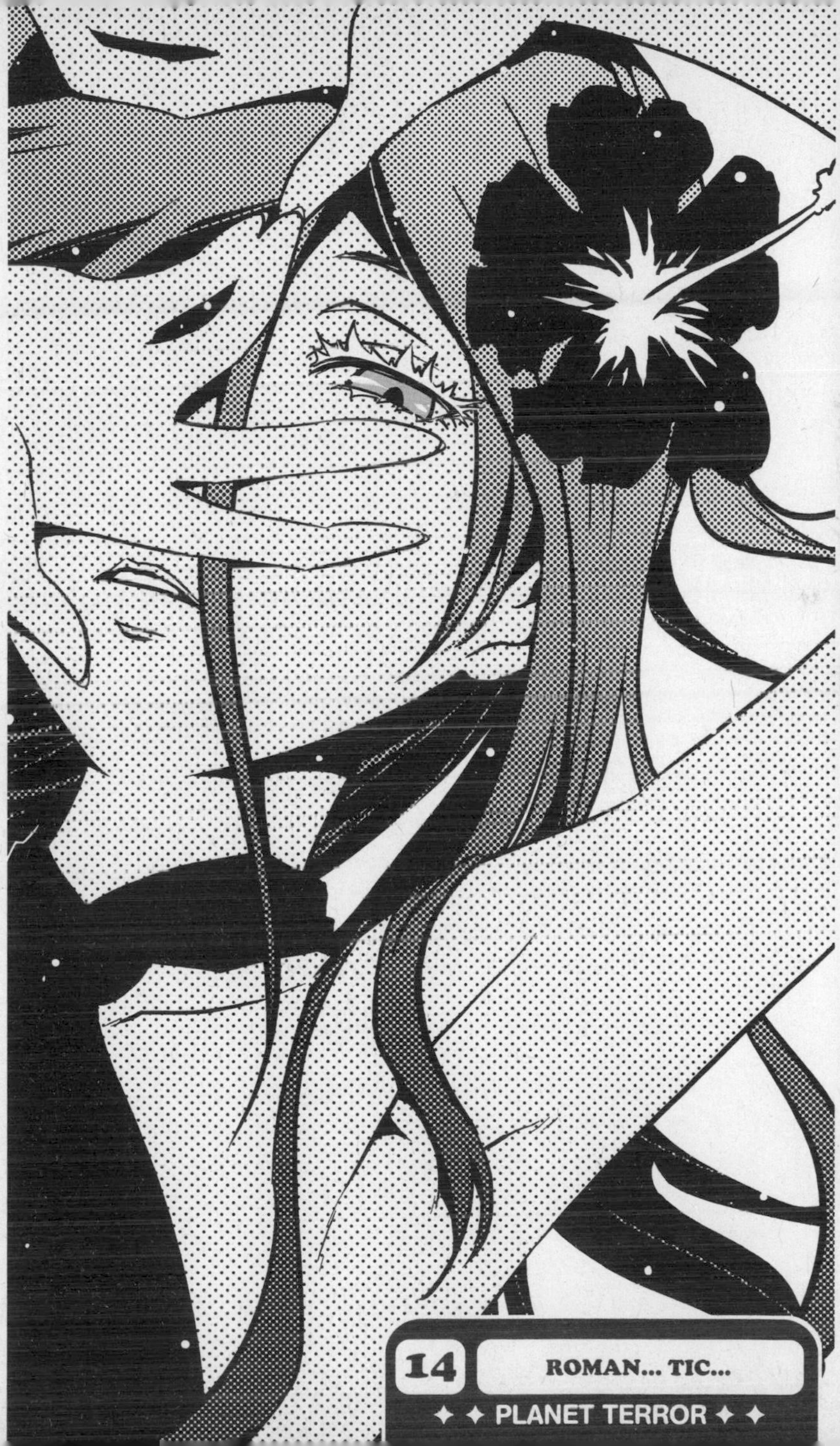
14
ROMAN... TIC...
PLANET TERROR

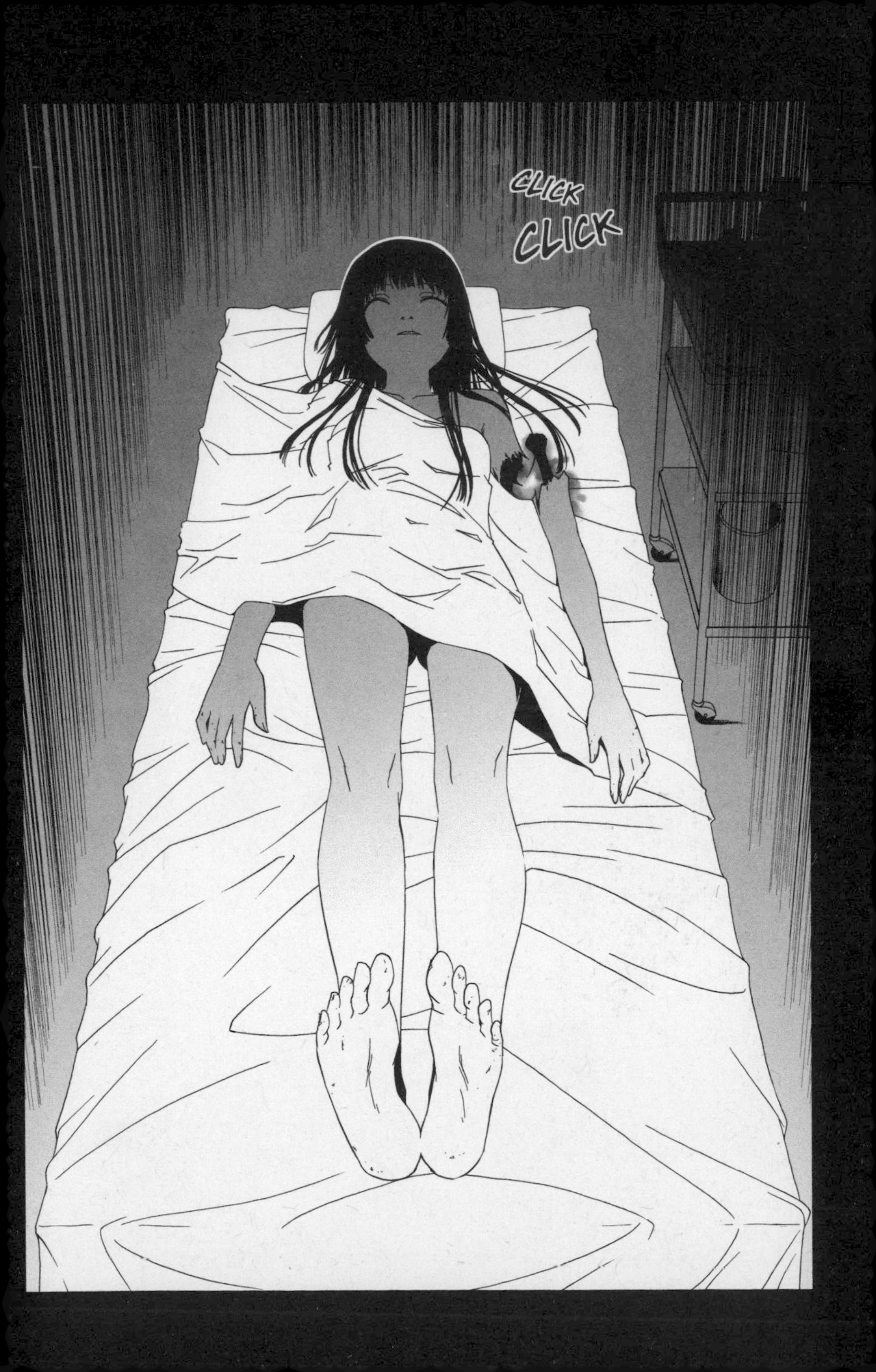
CLICK
CLICK

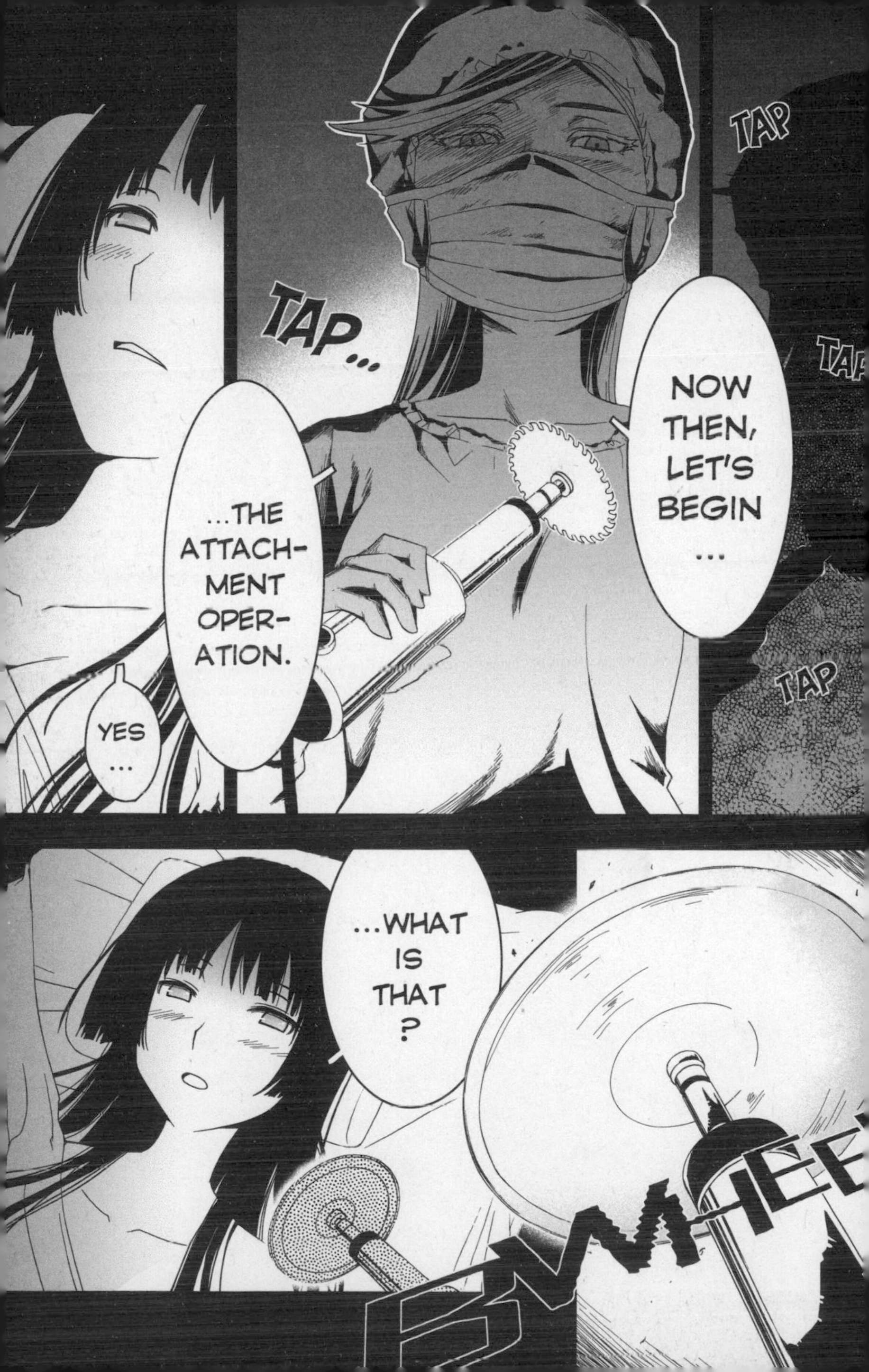
TAP
TAP
TAP
NOW THEN, LET'S BEGIN...
TAP...
...THE ATTACHMENT OPERATION.
YES...
...WHAT IS THAT?
BWHEE

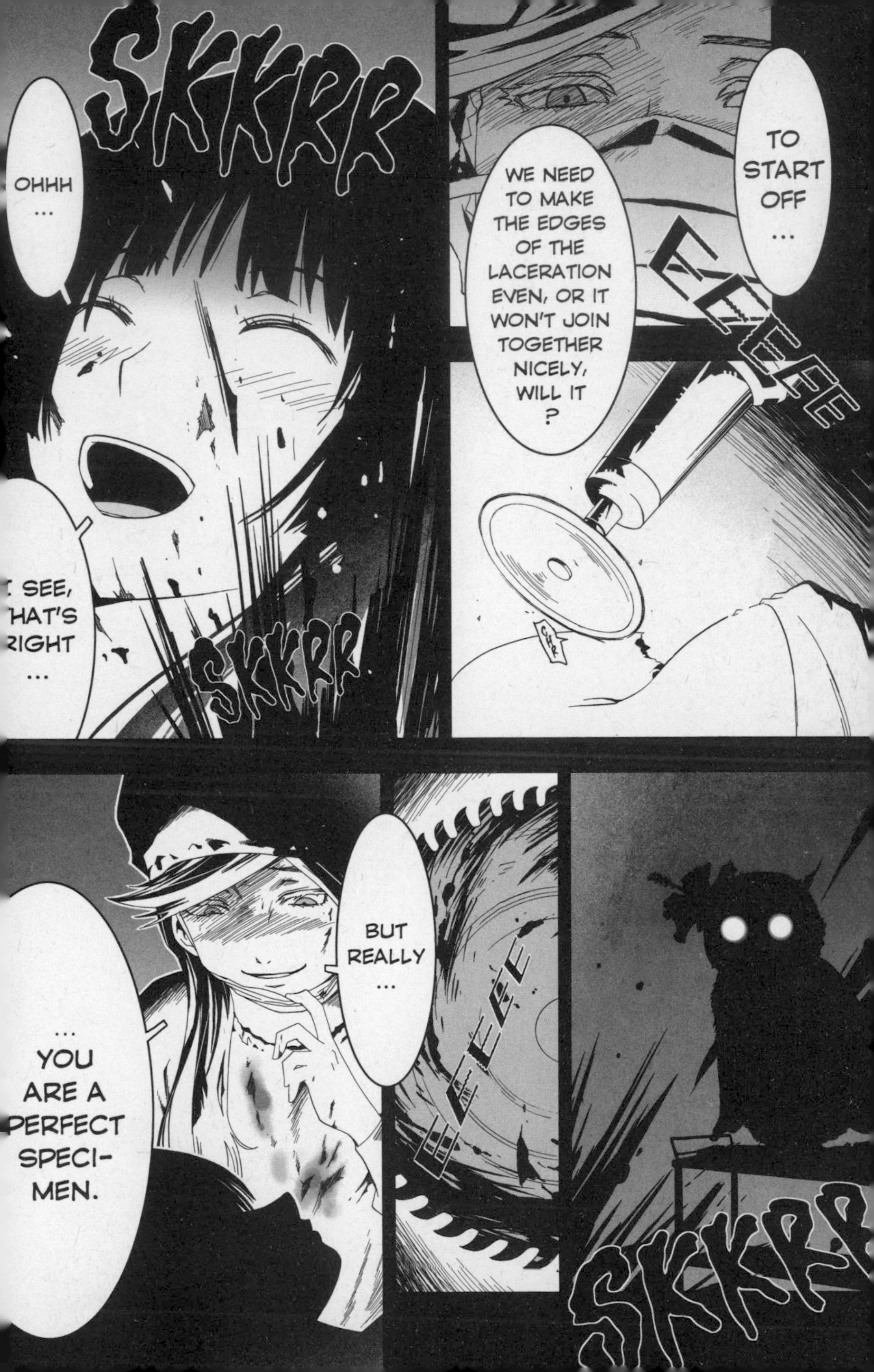
TO START OFF ...
WE NEED TO MAKE THE EDGES OF THE LACERATION EVEN, OR IT WON'T JOIN TOGETHER NICELY, WILL IT ?
EEEEE
CHR
SKKRR
OHHH ...
I SEE, THAT'S RIGHT ...
SKKRR
SKKRR
EEEEE
BUT REALLY ...
... YOU ARE A PERFECT SPECI-MEN.

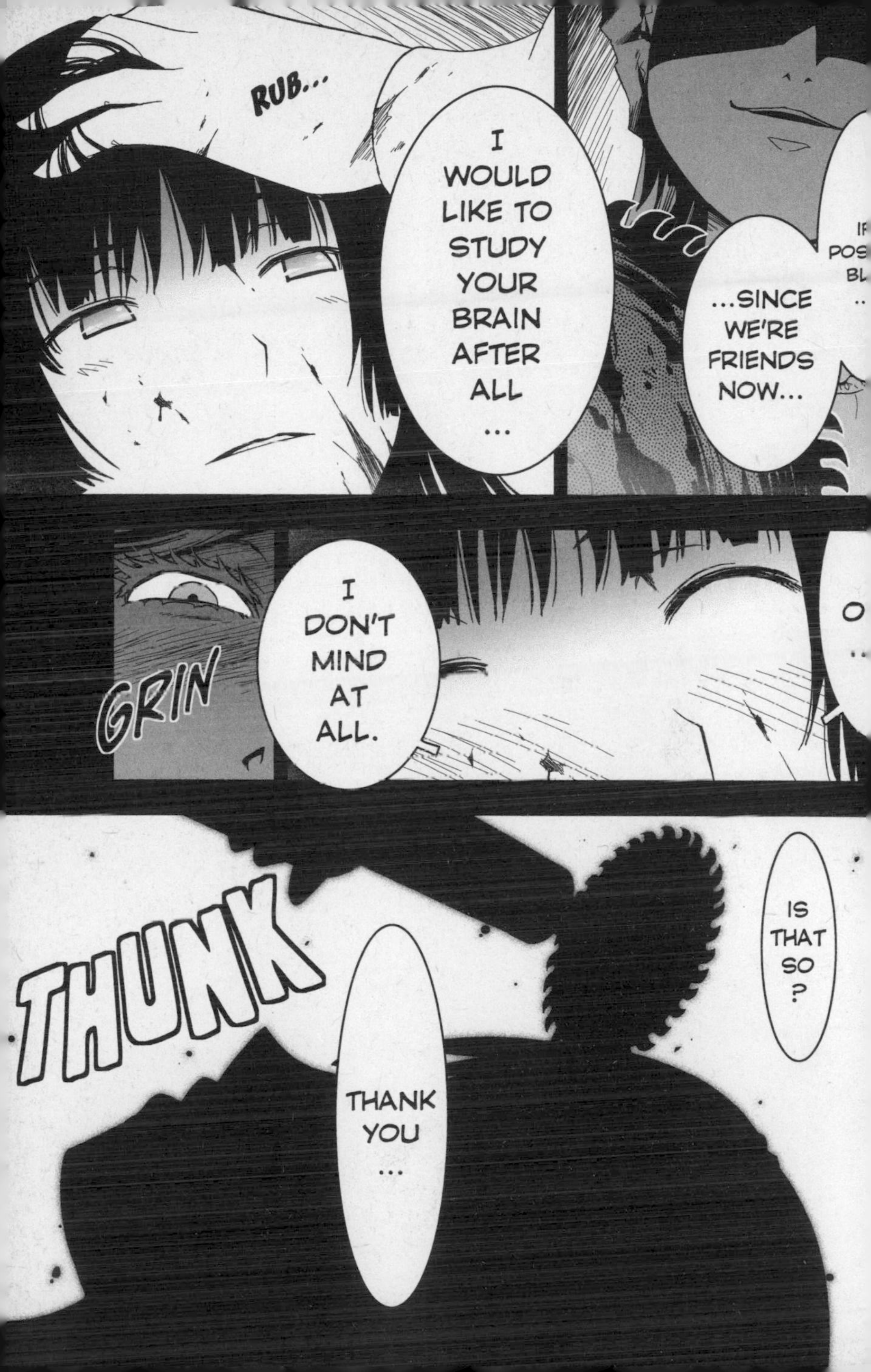
...SINCE WE'RE FRIENDS NOW...
I WOULD LIKE TO STUDY YOUR BRAIN AFTER ALL ...
RUB...
I DON'T MIND AT ALL.
GRIN
IS THAT SO?
THANK YOU ...
THUNK

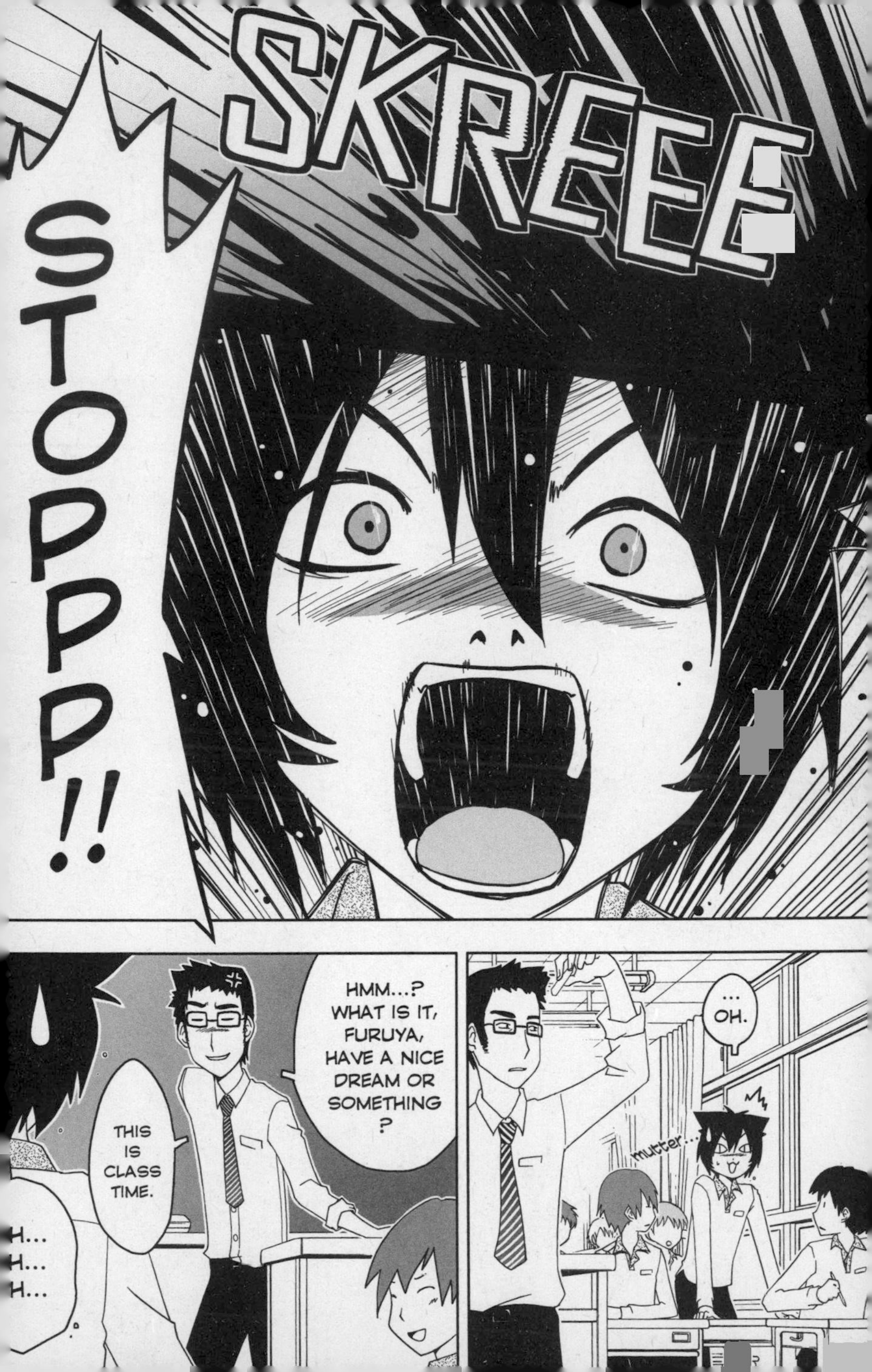
SKREEE
STOPP!!
... OH.
mutter...
HMM...? WHAT IS IT, FURUYA, HAVE A NICE DREAM OR SOMETHING?
THIS IS CLASS TIME.
H...
H...
H...

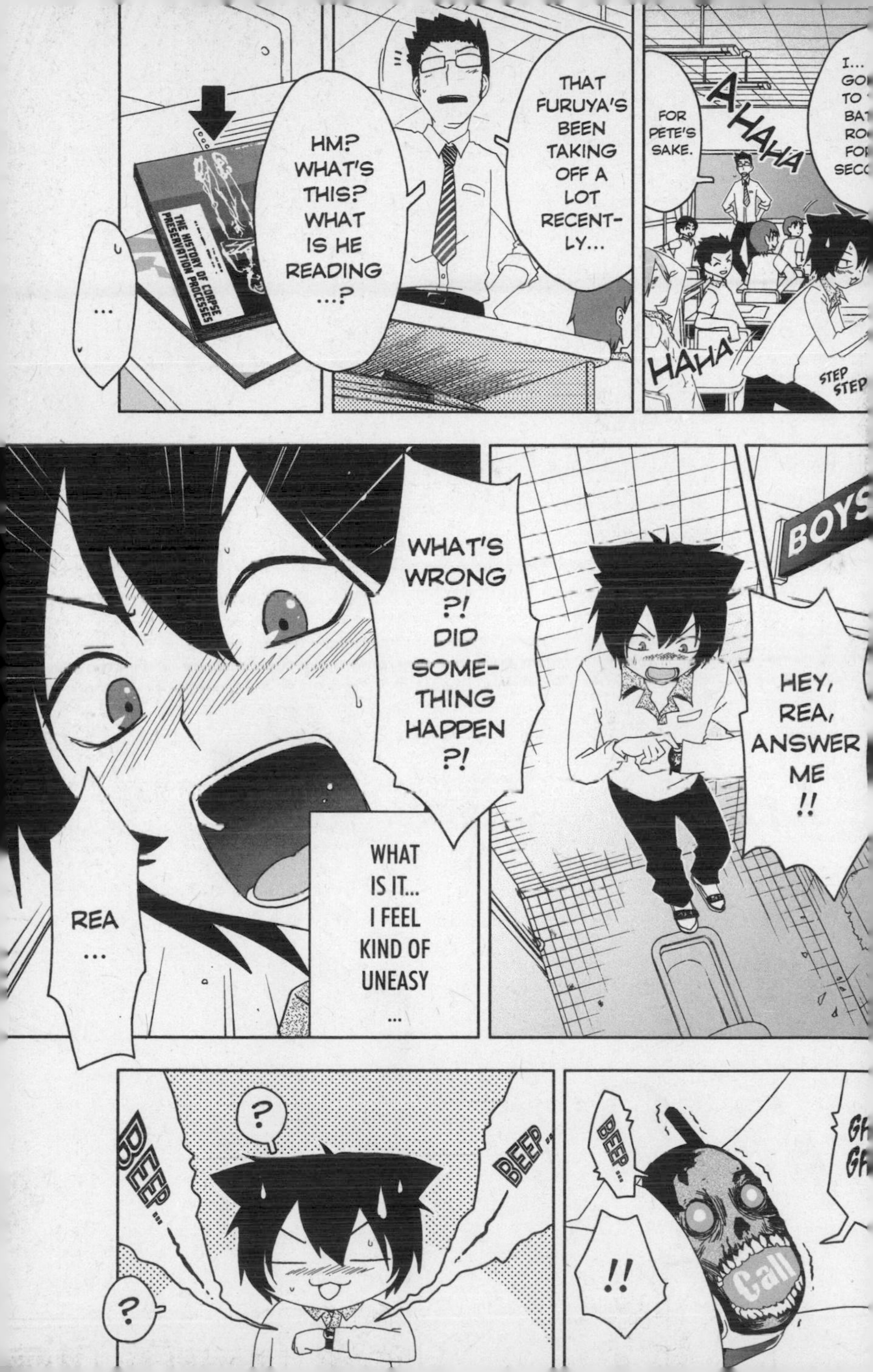
I...
AHAHAHA
FOR PETE'S SAKE.
HAHA
STEP STEP
THAT FURUYA'S BEEN TAKING OFF A LOT RECENTLY...
HM? WHAT'S THIS? WHAT IS HE READING ...?
THE HISTORY OF CORPSE PRESERVATION PROCESSES
...
BOYS
HEY, REA, ANSWER ME !!
WHAT'S WRONG ?! DID SOMETHING HAPPEN ?!
WHAT IS IT... I FEEL KIND OF UNEASY ...
REA ...
BEEP...
!!
Call
?
BEEP...
BEEP..
?

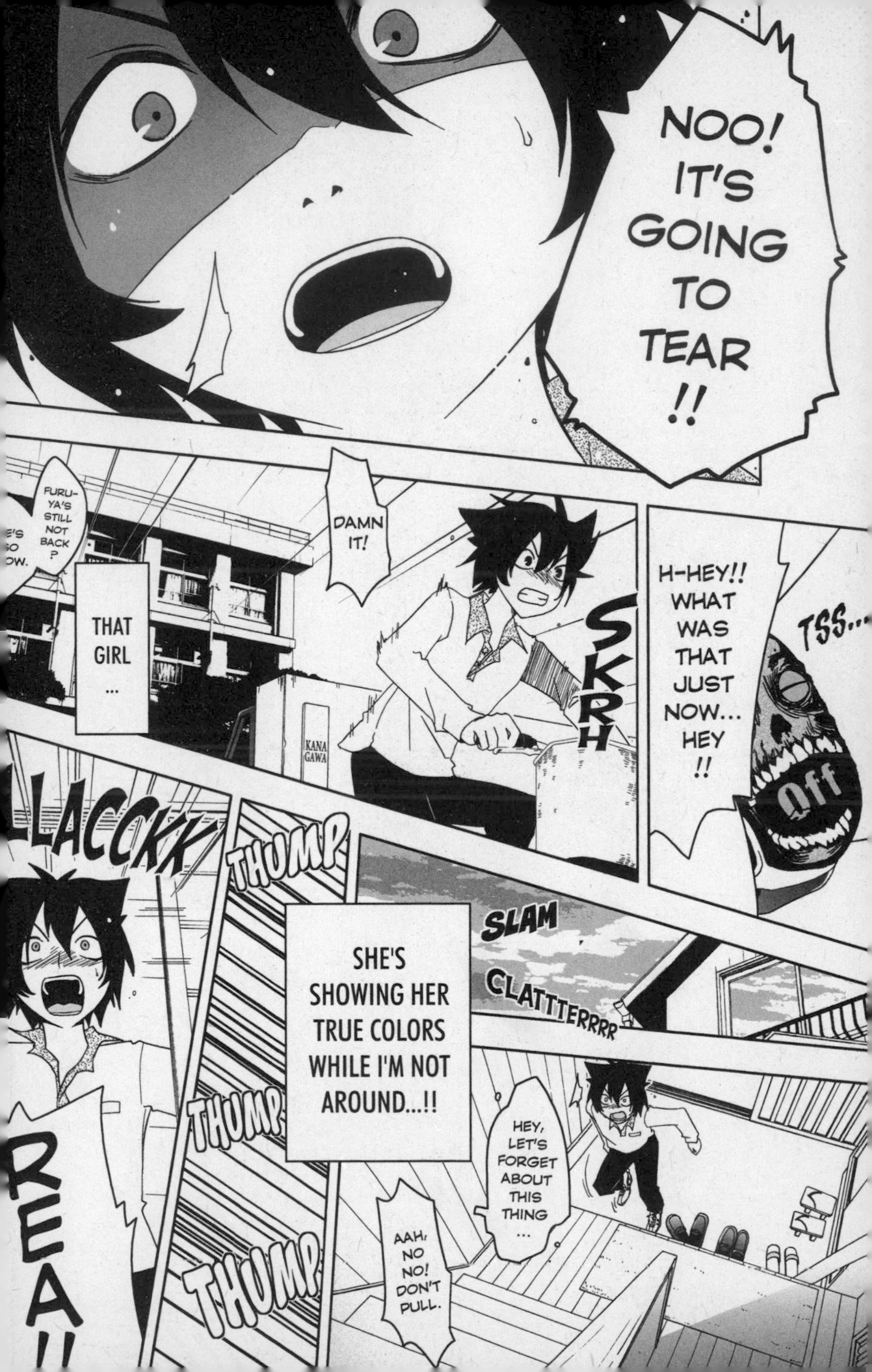
NOO! IT'S GOING TO TEAR !!
TSS...
H-HEY!! WHAT WAS THAT JUST NOW... HEY !!
SKRH
DAMN IT!
THAT GIRL ...
FURU-YA'S STILL NOT BACK ?
KANA GAWA
SLAM
CLATTTERRRR
SHE'S SHOWING HER TRUE COLORS WHILE I'M NOT AROUND...!!
HEY, LET'S FORGET ABOUT THIS THING ...
AAH, NO NO! DON'T PULL.
THUMP
THUMP
THUMP
LACCKK
REA!!

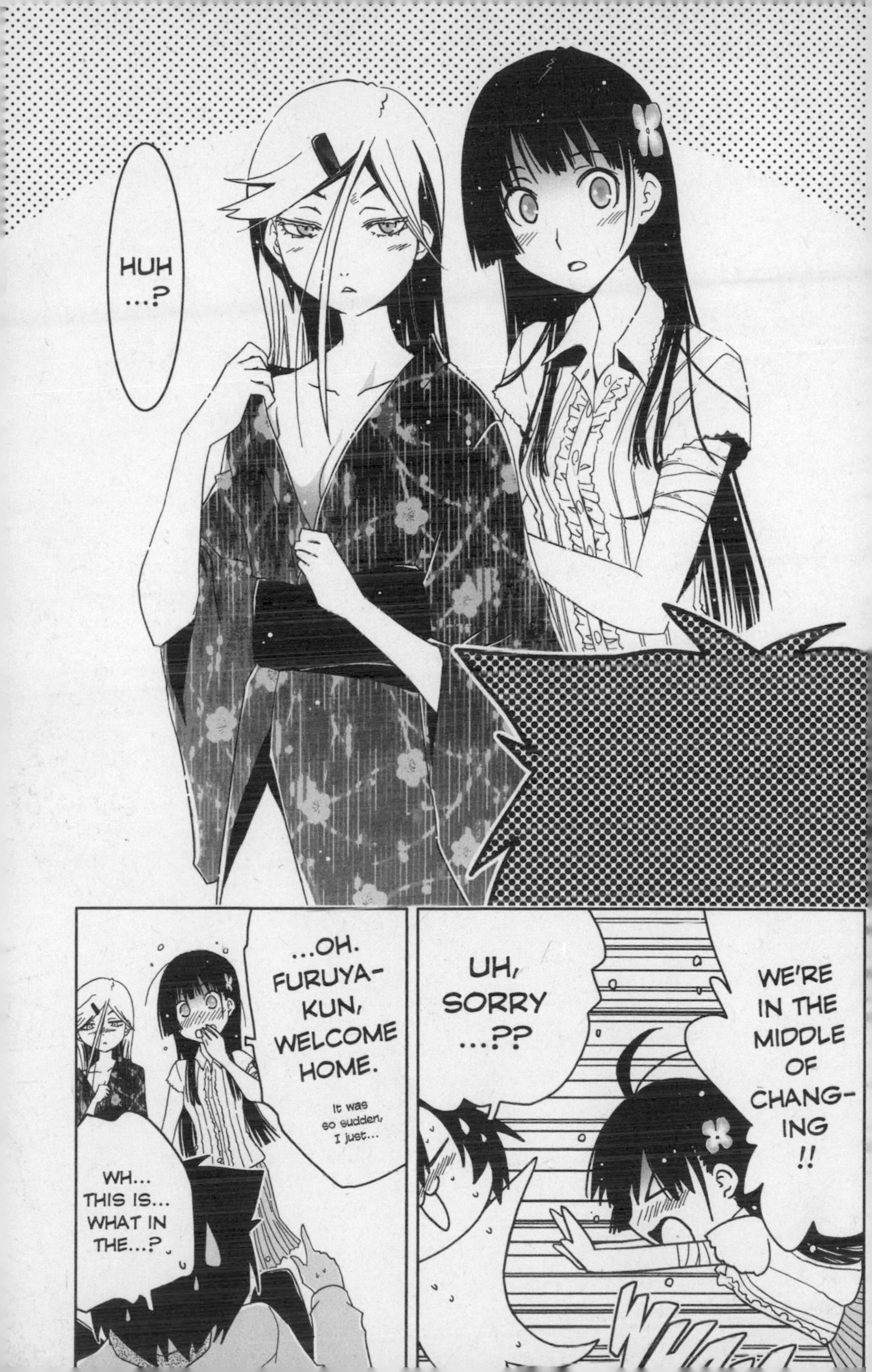
HUH ...?
WE'RE IN THE MIDDLE OF CHANG-ING !!
UH, SORRY ...??
...OH. FURUYA-KUN, WELCOME HOME.
It was so sudden, I just...
WH... THIS IS... WHAT IN THE...?

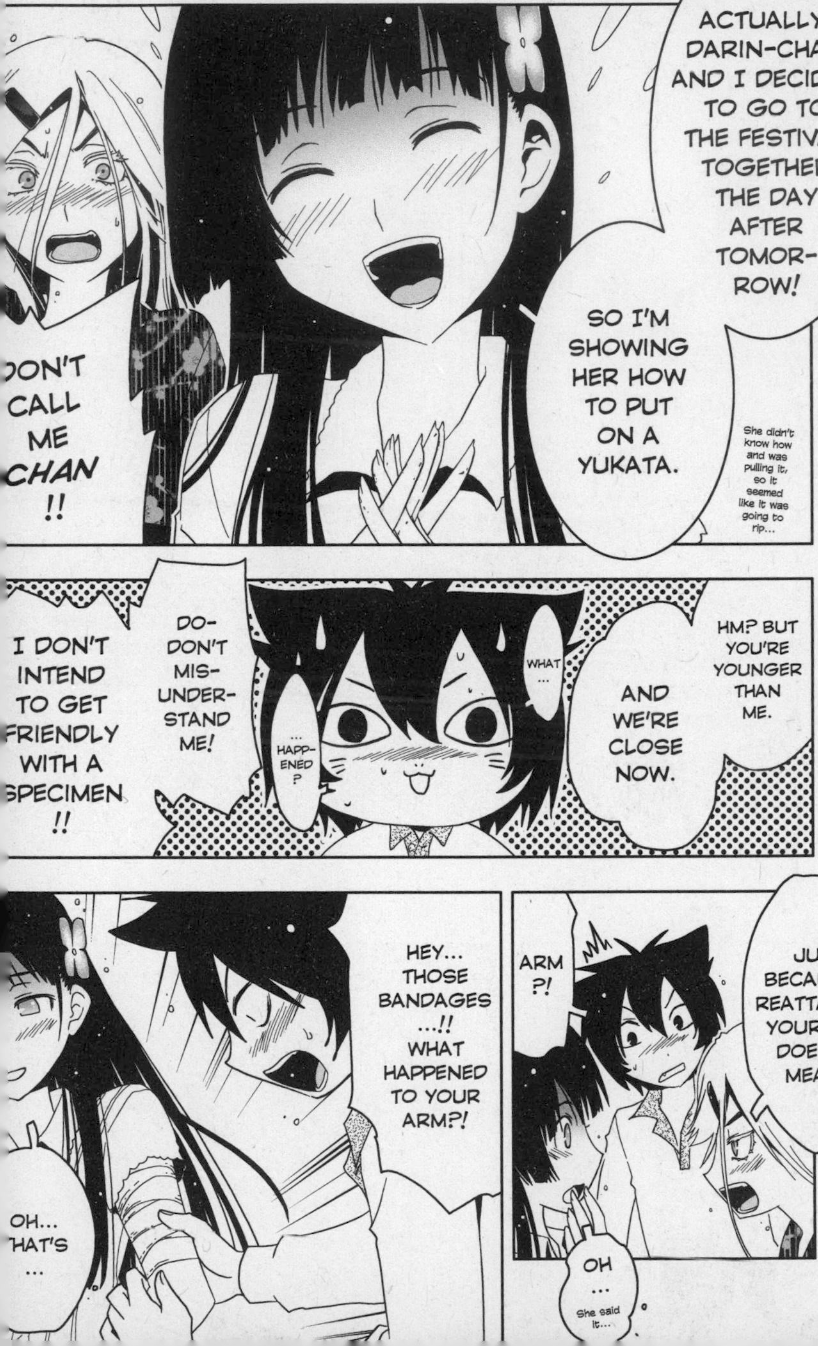
ACTUALLY, DARIN-CHAN AND I DECIDED TO GO TO THE FESTIVAL TOGETHER THE DAY AFTER TOMOR-ROW!
SO I'M SHOWING HER HOW TO PUT ON A YUKATA.
She didn't know how and was pulling it, so it seemed like it was going to rip...
DON'T CALL ME CHAN!!
HM? BUT YOU'RE YOUNGER THAN ME.
AND WE'RE CLOSE NOW.
WHAT...
...HAPP-ENED?
DO-DON'T MIS-UNDER-STAND ME!
I DON'T INTEND TO GET FRIENDLY WITH A SPECIMEN!!
JUST BECAUSE I REATTACHED YOUR ARM DOESN'T MEAN...
ARM?!
OH...
She said it...
HEY... THOSE BANDAGES...!! WHAT HAPPENED TO YOUR ARM?!
OH... THAT'S...

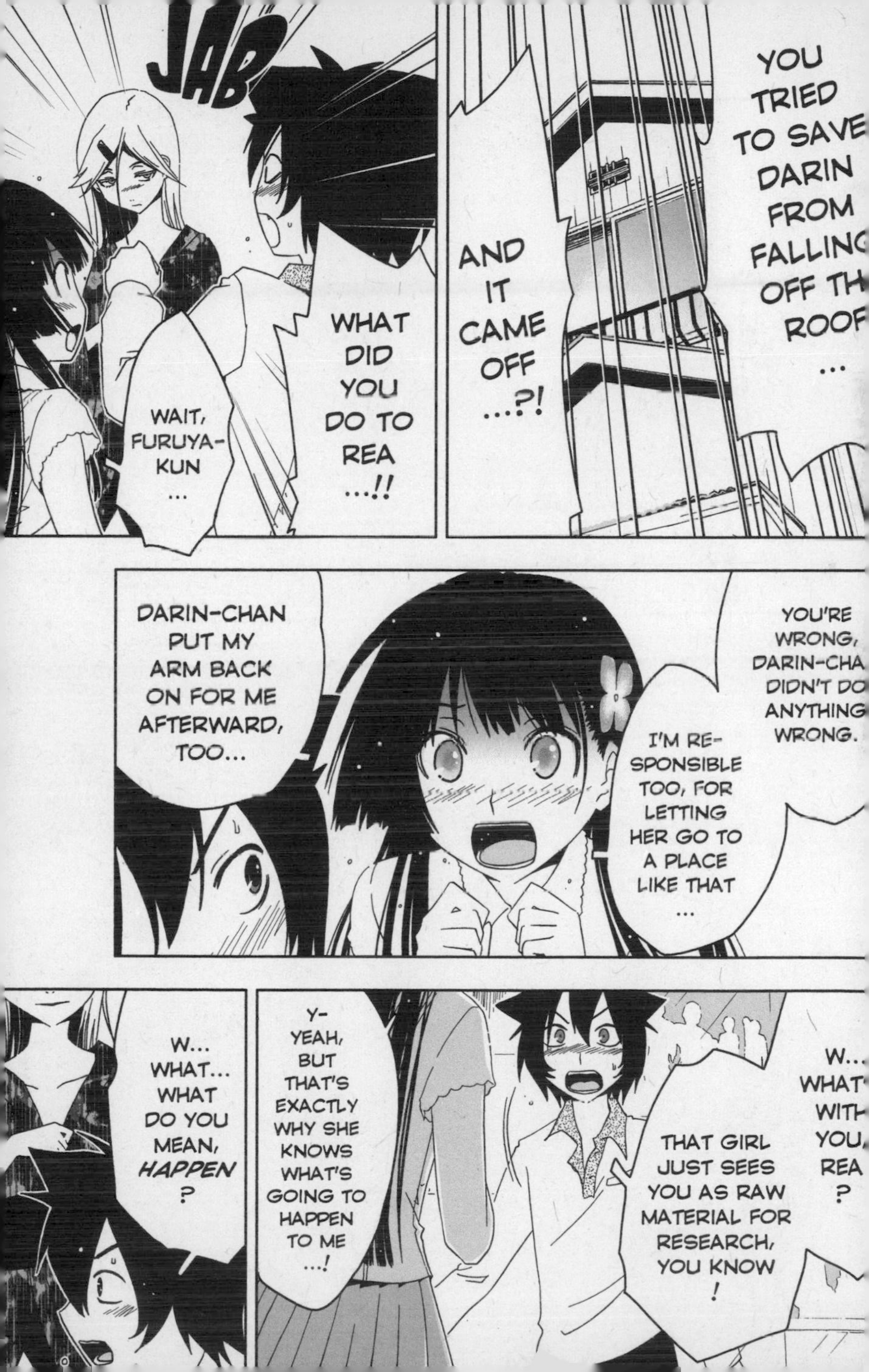
YOU TRIED TO SAVE DARIN FROM FALLING OFF TH ROOF ...
AND IT CAME OFF ...?!
JAB
WHAT DID YOU DO TO REA ...!!
WAIT, FURUYA-KUN ...
YOU'RE WRONG, DARIN-CHA DIDN'T DO ANYTHING WRONG.
I'M RE-SPONSIBLE TOO, FOR LETTING HER GO TO A PLACE LIKE THAT ...
DARIN-CHAN PUT MY ARM BACK ON FOR ME AFTERWARD, TOO...
W... WHAT WITH YOU, REA ?
THAT GIRL JUST SEES YOU AS RAW MATERIAL FOR RESEARCH, YOU KNOW !
Y-YEAH, BUT THAT'S EXACTLY WHY SHE KNOWS WHAT'S GOING TO HAPPEN TO ME ...!
W... WHAT... WHAT DO YOU MEAN, *HAPPEN* ?

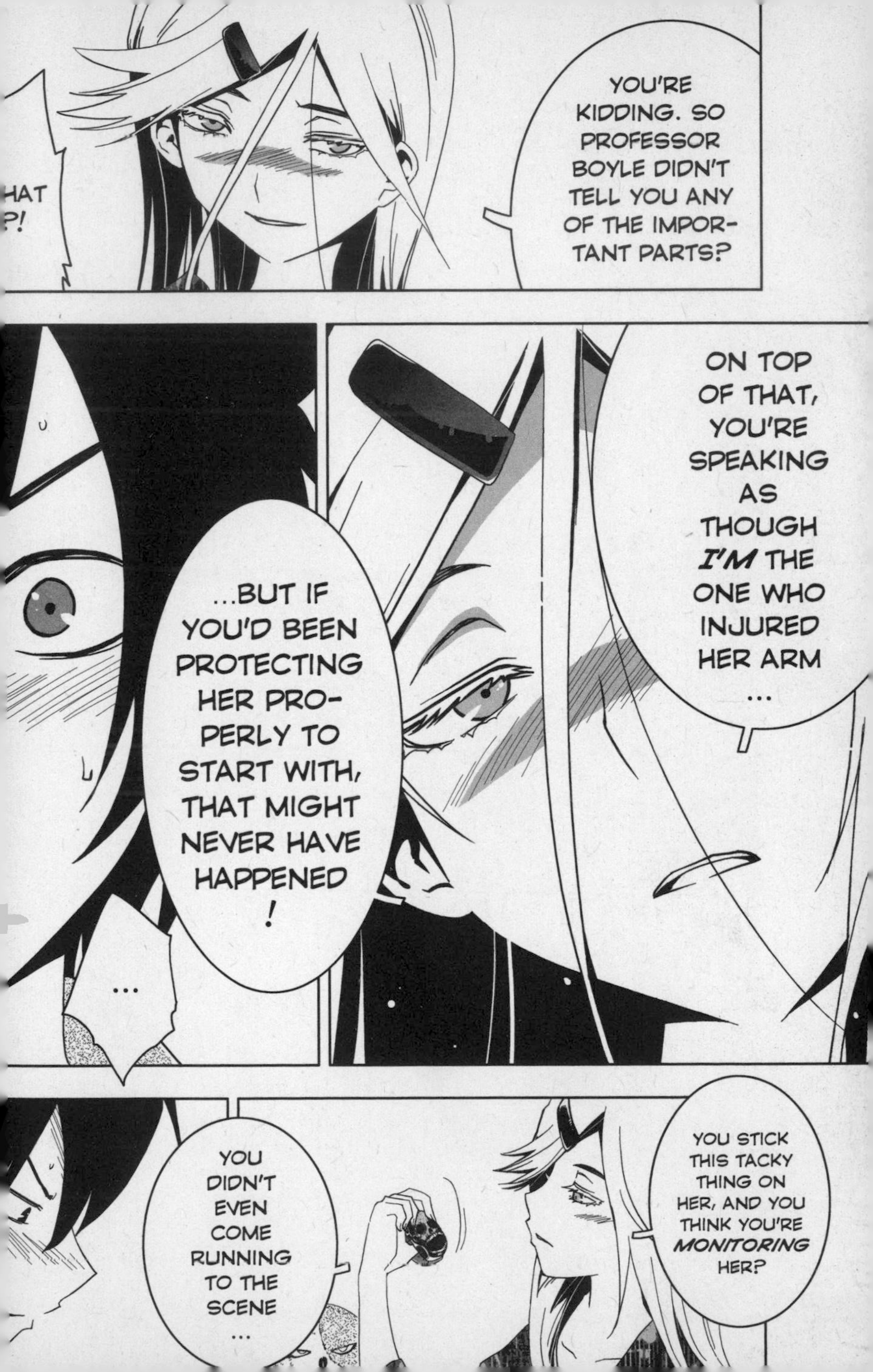
YOU'RE KIDDING. SO PROFESSOR BOYLE DIDN'T TELL YOU ANY OF THE IMPORTANT PARTS?
ON TOP OF THAT, YOU'RE SPEAKING AS THOUGH *I'M* THE ONE WHO INJURED HER ARM ...
...BUT IF YOU'D BEEN PROTECTING HER PROPERLY TO START WITH, THAT MIGHT NEVER HAVE HAPPENED !
...
YOU STICK THIS TACKY THING ON HER, AND YOU THINK YOU'RE *MONITORING* HER?
YOU DIDN'T EVEN COME RUNNING TO THE SCENE ...

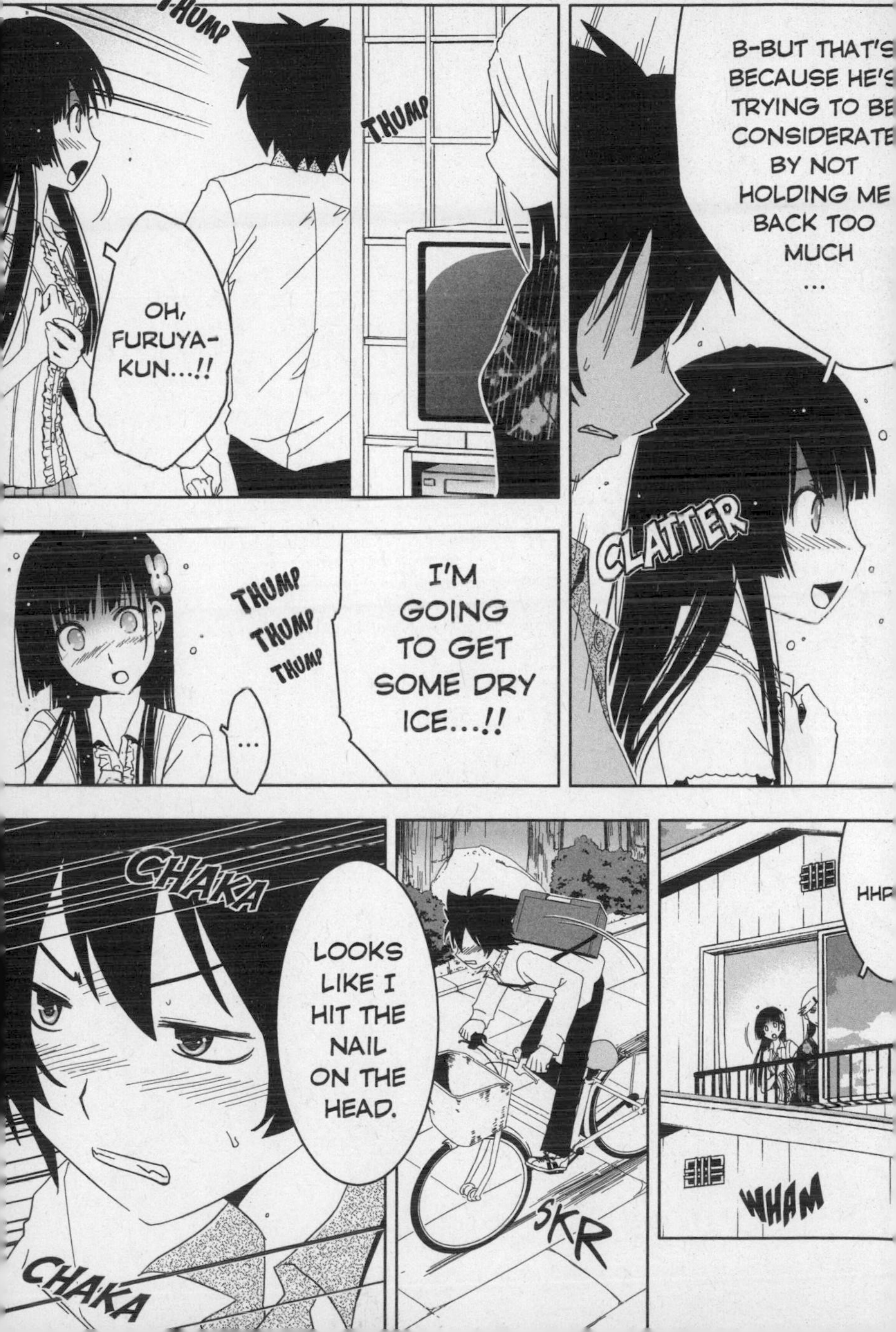
B-BUT THAT'S BECAUSE HE'S TRYING TO BE CONSIDERATE BY NOT HOLDING ME BACK TOO MUCH ...
CLATTER
THUMP
THUMP
OH, FURUYA-KUN...!!
I'M GOING TO GET SOME DRY ICE...!!
THUMP THUMP THUMP
...
HHP
WHAM
SKR
CHAKA
LOOKS LIKE I HIT THE NAIL ON THE HEAD.
CHAKA

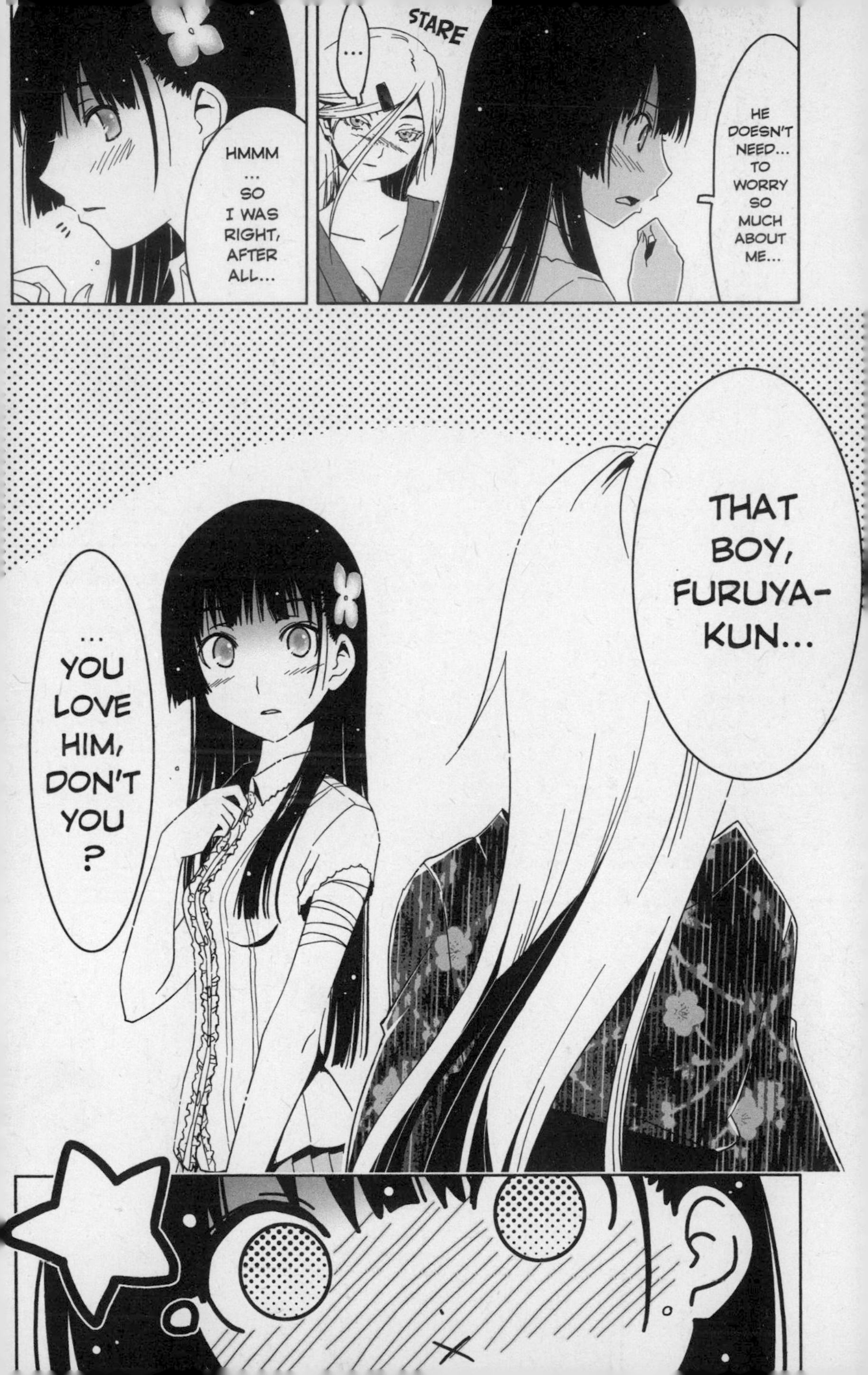
HE DOESN'T NEED... TO WORRY SO MUCH ABOUT ME...
STARE
...
HMMM ... SO I WAS RIGHT, AFTER ALL...
THAT BOY, FURUYA-KUN...
... YOU LOVE HIM, DON'T YOU ?

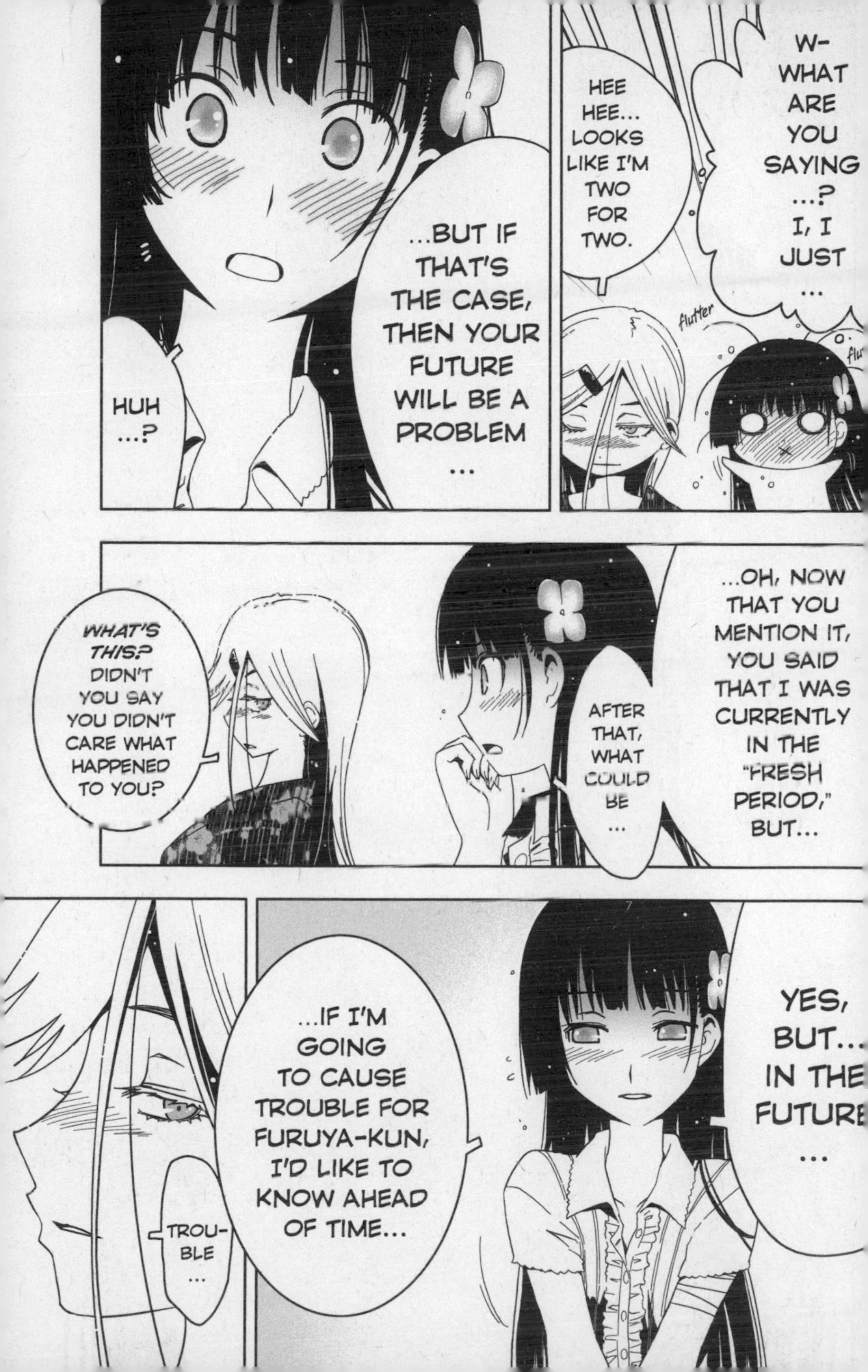
W-WHAT ARE YOU SAYING...? I, I JUST...
HEE HEE... LOOKS LIKE I'M TWO FOR TWO.
flutter
...BUT IF THAT'S THE CASE, THEN YOUR FUTURE WILL BE A PROBLEM...
HUH...?
...OH, NOW THAT YOU MENTION IT, YOU SAID THAT I WAS CURRENTLY IN THE "FRESH PERIOD," BUT...
AFTER THAT, WHAT COULD BE...
WHAT'S THIS? DIDN'T YOU SAY YOU DIDN'T CARE WHAT HAPPENED TO YOU?
YES, BUT... IN THE FUTURE...
...IF I'M GOING TO CAUSE TROUBLE FOR FURUYA-KUN, I'D LIKE TO KNOW AHEAD OF TIME...
TROU-BLE...

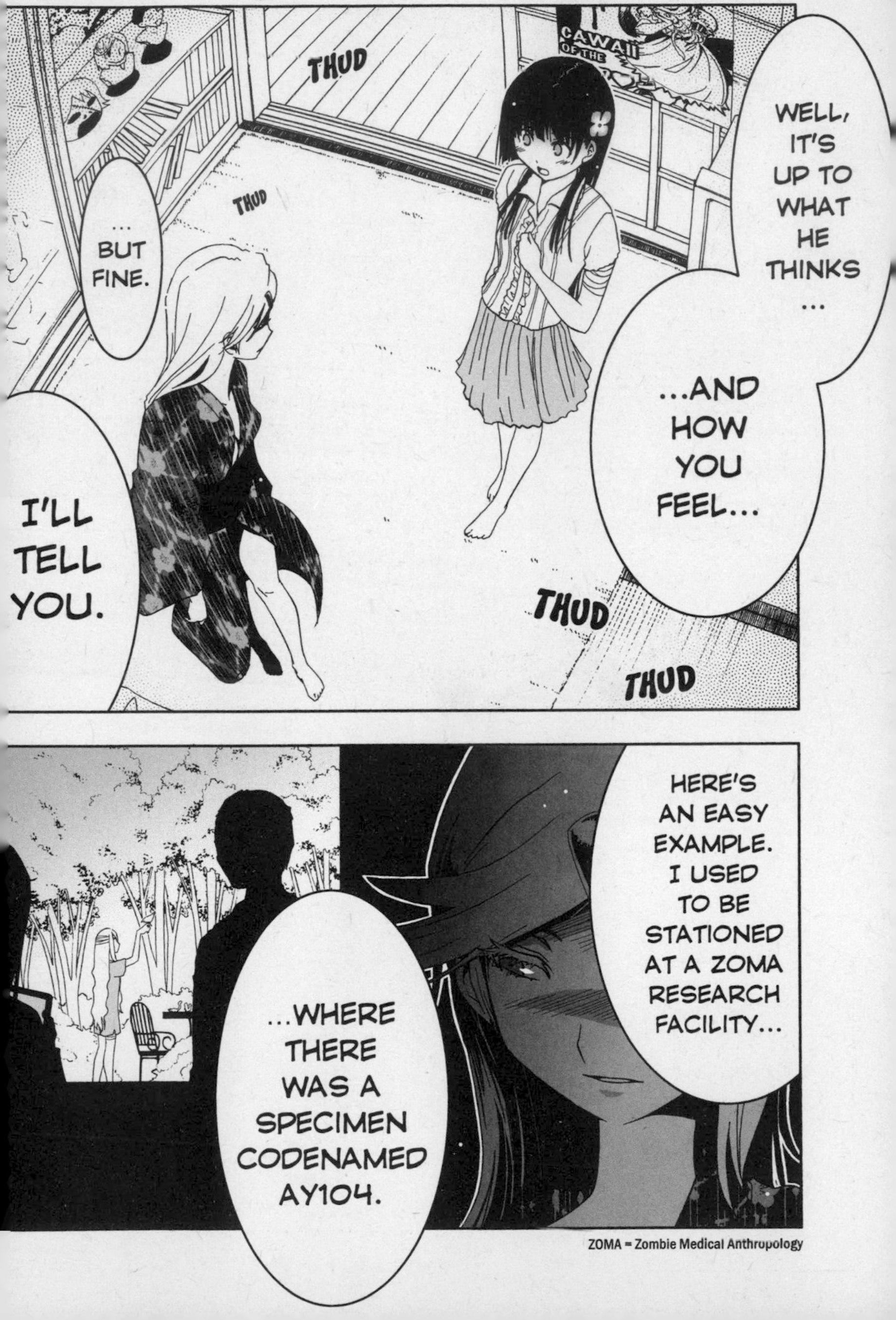
WELL, IT'S UP TO WHAT HE THINKS...
CAWAII OF THE
THUD
...AND HOW YOU FEEL...
THUD
...BUT FINE.
THUD
THUD
I'LL TELL YOU.
HERE'S AN EASY EXAMPLE. I USED TO BE STATIONED AT A ZOMA RESEARCH FACILITY...
...WHERE THERE WAS A SPECIMEN CODENAMED AY104.

ZOMA = Zombie Medical Anthropology

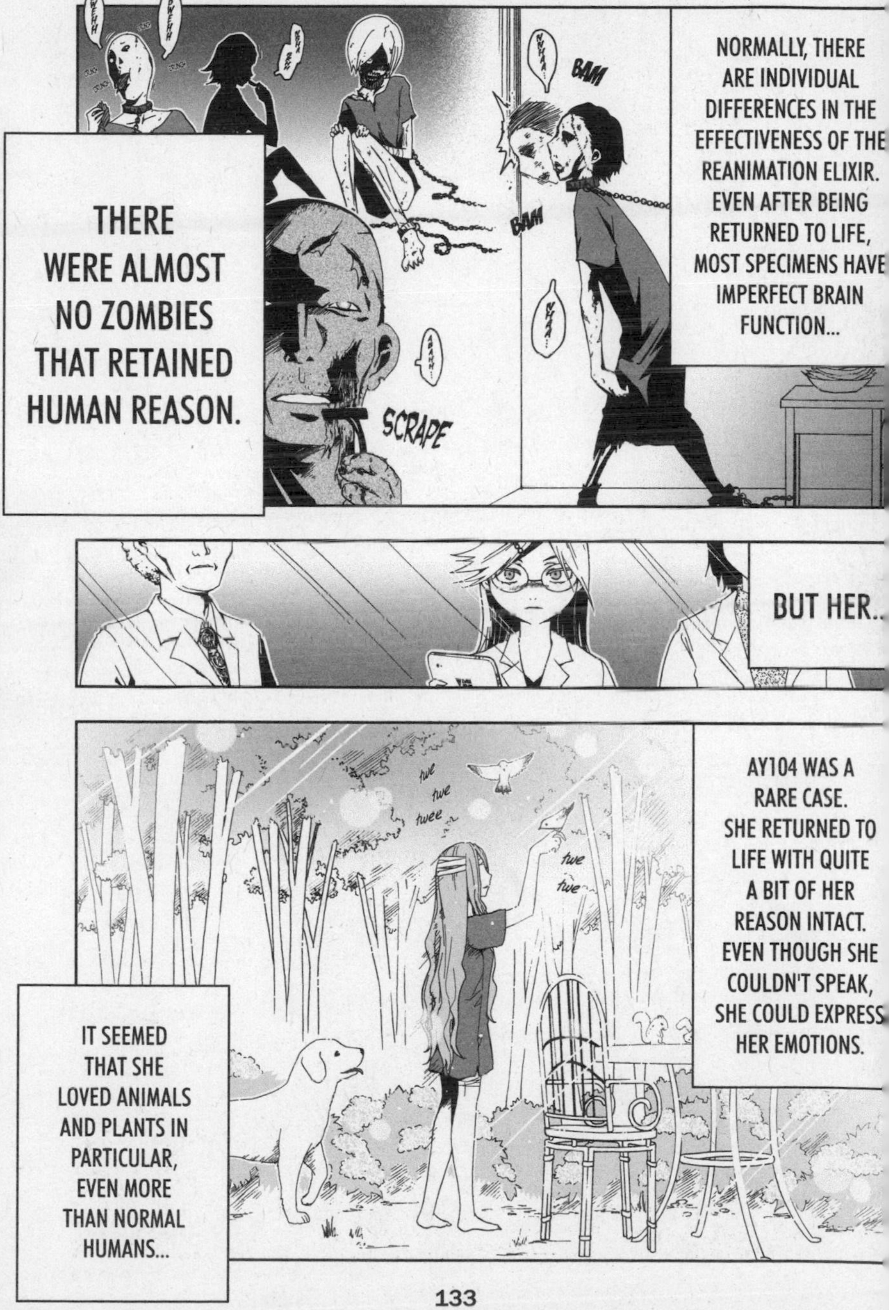
NORMALLY, THERE ARE INDIVIDUAL DIFFERENCES IN THE EFFECTIVENESS OF THE REANIMATION ELIXIR. EVEN AFTER BEING RETURNED TO LIFE, MOST SPECIMENS HAVE IMPERFECT BRAIN FUNCTION...
BAM
BAM
THERE WERE ALMOST NO ZOMBIES THAT RETAINED HUMAN REASON.
SCRAPE
BWEHH
BWEHH
BUT HER...
AY104 WAS A RARE CASE. SHE RETURNED TO LIFE WITH QUITE A BIT OF HER REASON INTACT. EVEN THOUGH SHE COULDN'T SPEAK, SHE COULD EXPRESS HER EMOTIONS.
twe
twe
twee
twe
twe
IT SEEMED THAT SHE LOVED ANIMALS AND PLANTS IN PARTICULAR, EVEN MORE THAN NORMAL HUMANS...

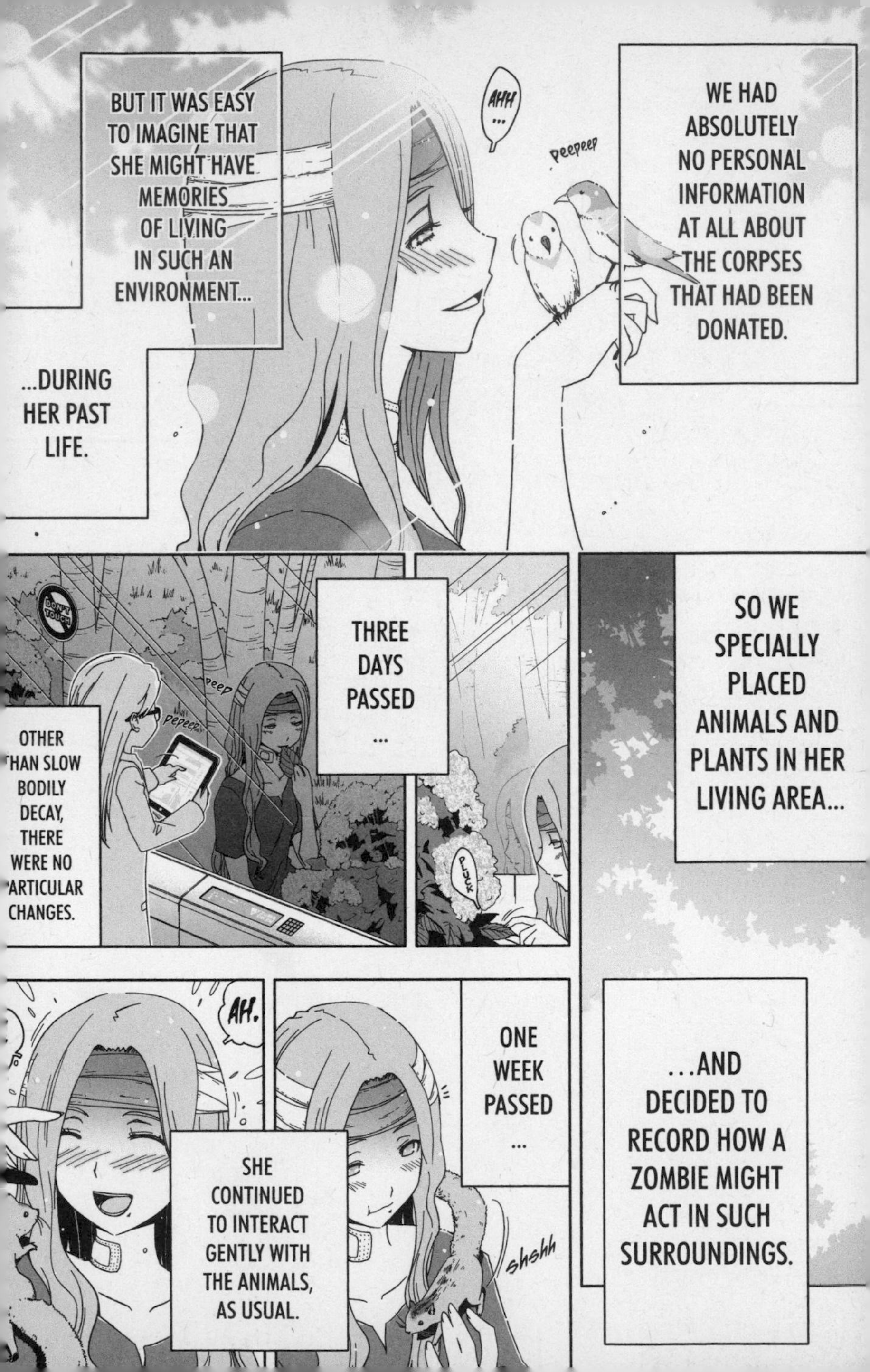
WE HAD ABSOLUTELY NO PERSONAL INFORMATION AT ALL ABOUT THE CORPSES THAT HAD BEEN DONATED.
peepeep
AHH ...
BUT IT WAS EASY TO IMAGINE THAT SHE MIGHT HAVE MEMORIES OF LIVING IN SUCH AN ENVIRONMENT...
...DURING HER PAST LIFE.
SO WE SPECIALLY PLACED ANIMALS AND PLANTS IN HER LIVING AREA...
PLUCK
THREE DAYS PASSED ...
DON'T TOUCH
peep
pepeep
OTHER HAN SLOW BODILY DECAY, THERE WERE NO ARTICULAR CHANGES.
...AND DECIDED TO RECORD HOW A ZOMBIE MIGHT ACT IN SUCH SURROUNDINGS.
ONE WEEK PASSED ...
shshh
AH.
SHE CONTINUED TO INTERACT GENTLY WITH THE ANIMALS, AS USUAL.

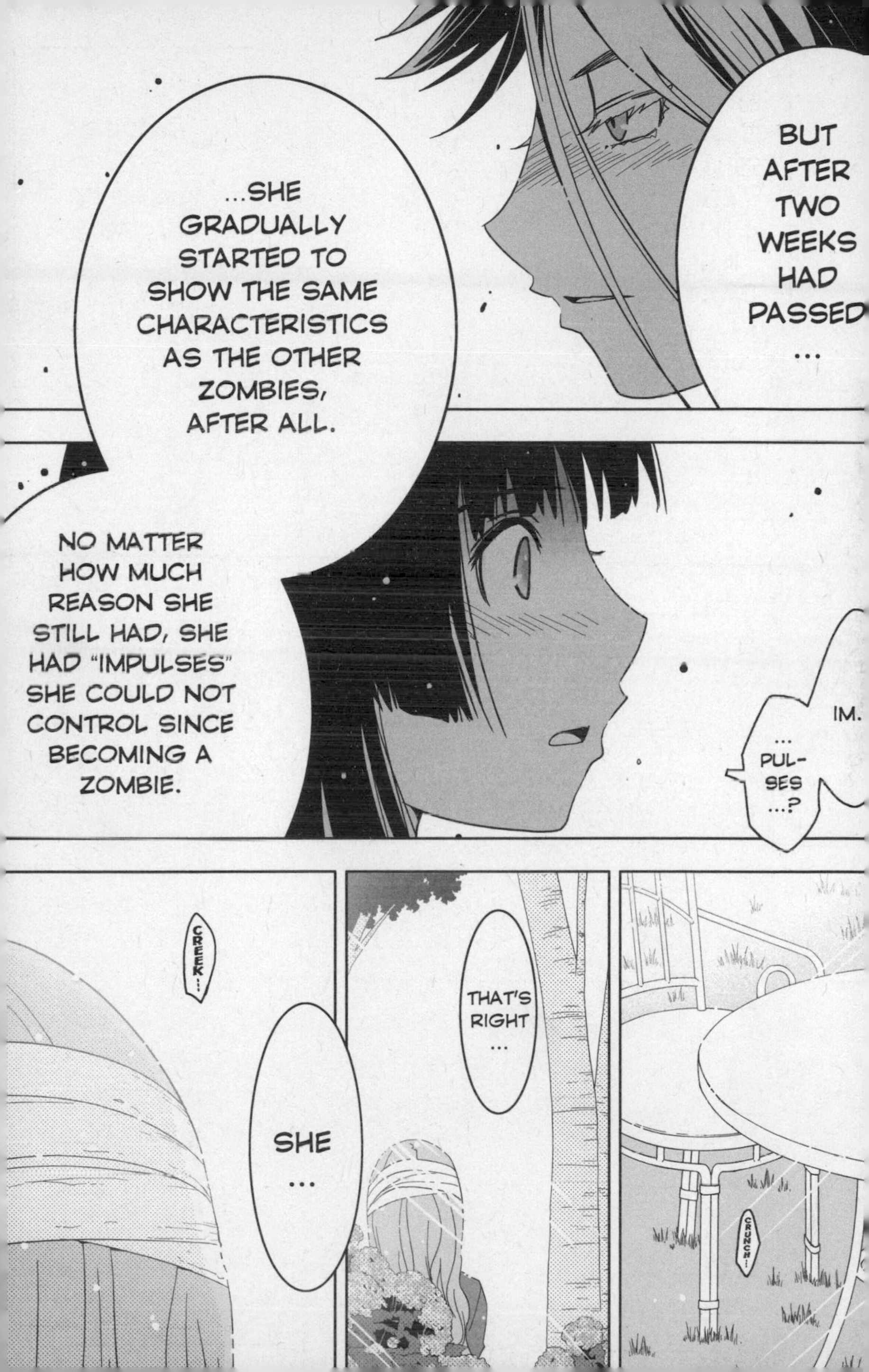
BUT AFTER TWO WEEKS HAD PASSED...
...SHE GRADUALLY STARTED TO SHOW THE SAME CHARACTERISTICS AS THE OTHER ZOMBIES, AFTER ALL.
NO MATTER HOW MUCH REASON SHE STILL HAD, SHE HAD "IMPULSES" SHE COULD NOT CONTROL SINCE BECOMING A ZOMBIE.
IM... PUL-SES...?
CRUNCH...
THAT'S RIGHT...
SHE...
CREEK...

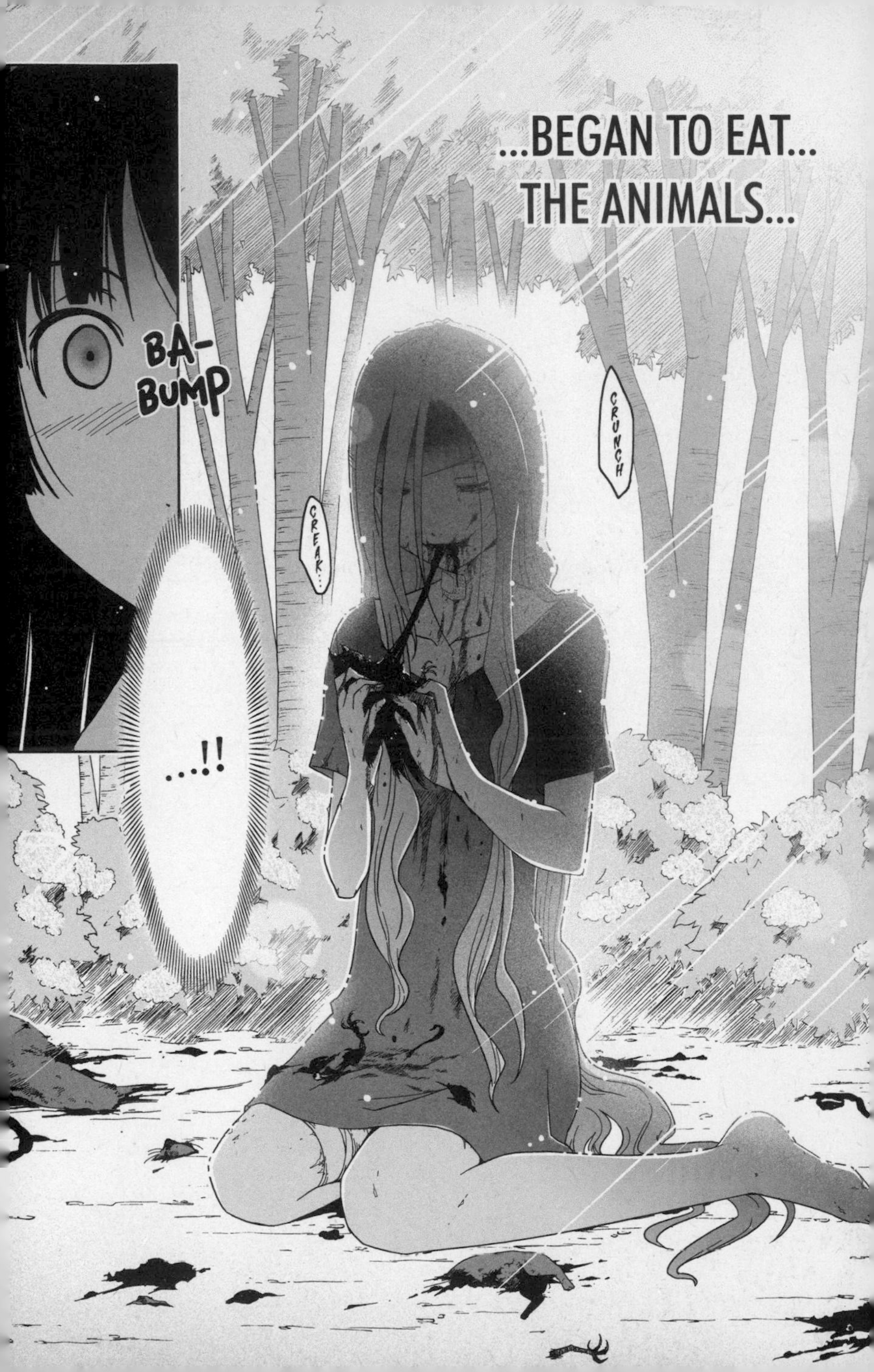
...BEGAN TO EAT... THE ANIMALS...
CRUNCH
CREAK...
BA-BUMP
...!!

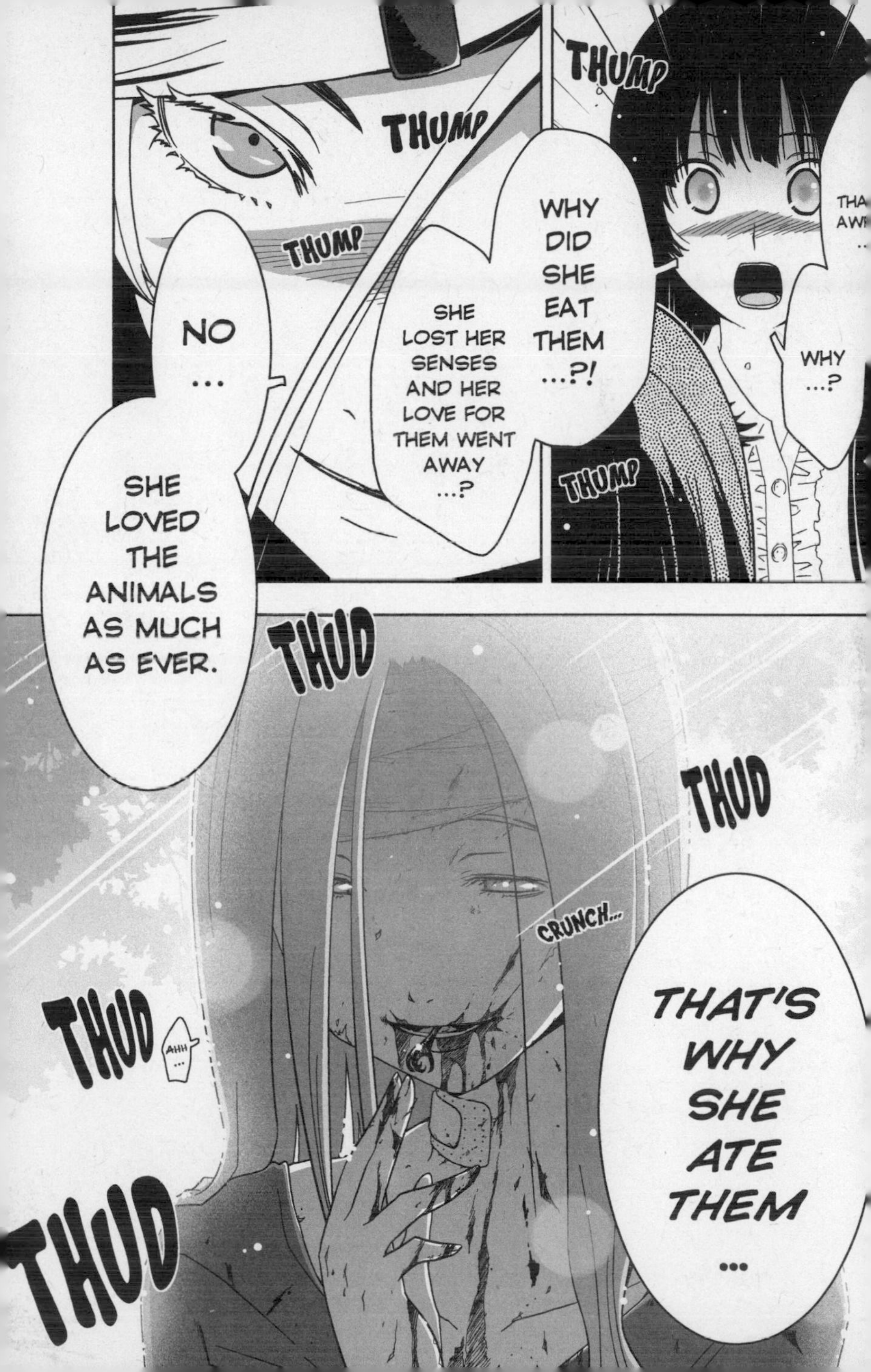
THUMP
WHY ...?
WHY DID SHE EAT THEM ...?!
THUMP
SHE LOST HER SENSES AND HER LOVE FOR THEM WENT AWAY ...?
THUMP
THUMP
NO ...
SHE LOVED THE ANIMALS AS MUCH AS EVER.
THUD
THUD
THAT'S WHY SHE ATE THEM ...
CRUNCH...
THUD
AHH ...
THUD

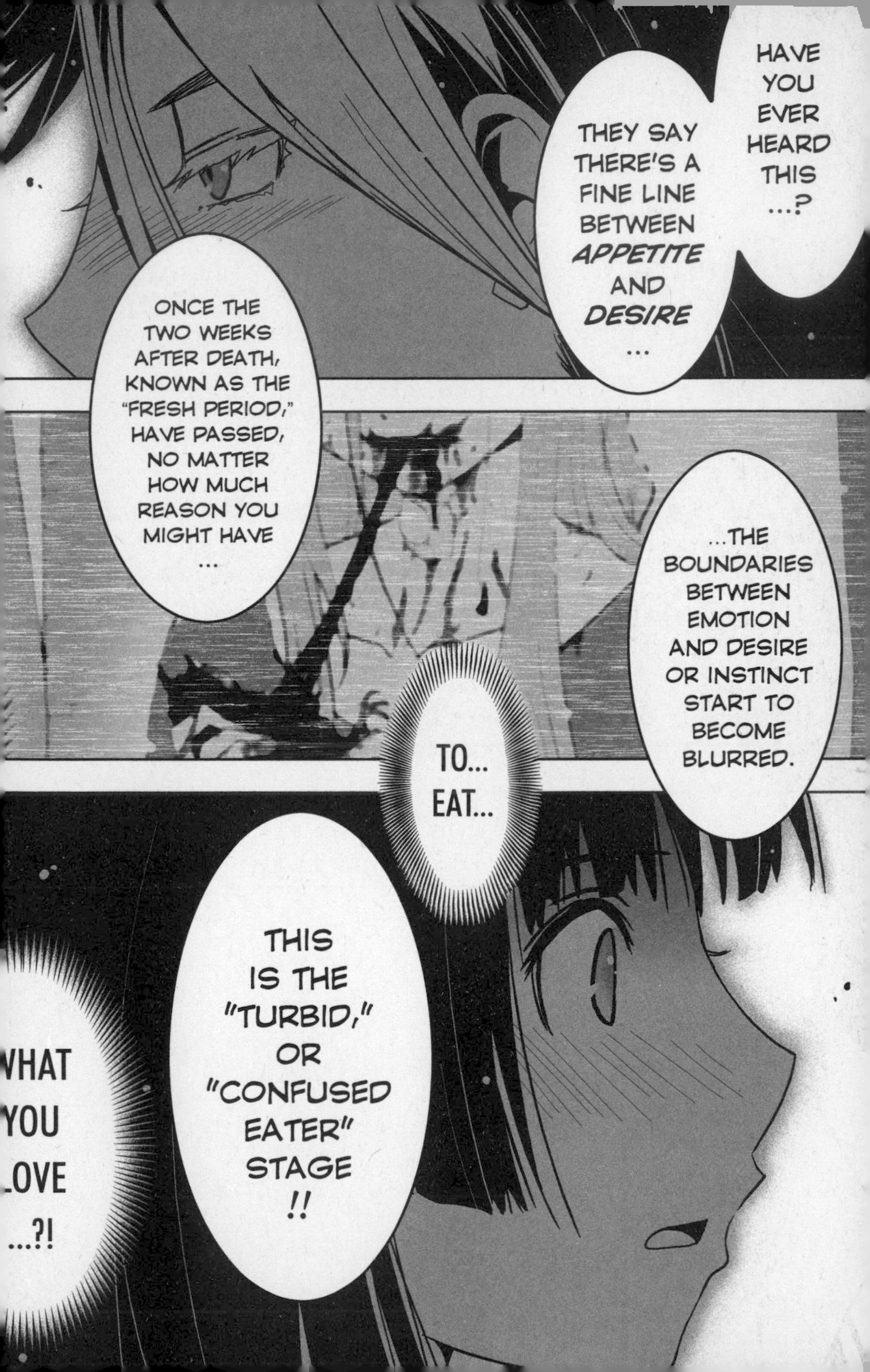
HAVE YOU EVER HEARD THIS ...?
THEY SAY THERE'S A FINE LINE BETWEEN *APPETITE* AND *DESIRE* ...
ONCE THE TWO WEEKS AFTER DEATH, KNOWN AS THE "FRESH PERIOD," HAVE PASSED, NO MATTER HOW MUCH REASON YOU MIGHT HAVE ...
...THE BOUNDARIES BETWEEN EMOTION AND DESIRE OR INSTINCT START TO BECOME BLURRED.
TO... EAT...
THIS IS THE "TURBID," OR "CONFUSED EATER" STAGE !!
VHAT YOU OVE ...?!

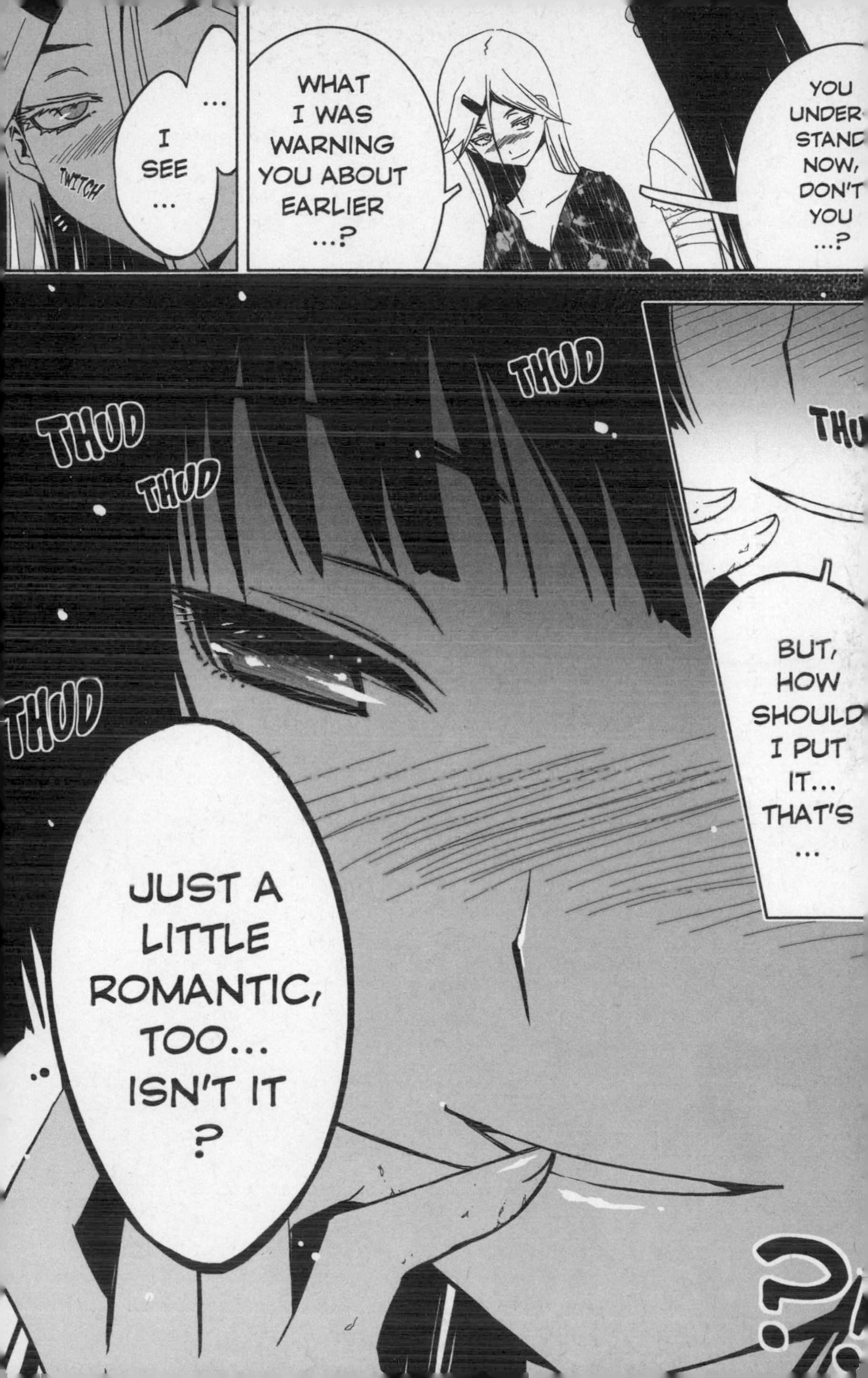
YOU UNDERSTAND NOW, DON'T YOU ...?
WHAT I WAS WARNING YOU ABOUT EARLIER ...?
... I SEE ...
TWITCH
THU
BUT, HOW SHOULD I PUT IT... THAT'S ...
THUD
THUD
THUD
THUD
JUST A LITTLE ROMANTIC, TOO... ISN'T IT ?
?!

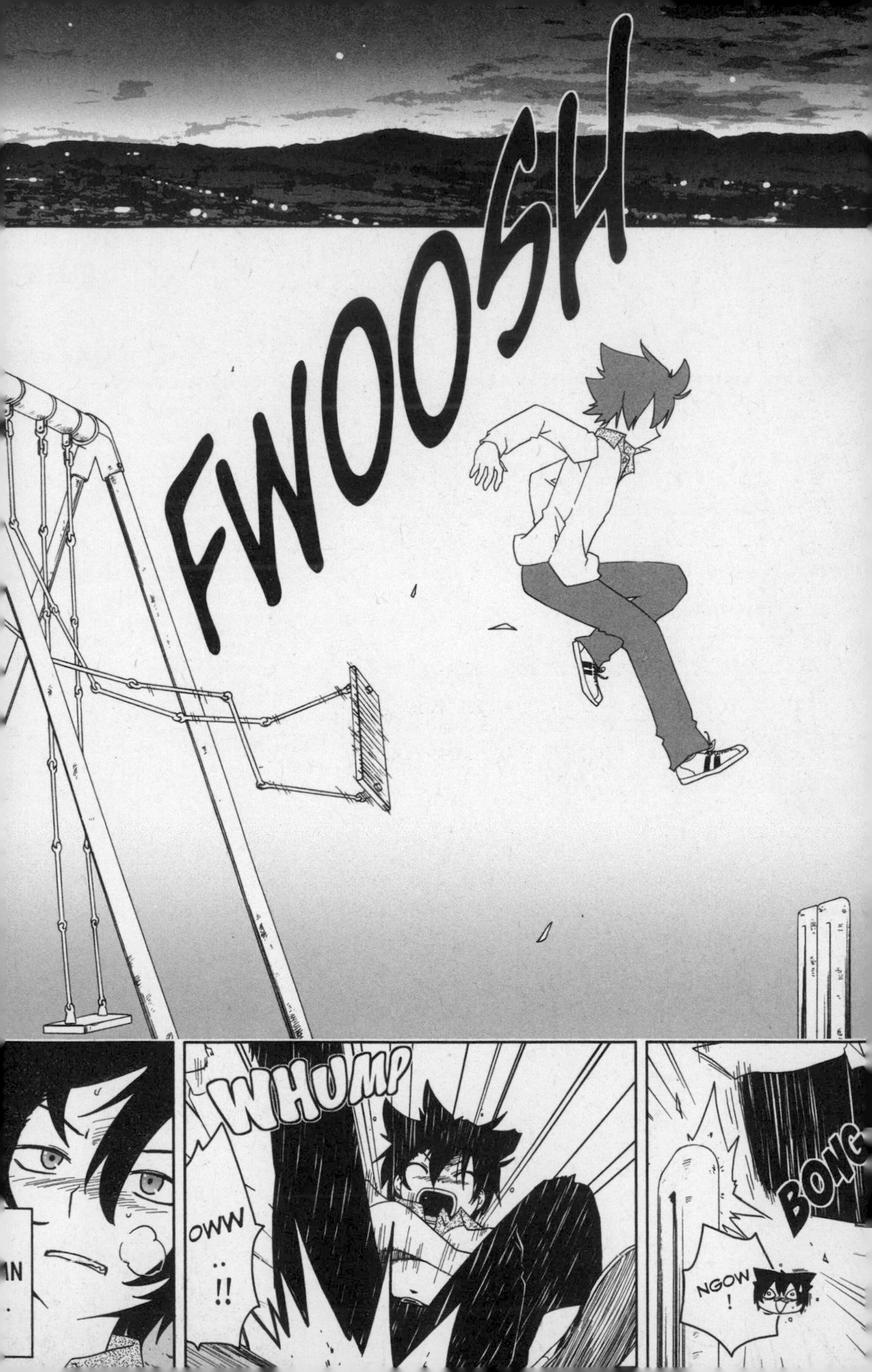
FWOOSH
BONG
NGOW!
WHUMP
OWW..!!

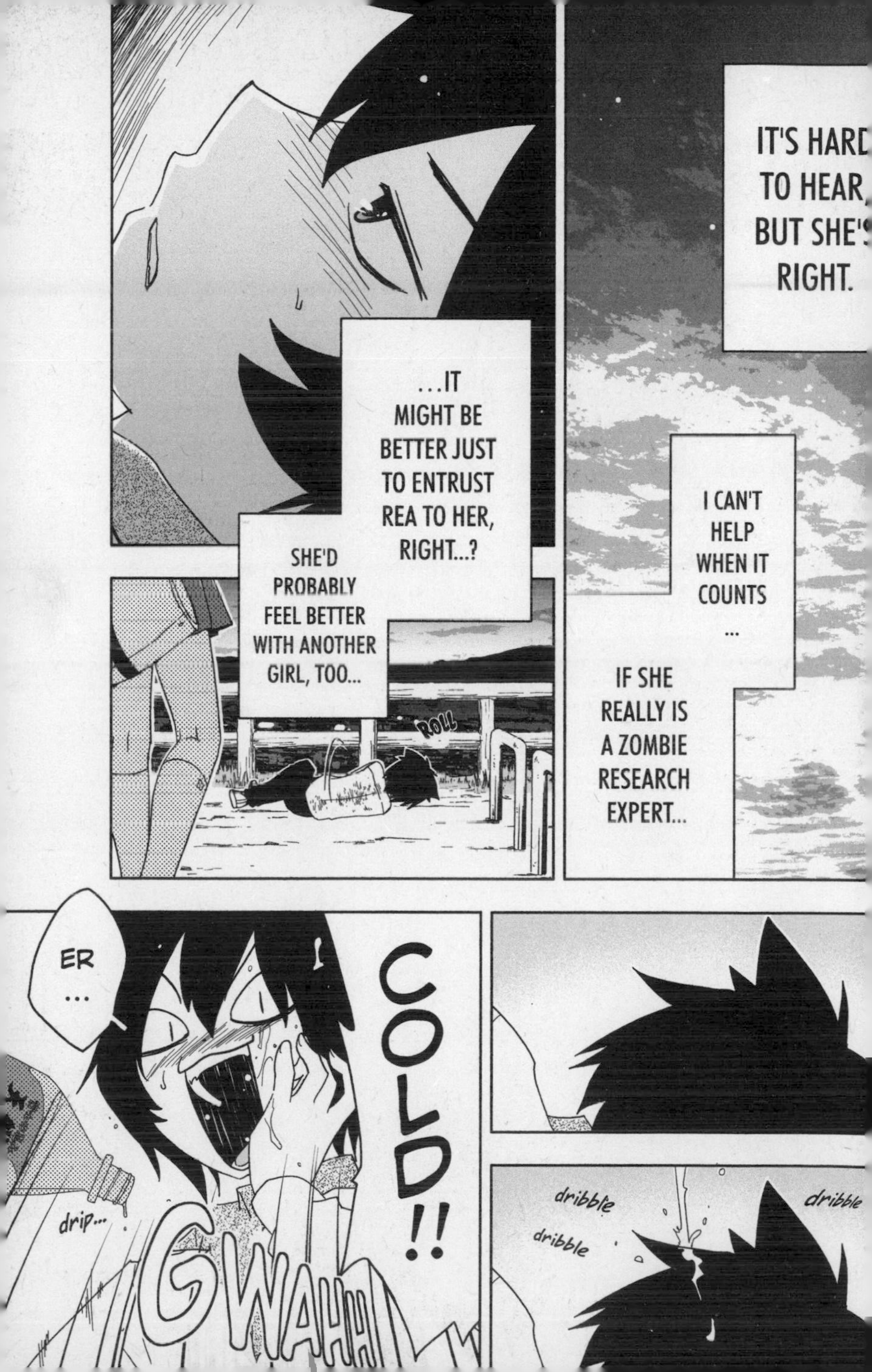
IT'S HARD TO HEAR, BUT SHE'S RIGHT.
I CAN'T HELP WHEN IT COUNTS...
IF SHE REALLY IS A ZOMBIE RESEARCH EXPERT...
...IT MIGHT BE BETTER JUST TO ENTRUST REA TO HER, RIGHT...?
SHE'D PROBABLY FEEL BETTER WITH ANOTHER GIRL, TOO...
ROLL
dribble
dribble
dribble
ER...
COLD!!
GWAHH
drip...

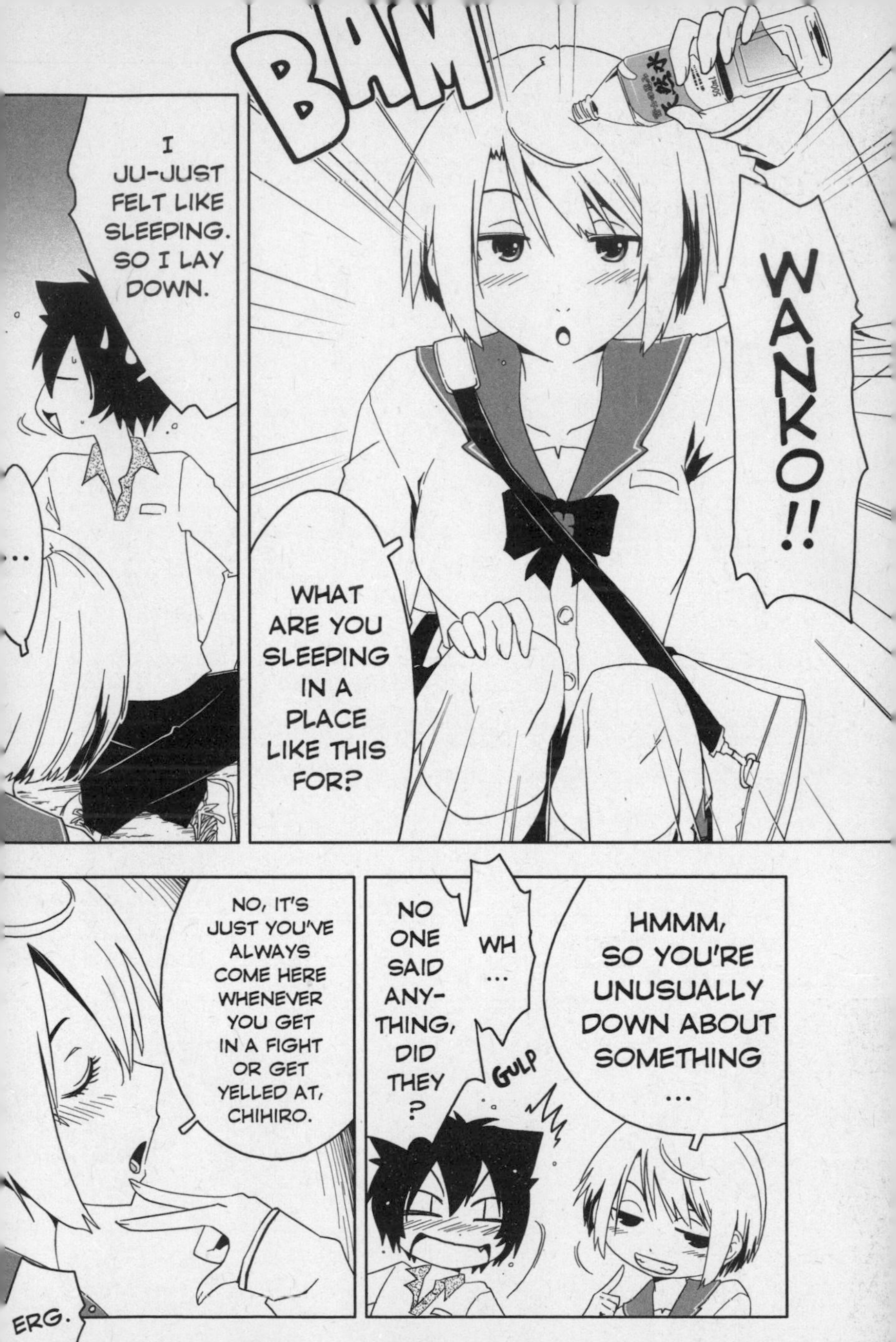
BAM
WANKO!!
WHAT ARE YOU SLEEPING IN A PLACE LIKE THIS FOR?
I JU-JUST FELT LIKE SLEEPING. SO I LAY DOWN.
...
HMMM, SO YOU'RE UNUSUALLY DOWN ABOUT SOMETHING ...
WH ...
GULP
NO ONE SAID ANY-THING, DID THEY ?
NO, IT'S JUST YOU'VE ALWAYS COME HERE WHENEVER YOU GET IN A FIGHT OR GET YELLED AT, CHIHIRO.
ERG.

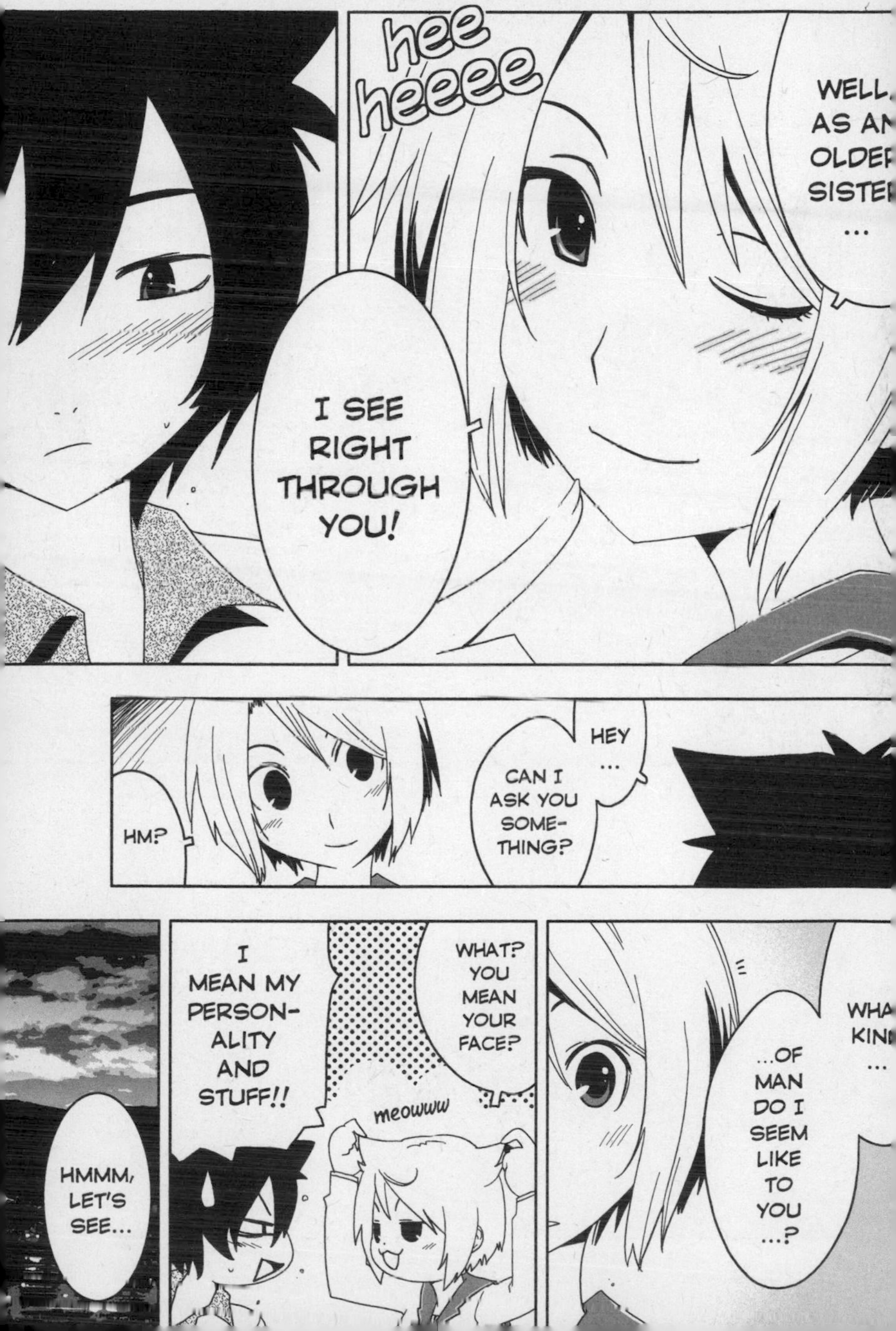
WELL, AS AN OLDER SISTER...
hee heeeee
I SEE RIGHT THROUGH YOU!
HEY...
CAN I ASK YOU SOME-THING?
HM?
WHA KIN...
...OF MAN DO I SEEM LIKE TO YOU ...?
WHAT? YOU MEAN YOUR FACE?
I MEAN MY PERSON-ALITY AND STUFF!!
meowww
HMMM, LET'S SEE...

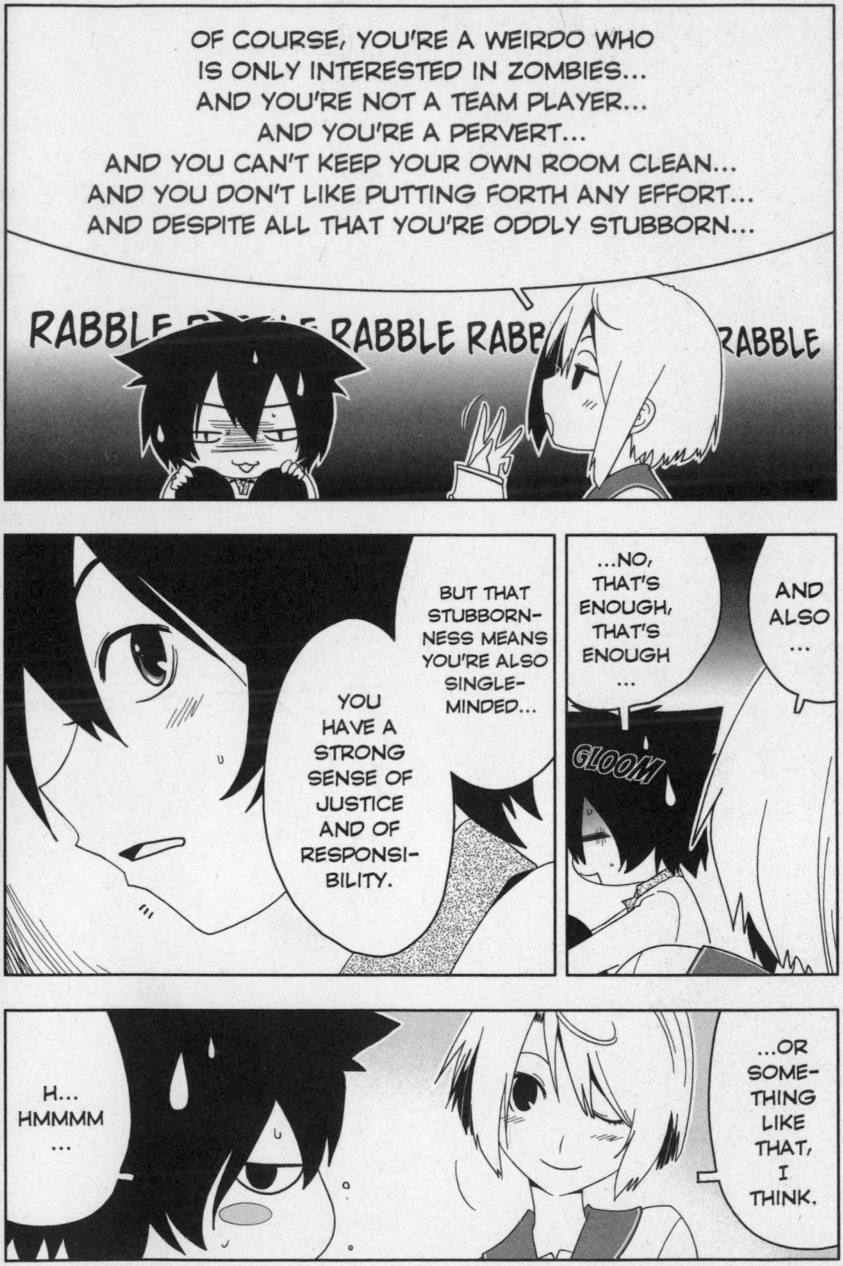
OF COURSE, YOU'RE A WEIRDO WHO IS ONLY INTERESTED IN ZOMBIES... AND YOU'RE NOT A TEAM PLAYER... AND YOU'RE A PERVERT... AND YOU CAN'T KEEP YOUR OWN ROOM CLEAN... AND YOU DON'T LIKE PUTTING FORTH ANY EFFORT... AND DESPITE ALL THAT YOU'RE ODDLY STUBBORN...
RABBLE RABBLE RABBLE
AND ALSO...
...NO, THAT'S ENOUGH, THAT'S ENOUGH...
GLOOM
BUT THAT STUBBORNNESS MEANS YOU'RE ALSO SINGLE-MINDED...
YOU HAVE A STRONG SENSE OF JUSTICE AND OF RESPONSIBILITY.
...OR SOMETHING LIKE THAT, I THINK.
H... HMMMM...

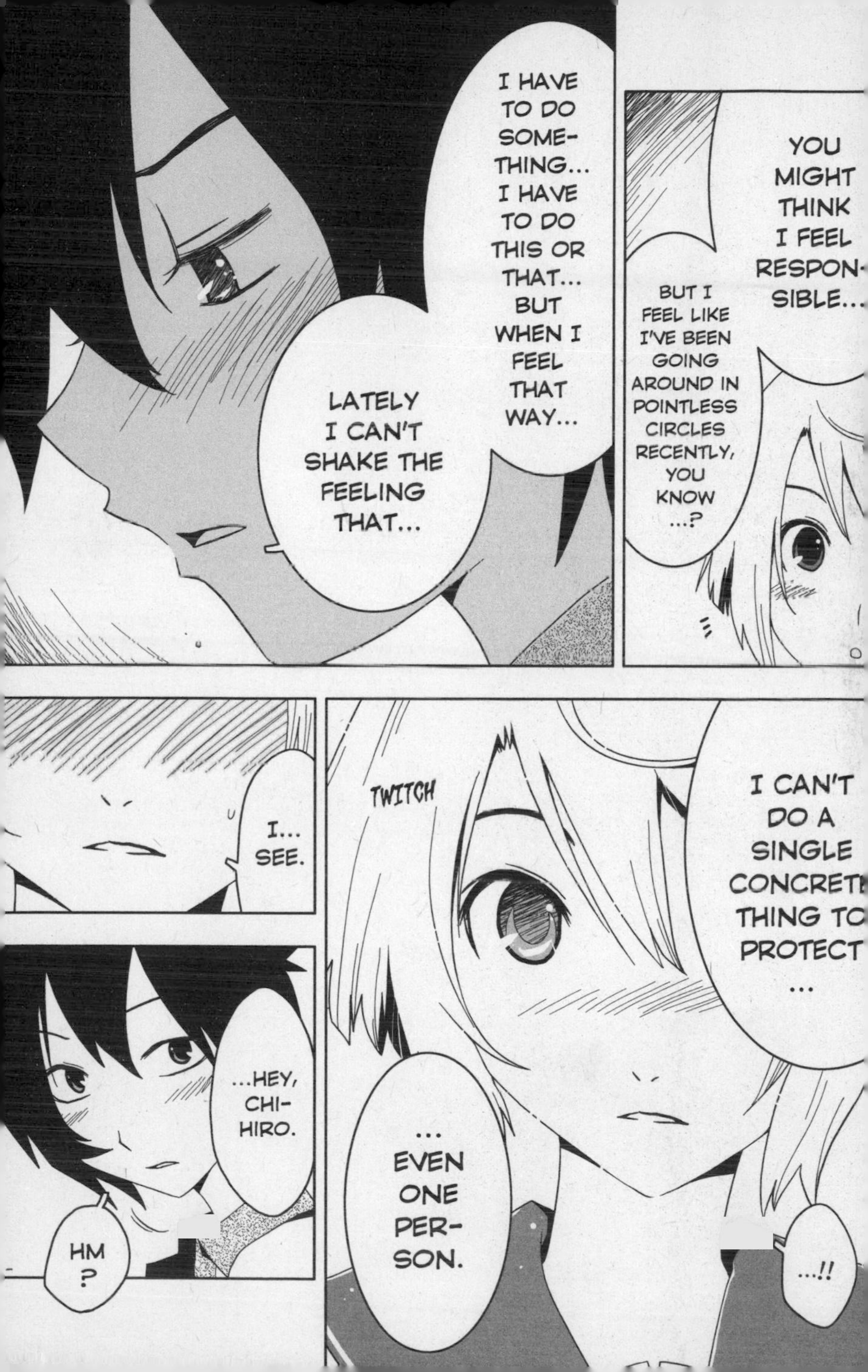
YOU MIGHT THINK I FEEL RESPONSIBLE...
BUT I FEEL LIKE I'VE BEEN GOING AROUND IN POINTLESS CIRCLES RECENTLY, YOU KNOW ...?
I HAVE TO DO SOMETHING... I HAVE TO DO THIS OR THAT... BUT WHEN I FEEL THAT WAY...
LATELY I CAN'T SHAKE THE FEELING THAT...
TWITCH
I CAN'T DO A SINGLE CONCRETE THING TO PROTECT ...
... EVEN ONE PERSON.
...!!
I... SEE.
...HEY, CHI-HIRO.
HM ?

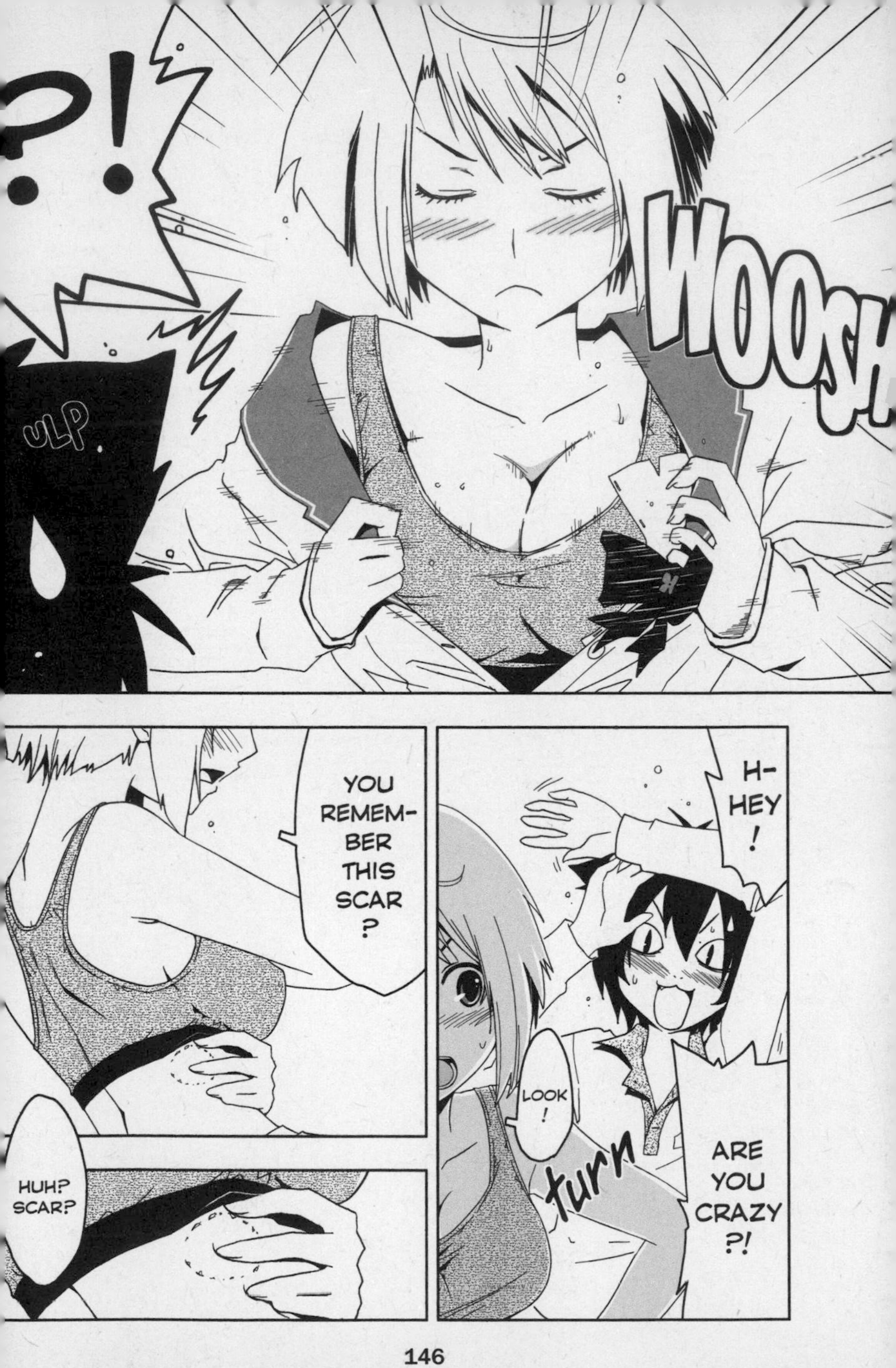
WOOSH
?!
ULP
H-HEY!
LOOK!
turn
ARE YOU CRAZY?!
YOU REMEMBER THIS SCAR?
HUH? SCAR?

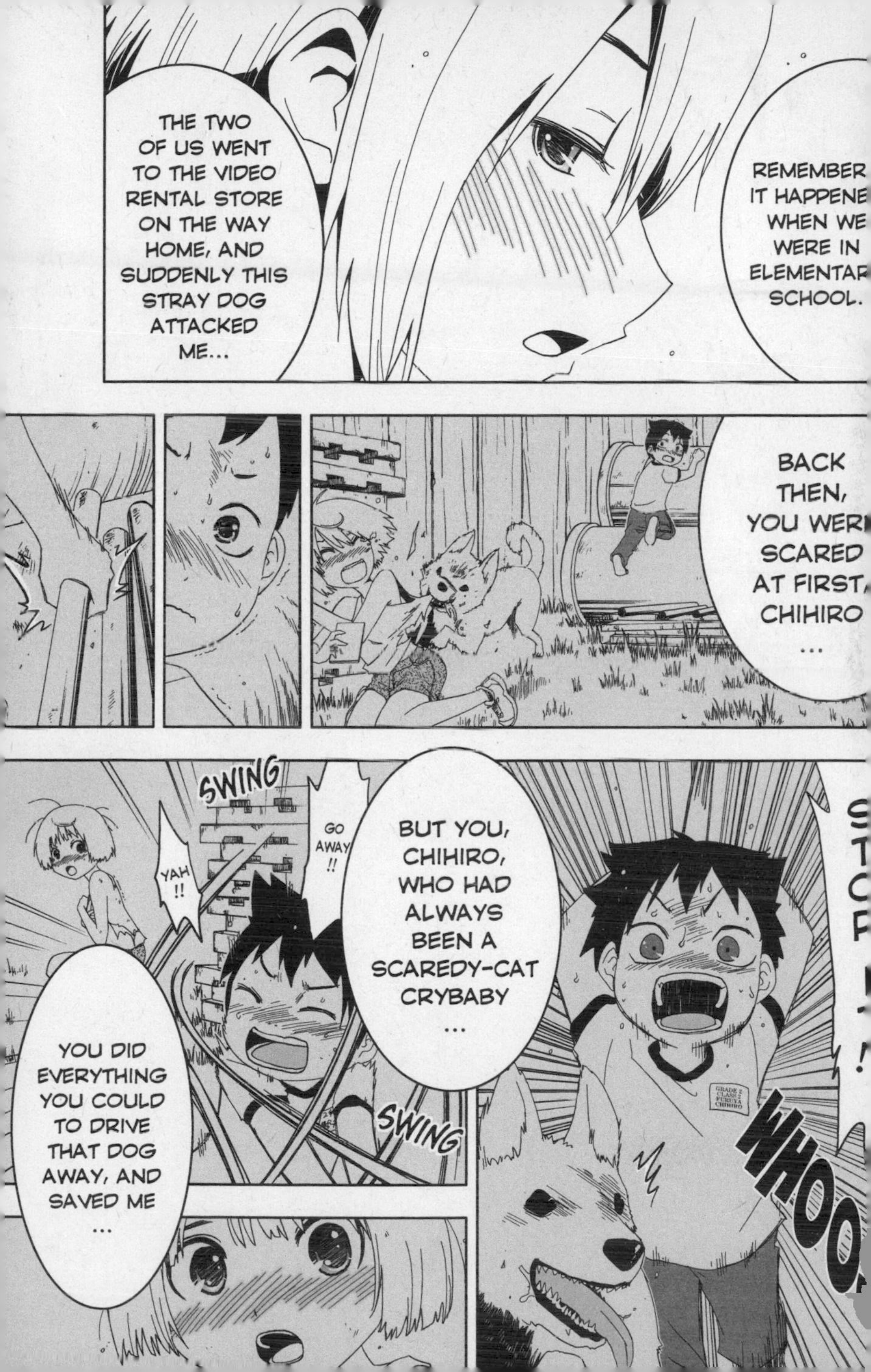
REMEMBER IT HAPPENE WHEN WE WERE IN ELEMENTAR SCHOOL.
THE TWO OF US WENT TO THE VIDEO RENTAL STORE ON THE WAY HOME, AND SUDDENLY THIS STRAY DOG ATTACKED ME...
BACK THEN, YOU WER SCARED AT FIRST, CHIHIRO ...
STOP!
WHOO
GRADE 2 CLASS 2 FURUYA CHIHIRO
BUT YOU, CHIHIRO, WHO HAD ALWAYS BEEN A SCAREDY-CAT CRYBABY ...
SWING
GO AWAY !!
YAH !!
SWING
YOU DID EVERYTHING YOU COULD TO DRIVE THAT DOG AWAY, AND SAVED ME ...

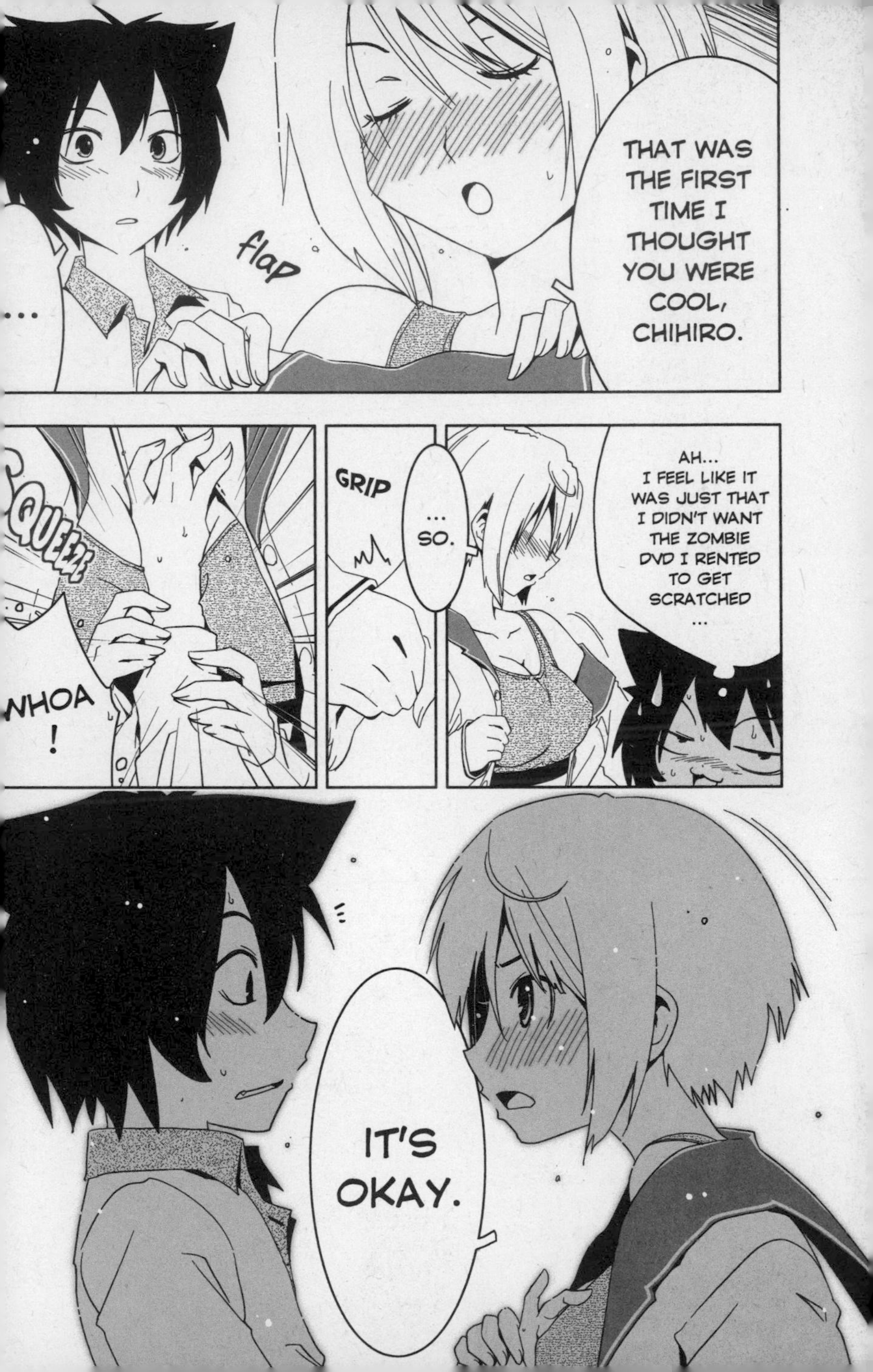
THAT WAS THE FIRST TIME I THOUGHT YOU WERE COOL, CHIHIRO.
flap
...
AH... I FEEL LIKE IT WAS JUST THAT I DIDN'T WANT THE ZOMBIE DVD I RENTED TO GET SCRATCHED ...
... SO.
GRIP
SQUEEZE
WHOA!
IT'S OKAY.

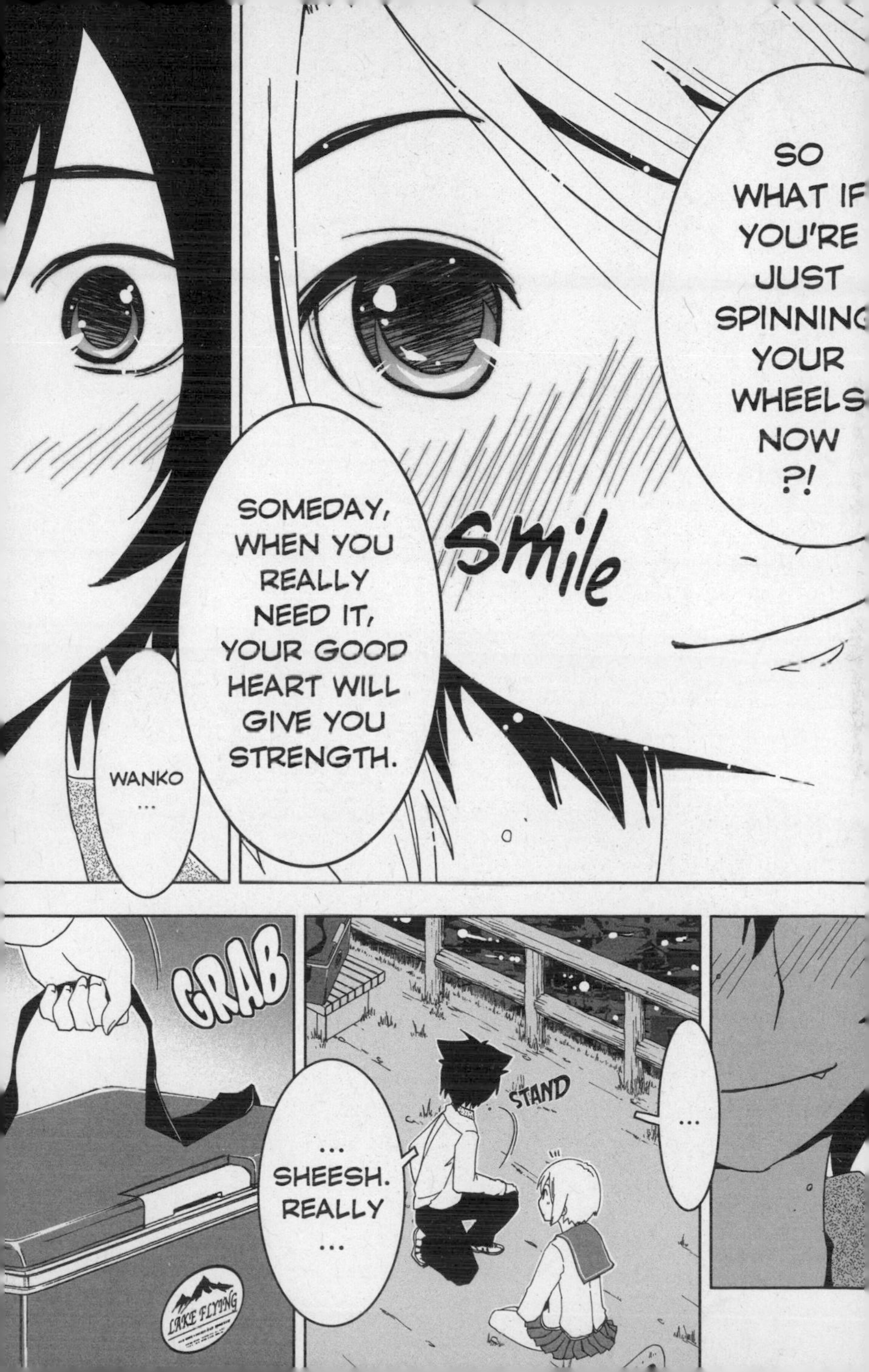
SO WHAT IF YOU'RE JUST SPINNING YOUR WHEELS NOW ?!
Smile
SOMEDAY, WHEN YOU REALLY NEED IT, YOUR GOOD HEART WILL GIVE YOU STRENGTH.
WANKO ...
...
STAND
... SHEESH. REALLY ...
GRAB
LAKE FLYING

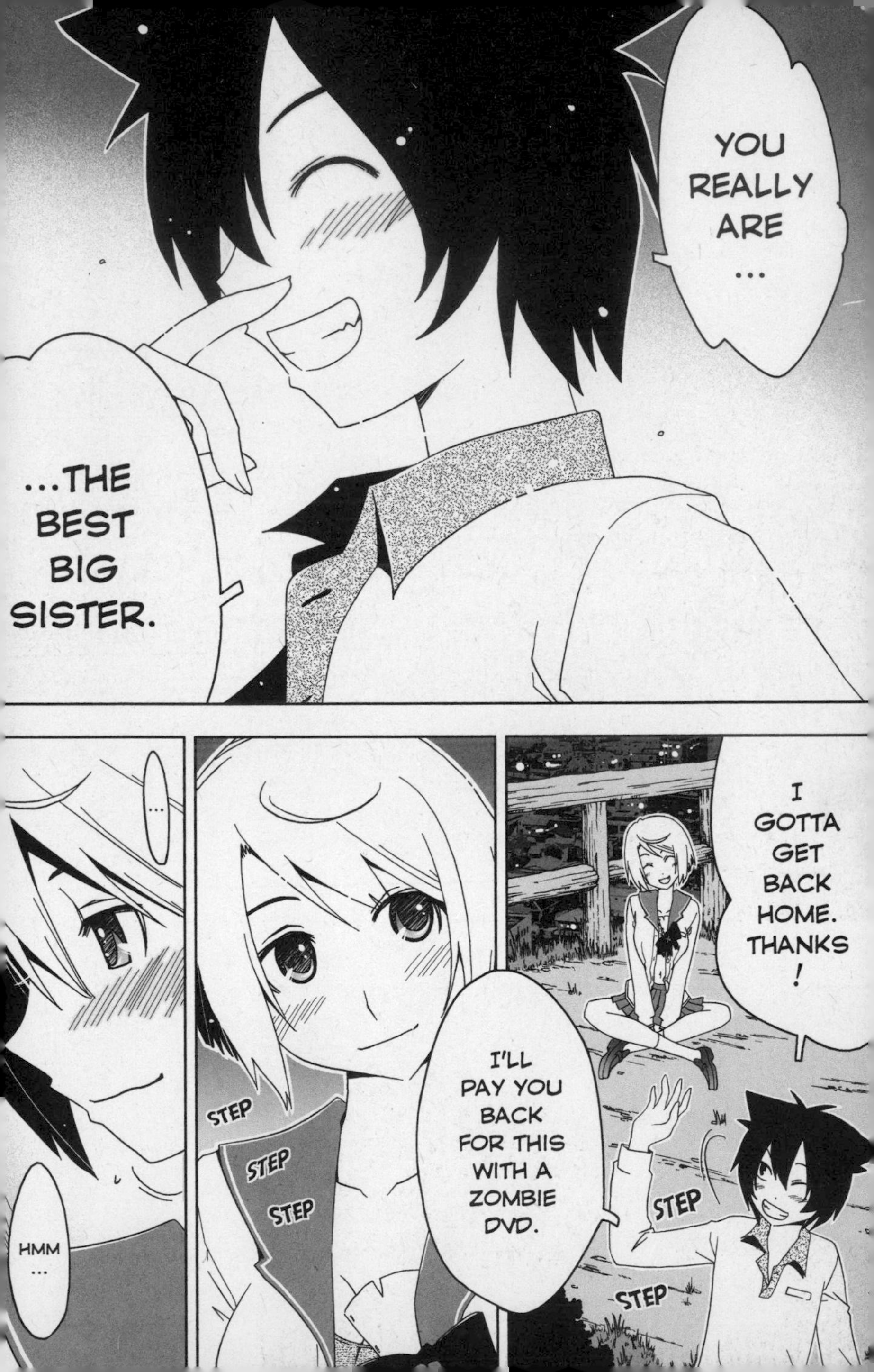
YOU REALLY ARE ...
...THE BEST BIG SISTER.
I GOTTA GET BACK HOME. THANKS!
I'LL PAY YOU BACK FOR THIS WITH A ZOMBIE DVD.
STEP
STEP
STEP
STEP
STEP
STEP
...
HMM ...

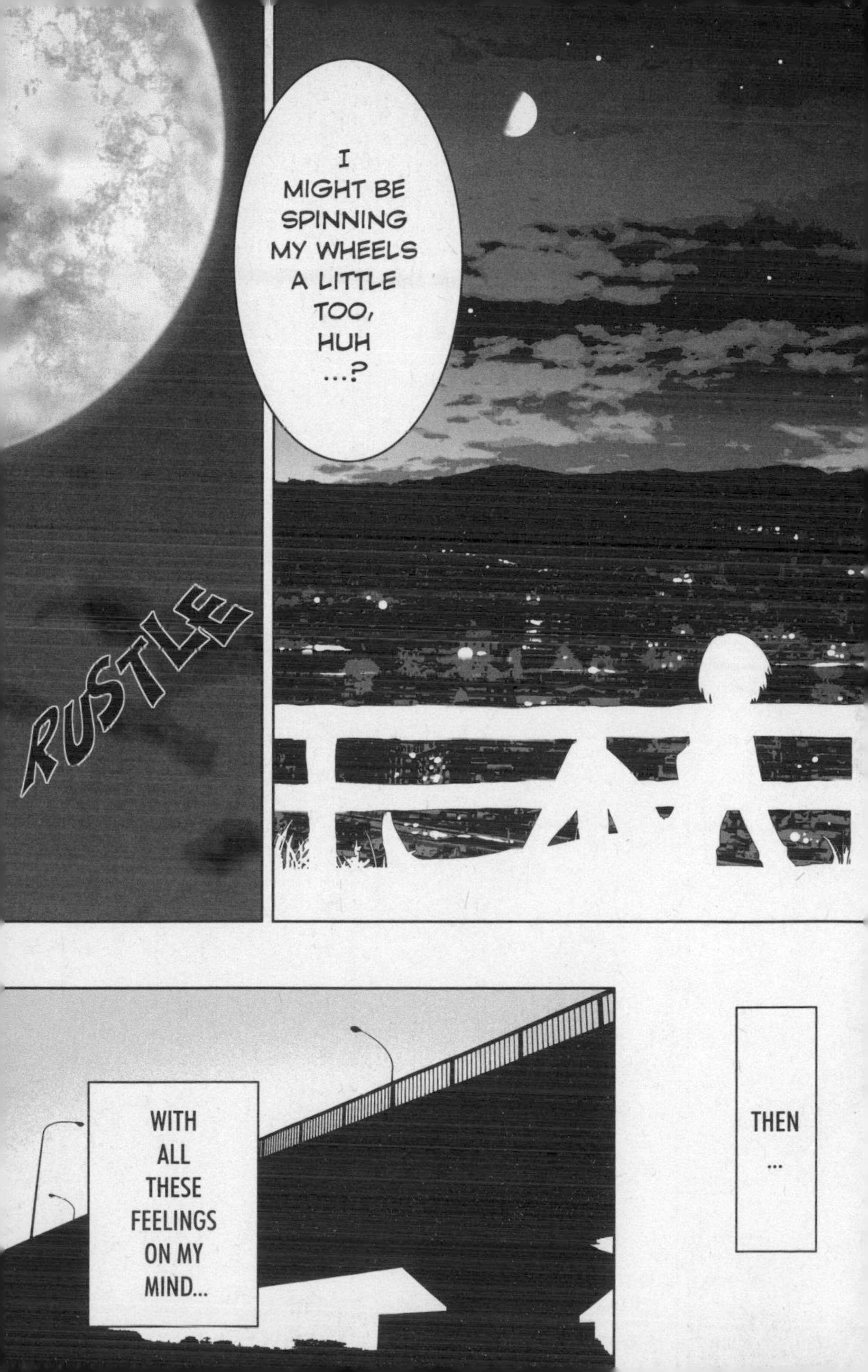
I MIGHT BE SPINNING MY WHEELS A LITTLE TOO, HUH ...?
RUSTLE
THEN ...
WITH ALL THESE FEELINGS ON MY MIND...

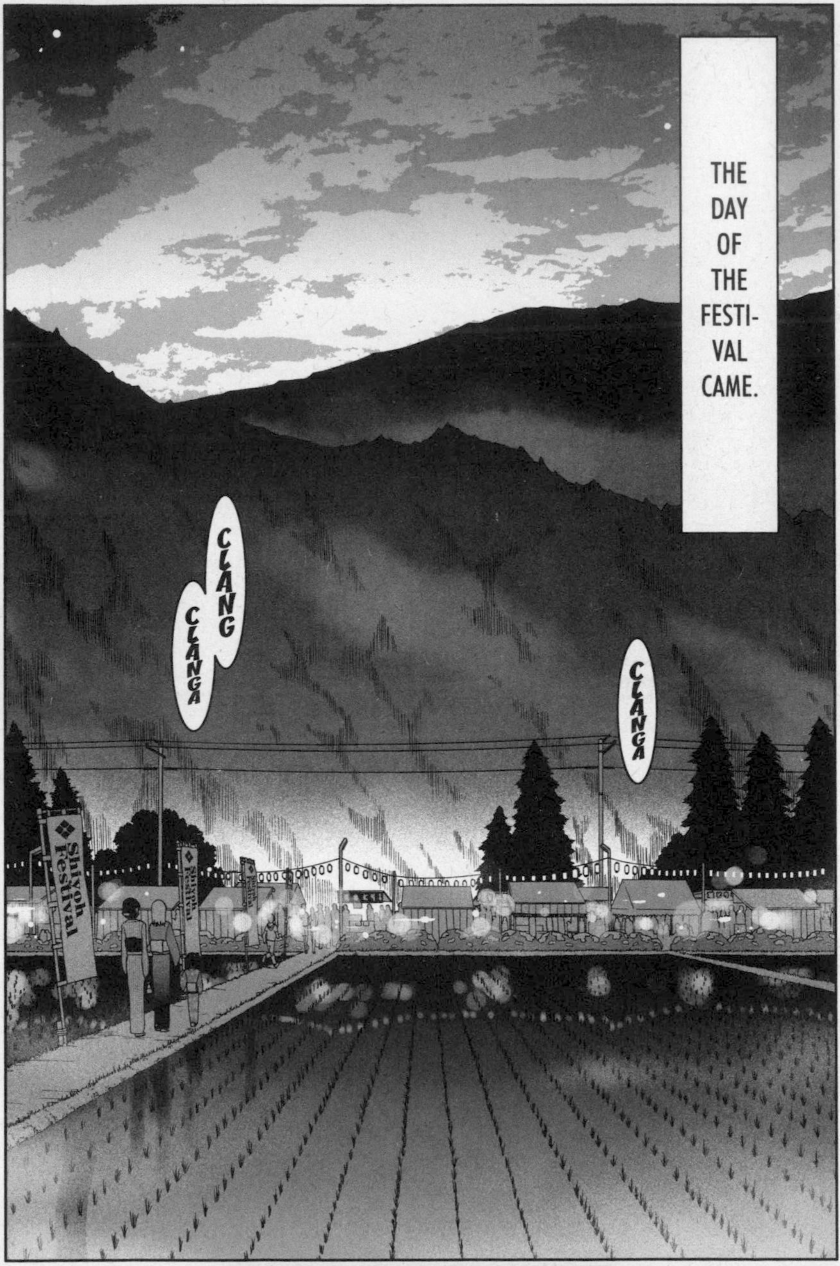
THE DAY OF THE FESTI- VAL CAME.
CLANGA
CLANG
CLANGA
Shiyoh Festival

TO BE CONTINUED IN VOLUME 4

Mitsuru Hattori presents SANKAREA

A HA HA HA HA HA HA HA

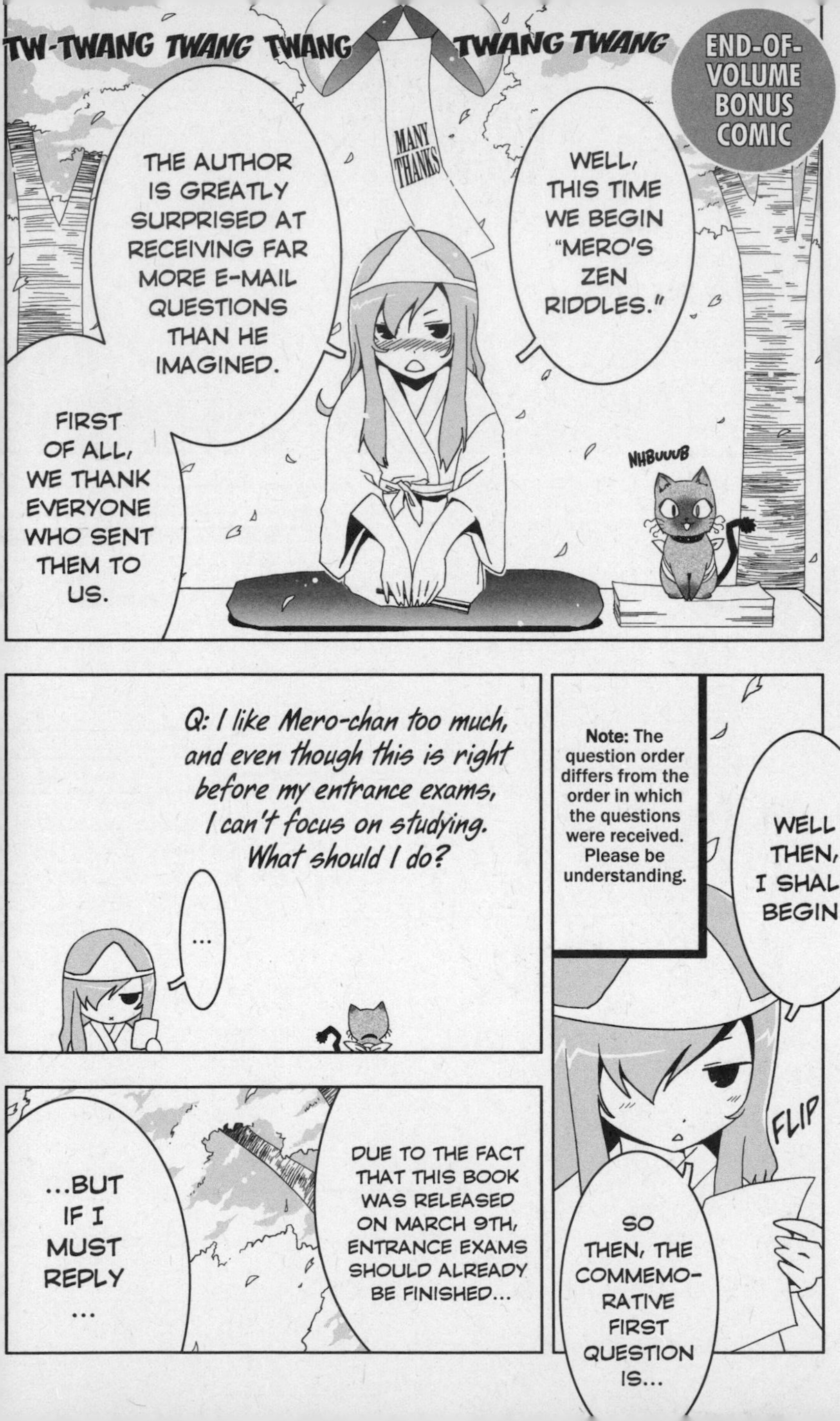

END-OF-VOLUME BONUS COMIC
TWANG TWANG
TW-TWANG TWANG TWANG
WELL, THIS TIME WE BEGIN "MERO'S ZEN RIDDLES."
MANY THANKS
THE AUTHOR IS GREATLY SURPRISED AT RECEIVING FAR MORE E-MAIL QUESTIONS THAN HE IMAGINED.
NHBUUUB
FIRST OF ALL, WE THANK EVERYONE WHO SENT THEM TO US.
Note: The question order differs from the order in which the questions were received. Please be understanding.
WELL THEN, I SHALL BEGIN.
FLIP
SO THEN, THE COMMEMO-RATIVE FIRST QUESTION IS...
Q: I like Mero-chan too much, and even though this is right before my entrance exams, I can't focus on studying. What should I do?
...
DUE TO THE FACT THAT THIS BOOK WAS RELEASED ON MARCH 9TH, ENTRANCE EXAMS SHOULD ALREADY BE FINISHED...
...BUT IF I MUST REPLY ...

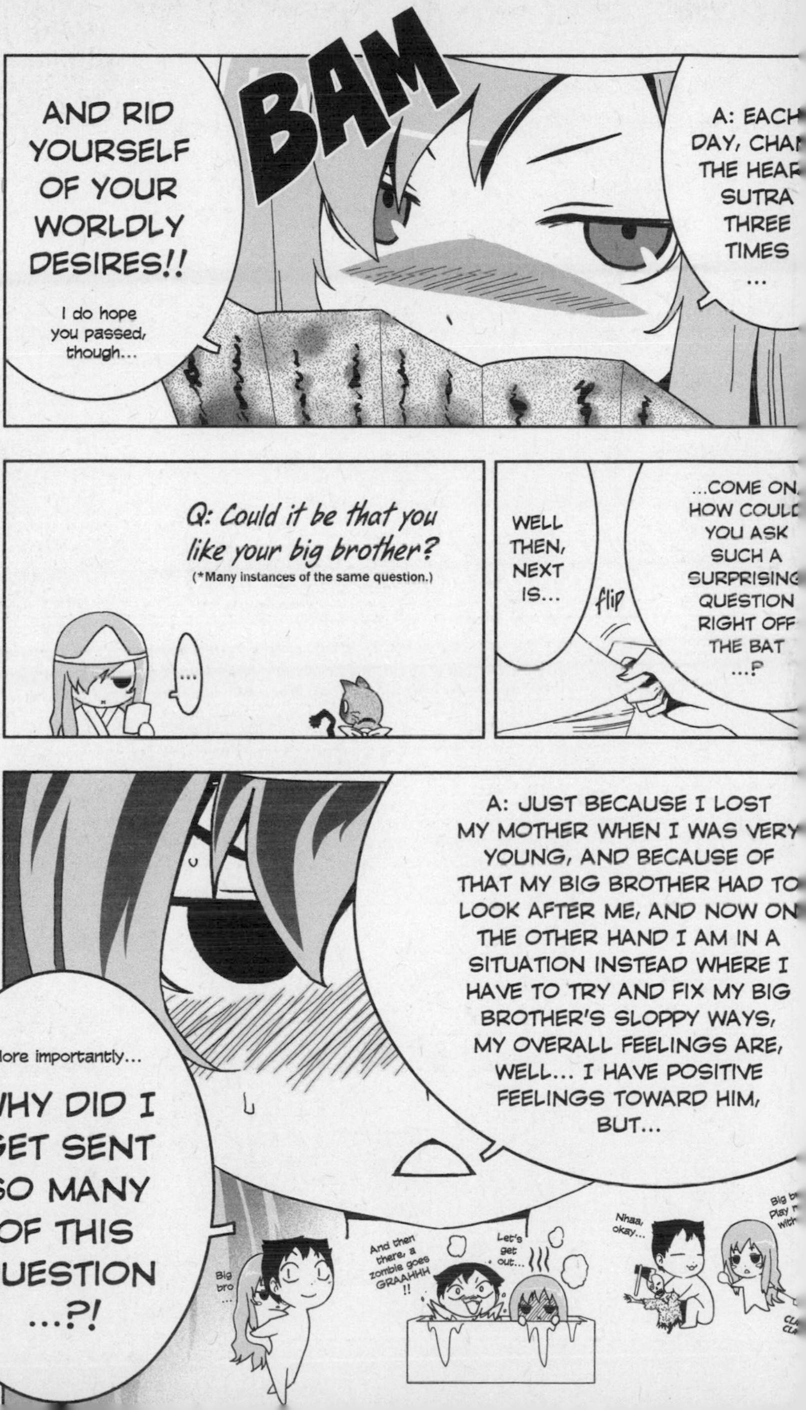
A: EACH DAY, CHA THE HEAR SUTRA THREE TIMES ...
BAM
AND RID YOURSELF OF YOUR WORLDLY DESIRES!!
I do hope you passed, though...
...COME ON, HOW COULD YOU ASK SUCH A SURPRISING QUESTION RIGHT OFF THE BAT ...?
flip
WELL THEN, NEXT IS...
Q: Could it be that you like your big brother?
(*Many instances of the same question.)
...
A: JUST BECAUSE I LOST MY MOTHER WHEN I WAS VERY YOUNG, AND BECAUSE OF THAT MY BIG BROTHER HAD TO LOOK AFTER ME, AND NOW ON THE OTHER HAND I AM IN A SITUATION INSTEAD WHERE I HAVE TO TRY AND FIX MY BIG BROTHER'S SLOPPY WAYS, MY OVERALL FEELINGS ARE, WELL... I HAVE POSITIVE FEELINGS TOWARD HIM, BUT...
Nhaa, okay...
Let's get out...
And then there, a zombie goes GRAAHHH !!
Big bro ...
More importantly...
WHY DID I GET SENT SO MANY OF THIS QUESTION ...?!

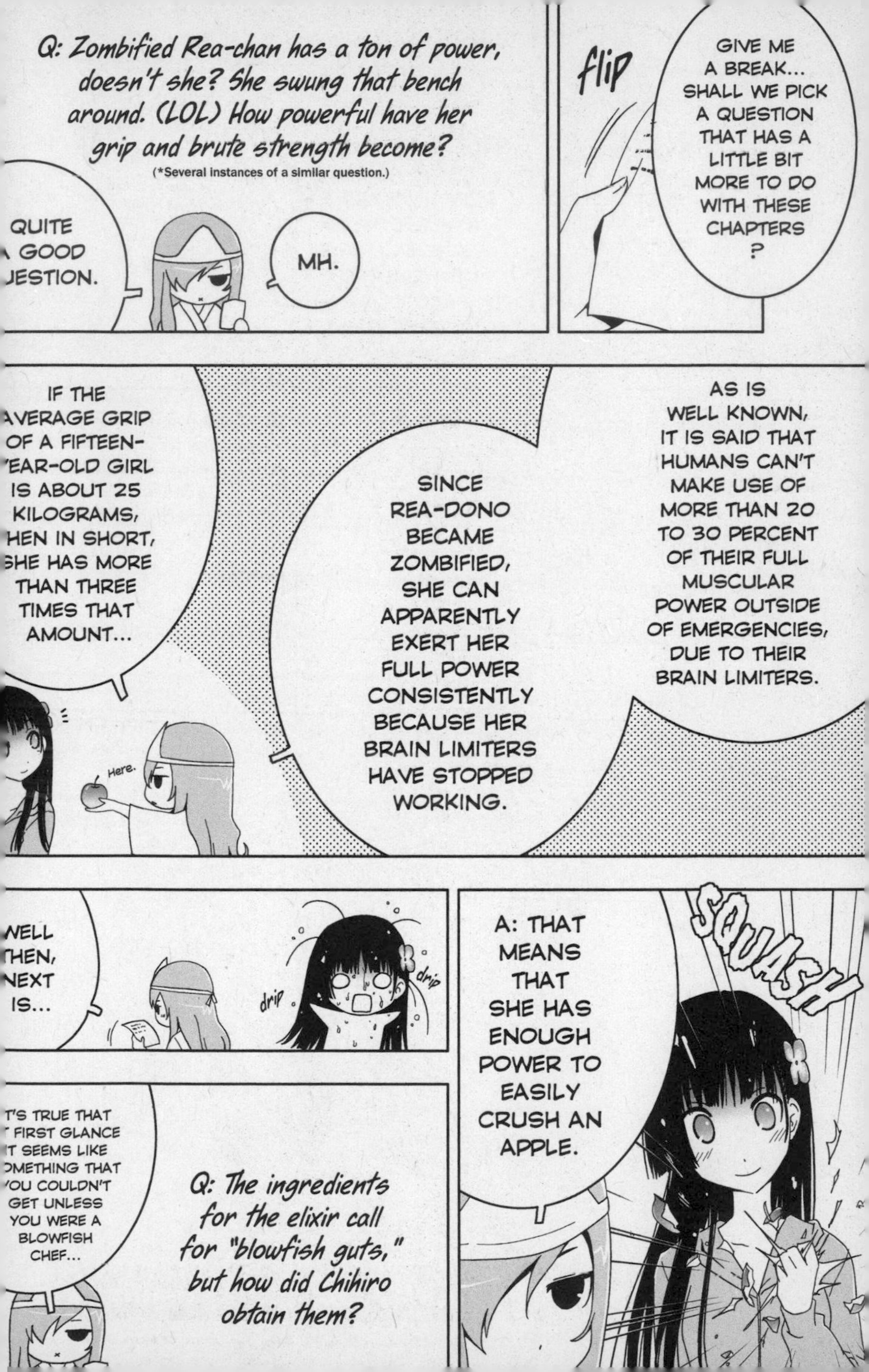
flip
GIVE ME A BREAK... SHALL WE PICK A QUESTION THAT HAS A LITTLE BIT MORE TO DO WITH THESE CHAPTERS ?
Q: Zombified Rea-chan has a ton of power, doesn't she? She swung that bench around. (LOL) How powerful have her grip and brute strength become?
(*Several instances of a similar question.)
MH.
QUITE GOOD ESTION.
AS IS WELL KNOWN, IT IS SAID THAT HUMANS CAN'T MAKE USE OF MORE THAN 20 TO 30 PERCENT OF THEIR FULL MUSCULAR POWER OUTSIDE OF EMERGENCIES, DUE TO THEIR BRAIN LIMITERS.
SINCE REA-DONO BECAME ZOMBIFIED, SHE CAN APPARENTLY EXERT HER FULL POWER CONSISTENTLY BECAUSE HER BRAIN LIMITERS HAVE STOPPED WORKING.
IF THE VERAGE GRIP OF A FIFTEEN- EAR-OLD GIRL IS ABOUT 25 KILOGRAMS, HEN IN SHORT, HE HAS MORE THAN THREE TIMES THAT AMOUNT...
Here.
SQUASH
A: THAT MEANS THAT SHE HAS ENOUGH POWER TO EASILY CRUSH AN APPLE.
drip
drip
WELL HEN, NEXT IS...
Q: The ingredients for the elixir call for "blowfish guts," but how did Chihiro obtain them?
T'S TRUE THAT FIRST GLANCE T SEEMS LIKE OMETHING THAT OU COULDN'T GET UNLESS YOU WERE A BLOWFISH CHEF...

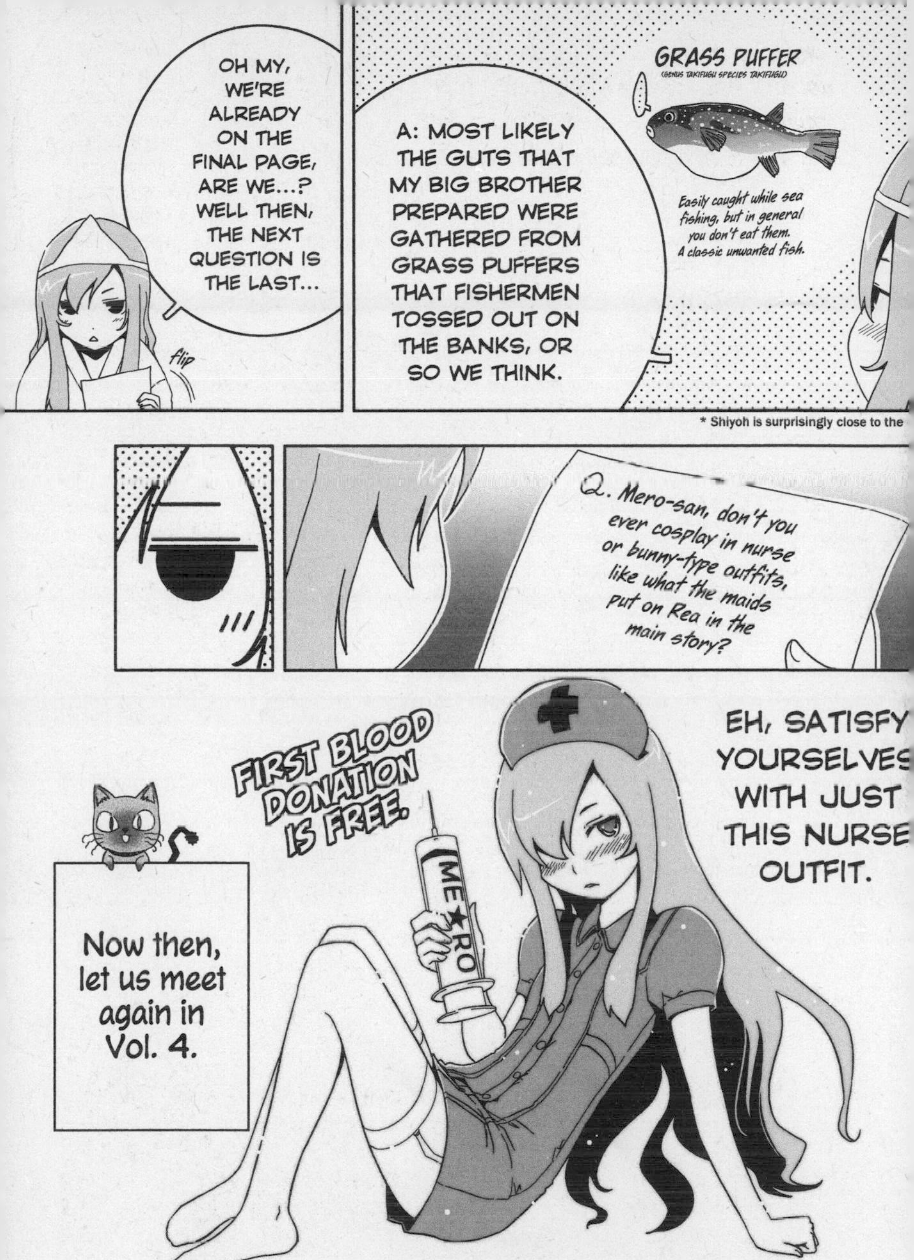
GRASS PUFFER
(GENUS TAKIFUGU SPECIES TAKIFUGU)
Easily caught while sea fishing, but in general you don't eat them. A classic unwanted fish.
A: MOST LIKELY THE GUTS THAT MY BIG BROTHER PREPARED WERE GATHERED FROM GRASS PUFFERS THAT FISHERMEN TOSSED OUT ON THE BANKS, OR SO WE THINK.
OH MY, WE'RE ALREADY ON THE FINAL PAGE, ARE WE...? WELL THEN, THE NEXT QUESTION IS THE LAST...
Flip
* Shiyoh is surprisingly close to the
Q. Mero-san, don't you ever cosplay in nurse or bunny-type outfits, like what the maids put on Rea in the main story?
EH, SATISFY YOURSELVES WITH JUST THIS NURSE OUTFIT.
FIRST BLOOD DONATION IS FREE.
ME★RO
Now then, let us meet again in Vol. 4.

"Mero's Zen Riddles" e-mail address:

(Put something like "Zen Riddles" or "Questions for Mero" in the subject line.)

kodanshacomics@randomhouse.com

*Questions we couldn't answer this time may be picked up in the next volume or after, as well.

investigate

Sankarea discovered something.
TUG TUG
POP
BOO
nooooo...
BOO
Sankarea was cursed.

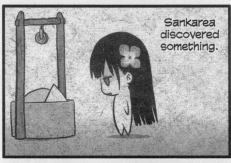

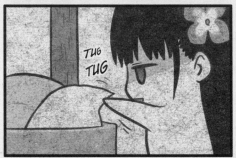

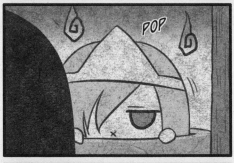

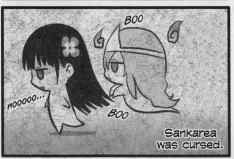

TRANSLATION NOTES

Honorifics: This series retains the Japanese honorifics. Here's a guide:

-san: Polite, equivalent to "Mr." or "Ms."

-sama: A term of great respect.

-kun: Used for boys or people in a lower position.

-chan: A sometimes cutesy term of endearment for girls.

-dono: A very respectful and now old-fashioned term.

-sempai: Refers to a student who entered school before you, or a colleague who entered the company before you. (The equivalent for your juniors is "kohai.")

p. 2, Heart Sutra

Sutras are Buddhist sermons or prayers. The Heart Sutra is probably the best known and most popular of all the Buddhist Sutras. Though they were originally written in Sanskrit, the version known in Japan has been transcribed into Chinese characters.

p.13, Cheerios

In the original Japanese, Yasutaka misunderstands the girl looking for Furuya's family's temple, Shiryohji, because the name "Shiryohji" can be spelled with characters that mean "ghost temple." The author probably picked the name intentionally for that very reason. We changed it to "Cheerios" because it sounds kind of like "Shiryoh."

p.p. 46, 18

Zombie owl 18's name is pronounced "towa" in Japanese. Since he's a zombie from her facility, it might be his specimen number.

p. 49, Uboa

Grandpa's cries (and his appearance) here seem to be a reference to a particularly memorable monster named Uboa in the underground hit Japanese indie PC game, Yume Nikki.

p. 59, Saponification

Human bodies have been recorded as turning into a soapy or waxy substance (often known as "grave wax"), in a process that can also be called adipocere formation. A famous example of this is the so-called "Soap Lady" on display at Philadelphia's Mütter Museum.

p.61, Yukata

A yukata is a very light, cotton kimono, worn by both sexes but more commonly by girls than boys. They're synonymous in Japan with the summer months and festivals in particular. The come in a variety of colors and patterns, both traditional and modern.

p.68, Muoh

A reference to a real Japanese long-running paranormal magazine, called Muu.

p.73, Namuu (Namu Amida Butsu)

A prayer involving saying the name of the Buddha, commonly used in Pure Land Buddhism. It is often shortened to just the first word in Japanese.

p.86, Meishin

As seen in the first volume, Sanka Girls' Academy holds a meditation exercise before homeroom that involves simply sewing a needle and thread through a piece of cloth over and over again for a set period of time. They call it "meishin" or "meditation needle."

Kodansha Comics Trade Paperback Original.

ublished in the United States by Kodansha Comics, an imprint of Kodansha SA Publishing, LLC, New York.

ublication rights for this English edition arranged through Kodansha Ltd., 'okyo.

irst published in Japan in 2011 by Kodansha Ltd., Tokyo, as *Sankarea*, volume 3.

SBN 978-1-61262-353-5

rinted in the United States of America.

www.kodanshacomics.com

8 7 6 5 4 3 2 1

'ranslation: Lindsey Akashi
ettering: Evan Hayden
diting: Ben Applegate